Expanding the Horizon of Electroacous

Innovations in music technology bring with them a new set of challenges for describing and understanding the electroacoustic repertoire. This edited collection presents a state-of-the art overview of analysis methods for electroacoustic music in this rapidly developing field. The first part of the book explains the needs of differing electroacoustic genres and puts forward a template for the analysis of electroacoustic music. Part II discusses the latest ideas in the field and the challenges associated with new technologies. Part III explores how analyses have harnessed the new forces of multimedia and includes an introduction to the new software program EAnalysis, which was created as the result of an Arts and Humanities Research Council grant. The final part of the book demonstrates these new methods in action, with analyses of key electroacoustic works from a wide range of genres and sources.

SIMON EMMERSON is Professor of Music, Technology and Innovation at De Montfort University, Leicester. As a composer, he works mostly with live electronics, recently Sond'Arte (Lisbon) and acousmatic work for Inventionen Festival (Berlin). His books include *The Language of Electroacoustic Music* (1986), *Music, Electronic Media and Culture* (2000) and *Living Electronic Music* (2007). In 2009–10 he was DAAD Edgard Varèse Visiting Professor at the TU, Berlin.

LEIGH LANDY directs the Music, Technology and Innovation Research Centre at De Montfort University. His scholarship is divided between creative and musicological work and his compositions have been performed around the globe. He is editor of the journal *Organised Sound* and author of several books including *Understanding the Art of Sound Organization* (2007) and *Making Music with Sounds* (2012). He directs the ElectroAcoustic Resource Site (EARS) projects and is a founding director of the Electroacoustic Music Studies Network (EMS).

Expanding the Horizon of Electroacoustic Music Analysis

Edited by
SIMON EMMERSON
De Montfort University, Leicester

LEIGH LANDY
De Montfort University, Leicester

CAMBRIDGE
UNIVERSITY PRESS

University Printing House, Cambridge CB2 8BS, United Kingdom

One Liberty Plaza, 20th Floor, New York, NY 10006, USA

477 Williamstown Road, Port Melbourne, VIC 3207, Australia

314-321, 3rd Floor, Plot 3, Splendor Forum, Jasola District Centre, New Delhi-110025, India

79 Anson Road, #06-04/06, Singapore 079906

Cambridge University Press is part of the University of Cambridge.

It furthers the University's mission by disseminating knowledge in the pursuit of education, learning and research at the highest international levels of excellence.

www.cambridge.org
Information on this title: www.cambridge.org/9781107544055

© Cambridge University Press 2016

First published 2016
First paperback edition 2018

A catalogue record for this publication is available from the British Library

Library of Congress Cataloging in Publication data
Expanding the horizon of electroacoustic music analysis / edited by Simon Emmerson
and Leigh Landy.
    pages   cm
Includes bibliographical references and index.
ISBN 978-1-107-11832-4 (Hardback : alk. paper)
1. Computer music–Analysis, appreciation.   2. Electronic music–Analysis,
appreciation.   I. Emmerson, Simon, 1950-   II. Landy, Leigh, 1951-
ML1380.E96 2016
786.7–dc23   2015028651

ISBN 978-1-107-11832-4 Hardback
ISBN 978-1-107-54405-5 Paperback

Contents

v

Figures

Contributors

Panos Amelides, *Bournemouth University*

Manuella Blackburn, *Liverpool Hope University*

Pierre Couprie, *Université Paris-Sorbonne*

Simon Emmerson, *De Montfort University*

John Robert Ferguson, *Griffith University*

Michael Gatt, *Kingston University*

Kersten Glandien, *Brighton University*

Leigh Landy, *De Montfort University*

Andrew Hugill, *Bath Spa University*

Gary S. Kendall, independent researcher and composer

Raúl Minsburg, *Universidad Nacional de Lanús* and *Universidad Nacional de Tresde Febrero, Argentina*

Katharine Norman, composer and writer

Tae Hong Park, *New York University*

Ben Ramsay, *Bath Spa University*

Ambrose Seddon, *Bournemouth University*

Sophy Smith, *De Montfort University*

John Young, *De Montfort University*

Michael Young, *De Montfort University*

∿ | Introduction

SIMON EMMERSON AND LEIGH LANDY

Additional online resources for this book can be found at: www.cambridge.org/9781107118324.

This book is the result of an Arts and Humanities Research Council funded project *New Multimedia Tools for Electroacoustic Music Analysis* (2010–13), designed to address a range of genres, drawing together existing methods, engaging the latest interactive and hypermedia tools, and applying them to compare their strengths and weaknesses. This contribution aims to introduce the reader to the background ideas which have, we trust, guided and given direction to this initiative. 'Analysis' means many things and these will depend on mutually interactive questions such as which tools/approaches, for which works/genres, for which users, with what intentions. It would be impossible for a single volume to cover all the possible options and combinations. We have tried to open the field out from a limited core set of genres and approaches (which have tended to dominate the literature in the last 20 years or so) to embrace an eclectic group of practices and to encourage a *range* of different points of view.

The project included the development of two new – and very different – applications. First, a multimedia software package, EAnalysis (Pierre Couprie), which takes visualisation of sound into new areas, allowing advanced annotation of its characteristics, not only for analysis but also for a wide range of uses; second a website, OREMA (Online Repository for Electroacoustic Music Analysis) (Michael Gatt), possibly the first forum for sharing and discussing analyses. The website was intended to develop a new model for analytical methods through sharing and interactive discussion and to open out the discussion from the narrow confines of academic journals and conferences.

We initially divided the corpus of electroacoustic music into genres (e.g. acousmatic, electronica, glitch, soundscape), but these have hybridised continuously – an *installation* may include *algorithmic* generation, be *interactive* and use *soundscape* and *acousmatic* materials. We clearly need a range of tools for analysis, as well as a range of approaches to their application.

Thus Part I of the book contains a single chapter by the editors intended to address 'the differing needs of the genres and categories' of electroacoustic music when it comes to analysis. We experienced a difficult balancing act between the desire for an eclectic breadth and the need to contain the field in a manner that the reader could make sense of. Defining clearly the questions that analysis asks is common to all types of music, but electroacoustic music has some very special approaches to its soundworld and practice that are clearly very different from longer established 'note-based' methods. We hope that the outcome as seen in the remainder of the book goes some way along this sometimes tricky high wire.

Part II of the book addresses new ideas for *thinking about what is going on* and how this affects the *tools we need*. These contributions look at 'high-level' issues or aim to challenge existing approaches to analysis. In his chapter 'Listening and meaning: how a model of mental layers informs electroacoustic music analysis', Gary Kendall challenges static representations of music structure, moving away from ideas of 'sound object' to 'sound as event'. He adapts a layered model of mental processing to music and grasps the difficult but essential notion of the 'emergence of meaning' from the listening experience. John Young tackles an area underrepresented in work to date, namely form (and structure), in his chapter 'Forming Form'. He re-examines different views of forming musical experience over time. Comparing 'moment form' and Wishart's 'morphic form', the sculptural and the rhetorical, and their relationship to narrative, he gives a special place to what electroacoustic music adds to this experience. Michael Young challenges traditional views on analysis of a fixed 'work' – in this case one that might be generated anew at each performance. In his chapter 'Interactive and generative music: a quagmire for the musical analyst', he suggests that machine participation in composition and performance changes the nature of the questions we ask about the music. It may not be possible simply to 'listen to the result' as if the way we got there did not matter. Finally in this part, Raúl Minsburg addresses some high-level issues in his contribution 'Some ideas concerning the relationship between form and texture'. He argues that, historically, texture has been too little discussed, that is, how we perceive *layers* of music and their contribution to changing *complexity*, and that this is a key element for the building of formal structures. Using examples of work from South America he suggests a strong relationship of *textural modulation* to form.

Part III looks more specifically at the practical development of new tools. While the tenor of much of this book is strongly listener focused, Tae Hong Park argues the case for machine application, describing his ideas in 'Exploiting computational paradigms for electroacoustic music analysis'. His ongoing work on Systematic and Quantitative Electro-Acoustic Music

Analysis (SQEMA) is applied to a group of contrasting pieces, showing how new multimedia analytical applications can reveal important features of the music. There follow two contributions from the project team members introduced at the opening. In 'OREMA: an analytical community', Michael Gatt examines the origins and rationale behind the OREMA (Online Repository for Electroacoustic Music Analysis) website and its aims to add a 'wisdom of the crowd' dimension to the toolbox. Pierre Couprie's 'EAnalysis: developing a sound-based music analytical tool' examines the aims and objectives behind this new software and how the challenges of new media may be harnessed to give us better ways to represent the music.

Then in Part IV the authors present analytical examples illustrating a wide variety of genres and approaches – each has unique demands on the analytical method.[1] As an example of how analytical work can address different audiences, Leigh Landy develops the theme in discussing 'Trevor Wishart's *Children's Stories II* from *Encounters in the Republic of Heaven*: an analysis for children of a sample-based composition' using a language designed to communicate with school-aged people and their teachers. In a chapter which aims to come to terms with 'new wave' developments in materials, instruments and performance that came about in the 1990s derived from more mainstream popular practice, Ben Ramsay looks at an example of 'IDM/electronica' in 'Analysis of *Foil* by Autechre (from *Amber* (1994))', showing how sound identities and relationships are established in this genre. Acousmatic music has many streams and traditions. Ambrose Seddon focuses on how recurrence may be related to timbral evolution and real-world references in his chapter 'Temporal recurrence in Andrew Lewis's *Penmon Point*'. John Ferguson's contribution ('Michel Waisvisz: *No Backup/Hyper Instruments*') discusses how to come to grips with new invented electroacoustic instruments designed primarily for improvisation, where analysis demands the inclusion of the performative. There follows a chapter on another genre to demand greater account of context. In 'Analysing Sound Art: Douglas Henderson's *Fadensonnen* (2009)', Kersten Glandien examines a work of sound sculpture which challenges established norms of analysis – the work weaves together experience of both the physical and sonic spaces it defines.

Two succeeding chapters look at genres which 'sample' sound and actively use our recognition of sources in their discourse. Manuella

---

[1] Not all feel the need for an EAnalysis or Acousmographe representation.

Blackburn's 'Analysing the identifiable: cultural borrowing in Diana Salazar's *La voz del fuelle*' focuses on 'cultural borrowing' – the use of recordings of tango, what that might indicate and how this influences the way we follow the work. Sophy Smith has pioneered analysis of turntable music. Here she explores in detail a team turntable routine by Kireek ('*Kireek 2011* Championship routine analysis'). She has developed a notation for this virtuoso gestural world and shows how the routine is performatively structured. Simon Emmerson looks at an example of more recent developments in the notated instrumental Western tradition in his contribution 'The analysis of live and interactive electroacoustic music: Hans Tutschku – *Zellen-Linien* (2007)'. Starting from the listening experience alone, he works back only later to the composer's notes and eventually the score.

Analysis of two very contrasting genres of soundscape conclude the book. Andrew Hugill and Panos Amelides examine 'Audio-only computer games: *Papa Sangre*' – arguing for their inclusion as sound art, with strong environmental, narrative and affective dimensions, enhanced by the acousmatic nature of the experience. They suggest that 'play' can become performance. Finally Katharine Norman returns to the world around us and how we listen to it with her chapter 'Some questions around listening: *Vancouver Soundscape Revisited* by Claude Schryer'. She weaves together recognition, memory (individual and collective), space and time all as components of a listener's imaginary soundwalk.

(No) Conclusion

All parts of this book offer both general and genre-specific examples of the state of developments today and will hopefully provide an incentive to expand the horizon of electroacoustic music analysis further in the years to come.

It aims to open doors to new futures and we have seen – and will continue to see – considerable further development of software since the conclusion of the original project (September 2013). The world of electroacoustic music is broad and, compared with many other forms of music, still quite young. Integration with analytical tools used for different purposes in note-based music deserves further attention and tools for analysis going across the new media arts are expected to develop apace.

There may be no Schenker equivalent in electroacoustic music analysis as each genre has such different approaches to substance, process, form and performance. What we have tried to do is to assemble a toolkit by example. While such a collection is necessarily incomplete, we aim to introduce this wide range of new options, crucially shared under a single cover such that you, the reader, may make choices – and perhaps develop and share additional tools for future work.

The website to accompany this book, which will be launched at publication, will contain colour images (of figures printed in black and white in this volume) as well as sound examples.

The analysis of electroacoustic music: the differing needs of its genres and categories

SIMON EMMERSON AND LEIGH LANDY

Introduction: genres and categories

The ElectroAcoustic Resource Site (EARS) (www.ears.dmu.ac.uk) lists 81 genres and categories of electroacoustic music – these are effectively naming conventions, clustering into two categorisations which are in no way exclusive: a *genre* is a musical or artistic grouping (e.g. *soundscape* or *acousmatic*), whereas a *category* is grouped around a *performance situation*, an *aspect of technology* or an *approach* (e.g. *installation, microsound, algorithmic*). But sometimes the distinction of genres and categories cannot easily be maintained. A word used to describe a category may migrate in meaning to describe a genre – some might argue this is true of 'acousmatic'!

While we have positioned the approach of our Arts and Humanities Research Council project (and this book) firmly from the listener's perspective, there can be no *tabula rasa* – we all have memories, knowledge and feelings to bring to the listening encounter. So, for example, does knowledge of a *generative* algorithm influence perception and hence analysis? Analysis may furthermore include *socially situated* characteristics of production, perception and consumption. *Glitch* and *hacking* works analysed from their sound alone would surely lose a substantial part of their meaning. How do we capture these additional dimensions, including emotional response? What other traces should run in parallel to transcription of the sound? Any analytical procedure must balance the gravitational pull of genre or category with a networked, relativistic world of characteristics which reconfigure depending on initial questions (which we shall discuss below).

We therefore have a dilemma – there is no single way forward for analysis in this field and the plethora of possibilities threatens to drown the listener and reader. We thus had to establish limits and boundaries, but in such a way, we hope, that the reader can create his/her own pathway – perhaps from a hybrid of approaches – through this rich landscape. Our first limit is that the approach to analysis is (as already stated) primarily listener focused – the composer's intentions, methods and approaches may influence but not define the experience of the music. We aim to make analysis an *active support* for listening and composition. Hence this book is intended for wide use within composition, teaching, analysis and musicology at all levels, including non-specialist users. Our project has brought together existing research, attempting to assess its range and efficacy. From this we have tried to identify needs and to 'fill gaps' in the assembled toolkit.

Research methods

The first stage of any such project involves the assembly and comparative evaluation of existing analytical tools. After assembly of the toolbox, we will be in a better position to see if there are gaps – that is, topics, genres, materials which are not fully addressed or do not have relevant tools available. We must then address how best we *represent* the data needed for analysis for each genre or category and how this limits the analytical questions. The tools and the questions are thus strongly interactive. This all informed the project's software development and innovation (EAnalysis), and hence the content of this book.

But this book has a further function beyond simply being the outcome of this research project. The analytical discussions are not intended to be dry and unapplied, but immediately to encourage more engagement and under-standing of the music *through listening*. All music examples are publicly available on CD or reliable download.[1] Thus the completion of the research 'method' lies with the reader-listener. The analyses focus on aspects of the work *that can be heard* – not those that can *only* be detected by machines.

Some important points of departure: the four-part question and a template for analytical discussion

The question that we posed when applying for funding for this project was: What do we want from analysis of electroacoustic music and how might we get it? This raises a number of questions. In fact, we could simply go back to the heart of the matter and ask: What is music analysis? *The New Grove Dictionary* includes the following definition: '[A]nalysis may be said to include the interpretation of structures in music together with their resolution into relatively simpler constituent elements and the investiga-tion of the relevant functions of these elements' (*New Grove* 2001). This, in itself, does cover a large part of the territory that we wanted to investigate.

---

1 In addition, several contributors have prepared (with permission) sound and video examples to be found on the website accompanying this book.

Interesting here is the central focus on structure, perhaps the weakest point in terms of methods and tools used in electroacoustic analysis thus far. Moving from structure to detail makes sense in a great deal of music, but there are two issues that might be raised in order to suggest that this definition might not be ideal for our purposes. First, part of the reason why structure (and form) has proven so problematic in much electroacoustic music analysis has to do with the fact that a fair share of this music is what might be called 'bottom-up composition'. With this approach the building blocks are the small-scale sound materials, often painstakingly assembled without a pre-formed structure common to many forms of traditional music. Therefore, many structures are unique and difficult to identify convincingly. There is another issue, too. As will be discussed shortly regarding our so-called 'four-part question', an analysis need not focus on the entirety of a work, but instead on one or more aspects of the composition. Structure may not be amongst these unless it is of influence to the understanding of the analytical goals or intentions.

Closer to home, it was Emmerson who helped launch (at least in English) the discussion regarding 'the language of electroacoustic music' in 1986. Do we know much more about this subject over a quarter of a century later? The questions that led us to embark on this project included: Why have there been so few analyses made of electroacoustic music? Why are many of these based on the poiesis, that is, the construction of a work, as opposed to being related to its reception? Why have so few tools and methods been proposed for electroacoustic music analysis[2] and, with this in mind, is it right that so many analyses rely heavily, on the one hand, on Schaeffer's and Smalley's contributions (e.g. Schaeffer 1977; Smalley 1997, 2007) or, on the other hand, on sonograms and other graphic forms of representation (Licata 2002 and Simoni 2006, amongst others)? To what extent are approaches used in note-based music analysis relevant to this project?

Part of the problem, as summarised in Landy's 2007 book, *Understanding the Art of Sound Organization*, is that a great deal of high-level research has been done in the field of electroacoustic music studies, but there has been too little foundational work presented. We do not possess a large choice of tools for this type of analysis. Perhaps poietic analysis is more straightforward – we have so much more information from the composers themselves, as well as descriptions of technical means. Schaeffer's and

---

[2] Michael Gatt's OREMA and Pierre Couprie's EAnalysis (Couprie 2012) have assembled most of these – some are discussed below.

Smalley's work is based on morphological categorisation and evolution, that is, a bottom-up approach which rarely looks at mid- and large-scale structural entities. Their application to the listening experience seems to be easily made, and it is quite likely that it is for this reason that their approaches have been called upon fairly regularly.

Falling back on note-based tools can be dangerous. Is the sound event, however defined, the same as the musical note? Clearly not; more likely a cluster or accumulation of notes would be more appropriate. Much note-based analysis is based upon expectancy or grammatical issues. Expectancy in electroacoustic music is a growing area of analytical concern, but has hardly been developed. This is perhaps ironic, as the notion of the 'electroacoustic cliché' has existed for quite some time. To our knowledge, this has not been formally studied thus far. In any event, discussions between analysts of traditional music and of electroacoustic music are long overdue. Fortunately, new types of analytical approaches are being developed, such as Michael Clarke's interactive analysis (see, e.g., Clarke 2006, 2010) where the analyst creates a simulation of how a composer created some of their materials and the user can relive the experience as well as try alternatives using the same technique. Again this is very much based on bottom-up building principles.

In attempting to define analysis for the many genres and categories examined in this book, we took an empirical view. As suggested above, one does not normally analyse a piece of music from every conceivable angle; the analyst has specific intentions. An analysis is based on the sum of those intentions. To create a working empirical model, a *four-part question* has been formulated that is offered as a basis to determine what one might seek when investigating electroacoustic works from the listener's point of view. (It is indeed true that this question can be applied to other types of music, but it is crucially needed in a world which has little history and few developed tools.) There is no particular order of importance:

. For which users?
. For which works/genres?
. With what intentions?
. With which tools and approaches?

Let us discuss these now one by one. As far as *for which users* is concerned, one might think of describing potential users based on specialists (musicologists, musicians, educators) or non-specialists (e.g. school children). Another way of looking at this would be to support understanding related to: research, composition/practice and teaching. Let's tease this out briefly. *Research* needs the least amount of elaboration as most analysis has been undertaken with this specific goal in mind. Thus the goal is the greater understanding of certain aspects of a given work, not necessarily with any particular application envisioned. *Composition/practice* is an area that has not yet been considered by many involved with analysis in this field. One can analyse a work before the act of composition to understand aspects of one's own or another person's work that might influence the piece in question. One can also analyse a work after it has been completed to identify characteristics that were not consciously part of the compositional process. Finally, and this is perhaps the most radical of the three approaches mentioned here, one can analyse what is taking place in a work during performance. For example, a laptop ensemble's members may be able to track what they are playing and, on the fly, select materials used and either return to them or modify them during performance. As far as this book is concerned, this falls under the category 'future plans', as it is not in our current remit. *Teaching* refers to both specialists (e.g. at higher education level) and non-specialists in schools. Analysis can be used in teaching not only to support the general understanding of a work, but also to exemplify new general ideas and concepts.[3]

The question *for which works/genres* will be treated at some length in the following section. The list of *tools and approaches* is quite finite currently. We have already cited Schaeffer's 'typomorphologie' and Smalley's 'spectromorphology' and 'spatiomorphology'. Then there are Roy's and Thoresen's additions related to these (Roy 2003; Thoresen 2007). Furthermore there is UST ('unités sémiotiques temporelles', MIM 1996) on offer, not to mention Emmerson's 'language grid' (Emmerson 1986) and Landy's 'something to hold on to factor' (Landy 1994). Other tools have been created for timbral contemporary music including instrumental note-based works. A list of these can be found on the OREMA site that will be introduced in detail in Chapter 7 (www.orema.dmu.ac.uk/?q=analytical_toolbox). None of these has been widely applied in electroacoustic music analysis. Beyond this, there are new computational ones being developed; ones to do with structure beyond the level of gesture; ones to do with live performance, installations or audio-visual works. As these are developed,

---

[3] For example, in the EARS 2 Pedagogical project (Landy *et al.* 2013; ears2.dmu.ac.uk), brief analyses are presented to young learners (for example 11–14 years old) to introduce them to particular concepts and to aid their appreciation of this type of music. An example of how this might be done is presented in the Wishart analysis in Chapter 9 of this book.

they should be tested to investigate where they optimally apply. Our goal is to offer as many of these as we can on EAnalysis (the program developed as part of this project and introduced by Pierre Couprie in Chapter 8) and add newly developed ones that can also be implemented in the future. However, these tools and approaches do not exist in isolation and should always be related to an analytical intention.

Analysis can have one goal or many interconnected ones. The question *with what intentions* is our means of articulating these goals. Intentions might include aspects such as to reveal structuring, layering, narrative discourse, sound qualities[4] and their evolution in time, and gestures at the local level. We might aim to examine movement from one type of listening to another (e.g. between contextual and musical), drawing in social, emotional or meaning elements, and any of these in combination with other performance-related and sonic aspects. Furthermore, a composer's dramaturgic intention and/or compositional aspects may need to be triangulated as part of an analysis.

The following list of 'headers' has been put together to form a proposed template for analysis. This template has been proposed in order to offer people a potential model for the consistent presentation of analyses based on defined intentions yet flexible when specific concerns are of importance. All authors presenting analyses in Part IV received it and used it as a benchmark appropriately to their genre.

- Representation
- Materials
- Listening behaviour
- Behaviour of materials
- Ordering
- Space
- Performative elements
- Intention/reception, social, emotional and meaning-related aspects
- Elements specific to a given genre or piece.

Representation. Many analysing electroacoustic music like to include or even to be led by some form of visual representation. Examples vary from handmade diffusion scores subsequently used for analysis and sonograms

---

[4] 'This is used as an umbrella term [...] referring to a single or composite sound's aural characteristics. Instead of discussing source and cause, in this case one describes the sound's colour or timbre, aspects related to its texture and any other description related to its sonic as opposed to contextual value' (Landy 2012: 195–6).

(or similar) including specially prepared output files from such as the GRM's Acousmographe to the much more complex visualisations possible with EAnalysis transcription and annotation. The question of importance here is: What are the most effective form(s) of representation? The answer is largely dependent on what has been proposed based on the four-part question. EAnalysis continues to be developed so that it will be seen to be highly flexible to optimise its usefulness. Although it is by no means solely a representation tool, it offers a wide variety of types of representation to aid an analyst's work.

Materials. What types of sounds have been used and what sound morphologies are present? In aesthesic and, to an extent, poietic analysis, this can be a non-trivial request. We have very few systems for categorising sound materials. Some sound descriptions are based on surmised source and cause, while others are not, relying solely on spectral and other acoustic data; yet others are more metaphoric of the visual and emotion domains. Presenting materials on a simple list may be a useful first step, but this needs to become a well-organised taxonomy which can be combined with other items of the template, such as sound behaviours, ordering and the like.

Listening behaviour. The way the listener interprets sound material, its behaviour and function within sound structures is the subject of modes of listening, whether Schaeffer's 'quatre écoutes' or any other alternative that has been presented by numerous authors (e.g. Truax 1984; Norman 1996). Listening strategies are rarely identical amongst listeners to music or even from one aural experience of a work to another. Some shifts of material within pieces do indeed trigger an altered means of listening. Real-world musical material may call for heightened or contextual listening whilst more abstract material may invite reduced or musical listening. In other words, the recognisability of sounds may affect the listening experience. Finding relationships between listening behaviour and the musical language involved can be a very gratifying aspect of electroacoustic music analysis.

Behaviour of materials. This item picks up on the morphology aspect raised under materials (above). As in any kind of music, once material has been introduced, it tends to reappear under several guises. Therefore, behaviour has to do with the development of sound qualities. It also has to do with the combination of materials; for example, sometimes, when two material types are presented concurrently, they blend to create a single sound quality. In other situations, this may not be the case and they take on an individual role in the collection of sounds present. For example, when using contextual elements where source identification is suggested, what is the relationship between foreground and these more contextual sounds? Behaviour of materials is a focus in a great number of analyses, as it should be; it is often combined with discussions under the next heading (they form an interacting pair) – ordering.

Ordering. This item focuses on the order of sound events and their organisation. It can be investigated in terms of both horizontal and vertical components. Furthermore, it involves audible salient characteristics related to sonic and structural behaviour as well as discourse. Once patterns are discovered, their evolution in terms of ordering can be investigated. Patterns may be discovered at many levels within the work. Ordering investigates small- to full-scale means of structuring.[5]

It is perhaps in this item, more than others, that relationships with note-based music can be discovered. For example, much analysis of twentieth-century European art music, like the compositions themselves, focuses on the isolation of musical parameters. Perhaps the best known are analyses of 12-tone (or pitch-set) works in which primarily pitch is taken into account. However, pitch is not the only isolable parameter relevant to instrumental or electroacoustic music. Duration (of events, gestures, sequences, other structural entities) forms its complement. Other parameters of relevance include dynamics, density, order/disorder, simultaneities (analogous with traditional harmony), horizontal relationships such as layering (analogous with traditional counterpoint) and space (see below).

Large-scale structure identification along with narrative and discourse elements of a work are underdeveloped aspects of electroacoustic music analysis. This is possibly due to the fact that many works constructed bottom-up are difficult to analyse at this level. Textural compositions, focused on layering, deserve another approach to structure than that applied in most note-based music analysis. Many (by no means all) works based on a priori structuring rules fall under the heading of formalised composition. The interesting challenge here is that the majority of formalised electroacoustic works are based on algorithmic methods that are not readily deciphered aurally. This is another reason why structural analysis is in need of development in this field.[6]

---

[5] One aspect of this, which is an aim of ongoing research, is the development of computational sound/sonic behaviour spotting (Casey 2009).

[6] Ironically, this raises the question of how easy works without identifiable structures are for listeners, but that is a subject for another book.

Space. Discussion of spatialisation has been a recent development in electroacoustic music analysis, yet it is one of the most audible and interesting aspects of the art form. The treatment of space and spatial movement is an integral part of electroacoustic composition and should be reflected in analysis. Terminology has evolved related to spatialisation, not least Smalley's vocabulary related to spatiomorphology (1997, 2007), which can be put to good use when applying this template. Some works from the psychoacoustic literature (Handel 1989; Bregman 1994) will also allow us to explain the relationship of the musical materials to perceptions of space, structure and 'scene'. In mixed and live electronic works, there are social spaces around the performers and audience, the venue and environment (Emmerson 2007). Even in fixed works which are actively diffused, recordings have been made and compared of a single composition diffused differently to identify different interpretation strategies.

Performative elements. Aspects of electroacoustic music, related to musicians making live, in particular improvised, performance, may need special attention. There may be no score or fixed media. Issues of performance, or 'liveness', cannot be separated from the sounding result of, for example, a live electronics performance. Where improvisation is involved, it is certainly useful to investigate more than one performance (whether of a given piece or a specific ensemble) when it comes to analysis. The language of performance, the level of on-the-spot decisions and their musical coherence, may form part of the many aspects related to performance that belong to this template. Using video recordings of performances is useful when considering performative elements (and was an early inclusion in the development of EAnalysis).

Intention/reception, social, emotional and meaning-related aspects. Amongst the things we may hold on to when listening, and which contribute to analysis, are extra-musical aspects, such as dramaturgic intentions. The intention/reception loop is a means of gauging successful musical communication whenever a musician is willing to share intention information. There are many levels of such potential communication: dramaturgic, emotional and meaning-related aspects are perhaps the most important. These are often best analysed by working with groups of listeners of the same or of differing backgrounds to learn to what extent the reception of works offers coherent response data.

Another aspect of a good deal of electroacoustic music relates to the social circumstances of performance. Not all electroacoustic music genres are intended for traditional concert presentation. Some types may be presented in clubs, galleries and the like, for example, sound installations, some of which may be site-specific. Social settings inform the musical experience either through the community sharing the musical values of a genre or for other reasons. These need to be integrated into electroacoustic analytical studies.

Elements specific to a given genre or piece. Although this template attempts to cover as much common ground as possible, there is in general no isomorphic relationship between intentions, tools and genres. There are genres, even specific pieces, that pose particular questions that are not of universal relevance, such as audio-visual coordination in installations and visual music or specific questions related to interactivity, such as comprehensibility to the audience or the participant.

Therefore, there are certain intentions that are more relevant to some genres than to others. Let us look at *sampling culture* to exemplify this. *Which tools and approaches* are of particular importance to this body of music? In some cases these take on a specific importance, even though they might be of relevance to other genres, while in other cases, they are of particular relevance only to the genre, itself.

- Which (types of) sources?
- How are they treated? (E.g. with respect, ironically.)
- Are they used legally? (If not, was this deliberate?)
- Have they been modified? If so, to what extent are they still recognisable?
- What role do they play in the work/performance?
- How have they been integrated into the composition/performance?

In particular the second and third questions above are specific to sample-based music. The others are more generic but take on a special function in many such works. A list related to any other electroacoustic genre or category would look quite dissimilar to this one. These questions are all discussed in the analysis of Trevor Wishart's sample-based composition in Chapter 9 of this book.

This template has been proposed as a starting point for investigations and subsequent presentations of analyses of electroacoustic works. It has also been conceived to offer some consistency in terms of the presentation of electroacoustic analyses regardless of the answer to the four-part question. It is not complete, nor is it intended to remain in its current form. It will evolve as new genre hybrids on the one hand and technological tools on the other are developed.

As suggested earlier, an analysis may include investigations of more than one aspect. One might consider analyses involving *three intentions for one piece*. In this example, one might conceive of someone investigating the relationship between order/disorder and narrative discourse in a specific work or the relationship between layering and simultaneities or the relationship between source identification and structure in the same work. It is equally conceivable that one apply *a single tool across three dissimilar genres*. One might consider investigating sound recurrence and variation through sound spotting in an acousmatic, a lower case or a Sound Art work. It would be easy to conceive of hundreds of such examples. These examples show the breadth and flexibility of the four-part question.

The four-part question and its associated template allow us to look at electroacoustic analysis holistically. It is clearly true that the four-part question could be used for any type of music. It has been proposed here to help people identify exactly what they might seek from an analysis of an electroacoustic work or genre. These two together have made it possible for us try to delineate an area of electroacoustic music analysis. They formed an important part of the project's foundation and that of the current book, and offer a point of departure for those interested in undertaking analytical studies.

Genres and categories: differing demands

Now we have attempted to delimit the field in the questions and template discussed above, let us turn to the varying needs of the genres and categories themselves. Genre and category (as we have defined them) may be seen as essentially social constructs, in some ways comparable to subcultures which are based on shared practice. As has been much discussed by ethnomusicologists over the years, this can create problems of 'insider/outsider' decoding – members of a given social group may articulate the important features of their culture in very different ways to an outsider. These have been termed 'etic' and 'emic' differences. Etic refers to a *measurable* difference, emic to a *significant* difference. Thus the idea of emic is based on salient features as defined by the community of practice. But this raises some interesting issues – is it not possible for a community to work in a particular way *unaware* (or at least not consciously aware) of some features of their work which seem obvious (salient) to outsiders? In the tradition we know as 'acousmatic', practitioners claim to judge combinations of sounds on the 'ear', that is, 'what sounds right'. They rarely say much more on what that sounding right actually entails. It may thus have to be much more an outsider's view as to how we answer that question.

What kinds of things do we want to examine? What are the salient aspects and how do we describe them? Our research has thrown up some unexpected applications of words and meanings. One theme that has emerged is the steady migration of a language derived from one genre (or category) applied to another – this may lead to some confusion which may need to be tested to see what might be valuable. The following terms are all found in the literature to mean roughly the same thing – *parameters, variables, qualities, attributes, properties, features*. We must remember, however, that these have been largely developed with respect to analysis of the sound signal or its transcribed (visualised) substitutes. Applied more broadly to interpretation and more subjective listening traits, the meanings shift. Thus the salient features of a genre need to encapsulate not only the soundworld, but also the world of interpretation and sites of reception.

Hence each genre or category is 'generated' by its salient features.[7] These features work effectively like tags which configure into 'clouds' for a given genre practice. These demand languages of description – that is, vocabularies – which in turn help define suitable tools for analysis. The following list reduces the large range of analytical issues described above in the 'template' to four key areas – material, construction, interpretation, site and place. These interact continuously but help define the vocabularies we have seen emerging in the last 50 years for the definition of genre. None can strictly be separated – a genre may privilege one or another but all will play a part to some degree.

Material and its organisation

There is an assumption in this undertaking that we are dealing (with some small exceptions) with what Landy has described as 'sound-based musics' – that is, those where pitches (or 'notes') play a secondary role (if any) to sound qualities. Also we confine ourselves to musics where technology plays an important mediating role. Thus sounds are our subject – and such genres will need an agreed representation and description.

---

[7] Not the other way round.

That said, we note that some of the contributors to the analytical part of this volume resisted 'outside time' representations of their chosen music when discussing the organisation of the sounding flow.

There was a range of reasons – mostly that 'fixing' time in this way gave a false sense of music as 'architecture'. By appearing to fix structure and form in this way, the time dimension is frozen in space and (it is argued) its perceptual essence lost. The alternative view prefers to describe music rather as a living organism having 'growth' and 'behaviour', and the listener as part of a process emerging from the accumulation of experience over time. The 'sound object' gives way to the 'sound event'.

The advent of analysis tools that include full playback facilities has made a substantial difference in this respect. Programs such as Sonic Visualiser, Acousmographe and this project's EAnalysis return the time domain (listening) to near the forefront of use features. In forthcoming versions of books such as this read on portable devices, all musical figures will have the capacity to play back their materials.[8] Taken to an extreme, we might not need to discuss music *with words* at all – leaving its experience unsullied by mere verbal or graphic interpretation. But words are a form of representation (however limited) which can guide us over time through an enhanced experience.

Interpretation

Ecologically informed thinking ensures we do not erroneously separate interpretation from perception itself in some arbitrary manner. It is intimately bound in with how we discuss materials and organisation. Most clearly this is true on those many earlier discussions that deal with surmising sources and causes in acousmatic music. We are at the same time describing a sound quality and its behaviour, but with respect to some imagined object and agency, 'out there'. We play games with the real, the imaginary and the imaginative. Denis Smalley has suggested (1996) that we need reference to what he calls the real world's 'indicative fields' to make sense of the acousmatic musical flow. Then a further sense of interpretation was introduced by Luke Windsor (after Gibson) (2000), who introduced *affordance* to the musical vocabulary. This may be interpreted

---

[8] Of course, this is possible today and effective in e-journals – but copyright issues still inhibit widespread adoption.

both literally (the music affords us listening) and imaginatively (the music may 'tell stories' and afford us empathic responses).

The domain of the more personal response – of narrative, meaning, affect and feeling – has been difficult to grasp and largely ignored until recently in analytical discussion of contemporary music in general and electroacoustic music in particular. In commissioning the analyses contained in this volume, we encouraged all the authors to address this area. Not surprisingly, those who wished to forefront symbolic and extra-musical reference found this to be no problem but we sense a continuing need to develop (over a longer timescale than we have available) a community discussion on what many of these musical genres convey or mean.[9]

Site and place

What is the music *in this place* communicating to us as individuals and as a community and how best do we communicate that amongst ourselves? All music is interpreted and presented some*time* and some*where* and this will always affect what takes place. But this trivialises the degree to which site and place can be fully *part* of the musicking. Where I am and who I am with when I listen to music (or participate in its making) effects salient features and qualities of the result. While clearly true of site-specific installations – where the materials and their organisation are determined largely by the site itself – it is equally true for freer forms of live music making such as improvisation.[10] Here there may be a strong sense of theatre and dramaturgy, an essential empathy between audience and the performers which may be hard to capture and account for.

However, there remains a legacy of 'absolute music' which persists in some genres – those that claim a 'high art' heritage usually. In this view, the music exists outside of its performance time and place – a Platonic ideal to be aimed for in performance, though rarely achieved. In the fixed media acousmatic genre, this is sometimes equated with a 'neutral/perfect' studio listening experience such as the composer might have had, though others see the performance as 'completing' the composition and thus demanding that the performance space be taken into account (Harrison 1998).

We thus have a reciprocal and dynamic relationship: the genre as practice is defined by salient features and an appropriate vocabulary through

---

[9] In Chapter 2 of this volume Gary Kendall makes a further step along this long road.
[10] As Sophy Smith (Chapter 15) and John Ferguson (Chapter 12) discuss in this volume.

dynamic and evolving configurations of material, construction, interpretation, site and place.

'Poietic leakage'

While the orientation of this project is clearly to focus on the listener's
experience and how the music may be analysed from this perspective, it is
of course impossible completely to *exclude* the composer's intentions on
the one hand and the poietic aspects of social context on the other. Both of
these contribute to the construction of the music in some way, and the
knowledge the listener has of these will influence the resulting experience.
For example, this is clearly true when socially sited aspects of practice
become dominant – it may be that a very real social critique is embedded
in the performance. Take *hardware hacking* – here the primary purpose
often lies in social activity, the practice *resists* acousmatic aestheticisation
of the sound alone and usually demands a visual dimension (perhaps
projection) and some knowledge of the real objects and social circumstances of the performance. An examination of music as social practice
clearly demands more than simply recorded sound. We may also listen
differently if we know (or are told) that a work is generated from a
particular (say a *swarm*) algorithm. This knowledge might be a helpful
part of the learning cycle – if several swarm pieces share characteristics, we
may in time learn to recognise these characteristics without prompting.
There are many more such examples of *poietic leakage* being vital to the
listening experience.

Some examples

We cannot here illustrate every genre and its needs – many are covered in
the discussions of Part IV. Here we aim simply to show how a range of
genres generate different visualisations and hence demand different
approaches to discussion. Each EAnalysis page shows contrasting examples
of salient features addressing material, construction, interpretation with
reference also to issues of site and place – in each genre similar features
may be present but with (very) different emphasis. Types of relevant
language and 'holes' in the descriptive vocabularies will be highlighted
and filled as the research progresses. We have in general suggested that
many 'taboo' issues of representation and description be abandoned as a

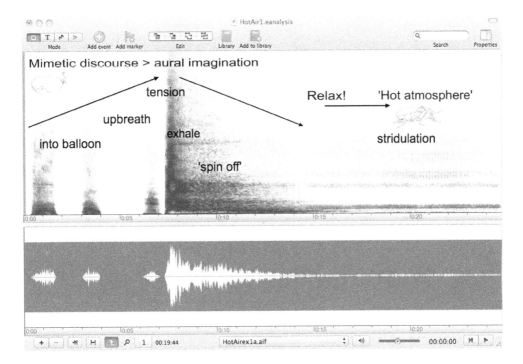

Figure 1.1 Jonty Harrison – *Hot Air* (opening)

way of 'freeing up' the discussion. Thus if we believe we hear a cicada sound, then perhaps a pictogram of a cicada will illustrate that this is indeed a real-world referent for the listener (Figure 1.1).[11] However, there is no (equivalent) pictogram for mains hum[12] – so one could instead use the written phrase (Figure 1.2).

Thus an example from a fixed media acousmatic tradition – *Hot Air* by Jonty Harrison – is rich with real-world references 'feeding back' into the more musically abstract discourse.[13] Its salient features and hence vocabularies of description reflect this wide range.

The glitch work *Cyclo (C2)* by Ryoji Ikeda and Carsten Nicolai is centred on technological artefact. The hum, spark sounds and glitches have extraordinarily characteristic spectra quite unlike the natural environmental sounds of the Harrison. We can also easily extract the rhythmic articulation and the 'call and response' patterns within the motifs. Sounds originally

[11] Colour versions of the figures in this chapter may be found on the website accompanying this book.
[12] Of course, other electrical symbols might be useable.
[13] This would be described as a 'balance of aural and mimetic discourse' in Emmerson (1986) and as 'expanded listening' in Harrison (1996).

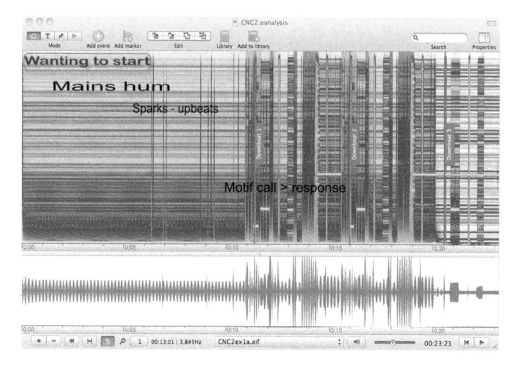

Figure 1.2 Ryoji Ikeda and Carsten Nicolai – *Cyclo (C2)* (opening)

associated with 'breakdown' or 'failure' are now commonplace and have migrated to other genres and sites of practice.

Our third example is the classic soundscape composition *Kits Beach Soundwalk* by Hildegard Westerkamp (Figure 1.3). Here we see how the piece is structured sonically – and how this follows the composer's 'voice-over' narrative. What is emphasised by the display is the frequency-dependent 'sculpting' of the sound – with the delicate environmental sounds 'floating' above the city – which has been surgically removed (filtered out) to allow the small sounds greater voice. The two dream sequences are clearly differentiated, the second incorporating quotations from Xenakis's *Concret PH* (unaltered) followed by Mozart's Clarinet Concerto (hi-pass filtered to match the surrounding frequencies). This all confirms our ear's suggestion of a kind of 'niche theory' (Krause 1987) in which the voices of nature speak more clearly through unmasked frequency bands. The pertinent feature here is the relationship of frequency band to perceived environmental cause.[14]

---

[14] This is expressly referred to in the voiceover – which 'demonstrates' the exaggeration and then filtering out of the city ('the monster').

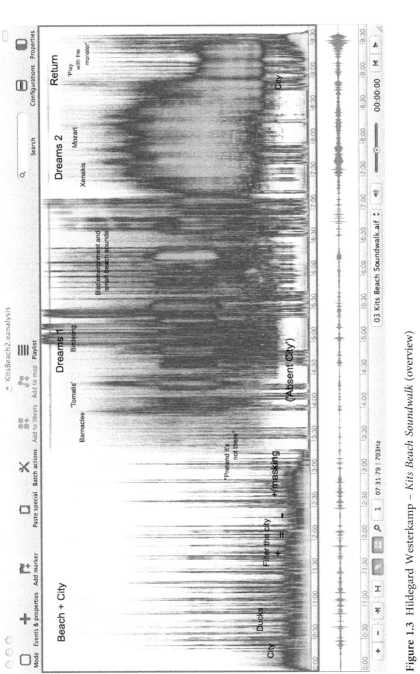

Figure 1.3 Hildegard Westerkamp – *Kits Beach Soundwalk* (overview)

Conclusion

We have developed a symbiotic model of genre and analysis with electro-acoustic music which is dynamic. Over time, genres of music change and hybridise. The genre as practice defines to a large part its salient features not all of which we will immediately grasp. Analysis seeks to uncover, explain and integrate our experience of the music (or sound art) and how it 'works'. This is a potentially vast task where there is no definitive analysis; we have thus attempted to bring a degree of order to this field by articulating a four-part question and a template. These we put to the authors of the contributions in Part IV who analyse examples from a range of genres. While they have each applied the ideas in a different way – some in common across a range of genres, others more specific to the artwork they have chosen – there is a core coherence which we believe unites their purpose.

References

Bregman, A. S. 1994. *Auditory Scene Analysis: The Perceptual Organization of Sound.* Cambridge, MA: MIT Press.

Casey, M. 2009. Soundspotting: A new kind of process? In R. T. Dean (ed.) *The Oxford Handbook of Computer Music.* Oxford University Press.

Clarke, M. 2006. Jonathan Harvey's *Mortuos Plango, Vivos Voco.* In M. Simoni (ed.) *Analytical Methods of Electroacoustic Music.* London: Routledge, 111–43.

2010. Wind chimes: An interactive aural analysis. In É. Gayou (ed.) *Denis Smalley: Polychrome Portraits.* Paris: INA/GRM, 35–57.

Couprie, P. 2012. EAnalysis: A new electroacoustic music analysis piece of software, in *Proceedings of the Electroacoustic Music Studies Network Conference, Stockholm 2012* (www.ems-network.org/spip.php?rubrique48).

Emmerson, S. 1986. The relation of language to materials. In S. Emmerson (ed.) *The Language of Electroacoustic Music.* Basingstoke: Macmillan, 17–39.

2007. *Living Electronic Music.* Aldershot: Ashgate.

Handel, S. 1989. *Listening: An Introduction to the Perception of Auditory Events.* Cambridge, MA: MIT Press.

Harrison, J. 1996. Liner notes, *Articles indéfinis* (CD), Empreintes Digitales: IMED 9627.

1998. Sound, space, sculpture: Some thoughts on the 'what', 'how' and 'why' of sound diffusion. *Organised Sound* 3(02), 117–27.

Krause, B. 1987. The niche hypothesis: How animals taught us to dance and sing. *Whole Earth Review* 57.

Landy, L. 1994. The 'something to hold on to factor' in timbral composition. *Contemporary Music Review* 10(2), 49–60.

2007. *Understanding the Art of Sound Organization.* Cambridge, MA: MIT Press.

2012. *Making Music with Sounds.* New York: Routledge.

Landy, L., Hall, R. and Uwins, M. 2013. Widening participation in electroacoustic music: The EARS 2 pedagogical initiatives. *Organised Sound* 18(2), 108–23.

Licata, T. (ed.) 2002. *Electroacoustic Music: Analytical Perspectives.* Westport: Greenwood Press.

MIM. 1996. *Les Unités Sémiotiques Temporelles – Élements nouveaux d'analyse musicale.* Marseille: Édition MIM – Documents Musurgia.

The New Grove Dictionary of Music and Musicians. 2001. Ed. S. Sadie and J. Tyrrell, 2nd edn. London: Macmillan.

Norman, K. 1996. Real-world music as composed listening. *Contemporary Music Review* 15(1–2), 1–27.

Roy, S. 2003. *L'analyse des musiques électroacoustiques: modèles et propositions.* Paris: L'Harmattan.

Schaeffer, P. 1977. *Traité des objets musicaux: essai interdisciplines.* Paris: Seuil (2nd edn; orig. 1966).

Simoni, M. 2006. *Analytical Methods of Electroacoustic Music.* New York: Routledge.

Smalley, D. 1996. The listening imagination: Listening in the electroacoustic era. *Contemporary Music Review* 13(2), 77–107.

1997. Spectromorphology: Explaining sound shapes. *Organised Sound* 2(2), 107–26.

2007. Space-form and the acousmatic image. *Organised Sound* 12(1), 35–58.

Thoresen, L. 2007. Spectromorphological analysis of sound-objects: An adaptation of Pierre Schaeffer's typomorphology. *Organised Sound* 12(2), 129–41.

Truax, B. 1984. *Acoustic Communication.* Norwood, NJ: Ablex.

Windsor, L. 2000. Through and around the acousmatic: The interpretation of electroacoustic sounds. In S. Emmerson (ed.) *Music, Electronic Media and Culture.* Aldershot: Ashgate, 7–35.

PART II

Ideas and challenges

2 | Listening and meaning: how a model of mental layers informs electroacoustic music analysis

GARY S. KENDALL

Introduction

Concerning the analysis of electroacoustic music

For me, the key question to be answered by the analysis of electroacoustic music is: How does the listener's experience of listening become *meaning-ful*? Amidst the novel timbres and spatial soundscapes, the raw electronics and clashing juxtapositions, the electroacoustic listener is instantly making sense of auditory sensations and experiencing meaning. For the more experienced listener, this may be a well-accustomed encounter that imme-diately gives rise to clear and nuanced meanings. This listener likely has a personal history of similar encounters, possibly spanning multiple genres of works and composers, and perhaps this listener is particularly familiar with some electroacoustic works that have become exemplars of the genre's idioms. For the novice listener, this could be a disorienting encounter with an aural landscape that juxtaposes the recognizable with the unknown, whose unfamiliar topography is best comprehended in terms of eccentric objects and fragmented narratives. What is so easily lost in this perspective is how similarly both the expert and the novice are experiencing meaning.

That meaning varies widely with individual listeners is clear. Meaning is a product of the individual listener's mental processes: whatever meaning the listener makes of the listening experience, that is its meaning to the listener. But as listeners become more familiar with a particular work of electroacoustic music, we should expect that these meanings become less divergent and more finely attuned to the specific implications of the work, essentially because the mental processes of the individual listeners are increasingly guided along convergent lines, even when we allow for their differences in personal history. Therefore, the analyst should be mindful not to ascribe meaning to the physical acoustic attributes of a work or to graphic representations based on signal analysis in which the listening experience is not captured. For analysis to be truly credible, it must be envisioned fundamentally in terms of human perception and cognition. This places a rigorous responsibility on our analytical techniques to justify

31

their relevance to the listener's mental activity and to avoid unexamined, implicit assumptions about what is meaningful to the listener.

Cognitive processes

Part of this continuing dilemma is the lack of a framework for discussing the subjective experience of art, that is, for putting its component parts up on the board for study. Clearly listeners have experiences that are meaningful and varied. But how does this come about and what are the mechanisms by which this happens? We understand that the listener's mental processes are at root neurological processes and that neuroscience provides an important framework, but we can also approach listening in terms of *cognitive processes*.

A major objective driving what might be termed the cognitive deconstruction of artistic experience is to analyze the functional architecture of its underlying component operations. (Donald 2006: 10)

This statement is representative of an effort within cognitive sciences to address humanity's distinctive aesthetic capacity and to elucidate the mental basis of this capacity. We posit cognitive processes in order to facilitate a discussion of such mental activity in terms of functional components like working memory, attention, or schemas. It is a goal of this chapter to clarify ways in which listening processes can give rise to meaning in electroacoustic music, specifically to highlight the importance of mental layers to the essence of how meaning arises while listening.

Mental processes and the five mental layers

Listening is a mental activity that is constantly unfolding. It unfolds moment to moment in time, and importantly it also unfolds in multiple, simultaneous layers. In order to address these issues, a *model of five mental layers* will be introduced: a model that is sufficiently complex to clarify how the notion of layers contributes to our understanding of the listening experience.

The five-layer model

The model of the five layers starts at the bottom with the simplest sensory processes and proceeds up layer by layer to the most synoptic and abstract level. Other authors within cognitive science have postulated similar ideas for a variety of purposes (Donald 2001). This model owes a large debt in particular to Per Aage Brandt (2004: 180–5; 2006: 173–6) who says:

our organization of what we will call *meaning* is a process that occurs on many levels simultaneously. On a scale extending from the most dense, massive, and 'concrete' sensations to the most transparent and 'abstract' notional conceptualizations, we may distinguish a series of strata interrelated by processes of integration. (Brandt 2006: 173)

Our purpose here is to account for listening processes, and for that reason the discussion of this model will not address many concerns that might otherwise be important to cognitive scientists. At the same time, our focus on listening enables us to greatly increase the level of specificity within Brandt's model. The five layers can be summarized as follows:

Layer 1. **Sensations** – Perceptual organization and constancy of immediate sensation.

Layer 2. **Gist** – Framework of things and space extended over several seconds enabling sustained awareness in the short term.

Layer 3. **Locus** – Self-governing actions in response to situations in the 'perceptual present' and slightly beyond.

Layer 4. **Contexts** – Framework for enlisting and assessing medium- and long-term, event-oriented schemas and expectations over an extended time frame.

Layer 5. **Domains** – Frameworks of background knowledge providing long-term constancy.

(Kendall 2014: 195)

While Brandt was in part influenced by considerations of neural physiology, this model is not about physiology per se. Rather, the model is being adapted here as a product of cognitive semantics, here acknowledging the multilayered, parallel nature of meaning making. In this sense, cognitive semantics is being taken as a highly relevant and informative inspiration for understanding meaning in electroacoustic music. Brandt (2006) himself makes the explicit connection to aesthetic experience and employed this framework in a discussion of the aesthetic experience of specific works of visual art. A major difference between the contexts of visual art and music then is the temporal flow and the 'in-the-moment' nature of music listening that finds no parallel in Brandt's analysis of the visual experience. The discussion ahead will specifically address issues of time. Then, too, Brandt (2004: 182) originally labeled the model's layers correspondingly as Qualia, Things, Situations, Notions, and Feelings. The relabeling of the layers for the specific context addressed here is generally in line with

Brandt's original thesis, with the exception of the last layer which Brandt later re-labeled as 'Emotions' (2006: 174). The exception to Brandt made here was primarily motivated by a different approach to feelings and emotions (Kendall 2014), which differentiates feelings and emotions by layer, rather than grouping them into one layer. And still, the major objective of this chapter is to extend Brandt's five-layer model in a way that supports the detailed analysis of electroacoustic listening.

Productions

Each layer can be described in terms of what it produces, that is, the kind of mental productions it constructs and manages. Each is producing potential meanings from within its own 'vantage point', percolating meanings from which dominant meanings will ultimately emerge. An overview of the productions relevant to electroacoustic music listening is shown in Table 2.1.

Let us illustrate the organization of these productions and their layers with a hypothetical example from everyday life, here demonstrating how the mind forms a single thread linking related productions across the layers. Our example starts with a series of clicking events that *Sensations* would group as an auditory stream whose localization could be affected by multimodal influences such as visual motion. This is the start of a thread that *Gist* would take up and understand as footsteps in the spatial context of a reverberant room, a thread that would likely be the foreground against background noise. Given this current situation in *Gist*, *Locus* decides where attention should be focused: on the thread of the footsteps that are approaching from the right or the thread of the voice that is speaking far off in the distance. Motion approaching personal space takes priority and mental resources are invested there. *Contexts* holds the medium-term pattern of this foreground thread, which is simply that we have already heard one, then several, people walk past us, each one pleasantly saying hello as they pass. *Contexts* anticipates this happening again now. *Domains* holds our background knowledge of personal greeting behaviors, maybe typical of the office setting, and the personal significance that such greetings hold for us. It supplies a sense of background to these events. This example is taken from the everyday, but it could just as easily be part of an electroacoustic work of art.

Harmonization

In order for moment-to-moment experience to have a sense of consistency, the productions of these autonomous layers must constantly be harmonized

Table 2.1 Productions of the five layers

---

1. Sensations

Perceptual binding and grouping: auditory streams, perceptual events, 'gestalted' forms
   (low-level attributes of the auditory scene)

Attributes of perceptual units, that is, perceptual features

Immediate trajectories of change

Influence of cross-modal integration

2. Gist

Instanced schemas for things (taken broadly and including people), short-term events
   such as image schemas and space (high-level attributes of the auditory scene)

The attributes associated with instanced schema (properties of objects, forces, events,
   etc.), filling their empty slots with defaults, thereby reducing ambiguity

Organization and grouping: foreground/background, strongly related things and events
   (percussion, footsteps, etc.)

3. Locus

Instances of action schemas for medium-term situations matched to situational
   characteristics

Attributes of such schemas including:
   - priorities for action
   - appropriate responses in focusing and ignoring, etc.
   - filling empty slots with defaults, thereby reducing ambiguity of action.

Executing action schemas and managing transitions when updates occur

Networks of associations among schemas providing context and deeper meaning

4. Contexts

Instances of medium- to long-term event-oriented schemas that extend the scope of
   consideration beyond locus. These include such temporal patterns associated with
   musical/auditory patterns, scenarios, narratives, etc.

Attributes of such schemas, filling in their slots possibly with defaults and reducing
   ambiguity. Predictions and expectations are a direct consequence

Managing/evaluating event schemas in the flow of experience

5. Domains

Schemas of long-term, domain knowledge, typically 'abstracted' knowledge, meta-
   knowledge

Parameters of schemas, filling in their slots possibly with defaults and reducing
   ambiguity

---

with one another. This is a dynamic process in which productions are
constantly shifting in response to external and internal changes. As illustrated in Figure 2.1, we could say that the path from *Sensations* to *Domains*
is driven by the onrush of sensory stimulation and that sensory input is
compressed and/or transformed at each step. The path from *Domains* to
Sensations is driven by internal representations that impose constancy and

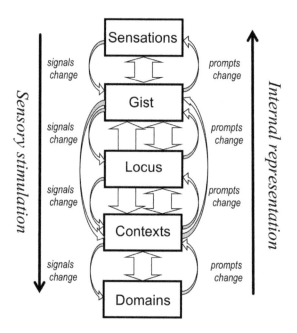

Figure 2.1 Harmonization within the five-layer model (Kendall 2014)

structure on the dynamic input. Brandt (2004: 182) labels the first 'dynamic processing' and the second 'figurative processing.' There are numerous tentative productions being birthed all the time, but the listener will become conscious of only a few. For something to rise to the level of conscious awareness, it must have achieved a significant degree of salience – generally it must be reinforced, especially by other layers. The operative inhibition of weak, tentative productions eliminates irregularity and perceptual noise in the system that ought to be ignored. Importantly, the proliferation of productions is counterbalanced by the constant pull toward consolidation both within and across threads as the mind is attempting to weave a coherent tapestry, at some times more successfully than at others.

To summarize how harmonization works, let's trace the path of a prototypical thread up and down the layers. *Sensations* produces perceptual bindings and groupings while *Gist* connects these to instances of schemas for things in space thereby compressing multifaceted sensory information into something more manageable. *Locus* takes these things and connects them with schemas for the governance of medium-term tasks like deciding what to attend to. *Contexts* is trying to match these ongoing situations to longer-term patterns that also generate expectations about the future. Finally, *Domains* sustains the background information that defines and maintains the long-term context. Tracing the thread's path down through the layers: *Domains* delimits the schemas that are appropriate to *Contexts*. *Contexts*'s schemas determine what medium-term governance is prioritized in *Locus*. *Locus* causes the *Gist*'s organization to shift in response and thus trigger *Sensations* to retune to different auditory attributes.

Time frames

The functional differentiation of the layers extends to their time frames. There are two independent considerations (which are often confounded in common discourse). The first we might call the *functional* time frame of the layer's focus and the second the *operational* time frame in which it responds to change. As a simple example, one might think about the form of Stockhausen's *Kontakte* that is 34 minutes long (functional time frame), and after 3 seconds (operational time frame) switches to the form of Varèse's *Poème électronique*. These two considerations reveal the relationship of the layers to memory: the sensory hold, working and long-term memory, represented in Figure 2.2.

The knowledge associated with each layer is accessed and stored in long-term memory, while the current productions are held in working memory. The 'perceptual present' is captured in the inner workings of the layers

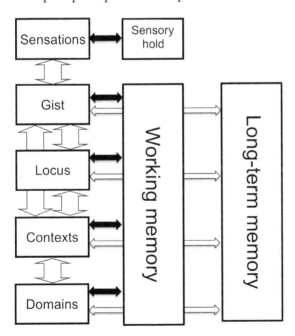

Figure 2.2 Five layers in relation to memory systems (Kendall 2014)

with working memory and varies between two and eight seconds, depending on the processing load (Pöppel 1997, 1998). Mental activity is always in the perceptual present, but what we think about can have a wide range of time frames. This is reflected in the way that each mental layer specializes in productions of varying duration. *Sensations* is the simplest because it registers immediate perceptual processes in sensory hold. The 'auditory present' has a duration of around 250 msec, less than the 'perceptual present' during which auditory attributes can be experienced as changing. *Gist* extends the auditory present over several seconds, giving short-term constancy to the auditory scene. *Locus* manages real-time tasks in the short to medium term, the time frame in which the body executes gestures, the perceptual present and slightly beyond. It accesses action schemas (including listening strategies) from long-term memory while its temporary productions are held in working memory. *Locus* seemingly has a clock, while *Contexts* operates in abstracted time, generally medium- to long-term schemas extending well beyond the perceptual moment. *Contexts* manages temporal schemas that create projections about the future. *Domains* we can think of as holding the permanent, background information for the present situation.

Attention vs focus

As this model reveals, each layer has its own 'viewpoint' on heard events. The model then enables us to make a distinction that is important for listening between *attention* and *focus*. (Wright and Ward (2008) make a similar distinction between overt vs covert attention.) We will say that attention is a question of *what* is listened to (mental thread), while focus is a question of *how* it is listened to (mental layer). If I should hear Xenakis's *Gendy 3* with my focus in *Gist*, I might find it simply noisy and rough. But if my focus is in *Domains*, which connects my listening to my background understanding of Xenakis and his works, then my experience is entirely different: Xenakis's choices have a nuanced and moving artistic significance. Focus on a single layer also brings with it the expanded resources to strengthen and expand mental connections. If focused in *Gist*, then that aspect of listening will be enriched and most likely produce an enduring memory. Most listeners shift focus unconsciously and effortlessly, never noticing the resulting leaps of perspective. These effortless jumps occur so easily in part because all layers are continually active and accessible.

The importance of focus is collaborated by Brandt (2004: 183–4), who describes the difference between practical and communicative 'styles of consciousness,' and how they are differentiated by the layer of their 'center of gravity.' The layer he labels Situations (what is referred to as *Locus* here) is related to 'practical consciousness,' and the combination of Qualia (Sensory) and Feelings to 'communicative consciousness.' We might relate 'practical consciousness' to everyday listening and 'communicative consciousness' to aestheticized listening (Oliveros 2005), a distinction carried by focus.

One of the most important constraints on moment-to-moment listening is that mental resources are limited. These are real limitations that can be measured in terms of available working memory, inherent neural delays, restricted neural representation, and so on. The influence of processing load on limited resources is especially obvious when observing real-time tasks like listening where one often has to glide over the details in order to keep up. *Gist*'s job of prioritizing one sound while ignoring others is the most effective way of managing limited resources.

Listening attention and focus will be responsive to a composition's content, and, as a corollary, we might say that the work itself will cue the listener to the *what* and *how*. Then, in repeated listenings one tends to repeat the same patterns of attention and focus; in fact, one essentially replays listening patterns. However, any number of things might induce the listener to change their habits; for example, to shift focus to a different layer. Well-practiced listening patterns require fewer mental resources, thus freeing resources for finding new meanings, especially in connection with alternative layers, say shifting from the immediate (*Gist*) to the long-term (*Domains*). The powerful influence of focus, attention, and learned listening patterns yields additional insight into how a novice listener's hearing of a work of electroacoustic music can be so different from an expert's.

Mental layers and the emergence of meaning

In the moment-to-moment flow of listening, just as in everyday life, the mind is constantly engaged in determining the meaning of things. A practical question that we are often implicitly posing is: What is going on? That question is most easily answered in terms of a limited number of options. The more that the details can be related to known models and categories, the easier it is to have a manageable experience. Meaning emerges from the web of relationships we construct, especially between the onrush of sensory stimulation and the systemization of internal representation. We expect different listeners to experience differing meanings. *Gist*, which is most closely related to *Sensations*, is the most likely layer to produce similar meanings across all listeners. *Contexts* and *Domains*, which are most closely tied to internal representations, are the most likely layers to produce differing meanings, especially connections between novices and experts. But, while experiences and meanings may differ, we should be able to model the essential mental activities of listeners similarly, possibly clarifying the differences between novices and experts in specific terms. The five-layer model enables us to separate each layer's contribution to meaning making. In this section, we will explore some repercussions of the five-layer model and how the layers specifically participate in the emergence of meaning.

Schemas

The electroacoustic listener's knowledge is both the direct knowledge of things and the background knowledge that shapes a sense of context. Many components of such knowledge can be modeled as *schemas*, most simply understood as repeated mental activities that are codified as a pattern. For example, we all have repeated patterns of thinking for things like trumpets and loudspeakers, for people like DJs and electroacoustic composers, and for events like disco parties and electroacoustic concerts. Schemas as such are essential to simplifying the complexity of direct experience by compressing information. They are also essential for thinking at more abstract levels of representation, for anticipating outcomes, and for understanding contexts. Depending on circumstances, there are distinctions associated with the terms 'schema,' 'frame' (Minsky 1975), and 'script' (Schank and Abelson 1977). We will use 'schema' as an umbrella term for what are, in fact, closely related mental phenomena. And while the concept is quite broad, we expect schemas to have some common structural features. For instance, we expect schemas to have slots (like little key holes) in which information of a particular type will be matched and fitted (quite possibly from other schemas) in order to activate the schema. Such slots often have default values that fill in missing gaps in specific ways, enabling us to make sense of situations in which our information is incomplete (something that was mentioned in Table 2.1). Schemas are also often connected to exemplars that represent idealizations; for instance, not just bells, but idealized bells. Especially important for the arts, schemas are also often coupled with feelings and emotions. So, if we imagine the schema for the sound of a baby crying, we can envision a slot for filling in the cause (with a default like hunger for a bottle), prototypical cries, and we can immediately sense our feelings when we hear this sound!

We made repeated references to schemas in our discussion of the five mental layers without fully clarifying how schemas are differentiated with respect to layer. When discussing *Gist*, we invoked schemas that capture our recurrent mental processes for objects, motion, space, force dynamics and events, inclusive of the *image schemas* that capture our most essential notions of objects and forces (Johnson 1987; Lakoff 1987; Lakoff and Johnson 1999). When discussing *Locus*, we largely invoked schemas that were procedural, which like scripts captured patterns of action, in this case, immediate listening strategies that are invoked in response to the current perceived situation. This knowledge is rich with signification – what should be important within a context and how important is it. At the level of *Contexts*, we emphasized schemas that enable the listener to recognize medium- to long-term patterns, especially important for anticipating out-comes, whether in physical reality or in musical works. And at the level of *Domains*, we discussed schemas that connect things that normally belong together, background knowledge and meta-knowledge, all of which are essential to providing a continuing sense of context. Clearly, all of these differing kinds of schemas are important, and the five mental layers help us to separate and understand their complementary interactions.

The way that sensory stimulation activates schemas and schematic connections is what we might think of as an initial, essential level of meaning making. As was illustrated in Figure 2.2, active mental processes within the layers access long-term memory and its vast interconnected network of schematic knowledge. However, this process happens neuro-logically, and triggering this access activates a functional categorization of schematic knowledge both within and across layers. Thus, a bright, high-pitched sound (*Sensations*) is made meaningful by being categorized as a musical sound, an instrument, a bell, a church bell, a small church bell, etc. (*Gist*). One of these, probably church bell, represents the most practical level for situational thinking (*Locus*), the basic-level category (Rosch 1978). That church bell schema has connections to other schemas relevant to *Gist*: the mechanics of producing sound, the player's gesture of playing, the feeling dynamics of the sound, etc. These connections in particular differ-entiate church bells from doorbells, and they effectively clarify the frame that we hold around church bells. At the same time, we can imagine many other connections being made to schemas at other mental layers: for the role of bells as signals for attention, for musical patterns with bells, for the role of bells in church services and other important social events. Thus, the activation of schemas at one mental layer may also activate schemas across the layers. Conversely, schemas present at one layer may influence which schemas are reinforced and activated in other layers. Narrowing the range of potential connections is a particularly important role for domain knowledge. The network of associations we form within a domain guides and limits our connections and projections. For example, if *Domains* is holding a schematic network for weddings, it will influence the schemas that may be activated by a bell sound. This is a consequence of the harmonization process across the layers that we described in the section 'Harmonization' (pages 34–7), a process that assists in managing limited mental resources by eliminating the less salient productions.

Mental spaces

While schemas are accessed from long-term memory, they are instantiated and made active in working memory, organized within *mental spaces*, that is, the temporary assemblies that are constructed, interconnected and modified in moment-to-moment thinking (Fauconnier 1994; Fauconnier and Turner 2002). The concept of mental spaces enables us to model the schematic connections that are made on the fly and moment to moment. For example, we expect that any noticeable auditory event instantaneously activates a mental space in working memory. Depending on context, this space will contain the schemas that frame the event (say, source category, type of agency) along with their connections to other potentially relevant schemas. We will call these *schematic associations* excess connections that may be reinforced depending upon context or what associations are particularly strong for the user. Thus, we can visualize that sensory stimulation at the level of *Sensations* evokes a mental space for a perceptual event recognized as striking a bell at the level of *Gist*. Depending upon the listener's predispositions and the context, especially the context of what else is in working memory, this space is potentially connected with other schemas and mental spaces – school bells, being startled, the school yard, feeling imposed upon by school, etc. – some of which may relate most closely to *Locus*, *Contexts*, and *Domains*. A new event or change of context will likely evoke changes in the mental spaces and their interconnections. How mental spaces affect one another, how new connections are made, how significance is recognized, etc. – this is the work of the mental layers that will dynamically reconfigure the mental spaces of working memory.

So, at the beginning of Jonathan Harvey's *Mortuos Plango, Vivos Voco* (Harvey 1981, 1990) when we hear the sound of church bells, a mental space is instantly created which frames church bells and which activates schematic associations. When considering typical listeners, we can expect that some of the listener's schemas are individual and personal (e.g. the bell I once touched, my memory of church bells at my cousin's wedding), while others are more cultural, shared, and easy to anticipate (e.g. bells in general, church bells in particular, how church bells are rung, the typical occasions for ringing church bells). It is important not to lose touch with the fact that the interconnection of mental spaces is a creative act of meaning making that can produce a variety of results. And, importantly for the arts, we can anticipate that this cultural/personal mix also encompasses the feelings associated with church bells: the cultural solemnity of church bells, personal feelings about churches, rituals, etc.

Soon after the entrance of Harvey's church bells, we hear the entrance of a boy soprano singing in Latin, and another mental space and its schematic associations are evoked in working memory. Much of its extended network of associations will overlap the first. The overlap immediately clarifies the conceptual background of the piece, especially in *Domains*. Areas without overlap may be less important to the piece's sense of meaning – associations of boys with childhood mischief, for example. These may never become sufficiently salient to participate significantly in the listener's sense of meaning. Other associations may participate in meaning because their incongruences are highlighted. For example, the lack of overlap highlights the sonic disparities between the bells and the boy at the level of *Gist*, which turns out to be very important in the continuation of the piece.

Blending

We can say that meaning in electroacoustic music sometimes emerges directly from schematic associations, that is to say, that meaning is a product of the schema's position within its network of interconnections. In the example of Harvey's *Mortuos Plango, Vivos Voco* above, we discussed the associations of church bells and boy sopranos, and we proposed that the context of the piece was clarified by the overlap of two schematic networks. Significantly, meaning also emerges from a network of mental spaces in the process called *blending*, sometimes called 'conceptual blending' or 'conceptual integration' (Fauconnier and Turner 2002). Fauconnier and Turner have developed models for the most common forms of blending called *conceptual integration networks*. The prototype integration network shown in Figure 2.3 has four mental spaces: two represent the spaces for the input elements that are being blended; one represents the space of the common elements that relate the two inputs, the *generic* space; and one represents a new space, the *blend*. In blending, selective content from the input spaces is

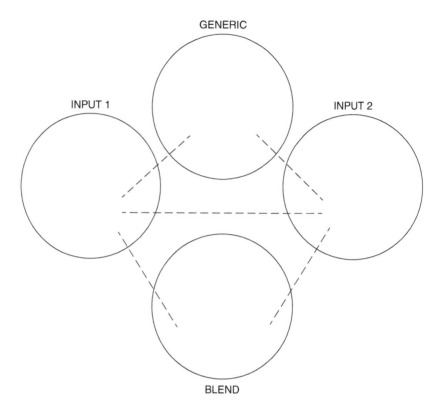

Figure 2.3 A connection of mental spaces representing a prototype integration network, after Fauconnier and Turner 2002

projected into the blend, which now contains relationships that cannot be represented by either input. Blending produces emergent structures not contained within the input spaces and most importantly emergent meanings that are unequivocally a product of the blend.

In *Mortuos Plango, Vivos Voco*, we already mentioned the sonic disparities between the bells and the boy soprano. Shortly after the opening section, new sound material is introduced that is a product of cross-synthesis between the sounds of the bell and the boy soprano. This is art: that which is a physical impossibility is realized through digital signal processing. How does one understand the deeply evocative sound of a hybrid bell-boy? It requires an imaginative act of meaning making. The blend of the two is an emergent entity with many hybrid properties (as illustrated in Figure 2.4) that is rich with schematic associations and not necessarily harmonious ones. For example, the bell is a passive object that must be acted upon by an agent in order to produce sound, while the boy soprano is the agent of its own sound production. Especially in the context

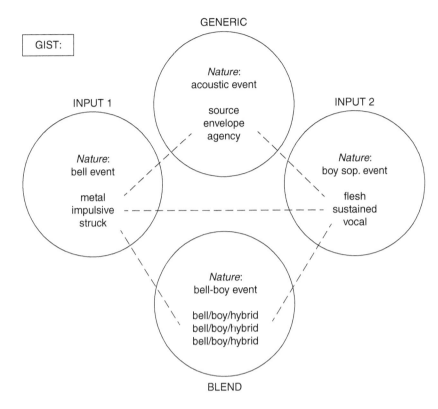

GIST:

GENERIC

Nature:
acoustic event

source
envelope
agency

INPUT 1

Nature:
bell event

metal
impulsive
struck

INPUT 2

Nature:
boy sop. event

flesh
sustained
vocal

Nature:
bell-boy event

bell/boy/hybrid
bell/boy/hybrid
bell/boy/hybrid

BLEND

Figure 2.4 Prototype of the blending of church bells and the boy soprano in Jonathan Harvey's *Mortuos Plango, Vivos Voco* (Kendall 2014)

of contemporary arts, blends often contain the incompatible or the oppositional, the novel with the profoundly obvious. Here the disparity is greatest at the level of *Gist*, where there is a discrepancy between the sound sources (metal and flesh), between acoustic envelopes (impulsive and sustained) and between agencies (struck and vocal). As the individual sections of the piece's 'moment form' unfold one after the other, the flexibility of the cross-synthesis enables the potentials of the bell-boy blend to be explored first one way and then another, creating novel events that mix bell, boy and hybrid attributes. Passive vs active agency is negotiated, as well as metal vs flesh source material. There are bells seemingly singing and clusters of boys sounding struck tones.

Context and domain knowledge

As becomes obvious from much we have said so far, meaning arises in a context. Speaking in regard to cognitive semiotics, Per Aage Brandt says:

Anything meaningful is meaningful in a 'context'; contexts supply relevant frames for the contents of our consciousness, and they thereby allow us to draw inferences from these contents ... contexts are structured within distinct semantic domains. (Brandt 2004: 33)

And while there is no universally accepted model for the organization of schematic knowledge, the notion of distinct domains of knowledge is useful to understanding how listeners relate content and context, especially how the network of schematic associations is negotiated by the layers of *Contexts* and *Domains* while listening. Drawing again from cognitive semantics and following the lead of Brandt, let us postulate at least three largely independent 'base' domains for the listener's knowledge that we can call *nature, culture* and *spirit*. Brandt in fact describes these as 'world types':

1. NATURE: the macro-physical, material and gravitational, geo-, bio-, and zoo-logical environment;
2. CULTURE: the collective horizon formed by groups of fellow human beings densely informed by intentional and mimetic behaviors of all kinds, practical or symbolic; ...
3. SPIRIT: the sphere of direct interaction with other minds by expressive contact, allowing for the sharing of thoughts and feelings with individuals in a face-to-face relationship.

(Brandt 2004: 23)

It is a good question whether *Music* too might be considered an independent domain, especially as evidenced by the relative autonomy of musical structure. (Consider how commentary on historical Western music and even popular music has focused almost exclusively on abstracted patterns of pitch and rhythm that only a musician can understand!) Of course, interconnections between aspects of music and other domains can be demonstrated; some music theorists have related musical intelligence to linguistics (Jackendoff and Lerdahl 1983) and others to ecological knowledge (Clarke 2005). A particularly interesting twist on ecological listening is David Wessel's *Antony* (1990; comp. 1977), which is a kind of perceptual Rorschach test in which objects and spaces are evoked by the most totally un-*natural* aggregates of sine waves. Purely electronic sounds like these lie in what we might call a subdomain of *nature* called *technology*.

Within the field of electroacoustical music, soundscape composition, for example, clearly focuses on the context of the *natural* domain. Barry Truax (2000) says that the first two characteristics of soundscape composition are the recognizability of source material and the listener's knowledge of the environmental and psychological context (relating to *Gist* and *Domains* respectively). And ironically, *nature* is also the base domain for Denis Smalley's seemingly antithetical concept of 'remote surrogacy,' in which a sound event is detached from its natural, causal agent (Smalley 1986, 1997). This fact points up what a central concern *nature* and *natural* events have been for electroacoustic composers. Natural ecology has played a central role in electroacoustic theory, whether it is the attempt to create 'sound objects' devoid of ecological meaning (Schaeffer 1966) or to hear electroacoustic compositions in the manner of natural soundscapes (Truax 2000). All of this extended attention to *nature* reflects a shared style of meaning making (analogous to Brandt's (2004: 183–4) styles of consciousness) that focuses mental activity within *Gist* while repeatedly evoking the domain of *nature*.

We have discussed how the cross-synthesis of the bell and the boy soprano in *Mortuos Plango* produces a bell-boy blend which reconciles discrepancies in source material and agency, properties that lie in the domain of *nature* and at the level of *Gist*. But there are also discrepancies at the level of domain knowledge. What is a conceptual bell-boy, not just a sonic one? The sonic blend compels the listener to make the leap to also form a conceptual blend. This is represented in Figure 2.5. The bell's schematic network interconnects with schemas in *nature* and *culture* that we have already discussed. The boy's network interconnects with those and also with *spirit* – we identify with the boy's internal thoughts and feelings (part of what Dan Dennett (1987) calls the 'intentional stance'). And here we come to the compelling artistic core, the emergent meaning of these blends. In alignment with the piece's background of church and spirituality, the listener is led to blending the animate and the inanimate. How that blend is understood by the listener must vary with personal history and receptivity. It may take the listener to the realm of the spiritual that was a primary concern for Jonathan Harvey. That was the association of both Michael Clarke (2006) and Patricia Lynn Dirks (2012) in their analyses of the piece. Dirks came to 'interpret the bell as representing the dead and the boy's voice, the living.'

Example: Stockhausen's *Telemusik*, 'Structure 16'

As an illustration of how the concepts discussed above might be applied in the analysis of electroacoustic music, we will describe a hypothetical hearing of a short excerpt from Stockhausen's *Telemusik*, the section identified in the score as 'Structure 16.' This is an attempt to describe a

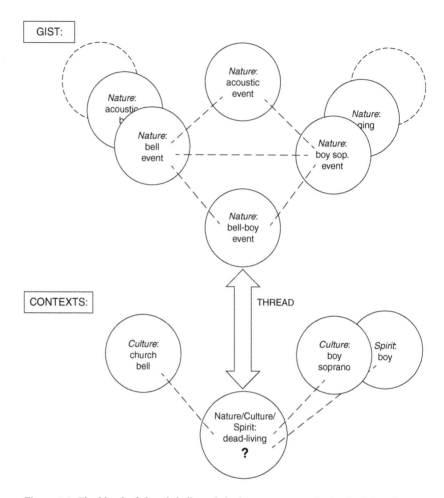

Figure 2.5 The blend of church bells and the boy soprano at the level of *Gist* also compels blend at the level of *Contexts*, a blend that crosses base domains. These world types, *nature*, *culture*, and *spirit*, are base regions of domain knowledge.

reasonably informed hearing, not necessarily an ideal one. 'Structure 16' is arguably the simplest of the 32 'Structures' that make up *Telemusik*. It begins like all of the others with the sound of a Japanese temple instrument, here a small metal bowl called a *rin* (Kohl 2002). And like the other 'Structures,' its length is a Fibonacci number of seconds – here actually the sum of a large and a small Fibonacci number (55+2 = 57 seconds). Excluding the initial percussive sound that marks the beginning of the section, the content of this 'Structure' is exclusively made up of high-frequency ring-modulated Gagaku music that is completely unrecognizable as such. What the listener does hear is glittering clusters between 5 and 7 kHz that are changing more or less every couple of seconds. Such high-frequency clusters are emblematic to *Telemusik*. In Stockhausen's *Hymnen*, similar sounds are mimicking short-wave radio signals, and from that perspective, *Telemusik* tunes into the 'vibrations' around the earth, in this case, picking up indigenous music from around the globe. In a less literal way, these clusters capture a continuous, dynamic flow of energy (as if the background sound of the world is not silence but a buzz). Similar sounds occur numerous times before 'Structure 16,' where the high-frequency ring modulation is interrupted three times by rapid, stepped changes in modulation frequencies that produce somewhat melodic sequences in a lower frequency range, 0.5–1.5 kHz. The score to 'Structure 16' is shown in Figure 2.6 (Stockhausen 1969).

Most interestingly, the last 20 seconds of 'Structure 16' are occupied only by uninterrupted high-frequency clusters. From an acoustic perspective, almost nothing happens for 20 seconds. But that hardly means that the listener's mental processes are inactive: any analysis based solely on the acoustics would skip right past the significance of such a passage. A sonogram of 'Structure 16' with numbered markers for critical moments in time is shown in Figure 2.7.

We will examine some of these moments in depth before scrutinizing those last 20 seconds. Marker 1 shows the activity at the end of 'Structure 15' that abruptly stops at marker 2. From the perspective of *Sensations*, there is a new perceptual event at marker 2 that is pitched, impulsive, and sustained. That perceptual event triggers a match to the schema for 'Bell' (from long-term memory) by which *Gist* makes sense of the perceptual event. The Bell schema also invokes a network of schematic associations among which are connections to world music and the ceremonial contexts evoked earlier by the piece and sustained in *Domains*. From the perspective of *Gist*, there is a Bell in the foreground, a new thread, that is posted to working memory. *Locus* reacts to this simple scene with high certainty and a simple strategy (drawn from long-term memory): attend to the thread of the foreground object, the bell. This is a more complex moment for *Contexts*, because everything that it was holding in working memory about the previous section is no longer in sync. But the meaning of the moment is confirmed by the bell strike which matches the schematic pattern learned earlier in the piece (and held in long-term memory) that such a sound marks the beginning of a new section. *Contexts*'s productions for 'Structure 15' (its schemas, blends, threads, etc.) must be closed off and incorporated into long-term memory. Long-term memory also holds the listener's background knowledge of Stockhausen, his music and its language – what is typical and prototypical. *Domains* sustains the relevant knowledge in

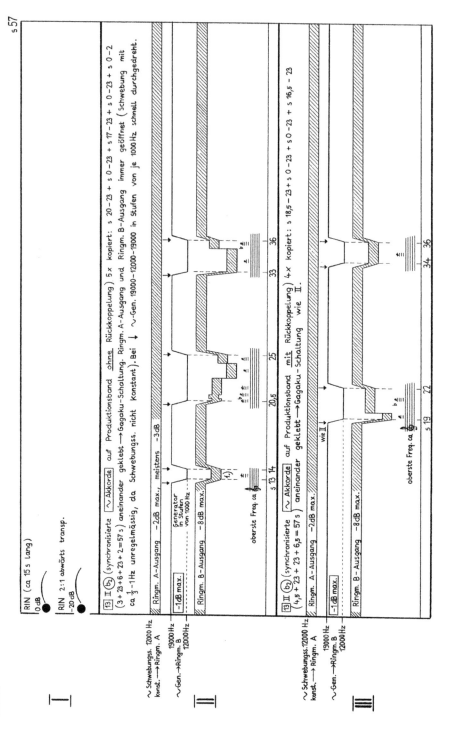

Figure 2.6 The score of Stockhausen's *Telemusik*, 'Structure 16'. Used by permission: Karlheinz Stockhausen "Telemusik für Elektronik Nr.20"
© Copyright 1969 by Universal Edition A.G., Wien, UE 14807

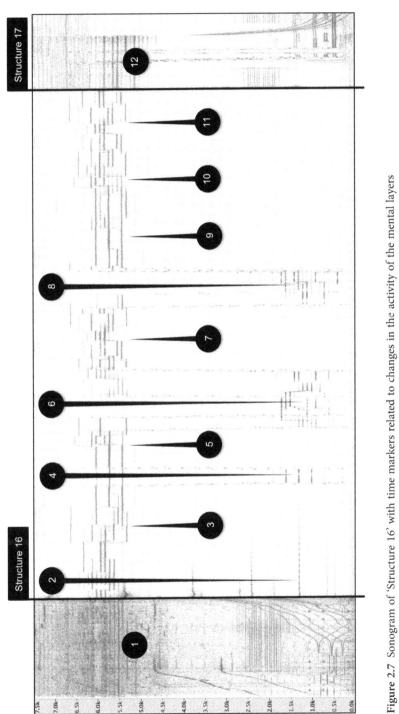

Figure 2.7 Sonogram of 'Structure 16' with time markers related to changes in the activity of the mental layers

working memory and consolidates new information about *Telemusik*, creating domain knowledge of the piece, such as its typical textures, or types of sounds. The present moment with the bell sound seems entirely consistent with previous knowledge of *Telemusik*.

At marker 3, some changes occur. *Sensations* registers an ongoing auditory stream that is high and rough, a second thread. With the cessation of the bell, *Gist*, *Locus*, and *Contexts* must sort out relationships: Is this bright, coarse cluster foreground? If so, *Locus* would switch attention to the clusters thread. But given the persistence of the Bell schema in the perceptual present (working memory), *Gist* takes the clusters as background. By this *Locus*'s strategy is less certain but simple: ignore the background thread and attend to the next foreground event. *Contexts* knows from earlier in the piece (long-term memory) that clusters do not likely change or create significant patterns; this influences *Locus*. So, all three layers are harmonized. *Contexts* must now make sense of this new section, so there is an open-ended search anticipating the start of some new schematic pattern within the section.

Marker 4 indicates the first melodic event. *Sensations* registers a pitched, mid-range event in addition to the continuing high, rough stream. *Gist* understands this as a new thread, a melodically segmented foreground event against the continuing and more continuous background thread. The event is similar to ones encountered earlier in the piece, and repeats a pattern of blending schemas from the domains of *Technology* and *Nature* (see Figure 2.8), a pattern that should already be assimilated within *Telemusik*'s domain knowledge. It is in one sense melodic and lies within a vocal range (domain of *Nature*), while in another sense it is clearly electronic when jumping through stepped frequencies, like clicking through settings of an oscillator (domain of *technology*). The lifelike quality of the sound probably derives from the fluctuating quality of the original Gagaku music. *Gist*'s blend compels the listener toward a conceptual blend at the level of *Contexts* in which this event is understood as technological and musical. *Locus* attends to the melodic thread with high certainty while ignoring the background. This gives *Contexts* the focus to take in the melodic event as the beginning of a new pattern, after which it can narrow its search and anticipate continuations. For most listeners, attention at this point is on the melodic thread and mental focus is in *Contexts* because it is the most important layer for making sense of the ongoing experience. That provides expanded mental resources with which *Contexts* is likely creating numerous productions (that will never become conscious and will eventually be discarded). By marker 5 when *Sensations* once again registers only

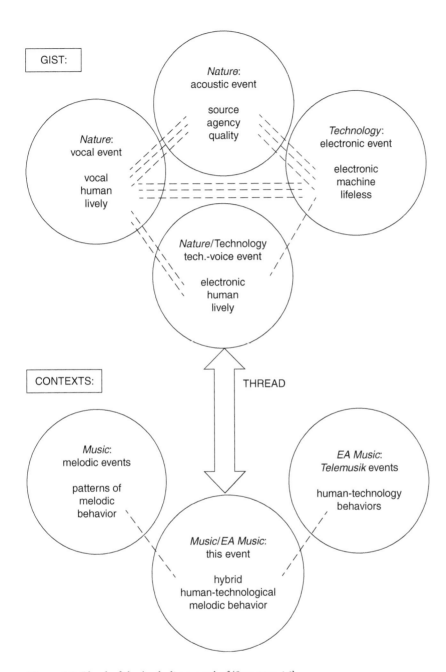

Figure 2.8 Blend of the 'melodic events' of 'Structure 16'

the ongoing stream, *Gist*'s foreground/background relationships are stable as well as *Locus*'s listening strategy.

The second melodic event at marker 6 is a continuation of the melodic thread still active in working memory, now a duet, which gives additional support to the vocal side of the blend. This is also a confirming moment for *Contexts* because possible schematic patterns are reduced to repetition-variation, which enables *Contexts* to more securely project continuations and to anticipate outcomes. Up to this moment, the sense across the mental layers has been one of certainty and confirmation. But after the second melodic event, uncertainty arises in *Domains* because the absence of other events and other threads is inconsistent with its long-term knowledge of *Telemusik*. This is far too sparse!

The third melodic event at marker 8 confirms *Contexts*'s projections and strengthens the anticipation of a consistent continuation to the thread. *Locus* is highly certain. But by marker 10, working memory is being stretched beyond the perceptual present, and nothing has happened. *Contexts* holds to a pattern that has not closed and now must search to find some new pattern or context that makes sense of this unanticipated lack of continuation within a typical time frame. *Locus* must refocus to find something in the foreground. *Gist* is signaled to re-evaluate, but with only the cluster present, the foreground/background distinction is ambiguous. By marker 11, the cluster thread shifts to foreground because there is nothing else to attend to. This pushes *Sensations* to retune and register any potential changes in the clusters as perceptual events, although nothing quite qualifies. *Gist* experiences the clusters now as an amalgam of activity.

For most listeners, attention has shifted to the clusters thread and mental focus has shifted to *Gist* because that layer is most important to making sense of the ongoing experience. *Locus* focuses on the clusters with a lack of certainty and *Contexts* attempts to find some pattern in this, but there is nothing to base a pattern on. There is no increase or decrease of any attribute; there is complete stasis. There is no way to make a projection about the future, and the listener's feeling may become somewhat apprehensive, lacking direction. The sparseness and the lack of continuation intensify *Domain*'s feeling of inconsistency with the rest of *Telemusik*. During these last 20 seconds, the thread that was previously background has become foreground. And, in the effort to make sense of things, focus has shifted from *Contexts* to *Gist*. Acoustically the clusters are just about the same as they were at the beginning of the Structure, but the listener's mental processes and the artistic meaning of the clusters has shifted significantly from what it was back at marker 6.

At marker 12 when 'Structure 17' begins with the sound of a wood block, the mental processes are very similar to the start of 'Structure 16.' *Contexts* recognizes the beginning of a new section and therefore closes its productions from the previous section. This means that the unusual sectional pattern for 'Structure 16' is incorporated into long-term memory. *Domains* too must integrate this unusual behavior in long-term memory so that the domain of *Telemusik* is expanded. Along the way, a trace of the listener's experience and the surviving productions of each layer have been written into episodic memory as a long-term record of the listening experience.

We have explored one hypothetical hearing. With repeated hearings, one would expect that many of the same mental activities would occur over and over again, especially activities that are driven by sensation: *Sensations*, *Gist*, *Locus*. The listener might also free up the mental resources to expand connections around the emergent meaning of its many blends or to marvel at the mystery of Stockhausen's odd decisions (domain of *spirit*). And repeated hearings could also deepen the experience of 'Structure 16,' as the unique incongruity is embraced, intensifying the artistic nuance that the listener has learned to anticipate.

Conclusions

The key question posed at the beginning of this chapter was: How does the listener's experience of listening become *meaningful*? We have adapted a model of five mental layers from Per Aage Brandt in an effort to capture the multilayered nature of listening. And, we have interpolated schema theory and blending theory into this model with examples from a well-known electroacoustic work, *Mortuos Plango, Vivos Voco*. And the potential of this expanded model has been illustrated by a very detailed analysis from another well-known work, *Telemusik*. It is not the purpose here to propose this detailed example as a general template for analysis, rather to illustrate the degree to which modeling the mental processes is essential to any understanding of how listening becomes meaningful. One lesson that this example from *Telemusik* clearly teaches, especially the last 20 seconds, is that electroacoustic analysis based solely on acoustic information, in either scores or sonograms, easily misses changes in the listener's mental processes that reflect changes of meanings that are fundamental and basic to the actual experience of listening. Therefore, future developments in analysis should take this essential lesson to heart!

In considering electroacoustic music, we have addressed meaning not only in its most general sense, but also in the context of an artistic experience. Electroacoustic music provides a distinctive domain for the discussion of cognition and meaning, especially in relation to blending theory where examples are typically drawn from non-auditory sources. The electroacoustic listener has meaningful experiences unfolding moment to moment without the need for conscious reasoning about sound; meaning is instantly grasped in sonic thinking. Then, too, a question that we have only touched on here is the nature of the mental activity that distinguishes the expert listener from the novice. How does the experience of listening shift from a disoriented encounter to nuanced meanings? To answer such a question, we must be able to describe the mental activities that produce nuanced artistic meanings. It is hoped that this chapter helps to provide a foundation for the future exploration of such questions.

References

Brandt, P. A. 2004. *Spaces, Domains, and Meaning: Essays in Cognitive Semiotics. Vol. 4: European Semiotics: Language, Cognition, and Culture.* Bern: Peter Long.

　2006. Form and meaning in art. In M. Turner (ed.), *The Artful Mind: Cognitive Science and the Riddle of Human Creativity.* Oxford University Press.

Clarke, E. F. 2005. *Ways of Listening: An Ecological Approach to the Perception of Musical Meaning.* Oxford University Press.

Clarke, M. 2006. Jonathan Harvey's *Mortuos Plango, Vivos Voco.* In M. Simoni (ed.), *Analytical Methods of Electroacoustic Music.* New York: Routledge.

Dennett, D. 1987. *The Intentional Stance.* Cambridge, MA: MIT Press.

Dirks, P. L. 2012. An analysis of Jonathan Harvey's 'Mortuos Plango, Vivos Voco.' http://cec.sonus.ca/econtact/9_2/dirks.html (accessed January 3, 2013).

Donald, M. 2001. *A Mind So Rare: The Evolution of Human Consciousness.* New York: Norton.

　2006. Music as communication. In M. Turner (ed.), *The Artful Mind: Cognitive Science and the Riddle of Human Creativity.* Oxford University Press.

Fauconnier, G. 1994. *Mental Spaces: Aspects of Meaning Construction in Natural Language.* New York: Cambridge University Press.

Fauconnier, G. and Turner, M. 2002. *The Way We Think: Conceptual Blending and the Mind's Hidden Complexities.* New York: Basic Books.

Harvey, J. 1981. *Mortuos Plango, Vivos Voco*: A Realization at IRCAM. *Computer Music Journal*, 5(4), 22–4.

　1990. *Mortuos Plango, Vivos Voco.* On *Computer Music Currents 5.* Wergo CD, WER 2025–2.

Jackendoff, R. and Lerdahl, F. 1983. *A Generative Theory of Tonal Music.* Cambridge, MA: MIT Press.

Johnson, M. 1987. *The Body in the Mind: The Bodily Basis of Meaning, Imagination, and Reason.* University of Chicago Press.

Kendall, G. 2014. The feeling blend: Feeling and emotion in electroacoustic art. *Organised Sound*, 19(2), 192–202.

Kohl, J. 2002. Karlheinz Stockhausen: Telemusik (1966). In T. Licata (ed.), *Electroacoustic Music: Analytical Perspectives*. Westport, CN: Greenwood Press.

Lakoff, G. 1987. *Women, Fire and Dangerous Things*. University of Chicago Press.

Lakoff, G. and Johnson, M. 1999. *Philosophy in the Flesh*. New York: Basic Books.

Minsky, M. 1975. Frame System Theory. In P. N. Johnson-Laird and P. C. Wason (eds.), *Thinking: Readings in Cognitive Science*. Cambridge University Press.

Oliveros, P. 2005. *Deep Listening: A Composer's Sound Practice*. New York: iUniverse, Inc.

Pöppel, E. 1997. A hierarchical model of temporal perception. *Trends in Cognitive Science*, 1(2), 56–61.

   1998. *Mindworks: Time and Conscious Experience*. New York: Harcourt Brace Jovanovich.

Rosch, E. 1978. Principles of categorization. In E. Rosch and B. B. Lloyd (eds.), *Cognition and Categorization*. Hillsdale, NJ: Lawrence Erlbaum Associates.

Schaeffer, P. 1966. *Traité des objets musicaux*. Paris: Seuil.

Schank, R. C. and Abelson, R. P. 1977. *Scripts, Plans, Goals, and Understanding: An Inquiry into Human Knowledge Structures*. Hillside, NJ: Lawrence Erlbaum Associates.

Smalley, D. 1986. Spectromorphology and structuring processes. In S. Emmerson (ed.), *The Language of Electroacoustic Music*. Basingstoke: Macmillan Press.

   1997. Spectromorphology: Explaining sound-shapes. *Organised Sound*, 2(2), 107–26.

Stockhausen, K. 1969. *Nr. 20 Telemusik* (score). Vienna: Universal Edition (UE 14807).

Truax, B. 2000. The aesthetics of computer music: A questionable concept reconsidered. *Organised Sound*, 5(3), 119–26.

Wessel, D. 1990. Liner notes for *Antony* (1977). On *Computer Music Currents 10*, Wergo CD, WE119.

Wright, R. D. and Ward, L. M. 2008. *Orienting of Attention*. Oxford University Press.

3 | Forming form

JOHN YOUNG

Introduction

One question Denis Smalley (1986) asked in Simon Emmerson's book *The Language of Electroacoustic Music* was: 'Has electroacoustic music uncovered any new forms?' The question was used openly as a way of suggesting that formal consensus may not be relevant to music that plays with spectromorphological flux and complexity.[1] But proliferating practice in the three decades since Smalley posed that question (or for, that matter, in the preceding four) cannot have spawned as many structural solutions as there are pieces, and the implication of discovery made by Smalley suggests that forms are found within the maturation of developing practice. With that in mind, this chapter sets out some ideas on ways that we might consider form in electroacoustic music. The discussion is centred largely around acousmatic music, with occasional references to other musical practices, to provide an element of coherence in light of the range of practices encountered within electroacoustic music at large, while at the same time allowing perspectives on several different strategies and approaches to the shaping of material to be viewed. The emphasis is generally on the listener's engagement with the final result. It is supported by the underlying notion that the questions and insights arising are pertinent to, and the result of methods employed by, the acousmatic composer, whose creative milieu embraces worlds of natural sound and those developed with synthesis and processing tools in a studio environment.

A notion of form in music is a way of thinking about how we engage with a sense of connectedness and completeness in a work. Roger Reynolds (2002) places 'wholeness' at the centre of this idea, suggesting that a composition is 'a dimensional experience that either leads a listener along a path or proposes a landscape for exploration in such a way that an arc, a

---

[1] Smalley (1986) suggested rejecting the term 'form' in case it should evoke confusion with a normative understanding of it as a set of structural design archetypes (perhaps even in a derogatory sense: 'formulas') that exist outside any particular compositional process.

trajectory of proposal, engagement, and response has been traversed by its end'. In this sense, form embraces characteristics of global shaping and its relationship to short-term clusters of events – gestures, phrases and the dynamic that exists between them. This pertains whether a work is of fixed, directed structure (with, at one extreme, archetypal designs such as ternary, binary or sonata) or a temporal frame in which constellations of sound events have a more open connection with each other (as in variable or open form pieces). A very broad picture of the relationship between low and higher organisational levels is offered by Snyder's (2000) three levels of musical experience, beginning with 'event fusion' where sound events themselves are differentiated, through 'melodic and rhythmic grouping' within the frame of short-term memory to the 'formal' level, namely any grouping longer than the capacity of short-term memory (Snyder takes the lower limit of short-term memory, 3–5 seconds, as the basis for starting to define this level). Earle Brown (1966: 49) offered one definition of form as 'a function of a complex process of not totally rational developments within a chain of cause and effect, extending from the original conception of the work, through the graphic representation as 'score', to performance realization as actual sound'. Form in this sense is not simply the arrangement of materials (whether fixed or transient) but a metaphorical expression of the interaction of sonic structures employed. An impression of form at any level, whether fixed or open in design, is dependent on an interaction between musical object and listener. As Stephen McAdams has suggested: 'form as experienced depends partly on the mind of the listener and partly on the structure presented to that mind' (1989: 181). This suggests that form is something independent of structure in the sense of 'the-way-the-sounds-follow-in-sequence'. It also suggests that a notion of form is a useful way to generalise global meaning (not just global structure) – so that, for example, we recognise the 'contrasting', 'developmental' and 'recursive' essence of sonata form as a stylised way of embodying teleology, tension (struggle) and resolution. Or at an even broader level, we might see Mahler painting large images of the path to redemption or be engaged by the diversionary, imaginative flair of Mendelssohn conjuring up an additional theme in the development section of a symphonic first movement. Accordingly, we might make a distinction between the idea of musical structure as a construct of distinct materials and processes, and the idea of form as the way in which the characteristics of structure derive lower-level meanings, relationships and imperatives. An interesting feature of this distinction, from one work to another, becomes the way variations in structural arrangement continue to support generally comparable formal designs.[2]

From a material perspective, though, the nature of the basic elements used in music has important influence on all the preceding discussion. Stephen McAdams summarises a discussion of the psychological constraints on form-bearing elements in music thus:

A form-bearing dimension should be susceptible to being organized into perceptual categories and relations among these categories should be easily encoded. A system of salience or stability relations should be learnable through mere exposure and should affect the perception of patterns along this dimension. Certain recurrent sequential patterns of values should be easily learned as a kind of lexicon of forms. In other words, relations along the dimension must be susceptible to being acquired as abstract knowledge. (McAdams 1989: 195)

The culturally embedded hierarchical organisation of discrete pitch as in Western tonal music exemplifies a system that meets these requirements.[3] But we encounter a new set of issues given that the breadth of materials available in electroacoustic music affords a rupture not only with received notions of musical organisation, but also with its very substance. Electroacoustic composers are able to create and utilise sounds that extend beyond the physical constraints of traditional musical instruments with a degree of plasticity that allows shaping of the very structure of sound to take on a heightened role in musical form (such as through manipulation of partials, transients, spectral envelope and micro-sonic levels of sound construction). Because sound recording obviates the need to have the physical origins of a sound (such as a factory or locomotive) present in the composing or final performing space, electroacoustic resources have facilitated a new relationship between intrinsic and extrinsic signification in music (Smalley 1997: 110). All this is embraced in what Smalley has called acousmatic space-form:

Space-form in acousmatic music is an aesthetically created 'environment' which structures transmodal perceptual contingencies through source bondings and spectromorphological relations. Further, it integrates attributes particular to musical culture and tradition (like pitch and rhythm for example). Acousmatic space-form inhabits domains somewhere between space as lived and enacted, and the spaces

---

[2] In this sense, notwithstanding earlier reference to the terminological preference he stated at the time, Smalley (1986: 89) acknowledged 'we have found that there must be a consensus about structuring processes if spectromorphological music is to find understanding among its listeners'.

[3] See also McAdams and Saariaho (1985) for additional discussion around this principle.

afforded through spectromorphological contemplation – by the perceived and imagined configurations of spectral and perspectival space. (Smalley 2007: 40)

The transmodality to which Smalley refers is indicative of the fact that within one work materials may not be overtly linked by a consistent perceptual thread of, say, focal pitch, woven into a consistent underlying harmonic and melodic scheme. Typically, a consequence of this electronic-ally mediated musical landscape is that what are often complex sonic surfaces create difficulties in applying traditional reduction-based analytical processes.

In summary, I am referring here to a notion of form not as a set of formulaic moulds that simply 'contain' music, but as a more organic principle by which sound identities, transformative and ordering processes can project fundamental structural morphologies and messages – as much an idea of *forming* as *the form*. For the purposes of this chapter, there are four perspectives on form that may offer some insight into overarching structural considerations in electroacoustic music: musical rhetoric, the idea of 'moment' form, the idea of 'morphic' form and the idea of narrative.

Rhetoric

Established ways of explaining music's low- and high-level structures have frequently described the form and function of musical events in quasi-linguistic terms, employing notions related to chunking and parsing, phrasing and directedness, as well as to interpretation of meaning such as open and closed phrase structures, as elaborated by Deryck Cooke (1959). More recently, and explicitly with reference to electroacoustic music, Gary Kendall (2008) has considered the nature of the musical 'event' using the perspective of linguistic constructs as a starting point, showing that these are used as cognates for deeper but analogous ways of characterising and comprehending music's materials and their flow in time. Such approaches imply that music can be regarded as functioning on a rhetorical plane – that there are ways of utilising inherent principles of musical construction in order to make an 'argument' as lucid or efficacious as possible, or indeed to draw a listener into a web of ideas and interrela-tionships. Whilst Cooke asserted that the actual methods of emotional expression in music are different to those of speech-language, he raised the idea that a form is the embodiment of that expression: 'some general but clearly defined attitude towards existence by the disposition of various terms of emotional expression in a significant order. *And musical form is simply the means of achieving that order'* (Cooke 1959: 212; italics in original). For Cooke's influential thinking, this is especially important since his thesis rests on a notion that form is linked to content by virtue of the expressive imperative of the composer, that only materials consistent with the expressive intentions of the composer are those which ideally find their way into a work. Thus Cooke's view contends that form = expression. And in that sense an expressive intent requires the discursive means and skills of persuasion. Therefore the practice of setting out musical ideas in time, or, perhaps more accurately, articulating time through sound with a view to the consequent expressive and structural functions, might be considered one of constructing rhetoric. More explicitly, the category of rhetoric comprises one of the four overall quadrants of Stephane Roy's (2003) *grille fonctionnelle,*[4] itself divided into two subcategories characterising relational rhetoric and rhetoric of rupture. This category of Roy's *grille fonctionnelle* defines 19 specific rhetorical functions, such as: anticipation, reiteration, imitation, deviation, sign, bracketing (*parenthèse*) and the paired functions of call/response, theme/variation and opposition (*antagonisme*) which can be simultaneous/successive. All these terms are powerfully loaded as agents of meaning and arousal of feeling states beyond the simple reception of sound. Meyer's (1973) elaboration of the notion of implication in music is a profound influence here and also connects to Smalley's (1986, 1997) models of spectromorphological motion and structural function. So as a way of thinking about form, a rhetorical perspective on musical discourse provides a link between the surface style of presentation and deeper structural motivations and metaphors.

The relationship between Meyer's style of thinking about musical functionality and writers such as Roy and Smalley suggests that we should find complementary examples of rhetorical devices between classical and electroacoustic genres. A striking example can be found by comparing the opening measures of Beethoven's C minor Violin Sonata (played by the piano alone) with Trevor Wishart's *Tongues of Fire* (1994b). In these examples two pithy gestures demand attention, then open out into more extended continuations. In Beethoven's case, the sequential melodic profile of the first two gestures and its implied harmonic change is a clearly significant part of the way tonal motion is created. In Wishart's case, the

---

[4] Namely orientation, stratification, process and rhetoric. Roy (1998) alludes to an additional category of rhythm, which is excluded from the 2003 *grille fonctionnelle*. The category of 'sign' (*indice*) is itself more complex than indicated by Roy; this is further discussed later in this chapter.

exact repetition of the very complex voice-based gesture allows another take on the material, as though we had said 'Sorry, what was that again?' and the rapidly articulated spectromophological content of the gesture has the slightly ungraspable nature of a Warren loop, since there are perceptibly several spectral-gestural cells within it.[5] The punches out of and into silence also tell us that the ensuing discourse will be a turbulent one, implying a large-scale formal working of the material (which is true of both works).[6] In Wishart's case the ensuing extension of this opening repeated object is immediately developmental, projecting layers of accumulating energy, through an apparent smearing of the gestural structure of the sounds and consequential growth in spectral richness. This implication of scale in *Tongues of Fire* is also consolidated by the explosive projection early in the work of modulated pitched resonance, establishing a psychological distance between it and the staccato opening gestures that requires an extended interaction between materials to effect some from of resolution of their disparity. As musical rhetoric on a larger scale, this is stylistically classical, and culturally a call in one sense to McAdams's 'lexicon of forms' referred to earlier. What links the opening of these two works, considering their historical remoteness from each other, is an almost alarming similarity in the amount of time for each gesture to unfold and their bracketing in silence.[7] Where they part company is in the contrast between the tonal functionality and melodic transparency of the Beethoven (with its primary chord implications providing, in traditional tonal terms, a broader level of motion as harmonic rhythm) and the almost unfathomably compressed character of Wishart's gestures.

Marta Grabócz (1997) has argued that much electroacoustic music relies on traditional formal designs as a means of containing radically new sounds within understood and digestible structural frameworks. At the time of writing, she proposed that only in the previous ten years were new concepts of formal design substantially evident. From this she outlined three innovative 'structural ideas' (structure in this sense being used synonymously with 'form'): extra-musical models, structures featuring stasis, and articulation of music from graphic patterns. Despite being

---

[5] Repetition is also a feature of the Beethoven, but only on the entry of the violin after the initial short–short–long gesture statement of the piano.

[6] It could also be argued that the silences in the opening of *Tongues of Fire* are in metaphorical terms 'loud' silences, since the nature of what will follow these utterances is very difficult to predict.

[7] In this case I am referring in particular to the version of Kremer and Argerich (1994), where the tempo and urgency of delivery makes the comparison especially compelling.

useful typologies, those are essentially either compositional/generative processes or characterisations of musical materials – elements from which formal innovation might spring. In fact the diversity of contemporary practice presents a range of different emphases on the way musical products themselves are made and heard (consider sonification of non-audio data streams, chance procedures and improvisation, and forms derived from recorded environmental sounds) such that *form, nature and structure of materials* and *processes* are actually difficult to disentangle and attribute definitively as shaping and generative forces; in short, the fact that complex sound objects and referential sounds are not necessary as aesthetically (and culturally) neutral as 'notes' perhaps requires a listener to engage in an interpretative forming process.

While this is not a new dimension to musical analysis – form and content have always had symbiotic roles – the diversity of sound materials often found in the same electroacoustic work signals this as a primary question to address in attempting to understand relationships between materials and lower-level structural morphologies. It would seem then, that in *Tongues of Fire*, Trevor Wishart has, perhaps instinctively, deployed an established attention-grabbing rhetorical device to announce highly complex sonic material with a continuation that displays a kind of morphological smearing of the sound 'theme', also playing on the suggestion of vocal provenance. The gestural terseness that characterises the openings of both Wishart's and Beethoven's works above has architectural significance as a brusque punctuating motto and as a building block for more extended shapes. So although the rhetorical shaping at the opening of *Tongues of Fire* touches on tradition, Beethoven unfolds through interplay of rhythmic and tonal motion, while Wishart does so with an emphasis on spectromorphological malleability.

Moment form

Stockhausen (1991: 63) characterised the idea of moment form in this way:

When certain characteristics remain constant for a while – in musical terms, when sounds occupy a particular region, a certain register, or stay within a particular dynamic or maintain a certain average speed – then a moment is going on: these constant characteristics determine the moment.

The idea of the moment in electroacoustic music is a powerful tool, since it unites ways of thinking about sound objects and a *raison d'être* for the way they are used in time. The idea of sustaining moment form by shifting static arrangements can provide the platform for active listening 'inside' sound while, as Jonathan Kramer (1978: 177) pointed out, also being a vehicle for profound forms of discontinuity. In his words: 'the unexpected is more striking, more meaningful than the expected because it contains more information'. If we accept this, then the nature of the materials and the particular qualities of discontinuity that moment-shifts may evoke is clearly a significant factor in the affective potential of forms made in this way. John Dack (1999) has observed that 'Stockhausen's adoption of moment form need not discard perceptible processes with goals; they simply refuse to participate in a globally directed narrative curve', pointing to the fact that as an organising principle it has the potential to expose a sense of *arrangement* of structural components as individual entities and inviting the listener to engage in a questioning and creative 'forming' mode of listening. In that sense, Kramer (1988) suggests that moment forms behave differently to the way in which durations of individual sections in a piece of tonal music tend to imply the overall duration and scale over which it will unfold. Forward projection of probable timescale and the associated psychological preparations we make (from epic journey to diversionary miniature) are difficult to gauge in the arbitrary atmosphere of moment forms. Yet Pressnitzer and McAdams (2000) have asserted that 'A listener will always try to structure the acoustic world that confronts his or her ears, whatever the situation of listening strategy' – affirming a need to study both the way compositional decision-making tells us something about the process of forming structural pathways in music and ways in which commonalities of form can be discerned in spite of the idiosyncrasies of any specific work. How we perceive any particular moment depends on the distinctiveness and memorability of previous and surrounding events, or whether there is a recognisable pattern in the morphology of change that may give us a sense of syntactical coherence. As such it might be regarded as an embodiment of the idea of compositional process as form in the state of 'being discovered' and open to interpretation as micro-narratives, sequences, states of sonic matter and contrasts thereof. From the procedural perspective of the composer, moment form has a special potential through the use of technology because it touches with the idea of sound sculpting and juxtaposition through detailed editing and interleaving of sounds. The spirit of moment form has a particular potential in acousmatic music where individual sound gestures or textural identities may be presented in a way to direct attention inward to the idiosyncratic, fleeting, self-contained spectromorphological qualities of a sound. In turn that may influence the way large-scale form is sustained by articulating a work into strongly unified movements focused on play within particular object-based, spectral or morphological constraints, as in many large-scale works in the French acousmatic canon.[8]

A good example of an acousmatic work influenced by a moment form approach is Ray Guillette's *Hommage à Pollock No. 2* (1999; comp. [1991]). Its six-and-a-half-minute duration is characterised by continuous inter-leaving and layering of attacks in individual pulses and streams, and more fluid liquid-like sounds. In the first four minutes of the piece there is no decisive correlation between the gestural elements which present a whim-sical, haphazard series of sonically compelling moments, punctuated with short, irregular silences. Forward projection of the nature of future sound events is undermined by the constant variations in emphasis and colour, which also mitigates against forming retrospective connections, except in the most general sense: a feeling of more or less pitched quality to attacks, single versus streamed or the apparent proximity of sound events from the listener within the markedly three-dimensional spatial perspective. But within this some distinctive moments attract attention, such as the pulses of same pitch stream at 2'38" which, as tangible reiteration, form a notably rhetorical moment, while the focal pitch of a 'plucked string' chord at 3'13" stands out for the novelty of its spectral luminosity. In a twist of the form, a galvanising pitched drone from 4'18" heralds the commencement of greater causal interaction between sounds, which the composer likens to 'individual lines, dots and pools congeal[ing] into an intended structure' (Guillette 1999).

Morphic form

Trevor Wishart's (1994a) genre of 'morphic' form extends from the poten-tial of electroacoustic music to develop materials through processes of continuous transformation of sound identity and timbre. Sound trans-formation tools found in electroacoustic music may encourage this kind

---

[8] Kramer (1988) detects embryonic moment form in music from the inter-war years by Stravinsky and Messiaen. The fixed media of *musique concrète*, in affording direct perception of non-contextual and juxtapositional sequences of material, surely also both influenced and provided tools for the exploration of moment form. The shaping of sound in real time in various electroacoustic improvisational settings, where a formal process may be pre-structured or entirely serendipitous, is further witness to the ways the fluid 'sculpting' of material may guide the evolution of a work.

of approach since notions of sonic transfiguration and metamorphosis can take on a new, causally centred meaning (in the sense of sound as aural product of interactions between a sounding body and some energy input). This evokes the idea of the continuum as a unifying psychological construct (e.g. in terms of timbre and spectral types), which, if established, can be understood as both departing from a particular state or identity and moving in the direction of another. This has the advantage for the design of form in that a sense of transformational direction, with possible goal states, can be imagined or anticipated before an arrival state is actually known – from a traditional perspective, at least, an important ingredient in musical expectation and the creation and resolution of tension. There may be generalisable principles about the way continua can function, but we should be careful about the way these are characterised. For example, Wishart (1994a) has used the metaphor of 'key change' to describe the morphing of vocal sounds into wood-like sounds at one point in *Tongues of Fire*. While the shift in provenance he creates is tangible, this description misses the fact that in a tonal key change the result is still a set of equivalent relations between the pitch elements in the old and new keys and often the most interesting feature is not solely the sound of the new key, but the sensation of the point of change itself (certainly when we are talking about equal temperament). The voice-to-wood sound source transformation evokes a shift of apparent sources between which there are not equivalent relations. A further practical difficulty with the continuum model is that it is both imaginary and limited by what can actually be achieved in the studio. A composer may have the advantage of 'play' with sound that informs the final result in a way the listener never gets to experience, or may encounter the frustration of imagining sonic extensions that they do not have the wherewithal to achieve. So there are formal issues in presenting the 'image' of a continuum such that a listener can engage with it and enter into its dialectic.

Ideas of the *moment* and the *morphic* perhaps together have new significance with respect to form in electroacoustic music – with some interesting consequences. For example, in the work of spectralist composers, if we regard the singular identity of a timbre as being something formed and coherent in its own terms, it is clear that musical discourse can arise from the deconstruction of that *identity*, which might conform to McAdams's (1989) requirements for form-bearing dimensions in music (see above).

An essential feature of the spectralist approach is its acknowledgement of the phenomenon of spectral integration as something whose logic is instinctively 'known' outside any compositional context and can therefore be used in comprehending the composer's processes and patterns. Seeds of the 'moment' value of spectral thinking can be seen in Messiaen's *Mode de valeurs et d'intensités* (1949) from *Quatre études de rythme*. The pre-compositional serial/modal foundations of the work are well articulated in the literature (Hill 1995) and in fact set out in the preface to the score. At one level the effect is of a serial cut-up – note-droplets which project a tonally neutral pointillist piano canvas, in which the salient organisational feature is that (gamelan-like) the long durations correspond to the low end of the pitch range and the short ones are concentrated at the top, tending occasionally to be heard as momentary crystallisations of motivic units. It is a musical ecosystem that has been created here, with specific note-events occupying their own dynamic, durational and fixed-register niches helping us to grasp them as identities even when sufficiently connected to form groups. An image of random pitch dispersal is fashioned as the dispersion of the tones acts against the consistent formation of coherent voices. The concentration on the quality of each note, particularly through the textural contour created by unmediated dynamic shifts, means that single notes and some rapid groupings can themselves be thought of as 'moments'. Crucially, at another level this is enriched by the transient pooling of tones related as natural harmonics which gel in moments of transparent spectral fusion, the resonance of more extended low pitches assisting the blend that occurs at these points. These 'moments' articulate a level other than the notes themselves: they signal that there are conditions under which the tones cease to act as individual values and consolidate into a quasi-timbral unity – as formal signposts and lures to expectation (when will the next such moment emerge?). A stasis is conjured at these points as the grounding force of harmonic fusion seems to still-frame the passage of time.

Conceptually and technically, ideas around the deconstruction and fusion of timbre continue to be fundamental to electroacoustic thought, with considerable cross-fertilisation between instrumental and electro-acoustic domains spurred by what Murail (2005: 123) has related as 'the very essential idea that the musical "atom" is not the notehead written on staff paper'. A case in point is the first movement of Alejandro Viñao's *Chant d'Ailleurs* (1994; comp. 1991) in which continual processes of spectral reconstruction around the central source of a female singing voice rely on the steering of listening attention to particular regions within a spectrum and where manipulation of spectral balance or rhythmic articu-lation stimulate morphic development. Stages of timbral deconstruction make us aware of sound parameters as components are stripped away, but also disguise them through spectral sleight of hand when they reintegrate into new identities. Again, though, the central persona of the living voice provides a source-recognisable grounding. Moments of source consolidation within a spectrally morphic form also are a feature of John Chowning's work *Phoné* (1988; comp. 1980–1) as vibrato and synthesis of formants emphasise the fusion of digital FM timbres as perceptibly vocal. The most powerful feature of *Phoné* as an acousmatically experienced work is its integration of the morphic and the moment. Much of the work can be apprehended as a kind of constant and fluid spectral 'stuff', fusing and segregating in a myriad of ways (the morphic), but at certain points taking a revelatory turn into another world of meaning with a decisively human singing quality as imaginatively compelling moments.

Source recognition to define moments

In continuing this line of thought, I am going to suggest here that a recognised *source* may have a moment function, not solely in spectro-morphological terms, but also in referential terms. For example, *Phonurgie* by Francis Dhomont (2001; comp. 1998) opens in a powerfully rhetorical way with surges of impulsive resonant pitched gestures and textures emerging out of them. But at 4'48" a transition is made to a more earthly soundworld in an image of flapping birds' wings, emerging over an estab-lished broadband drone. Such a coherently realistic sound functions not just as a transition to a new morphological 'field' but also introduces a powerful shift of reference. As a 'grounding', the image takes over, and in a way time slows down in the work, even though the texture is very busy sonically – concentration instinctively goes to comprehending the scene. Formally, therefore, its function is not just as a contrasting morphological 'theme', but also as a deflection for us into another *kind* of listening. It tells us that the piece is not just about the structure of the sounds, but also about the formal context that embraces them, and the musical/imaginative sense that *allows* them to participate in the work. It makes of the work an imaginative world where this realism can coexist with abstract resonant morphologies, but we also have to construct for ourselves a scenario that imaginatively accommodates both the moment and the longer-term con-sequence of such a strong image created in that moment. But moments of this kind do not necessarily evoke a static response. It takes a short time to evoke a sonic image of this kind – and attention may shift in different directions, towards spectromorphological features of the sounds them-selves, in conjunction with attentiveness for change at the referential or spectromorphological level. For example, we might surmise that the birds could disperse leaving us to hear other previously hidden sounds within the scene, or the structure of the sounds may change (changes in pitch structure or envelope, for example), with the capacity to initiate a sequence of 'morphic' change. While a 'meaning' is available at the level of that juxtaposition alone, a deeper meaning (why have we been projected into this new 'environment'?) is ambiguous, open.[9] The overriding message is the powerful nature of the transition itself and the realisation that this kind of indicative shift is *possible*. Referential moments can also be very fleeting and we know they are a powerful way to invite listeners into a 'forming' way of listening – for example, in some of Jonty Harrison's music since the mid-1990s, where sound images confirm or playfully contradict the environment we think has been established in lively *mélanges* with abstract sounds. These sorts of referential shifts are one of the innovative features of electroacoustic forms. So if we seek in McAdams's terms above 'a system of salience or stability relations' that can be learned or grasped through 'mere exposure', referential shifts which function as defined formal moments or as seeds of morphological transformation are powerful motivators.

Innovative ways of developing formal design possibilities as a result of the structure of complex non-referential electroacoustic sounds themselves are more problematic, attributable to a large extent to the fact that this may involve asking listeners to engage with modes of listening that do not necessarily equate with what is (to date) normatively acquired through culture. In a very promising approach to explaining how the structure of sound might function formally, as part of a segmentation-based approach to structural analysis, James Tenney proposed the idea of a parametric profile for sound units of different durations (he terms them element, clang or sequence) in order to register fluctuation in 'parametric intensity' – a measure of the subjective significance or weight accorded to any musical parameter over time. A parameter he described as being: 'any distinctive attribute of a sound, in terms of which one (elementary) sound or sound-configuration may be distinguished from another' (Tenney 2006: 92). He also hypothesised that sounds evoke kinaesthetic responses in listeners and that the durations of these effects might vary according to changes in parametric intensity creating a cumulative effect on the interpretation of form. Given electroacoustic music's capacity for spectromorphological

---

[9] The 'wing' moment is answered by ambiguously pitched scattered attacks which offer a clear behavioural echo of the wing sounds, and these have a significant role in subsequent textural evolution of the work.

complexity and instability, this seems a potential tool to evaluate both the qualities of moments and their impact on form through the way listening might be steered in conjunction with the ensuing flow of morphological (read: morphic) evolution – though to be well developed this would require a suitable parametric lexicon. From a higher structural perspective, Kaija Saariaho's (1987) discussion of the mixed orchestral/electroacoustic work - *Verblendungen* (1982–4) offers the composer's view of an applied perspective along these lines. Extreme generalisations of parametric categories – 'orchestra', 'polyphony', 'rate of harmonic progression', 'pitch range', 'dynamics', 'homophony' and 'tape' (electroacoustic sounds) – have independent curves for the degree of importance ascribed to each through the course of the work. Saariaho admits that because some of these represent simple activity levels of the sounding agents ('tape' and orchestra) and others are more structurally qualitative in nature, the model serves more as a guide for the forming process, for which the overarching concern was 'an impossible overall form: a work which would begin at its highest point and whose infolding [*sic*] would be merely a winding down after the initial burst of energy' (Saariaho 1987: 107).

Tenney's ideas also resonate with the following statement by Christian Zanési in the programme note to *Stop ! l'horizon* (1996; comp. 1983):

I have the very distinct feeling that music is only a 'grand noise' and its interior sculpted in a thousand details. It opens like a living organism to let my hearing [original: *mon écoute*] wander around in it. Very soon a magnetic relation is established and all the sounds which constitute the grand noise draw me toward an orient. I accept this direction.

Later, much later, I reach a distant point on the horizon which pulls me towards it.

What Zanési has articulated here is an imaginative, almost sculptural, overview of a formal paradigm in which materials, although fixed in structure, are available for investigation, interpretation and contemplation, and which quite possibly presents the kind of musical and conceptual model that led Smalley (1986) to question the relevance of formal consensus. The three movements of *Stop ! l'horizon* are projected through rhetorical frameworks marked by interplay of materials that are mostly remote from identifiable sources such as clouds of complex noise, along with punctuating attacks that keep us close to a 'surface' of real objects such as resonant drum-like tones. Textures are alive with shifts in parametric intensity, particularly noise-pitch distinctions, inviting change in the nature of focus of listening. Richness of invention and sonic detail is crucial to such a vision, as is an appropriately expansive use of time to allow active listening to enter that detail. One might then characterise such an approach to form as a world of 'available moments', which are interrupted and layered. In short, Zanési achieves a balance between stasis and motion that keeps listening active and seeking direction, as well offering scope to relax into the immersive nature of this musical environment. The metaphor of a 'living organism' in which hearing can 'wander' also finds a parallel in the creative process. The ease with which sound materials can be developed and mutated using computers presents exactly the potential for extensive probing, reshaping and recombining of sounds objects that Zanési suggests within the listening process. Indeed, the electroacoustic medium's gift of a heightened freedom to disassemble and reassemble sounds in conjunction with the realisation that these sounds simply may not respond to process-ing in the way one imagines they will, or *need* to for the musical purposes envisaged for them, is a key reason a call for a clear understanding of form and forming principles is presaged here.

Narrative

Conceptions of narrative are central to time-based arts. Barthes (1977) regarded narrative as an 'international, transhistorical, transcultural phe-nomenon, simply there, like life itself': we find narratives because we view ourselves situated in a present, with a past and designs for a future and it is difficult to avoid the conviction that it is a fundamental dimension of human thought and understanding. The view of narrative presented here starts with the capacity for sound recording to function as a mirror held up to lived experience. Walter Benjamin (2002) pointed to the fact that reproduction of singular artworks shifts attention away from the need to ritually go to them for the experience. But the original application of reproduction technology makes another kind of shift, which is to focus on the reproduction of our perceptions. A camera or a sound recording device makes a fixed object out of our experience – it is very direct. This means that recording is more than the support mechanism for acousmatic sound in the sense elaborated by Schaeffer (1966), and neither is it solely a second-hand poor cousin of live or interactive performance. It forms a trace of experience and, to transliterate the sense in which Benjamin uses it, carries an 'aura of experience'. The nature of that experience can be questioned and revisited, but the data are a permanent document. Further-more the rhetorical function that a recorded sound may carry as a sign is dependent upon factors such as the apparent temporal context of the recording, such as presentation of a voice from the distant past offered within an otherwise contemporaneous setting (Young 2008).

The works I am going to discuss include words as a primary vehicle for narrative, with an emphasis on ways in which this has been used to form expressions of a personal or intimate nature. Marie-Laure Ryan (2004) suggests that 'of all the semiotic codes, language is the best suited to storytelling'. The word may be the trans-medial narration tool par excellence, but one thing I hope to show is that non-verbal sound has a crucial, more than accompanimental role in making distinct forms of narrative in acousmatic work, and that her three generalised criteria for narrative are applicable, namely:

1. Narrative creates a world, populated with characters and actions.
2. The world inhabited will undergo changes of state, through events that may or may not be imposed through human action – creating a temporal dimension.
3. The text allows reconstruction of an interpretative network of 'goals, plans, causal relations, and psychological motivations around the narrated events'.

Because the acousmatic space-form has the capacity to integrate the widest range of musical and real-world referents, it is well suited to the invention of complex narrative forms.

Narrative forms: three examples

Trevor Wishart's *Red Bird* (1992; comp. 1973–7) is well known and uses a very limited set of words in a symbolic way – they are a specialised set of objects within a wider range of referential primitives and sound constructs. Wishart conceived an overall narrative for the work, which he outlined graphically, but the potency of the sound-imagery and in particular the transformations used to create metaphorical meanings overshadows any purely linear implications of the narrative. However, Andrew Sachs's *The Revenge* (1978), created for the BBC as an experimental wordless radio play, uses very similar referential primitives to *Red Bird*, especially in the early part of the work. But the narrative is completely linear, namely an escaped convict seeks and exacts violent retribution on those who contributed to his imprisonment. There is some very effective projection of real-world contextualizing sound imagery in the work but, because the narrative is so linear and dedicated to the telling of the story, we are not taken into the kind of metaphorical world of *Red Bird*. For instance, when the prisoner escapes by swimming, we hear him gasp on plunging underwater, giving confirmatory context to the image/action. In *Red Bird* water has a literal presence but also a more symbolic and not a clearly indicative role – we feel our world submerged, but is it drowning or escape? In *The Revenge* we, auditors, are always in the same place as the character, observers at close quarters, but a deeper, more imaginative set of relationships between the sounds and the objects to which they refer is not made. *Red Bird* does achieve this because the discourse is not simply sequential but also transformational, that is to say, morphic in formal function. In *Red Bird* we enter the psychological world of the prisoner, not just as an individual but also as an emblematic one. Wishart summons an array of micro-narratives which collectively imply, but do not conclusively state, a larger narrative towards the eventual disposal of the prisoner.

The form of Luc Ferrari's *Presque rien no. 2, ainsi continue la nuit dans ma tête multiple* (2009; comp. 1977) is shaped around the notion of concentrated listening in a nocturnal environment: seeking to map out the darkened environment through sound. Ferrari and his companion are evidently located within the environment, commenting in hushed tones on the apparent physical and aural nature of the surroundings. Gradually elements of the space are described for us, but so is the aesthetic intent of the situation, as we are told right at the start that we are to 'try to penetrate a landscape', which is 'not easy'. Our attention is drawn to various perceptions of the sounds around the two people we perceive to be physically moving through this nocturnal landscape 'I thought we were more towards the road' . . . 'there is a strange insect' . . . 'it's nice here, not bad' . . . 'is there a train?' . . . 'Who is it in the distance?' Moving towards sounds of birds that cannot be seen, and with commentary on actions and objects within the landscape that are not sounding – a vine, a bush, towards the road, a brook that turns out to be not there: 'We are looking for something and then we find something else.'[10] But at the key point, Ferrari tells us that he has been enveloped by the night and is penetrated in an exchange – the night continuing in his 'multiple heads': the act of listening – his 'penetration' of the landscape allows his imaginative sense to take over, but it is an imaginative shift that appears to be prompted by elements of uncertainty and disorientation in the dark. And

---

[10] This aspect of the work's narrative could be taken as metaphor for the innate duality in acousmatic listening of an instinctive tendency to identify sound sources and the capacity to infer meaning from spectromorphological characteristics.

in that shift we are taken from an explanatory narration into a fulfilment of an imaginary, more normatively musical, a relationship with the environment, evoking the kind of deeper narrative of 'going inside' the soundscape and externalising sonic imagination, symbolised by the appearance of simple melodic instrumental phrases and a kind of electronically realised thunder in the second and third sections of the piece respectively. The strangely inconclusive ending, as though the protagonist has simply wandered off, and perhaps encountered something new (though by that stage he has left our company), leaves both narrative and metaphor unfulfilled. This work also demonstrates the artistic efficacy and originality of the microphone as a tool. It can be directed out to the world, but is also quite naturally turned back on the recordist himself – the microphone quite naturally lends itself to being a passive receiver of our narrative on the private world of experience.

John Cousins's *Doreen* (2007)[11] is a portrait of the composer's mother and concerns her meeting her future husband Ted during wartime, namely the powerful sexual attraction between Doreen and Ted. The work begins with a simple piano-accompanied rendition of the Billy Mayhew song *It's a Sin to Tell a Lie*. Sung by the very elderly Doreen, the subject of the work, the significance of the song is not fully articulated until the very end of the piece. At this point it contextualises the idea of memory – a 1930s song sung by an elderly woman places us in the present and creates a nostalgic atmosphere, setting an appropriate tone for the unfolding of memory. What follows is initially contextualised with the introductory words of an interviewer: 'What I'd like to do is to start with the Ngaio Town Hall and the band you used to play in.' Mention of 'during the war' and 'where I first met Ted' are spontaneously offered by Doreen in response to this, and these memory associations apparently triggered by mention of those past events provide us with an indication that we are about to enter a world reconstructed through reminiscing triggered by powerful associations of time and place, in itself a very intimate form of narrative. The story then unfolds through recollections of Doreen's band playing at recreational events for soldiers on leave from the local army camp. The piano accompaniment heard at the outset underpins most of this for the first eight minutes, providing a supporting counterpoint, in a fairly conventional documentary technique. The focus of the story moves towards details of Doreen and Ted's intense sexual connection, which, on mention of their

---

[11] The core materials of this work were subsequently incorporated into a larger audiovisual piece *Speak Memory* (2007).

watching a fireworks display, is interrupted by a shower of firework explosions. Woven within this is Doreen's uncontrolled laughter. At this point we are truly invited to enter the experiential world of this woman – the onset of the fireworks is sudden in the extreme and the laughter has a salacious, visceral quality which amplifies her earlier description of her 'whole body exploding' in love making.

This is, for the listener, a moment where the past of another comes to life. Another cue is the subsequent presence of an oppressive high-frequency tinnitus-like tone that recurs in sections that follow, which is itself something expressed by Doreen as part of her sexual experiences. So at these points, the narrative becomes story not just recounted verbally, but also inwardly felt in the process of re-engaging with past experience, *as reconstructed by the composer*. Doreen describes the pregnancy that followed, and alludes to consequential marriage. The fireworks have a dual role of representing the event and the sexual simile used by Doreen, but it also is evocative of the automatic retrieval of memory – the way the sense of events forces itself back into conscious thought. And of course this kind of reiteration and reintegration of materials is a very musical way to construct a form. The very last section is a short epigram from Doreen, beginning: 'I should never have married . . . but we did have something and it grew', which leaves the story open and unresolved, with the suggestion that the relationship was ultimately not completely satisfactory. It is at this point that the poignancy of the opening song is fully realised within the narrative.

In acousmatic music, the notion of narrative presents fundamental new opportunities for the ancient distinction between diegesis and mimesis: the story told and the story acted out. For via sound recording not only do we have access to oral histories both formal and informal, but also to sounds and images that carry us across the borders of memory and that is what makes these works particularly significant as acousmatic expressions.

Concluding remarks

A serious search to identify formal innovation in electroacoustic music is important to the field. It is closely linked to the development of descriptive and analytical tools per se. But if by form we mean ways that we relate local to global, micro to macro and the framing of meaning, taking into account the particular modes of listening encouraged by the genre, then an emergent concept of form is essential to the development of new modes of analysis – otherwise what are we using analysis to look for? Analytical methods frequently seek to identify particular features of sounds and particular kinds of relationships between them based on assumptions about the nature and function of 'musical' materials – and one of the problems in analysing electroacoustic music is that it frequently resists traditional reductive methods; for example, where complex models of timbre design are prominent. By evaluating the global patterns of musical organisation, imperatives for the enhancement of the analytical vocabulary and its application may be found.

The terms used here to outline a search for new musical forms are not solely the province of expressly technology-based work – witnessed by the roots of moment form as a more generically experimental approach to time in instrumental as much as in early electroacoustic music: the morphic orchestral works of Ligeti, the play of intrinsic/extrinsic referential layers found in the music of Ives or the autobiographical narratives of Mahler. However, the radical originality of sound recording as an instrument of creativity, and the extensive capabilities of electronic (especially digital) processing methods are among the most profoundly innovative tools provided by the electroacoustic remediation of music. But despite the far-reaching extension of materials made available by the electroacoustic medium, there should be no assumption that a complete break with traditional formal concepts is inevitable. Yet the capacity of electroacoustic music to help us find within ourselves new ways of listening calls for serious investigation into ways that this new listening can be fostered by composers. In a way this inevitable tension between the traditional and the innovative makes the issue most compellingly engaging and more fundamentally and cohesively musical.

References

Barthes, Roland (1977) *Image, Music, Text.* London: Fontana.

Benjamin, W. (2002) The work of art in the age of its technological reproducibility. In H. Eiland and M. W. Jennings (eds.) *Selected Writings, Volume 3, 1935–1938.* Cambridge, MA: Belknap Press of Harvard University Press, 101–33.

Brown, Earle (1966) Lecture given at the Internationalen Ferienkurse für Neue Musik, Darmstadt, 1965. *Music of the Avant-Garde,* 1, 49–51. (Originally published in Form in der Neuen Musik, *Darmstädter Beiträge zur Neuen Musik,* X, Mainz: Schott).

Cooke, Deryck (1959) *The Language of Music*. Oxford University Press.

Cousins, John (2007) *Doreen*. Subsequently incorporated into the audiovisual work *Speak Memory* (2007), available at http://www.studio174-nz.com/speak-memory.html.

Dack, John (1999) Karlheinz Stockhausen's *Kontakte* and Narrativity. *eContact* 2.2. http://cec.concordia.ca/econtact/SAN/Dack.htm.

Dhomont, Francis (2001) *Phonurgie* (1998). On Cycle du son. Montréal: Empreintes Digitales, IMED 0158.

Ferrari, Luc (2009) *Presque rien no. 2, ainsi continue la nuit dans ma tête multiple* (1977). On *L'oeuvre électronique*. Paris: Ina-GRM, INA_G 6017/26.

Grabócz, Marta (1997) Survival or renewal? Structural imagination in recent electroacoustic and computer music. *Organised Sound*, 2, 83–95.

Guillette, Ray (1999) *Homage [sic] à Pollock No. 2* [1991]. On Six Winners. Stockholm: Fylkingen Records, FYCD 1014.

Hill, Peter (ed.) (1995) *The Messiaen Companion*. London: Faber.

Kendall, Gary S. (2008) What is an event? The EVENT schema, circumstances, metaphor and gist. *Proceedings of the 2008 International Computer Music Conference*. Belfast. www.garykendall.net/papers/KendallICMC2008.pdf.

Kramer, Jonathan (1978) Moment form in twentieth century music. *The Musical Quarterly*, 64(2), 177–94.

(1988) *The Time of Music: New Meanings, New Temporalities, New Listening Strategies*. New York/London: Schirmer.

Kremer, Gidon and Argerich, Martha (1994) Beethoven Violin Sonata in C minor, op. 32 no. 2. Deutsche Grammophon 453743–2.

McAdams, Stephen (1989) Psychological constraints on form-bearing dimensions in music. *Contemporary Music Review*, 4, 181–98. http://mediatheque.ircam.fr/articles/textes/McAdams89a/.

McAdams, S. and Saariaho, K. (1985) Qualities and functions of musical timbre. *Proceedings of the 1985 Computer Music Conference*, San Francisco: International Computer Music Association, 367–74.

Meyer, Leonard B. (1973) *Explaining Music: Essays and Explorations*. Berkeley: University of California Press.

Murail, Tristan (2005) The revolution of complex sounds. *Contemporary Music Review*, 24(2), 121–35.

Pressnitzer, D. and McAdams, S. (2000) Acoustics, psychoacoustics and spectral music. *Contemporary Music Review*, 19(2), 33–59.

Reynolds, Roger (2002) *Form and Method: Composing Music*. New York/London: Routledge.

Roy, Stéphane (1998) Functional and implicative analysis of *Ombres Blanches*. *Journal of New Music Research*, 27(1–2), 165–84.

(2003) *L'analyse des musiques électroacoustiques: modèles et propositions*. Paris: L'Harmattan.

Ryan, Marie-Laure (2004) *Narrative Across Media: The Languages of Storytelling*. Lincoln, NE/London: University of Nebraska Press.

Saariaho, Kaija (1987) Timbre and harmony: Interpolations of timbral structures. *Contemporary Music Review*, 2(1), 93–133.

Sachs, Andrew (1978) *The Revenge*. Radio play first broadcast BBC Radio 4 June.

Schaeffer, Pierre (1966) *Traité des objets musicaux*. Paris: Seuil.

Smalley, Denis (1986) Spectro-morphology and structuring processes. In S. Emmerson (ed.) *The Language of Electroacoustic Music*. London: Macmillan, 61–93.

(1997) Explaining sound shapes. *Organised Sound*, 2(2), 107–26.

(2007) Space-form and the acousmatic image. *Organised Sound*, 12(1), 35–58.

Snyder, Bob (2000) *Music and Memory: An Introduction*. Cambridge, MA/London: MIT Press.

Stockhausen, Karlheinz (1991) *Stockhausen on Music*. London/New York: Marion Boyars.

Tenney, James (2006) *Meta Hodos and Meta Meta Hodos: A Phenomenology of 20th-Century Musical Materials and an Approach to the Study of Form*. Lebanon, NH: Frog Peak Music.

Viñao, Alejandro (1994) *Chant d'Ailleurs* (1991) for soprano and computer. On *Hildegard's Dream*. [Paris]: INA-GRM, INA C 1015.

Wishart, Trevor (1992) *Red Bird* (1973–7). October Music.

(1994a) *Audible Design: A Plain and Easy Introduction to Practical Sound Composition*. York: Orpheus The Pantomime.

(1994b) *Tongues of Fire*. York: Orpheus The Pantomime, CD Maxi-Single, OTP001.

Young, John (2008) Inventing memory: Documentary and imagination in acousmatic music. In M. Dogantan-Dack (ed.) *Recorded Music: Philosophical and Critical Reflections*. London: Middlesex University Press, 314–32.

Zanési, Christian (1996) *Stop! l'horizon* (1983). On Stop! l'horizon. [Paris]: INA-GRM, INA C 2001.

4 | Interactive and generative music: a quagmire for the musical analyst

MICHAEL YOUNG

Overview

The innovative, rapidly evolving fields of interactive and generative music present fascinating challenges for musical analysis. Many of these challenges are shared with experimental improvisation and sonic arts; diverse practices with distinct histories that have, to an extent, developed separately from the composition-orientated practices we normally associate with analysis, such as musical notation. To narrow the discussion, this chapter assumes that interactive and generative music is computer-based, whatever mutually informing relationships it enjoys with improvised music and other sound art forms. Music creation that exploits and depends on computers, that is, computational systems, raises questions about creative methodology, documentation and listener comprehension; in general, the impact of 'real-time' computation. The author approaches these issues as a composer and developer of interactive performance systems.

In the last 20 years or more there has been an explosion of music making in which computers are not just in evidence but can be acknowledged as co-progenitors. Computers are embedded into the act of music creation so profoundly they become not just facilitators but quasi-creators. For instance, in live electronic music a computer may act as an interpreter that mediates between a performer's action (e.g. via a tactile control device or musical instrument) and a synthesiser. The nature and complexity of this interpretation is integral to the performance process and the consequent production of musical events. For generative music, this is even more the case: automated generation might stand in for the activities of the composer and all the technical and intuitive methods we associate with the act of composition.

The preponderance of interactive and generative music today can be attributed to many factors, not least the accessibility of increasingly powerful hardware and computational capacity, previously available only to well-financed institutions. Nowadays all this technology is in the hands of composers, performers and music students using laptops, affordable controllers and, most recently, mobile devices. There has been a commensurate development of musician-friendly software offering alternative creative paradigms to the 'recording studio' model upon which ProTools, Logic and other DAW systems are based. Examples include Supercollider, Max/MSP, Pure Data and Ableton Live; software that can be traced back to early computer music programming. But now they are fully accessible, running on machines that compute audio at a rate required for live performance. The growing prominence of music computing in educational institutions reflects and fuels these developments, helping break down the conventional barrier between composer and technologist, that is, the discrete roles of musical creator and technical developer. Composers today might well expect to code their own software; the composer becomes software designer, not just software user. The software replaces many of the functions previously unique to human creative activity. Generative music apps written for iOS or Android (such as *Bloom* by Brian Eno and Peter Chilvers[1]) demonstrate an entirely new outlet for music creativity: musical aims, style and language are built into the software for the user to explore and – possibly – share the result. There is no definitive musical product, audience or 'author'. The musical analyst may need to become software analyst, appraising music computer coding independently of any specific instance of its use.

Music is a special case in a wider, cultural and social shift in which our own identity – as social and creative beings – increasingly integrates with digital technologies. We are acclimatised to computer systems in daily life. The growing, perhaps unwitting, acceptance of artificial intelligence in many quasi-social or functional settings is due to our ability to model communicative and cognitive processes. It seems entirely natural therefore that new music should explore, exploit and critically engage with this phenomenon. The increasing use of commonplace handheld devices in performance and production, amalgamating powerful sound-generating technology with social media and interactive systems, points to the future. These developments have arisen in tandem with a renewed interest in experimental and improvised forms of music and the recognition and promotion of non-institutional music creation (facilitated by the web and social media).

What we do not have yet, perhaps, is an accompanying shared understanding about how to appreciate and evaluate this vast and diverse creative endeavour. This chapter describes categories within generative and interactive music according to musical context, technical methodology

---

[1] www.generativemusic.com (accessed 8 April 2015).

and the apparent relationships between creative instigator and the result. Such understandings might point to how music analysis might be variously employed as a critical tool in this rapidly changing creative environment.

Analytical challenges

Interactive computer music, however elaborate and sophisticated in its technical development and design, is widely seen primarily as a perform- ance practice. But it is a practice that blurs all the boundaries between making, performing and listening. The performer engages in real time with a computer system, through a conventional instrument, user interface or control device. The audience appreciates this interaction, depending on how accessible the controlling actions might be to an observer. It could be hard to attribute agency (i.e. cause and effect) to the human or machine elements by listening and visual observation alone. This contrasts with the familiar world of instrumental-only performance and even fixed electro- acoustic music (where there is typically a clear delineation between the composition and live sound diffusion). Similarly, in a music where poten- tially all sound is amplified and processed, it might be hard to attribute the source of any sound heard (live instrument or computer?) let alone its ownership (composer or improviser?). But this is just one of the fascin- ations of live electronic music, as Harvey described:

When electronics are seamlessly connected to the solid instrumental world an expansion of the admissible takes place, and the 'mad' world is made to belong. (Harvey 1999: 80)

Generative music, in its pure form, is concerned with how we make, not perform, music; it is a computational, algorithmic process. There is no composer in a conventional sense, rather, there is a sonification of compu- tation. It is a technological manifestation of LeWitt's description of con- ceptual art in general:

all of the planning and decisions are made beforehand and the execution is a perfunctory affair. The idea becomes a machine that makes the art ... It is usually free from the dependence on the skill of the artist as a craftsman. (LeWitt 1967: 79)

Where generative music might differ from LeWitt is in his assertion 'art is not theoretical or illustrative of theories' and it does not depend on the 'skill of the artist as a craftsman'. In many approaches to generative music, the theory and craft are of immediate relevance: the music testifies to the attributes of the 'machine' and the skills, not just the intentions, of the software programmer.

The listener who witnesses generative music – computation-in-sound – is left to contemplate a world of paradoxes. The computational element, however important in the construction of the work, might in fact be dependent on unrelated creative decisions, including assumptions about music in general (instrumentation, synthesis method, musical style). A very common assumption in generative music is that music naturally consists of a series of symbols, that is, notes of fixed pitch, duration and timbre, and that the note choice should be constrained (e.g. to take the form of a diatonic scale). The work may be infinite in length (e.g. when presented in an installation format), so what constitutes a representative experience? The music might appear novel, and be accepted as an enrichment of our very idea of musical aesthetics. But this might be problematic because there is no reference point to judge its expressive, structural or aesthetic value, and no composer to ask, potentially. Some forms of generative music might compare to established styles or idioms, historical or contemporary, inviting either a negative or positive comparison.

Both interactive and generative music can lay claim to an independent history that pre-dates our information technology culture, and by centuries. Computation in music creation is as intrinsic to the phenomenon of music making as is its social, communicative functions. The challenge presented by current computer music is that it can both embrace and blur such fundamental attributes, which, formerly, were divided by culturally informed partisan notions: author versus presenter, compositional control versus social praxis, the intuitive versus the mathematical, and so on, all of which are highly loaded in terms of value, causal attribution and cultural capital.

So across this vast range of creative approaches a common issue emerges: Who is the 'composer', and should we care? Intentionality can only be inferred at the moment of performance or realisation, so it is impossible in either case – interactive systems in performance or generative systems in execution – to assert definitively that there is an original agency, a creative or expressive intention that correlates measurably and meaningfully to the outcome that audiences experience.

If the function of analysis is to explain, codify or in some other way legitimise the listener experience, then it can be undertaken without knowledge of creative intention, and this might be useful when considering computer-generated music.

A good analytical theory would need to model the dynamics of musical experience, which is a very difficult undertaking. Compositional theory only needs to focus on whatever is of most practical use to musicians who are performing, composing, or improvising music. (Rahn 2004: 135)

Listeners will apply their own creative faculties when interpreting their experience: all structural and expressive effect can be inferred. There are historical precedents for this approach, analytical methods applied beyond their original context (Schenkerian methods in atonal music, or recent quantitative methods developed in computer science). But a musical analysis, without focusing entirely on compositional theory *per se*, should aim to bridge between a work's known means and the final outcome experienced by the listener. Rahn quotes David Lewin's view that

since music is something you do, and not just something you perceive (or understand), a theory of music cannot be developed fully from a theory of musical perception. (Rahn 2004: 139)

Analysis might explain how the impression of structural efficacy and aesthetic effect results from an interaction, however distant, between intentional design and culturally informed reception. It may explain the relationships between known compositional principles, relevant to the time of creation, and the particular interpretation and extensions of these in the case of a specific creative work. Analysis may also seek to explain the relationship between construction and reception in terms of a given work's potential for status; its contribution to a wider field of cultural practice or academic research. Other generalisations may follow, with regard to a particular composer's or improviser's method, the musical style of its time, the wider structural principles and the analytic technique itself.

Analysis that illustrates how creative action and the listener's experience relate might do so without any evidence of the composer's wishes or biographical narrative; in other words, without any interest in intended communication. But it necessarily begins with some contextual under-standing. Inductive reasoning allows us to look for the same techniques evidenced in apparently comparable works. A wider understanding of cultural context could encompass notions of musical expression and organisation that impact on both composers and listeners alike, and could be documented elsewhere in critical and theoretical discourse. But all such inferences are secure in the knowledge there was an origin with which we can empathise: a living, breathing, feeling individual. Even if a composer or improviser had intentions that were complex or unwitting, it is easy to use our imagination, perhaps a conscious suspension of disbelief, to frame our own experience as listener or analyst in a way that presumes expressive and organisational purpose. We expect to enjoy music as human communication that validates our ideas about the value of artistic expression.

This is not so easy with interactive and generative music. We can still make many inferences, justifiably or beyond credulity for some. At the root of all creative computer systems is a software designer (who possibly regards him/herself as a creative artist in some sense), whether the software is coded from scratch or is implemented within a commercial platform. In generative music, we might hear algorithmic processes as if they are a proxy for what might otherwise be expected from more conventional, 'compositional' methods, however novel the outcome. There is therefore an agent to be imagined, perhaps very distantly related to the music, who conceivably invites empathy on the part of the listener. Complete disassociation is perhaps more likely: the computer itself, as a recognised co-creator, is likely to be as much a block to our understanding as an ambassador for human creativity. If generative music can truly produce music that could not be created in any other way, this questions our accepted notions of musical communication. Interactive music introduces other dimensions, the performer's independent role as another co-creator, the potential opacity of their interaction with the computer system (from a listener's perspective): all possibly quite separate from a composer or software designer's intentions.

If human agents are evident, either in proxy or as in person, we may be able to use analytical methods derived from traditional, classical practices. We can apply analysis on the assumption that there is an intention to communicate ideas to the listener. These opportunities remain until artificial intelligence, applied to creativity, genuinely excludes the need for a human originator at all. Although this remains an objective in computational creativity research, practice suggests that we are both far from an absolute position and uncertain of how we would recognise and evaluate this achievement should it ever arise.

Generative music categories

Generative music is wide ranging but might be categorised in broad terms as follows, as perspectives for musical analysis. These categories focus on creative context rather than generative technique, and – in a very generalised sense – increasingly remove authorial control away from the composer, who becomes the software coder.

Frame+swerve

Significant in the pre-history of generative computer music is the use of explicit calculations to produce musical materials: techniques used as more than just a compositional tool, exploring in sound the properties of the calculations, for which the output could be either electroacoustic or a notated instrumental piece. But compositional and aesthetic aims remain intrinsic. Ames describes such work as 'automated composition' (Ames 1987). There is a blending of traditional compositional practices with computational, possibly computer-generated, procedures.

In the early work of Xenakis, stochastic methods are calculated by hand to determine values within a structural framework, which are interpreted musically as events. These include the Gaussian methods in *Pithoprakta* (1956) and the Poisson distribution used in *Achorripsis* (1957), where mathematics translates into music albeit with a high degree of compositional control. Rahn describes the deep relationship between structural principles and their creative interpretation (or deviation) in the hands of the composer as 'frame+swerve' (Rahn 2004: 135). Analysis can focus on this relationship as in Arsenault's account of *Achorripsis* (Arsenault 2000). The ST series of works from 1962 onwards (such as *ST/10–1,080262* for ten instruments) takes the next logical step, using a computer program to calculate complex probability distributions that are again interpreted (not just objectively realised) as musical events.

Frame only

When a mathematically generated system constitutes the work, without any further level of interpretation, might be described as 'frame-only' music, because in essence it is a direct sonic realisation of the system. Analysis might show how far this is true in any specific case. Although Stockhausen's *Elektronische Studie II* (1954) was produced laboriously with sine tone generator and tape manipulation, its structural frame is so comprehensive that a fully automated, generative version is now executable on computer (as in Georg Hajdu's Max/MSP implementation[2]). But Stockhausen's framework clearly has musical purposes too; it explores new approaches to temperament and synthesis unique to electronic music at the time. So, although the computational basis of the work accounts for most attributes of the surface, that is, the musical foreground, there is a

[2] http://georghajdu.de/6–2/studie-ii/ (accessed 8 April 2015).

clear aesthetic purpose embodied in the enabling structure. And this purpose can be understood in the wider context of the composer's work, which analysis can reveal.

Experimental

The roots of generative music, as understood today, are in experimental methods well outside the conventionally musical. There is a long history of the repurposing of found or invented structures as a new way to create music (Nierhaus 2009). The experiment is to find out whether or not this repurposing can produce a semblance of music. The first known 'musical dice game' is credited to Johann Philip Kirnberger (Nierhaus 2009: 36), in which a series of random operations can assemble a new composition from a collection of pre-existing fragments. These 'combinatoric' compositions actually already contain, as game plans, much musical content laid out in a prescriptive fashion, so although there are many possible permutations, the outcome always complies with expected style and syntax. The impact is akin to our fascination with clockwork automata: self-operating systems that mimic – but do not recreate – a real-life human activity; in this case, the activity is composition.

In the contemporary period, experimental music has repurposed structural methods in order to find out what the result sounds like – an act of discovery that is intended to be demonstrative, as in Cage's well-known statement: 'An experimental action is one the outcome of which is not foreseen ... the action was a non-knowledge of something that had not yet happened' (Cage 1961: 39). Early work with generative computer music can be considered experimental in this way; in Hiller and Isaacson's string quartet *Illiac Suite* (1956) each movement is labelled *Experiment*.

The iterative nature of decision-making in generative music is fundamental to how this experimentation occurs. Iteration is the fundamental property of an algorithmic process. In algorithmic composition, musical events accumulate in sequence: the current 'state' of the composition (i.e. at a particular event at a point in time) is a determinant for the next 'state', and many alternatives might be available. Stepwise decisions may lead to an ultimately predictable result, or something unforeseen, which would perhaps be the real point. The four Experiments of the *Illiac Suite* employ random selection methods limited by rules or Markov modelling, so at every step the 'unforeseen' has in fact been significantly constrained. Experiment 3 is particularly experimental because the constraining rules are relatively unrestrictive, and do not leverage existing music theory. Hiller theorises this in general terms:

> The act of composing, therefore can be thought of as the extraction of order out of a chaotic environment ... successful musical compositions as a general rule are either centrally placed between the extremes of order and disorder.(Hiller and Isaacson 1993: 9)

There is a double function for analysis in such experimental work: to decode the constraint principles, in so far they can be inferred, and to account for how these interrelate and impact on the musical surface that the listener experiences. A third aspect is that this could be entirely disassociated from the generative method, because alignments with comparable music – for example, the contemporary string quartet idiom itself – are far more prominent.

More recent examples in this category could include Karlheinz Essl's *Lexikon-Sonate* (1995), which uses various forms of probability distribution to create complex durational and pitch behaviours for a computer-controlled piano. Essl's description summarises the workflow:

> There is no pre-composed text to be interpreted, and there is no need for an interpreter. Instead, the instructions for playing the piano – the indication 'which key should be pressed how quickly and held down for how long' – are directly generated by a computer program and transmitted immediately to a player piano which executes them. (Essl 1995)

Representing a significant trend, the *Lexikon-Sonate* points to a move away from the idea of the 'automated composition' to real-time execution, with emphasis on live realisation that fuses compositional act with performance (also see section 'Live algorithms, pages 93–5). Here is the profoundly *open* nature of generative work: there are as many equally valid instances of the piece that probability distributions, rules and other contingencies in performance allow. There are very many freedoms and constraints in operation together, both mathematical and performative, so a truly astronomical number of equivalent but different works exist in theory. Can the analyst be content with appraising only one?

Emulation

Research in artificial intelligence includes many examples of musical modelling; the computer-based emulation of historical composition procedures, or models based on deeper facets of organisation only revealed by computer analysis (i.e. beyond the cognisance of composers we associate with the musical style in question). The analysis can only be tested by application, producing new instances from the model. The first two Experiments in the *Illiac Suite* use textbook rules of Renaissance counterpoint as constraints. Kemal Ebcioglu's *CHORAL* is an expert system that harmonises chorale melodies in the style of J. S. Bach, using production and constraint rules that represent knowledge of the style; significantly, it also uses heuristic procedures that enable the system to backtrack and identify an optimal solution given the next required step. Ebcioglu argues this is analogous to the human compositional process (Ebcioglu 1993). So he implies the creative process is being emulated, not just the music itself. By contrast, the harmonisation system developed by Murray Allan (Nierhaus 2009: 78) uses a statistical method (a Hidden Markov Model) derived from a corpus of existing chorales. Decision-making is probabilistic, derived from this database, independent of any stylistic knowledge represented by rules.

In both cases the analyst's role is perhaps the same, like the music teacher who assesses a student's pastiche exercise: how far does the work comply with the target style, and does it do so without obvious quotation or reference to an existing 'real' composition?

By extension, entirely novel work can be produced, given an invented rule set or database. David Cope's *Experiments in Musical Intelligence* (EMI) system, using transition networks, was first developed for emulation purposes. By systematically cataloguing a wide range of existing musical styles, fragmenting and codifying these with reference to formulations of musical syntax, stylistically compliant, pastiche compositions could be assembled afresh. Cope has also produced original work with similar methods, as in *From Darkness, Light* (2004). Cope deflects the issue of authorship by attributing this work to a fictional entity: 'Emily Howell', the computer system itself. The analyst is free to apply any method that seems relevant to the style, irrespective of whether a composer like Howell is 'real' or not.

Emergent-creative

If a computer can produce unpredictable structures or effects that do not depend on pre-programmed musical rules – and are consequently much more distant from composer/designer's intentions – we might find this a more compelling insight into artificial creativity. 'Emergence' in generative music begins with a fascination with naturally occurring organisation (e.g. in biological systems), which appear to offer inventive methods quite independent of our own creative thinking processes. Our understanding of natural systems through computational modelling is that simplicity can engender great complexity and 'self-organisation' (Blackwell and Young 2004). So very basic, non-musical rules can offer an apparently simple starting point, as found in genetic algorithms, cellular automata or particle swarms. Complexity can emerge when such a dynamical system, incorporating many instances of interacting rules (or agents), progressively iterates. The degree of sophistication in such systems, when used to generate or develop musical ideas, is an aesthetic property; the true value is in the emergent process itself.

Todd and Werner employed a variety of models of sexual reproduction to evolve new melodies based on a corpus of folk music (Todd and Werner 1999). Miranda has explored cellular automata as a synthesis method and, in the *Cellular Automata Music* system (CAMUS), to generate patterns of rhythms and pitches as a basis for composition (Miranda 2007). Waschka's *GenDash* uses a genetic algorithm (GA) that makes variations of musical material, fully worked through as the structure of the work (Waschka 2007): the evolutionary process itself constitutes the unfolding musical structure. Clearly, it is of interest to the analyst whether or not this really is the case, that is, if we might see such work as a specialised form of process music or not (other applications of GAs are used in real-time improvised performance with more emphasis on process). In many examples, the algorithm is mapped directly to the surface of the music; the frame *is* the music, but the frame itself is neither predictable nor fixed but evolves according to its own *modus operandi*. Nevertheless, there are necessary value-driven choices to be made when using data produced by such algorithms to create sound. There are also choices embedded in the algorithm design itself, such as the fitness function used in a GA, which has a strong impact on the results by selecting data 'offspring' as each population is generated. The analyst might seek to infer what compositional judgements are implicit at various levels as this emergence unfolds. How far this generative process is at all identifiable is a significant issue.

Sonification

A feature of recent arts practice is to repurpose found data as sonic materials. In its purest form, sonification is a scientific method used to reveal structures within complex and large data sets that cannot be readily visualised (Kramer 1994; Worrall 2009). There is an artistic fascination in listening to the inaudible, especially if the data source is culturally or politically loaded; for instance, weather and other environmental data (Polli 2004; Bulley and Jones 2011).

Mathematical formulae that exhibit self-organising properties, such as chaotic and self-similar systems, can provide non-contextual data that invite creative reflection and application (Pressing 1988). The possibility that an aesthetic effect might arise from an intention-free source is intriguing. Pressing makes analogies between the distinctive behaviours of such formulae – strange attractors, bifurcations and limited cycles – and more familiar musical principles:

> Musical development or variation can be viewed as the transformation or distortion of a simple entity (a motive), often followed by some sort of return to the original motive. When certain values are chosen for the input parameters to these equations, very similar behavior can be obtained from them. (Pressing 1988: 35)

In this way the analyst might look for recognisable familiar musical features or structural patterns while acknowledging they arise, paradoxically, from abstract or natural phenomena. But the analyst is also likely to evaluate the creative methods designed into the sonification, as data are mapped to selected parameters for synthesis. There may be many assumptions about music, style and structure in this mapping – embodying the artist's own understandings and preferences – that has more impact on the sonic result than the intrinsic properties of the actual data.

Interactive music categories

The relationship between performer, composer (if any) and software designer is critical to interactive music. Musical analysis could consider the interactive process itself, or hear the product entirely independently of the process, or attempt to find correlations between construction and result. Computer music applications and the devices used in interactive systems might well present a barrier, and so such relations may be hard to gauge.

(Un)fixed media

Performance-based electronic music evolved dramatically during the 1980s to 1990s as audio processing became faster and better able to undertake the advanced synthesis and audio manipulations that previously were possible only in the composition studio. But live electronic music from this period is arguably a continuation of the genre of 'live performer with tape', established by impactful works such as Stockhausen's *Kontakte* (1960) decades before. Perhaps this is because the rich interactions between

instruments and studio-made material are so intrinsic to style and expression; the composer naturally wants to retain full control even in a live setting
where far more contingency is feasible. Manoury's flute and live electronics
composition *Jupiter* (1987) exhibits a wide range of interactive musical
behaviours (May 2006) and this required extensive, innovative software
development for real-time pitch tracking, synthesis and event scheduling.
But it is not too difficult to envisage a tape-only, fixed emulation of the
electronic element that would preserve a very great deal of the content. At
the very least, any performance is likely to be similar, clearly identifiable as
the composer's work, within the traditional, narrow boundaries of interpretation and realisation. So an analyst is free to disregard the interactive
element beyond what is clearly perceivable in sound: it is the musical
materials themselves that interact, irrespective of their cause or ownership,
demonstrating 'aesthetic liveness' (Croft 2007). For instance, what transformational relationships can be heard between recognisable instrumental
sources and processed or synthesised electronic sounds? We can discuss
Kontakte in exactly the same way.

Instrumental-reactive

Over the same period there has emerged a growing preponderance of new
controller devices that couple performance action with computerised synthesis. This is 'procedural liveness' (Croft 2007) because immediate agency
is required to produce live events. The computer is one element of a system
that includes the performer and the controller; for example, newly
designed devices for the musician or for cross-media work (such as visual
or haptic sensors in a dance) as well as onscreen computer interface.
Classical instruments have also been adapted with control systems or
sensors that gather data from normal actions (bowing, lip pressure, etc.).
There are many ongoing design and data capture issues (Wanderley and
Orio 2002). They also list various output uses: note-level control, shaping
sound processing and diffusion, a musical conductor-like role and
sampling/playback control. The overarching characteristic is that hardware
design, data capture and data manipulation are not just technical issues but
are substantially creative in themselves, by implication, in addition to the
musical aims that are *de facto* built into the audio software.

So there is a challenging and creative contradiction in this category: the
performance system as a whole is acting in proxy for the composer/
designer, enabling and encouraging the expressive and structural possibilities that are designed into the system. At the same time, such systems

might seem over-engineered if performers do not enjoy a satisfying degree of improvisational freedom in their actions, in order to learn the range of possibilities offered (and some control devices may not permit anything like the precision we associate with traditional instruments). Therefore it is not surprising, as in the case of Michel Waisvisz and the hands' system, for composer/designer and performer to be the same person. The old boundaries between instrument and composition are blurred, offering great creative potential (Krefeld and Waisvisz 1990). And, consequently, a great deal of music in this field is an improvisatory exploration of the system's abilities and creative constraints.

The analyst with access only to the musical output of such systems might find this performance practice frustratingly opaque. How can the performer's actions and the resultant data processing be disaggregated, their relationship evaluated and the result commented upon (Young 2010)? Conversation with the performers after a live performance, as a type of qualitative analysis, might be the only solution. Alternatively, there are analytic approaches for improvised music in general (e.g. Pressing 1987) which set such issues aside, emphasising product rather than process, looking for evidence of structural coherence. So an improvised performance might be appraised purely in terms of product, to assess how structural completion is (or is not) achieved, irrespective of the iterative actions between performer and computational system that led to it. But to take a performance entirely at face value, effectively comparing it with fixed, electroacoustic composition, might miss the whole point. We might hope for novelty and surprise – as well as coherence – in music constructed in such a complex way; innovation that the composer, sat alone in the studio, could not achieve.

Live algorithms: interactive *and* generative

This category reflects present-day practice and research that integrates generative methods – redefined by contemporary understandings of artificial intelligence – with interactivity in performance. This is far from the domain of Ames's 'automated composition'. Musical generation is both self-sufficient, drawing from sources such as machine learning, genetic algorithms and data mining, and strongly shaped by performance input during computation. Interaction is defined more rigorously to mean a truly reciprocal relationship between human and machine participants. This is a specialised, improvisation-orientated approach to computational creativity, termed as music for 'live algorithms' (Young and Blackwell 2013).

Two early examples are by Lewis and Biles. Lewis's *Voyager* is 'a non-hierarchical, interactive musical environment' for improvisation, players engaging with a 'virtual improvising orchestra' (Lewis 2000: 33). *Voyager* dispenses with direct control; it receives input by audio analysis of human musicians. Machine listening is a common, almost defining, feature of this category: interaction (action and reaction) occurs only within the music itself, not independently via controllers. *Voyager* generates note data (e.g. for a computer-controlled piano) from random generators constrained by a large rule set devised by Lewis; this in turn is influenced by performance data extracted from co-musicians. Biles's *GenJam* trades phrases between computer and jazz musician using a genetic algorithm to evolve material, on-the-fly; an early version used a human 'mentor' with separated training and performance stages. A later version uses an initial population of acceptable phrases (Biles 2007). So although the process focuses on live invention, the material is closely governed by stylistic constraints as defined by Biles.

More recently, there has been interest in music informational retrieval (MIR), machine learning and statistical modelling, allowing for a close integration between machine intelligence and musical understanding. The designer might have less direct influence over the generative behaviour of the system, which instead draws from the performer's improvisation, but can set boundaries for creative action nevertheless. Pachet's *Continuator* listens to a pianist's extended input and responds with its own improvisation that can be remarkably similar in style. A highly efficient statistical analysis, using a Variable Markov Model, develops in complexity as more musical information is obtained from the player, strengthened with a biasing method that favours certain attributes of the input performance (Pachet 2003). The necessary alternation between performer and computer is a musical restriction, however. The *OMax* system (Assayag and Bloch 2007) constructs new musical patterns based on live analysis, using the Factor Oracle Incremental Algorithm, which efficiently identifies patterns within longer strings, creating new material in tandem with the performer. The *FRANK* co-evolution system (Plans Casal and Morelli 2007) integrates Casey's information retrieval methods developed for *Soundspotter* (Casey 2009) with the evolutionary methods developed by Todd and Werner, allowing a free improvisation to develop between performer and computer, which draws on a large library of found musical sources. The author's own works for solo player(s) and computer – the *prosthesis* series (2007–present) and *Trio for Two Players* (2012) – employ feature extraction and unsupervised machine learning to derive information about the performer's improvisation, mapped progressively to pre-composed stochastic musical states programmed into the generative system; the player learns how to respond to this mapping (Young 2008). The linear structure in any given performance is a manifestation of the mutual learning process itself, and this is the central focus of interest.

'Live algorithms' aim to be autonomous, creative co-contributors. The composer's role, as a governing force, diminishes greatly. The analyst could approach the music is if it were human-only improvisation. If the machine output itself is instrumental rather than electronic, as in *Voyager* and the Continuator, there is sonic congruity between human and machine elements. In common with free improvisation, the analyst is concerned with evidence of structural cohesion, consistency of style and the impact of 'social' interaction on the evolution of musical material. The viability of such an analytic approach is a form of empirical criticism in itself: what live algorithmic systems demand is a rigorous, evaluative method that can demonstrate when autonomous properties are evident, or are not.

Analytic approaches

Opening the box

A key question is how far the software at the heart of interactive or generative music needs to be considered. This contextual knowledge seems necessary given the sheer diversity of methods and their rationale, but this may not require detailed insight into specific implementations. Collins contrasts a white-box versus a black-box approach: the software either is available and comprehensible, or not (Collins 2008). His analysis of James McCartney's *Synthetic Piano* (1998) points to the value of a white-box approach, citing the code itself alongside Collins's own pseudocode – this reduction is analysis in itself, revealing the code's functions in a more generic form – and cross-references this to sonogram analyses that highlight timbral features of interest. White-box software can be separately tested in practice to provide new output that can then be compared with prior, authorised versions. It might be valued for its own merit: the 'beauty of the code' (Collins 2008: 246).

But a black box might offer great analytic potential too: a musical analysis must focus on whatever structural elements can be inferred from a recording or notated score alone, illustrating the effective nature of the work.

Dealing with incompleteness

A single instance – a performance or realisation– is likely to be only a partial manifestation of any given system. Other instances might be similar or not. Intrinsic to many methods outlined above is their contingency and/ or infinite capacity. Many AI or fractal methods exhibit behaviour that is highly sensitive to the starting conditions (initial values in a chaotic system, fitness functions in a genetic algorithm). Although a purely mathematical definition of an algorithm includes determinability and a terminal point, endless loops are of course entirely feasible and can be so complex that there is no sense of repetition in practice. A generative sound installation need have no meaningful start or end, and no perceivable loops.

Interactive systems depend on user decision-making, on-the-fly, so no one performance can be held definitive, only representative. The results agree with Eco's (1989) conception of the 'open work in movement', works that 'consist of unplanned or physically incomplete structural units'; his compositional perspective is warranted because governing or influencing agents inevitably establish a delimiting 'field of relations' (in contrast to freely improvised music for instance).

A comparative analysis would systematically log differences between individual instances of a work, and this might be taken as a value judgement: the more variation evident, the more justified is the process that engendered it. But how many versions constitute a fair representation? We could question an elaborate improvisational or generative method that produces very similar results in every instance. Why has the composer/ designer simply not worked out the music fully, to ensure a preferred outcome? A fascination with the idea of diverse outcomes from the same initial conditions is perhaps the strongest motivator for all creative work in these fields, and speaks to our understanding of creativity in general.

Evaluating process

Systematic tools could be applied to decode and reveal an underlying generative process, as a kind of reverse engineering. For instance, if we know that Essl's *Lexikon-Sonate* is produced by certain constrained probability distributions, we could undertake a histogram analysis of any given rendition. This might be able to shed light on the properties of the distribution and how this changes during presentation (but the accuracy would depend on the population size available). The ease with which decoding is possible would also depend on how far processes are in the structural foreground.

As suggested in the section 'Instrumental-reactive' (pages 92–3), an interactive performance might be insufficiently transparent to allow any examination of process and the musician's role through the music alone. Work on interactive systems has tended to focus on the user experience, either in a technical sense (Wanderley and Orio 2002) or through qualitative analysis, in which performers are test subjects interviewed after their experience (Hsu and Sosnick 2009; Stowell *et al*. 2009). This can show how performers conceptualise their engagement with an interface and the computer's response, but may not help our understanding as an independent listener.

Pressing's systematic model of improvised music, parsing music into clusters that act as part of an emerging network of events (Pressing 1987), might be applied to computer music performance, particularly in the earlier category 'Live algorithms' (pages 93–5) where musicians have a distinct role as instrumentalists. We could track performers and computers as separately identifiable elements. Similarly, in live electronic compositions we can differentiate instrumental sound from effects processing or other computer-generated elements, such as Boulez's *Anthèmes II* (1997) or Manoury's *Jupiter*. An agent-orientated interpretation would look for interactions enjoyed between players and/or machines, by regarding the sound materials themselves as agents that work together in the wider landscape of the music (e.g. how one musical behaviour appears to instigate or respond to another). This is sonic evidence of a quasi-social praxis, to the extent that musical actions can be readily mapped to a particular human or machine contributor.

Evaluating the outcome

Music analysis need not concern the productive process (the *poietic*). But it is striking that much generative music begins with analysis – not only of other music but also of written/spoken language – as an enabling tool. It can be reapplied to make new work, to test methodological validity or simply for art's sake. Such analysis can be symbolic, tending to explore constructive methods, or subsymbolic (as in statistical modelling), looking for embedded structures irrespective of what was intended: this is a kind of computer-friendly *esthesic* dimension.

Computer-based audio analysis offers a range of tools for judgements pertaining to the listener experience. For instance, the timbral relationships perceivable in a live electronics work could be interrogated using FFT analysis to separate and compare identifiable elements (notated instrumental part, live processing, etc.), and this could be done without any prior knowledge of the intended strategies for synthesis and audio manipulation.

But other forms of quantitative computer-based analysis can reveal previously unknown structural properties that could also have a direct bearing on reception. For instance, Zipf's Law distributions (in which the number of occurrences of a specific element in a data set is inversely proportional to its ranking by frequency) can be found within established musical genres in a way that correlates with aesthetic satisfaction (Manaris *et al.* 2005). This could be readily applied to new musical products too.

As already noted, the act of sonifying any computational output or found data inevitably carries with it cultural and musical baggage: there is no pure approach that makes the composer/designer redundant. As noted above, an assumption evidenced in much generative music is that music in general should consist of notes – instrument-like events of fixed pitch and duration – and electroacoustic composition has well-developed norms of practice too. Musical analysis by whatever means is appropriate (pitch-set analysis, Generative Theory of Tonal Music (GTTM) based, Fast Fourier Transform (FFT) analysis) might be able to show how far the outcome evidences these underlying beliefs, in terms of structural and stylistic properties, which either accord with or entirely obviate the generative process itself.

A common theme in computational creativity is that perception, perhaps imagination, can be enough. Colton and Wiggins define this field as follows:

The philosophy, science and engineering of computational systems which, by taking on particular responsibilities, exhibit behaviours that unbiased observers would deem to be creative. (Colton and Wiggins 2012)

This is not simply a musical Turing Test, although models of such tests have been applied in limited musical scenarios (Stowell *et al.* 2009). Ariza discusses a far more demanding 'Lovelace Test' (Ariza 2009). This test requires complete opacity: for a computer programme to exhibit genuine creativity it must, by definition, be inexplicable to the original programmer.

Just as philosophers and computer scientists have debated the question of machine intelligence for decades . . . there continues to be debate as to whether true musical expression (conveying meaning or feeling) can be produced by a computer. The fundamental question in both cases is whether the appearance of intelligence or expression is sufficient to believe that intelligence or expression exists.(Dobrian and Koopelman 2006: 278)

Whatever our speculations about intentionality and machine creativity, the clear implication is that its behaviours must be explicable in terms already familiar to the listener. But as Dobrian and Koopelman emphasise, this is not a binary question: there are degrees of expressivity, interactivity and creativity during both creation and reception. These are the dimensions that analysis should aspire to explain. Or, to parody LeWitt (as quoted above): machines make ideas that *we think* are art.

References

Ames, Charles. 1987. Automated composition in retrospect 1956–1986. *Leonardo* 20(2), 169–85.

Ariza, Christopher. 2009. The interrogator as critic: The Turing Test and the evaluation of generative music systems. *Computer Music Journal* 33(2), 48–70.

Arsenault, Linda Marie. 2000. An introduction to Iannis Xenakis's stochastic music, four algorithmic analyses. http://hdl.handle.net/1807/13842 (accessed 7 April 2013).

Assayag, Gérard and Bloch, Georges. 2007. Navigating the oracle: A heuristic approach. *Proceedings of the International Computer Music Conference.* Copenhagen: MPublishing, 405–12.

Biles, John A. 2007. Improvizing with genetic algorithms: *GenJam.* In E. R. Miranda and J. A. Biles (eds.) *Evolutionary Computer Music.* London: Springer-Verlag, 137–69.

Blackwell, Tim and Young, Michael. 2004. Self-organised music. *Organised Sound* 9(2), 123–36.

Bulley, James and Jones, Daniel. 2011. Variable 4: A dynamical composition for weather systems. *Proceedings of the International Computer Music Conference.* Huddersfield: MPublishing, 449–55.

Cage, John. 1961. Composition as Process: II. Indeterminacy. In *Silence.* Middletown: Wesleyan University Press, 35–40.

Casey, Michael. 2009. Soundspotting: A new kind of process? In R. Dean (ed.) *The Oxford Handbook of Computer Music.* New York: Oxford University Press, 421–56.

Collins, Nick. 2008. The analysis of generative music programs. *Organised Sound* 13(3), 237–48.

Colton, Simon and Wiggins, Geraint. 2012. Computational creativity: The final frontier. *Proceedings of the 20th European Conference on Artificial Intelligence.*

Croft, John. 2007. Theses on liveness. *Organised Sound*, 12(1), 59–66.

Dobrian, Christopher and Koopelman, Daniel. 2006. The 'E' in NIME: Musical Expression with New Computer Interfaces. *Proceedings of the International Conference on New Interfaces for Musical Expression (NIME)*. Paris, 277–82.

Ebcioglu, Kemal. 1993. Expert system for harmonizing four-part chorales. In S. M. Schwanauer and D. A. Levitt (eds.) *Machine Models of Music*. Cambridge, MA: MIT Press, 385–402.

Eco, U. 1989. *The Open Work*, trans. Anna Cangogni. Cambridge, MA: Harvard University Press (original *Opera aperta*, 1962, rev. 1976).

Essl, Karlheinz. 1995. Lexikon-Sonate: An interactive realtime composition for computer-controlled piano. *Proceedings of the II Brazilian Symposium on Computer Music*. Canela, RS, Brazil.

Harvey, Jonathan. 1999. The metaphysics of live electronics, *Contemporary Music Review* 18 (3), 79–82.

Hiller, Lejaren and Isaacson, Leonard. 1993. Musical composition with a high-speed digital computer. In S. M. Schwanauer and D. A. Levitt (eds.) *Machine Models of Music*. Cambridge, MA: MIT Press, 9–22.

Hsu, William and Sosnick, Marc. 2009. Evaluating interactive music systems: An HCI approach. *Proceedings of the International Conference on New Interfaces for Musical Expression (NIME)*. Paris, 25–8.

Kramer, Gregory (ed.). 1994. *Auditory Display: Sonification, Audification, and Auditory Interfaces*. Reading, MA: Addison-Wesley.

Krefeld, Volker and Waisvisz, Michel. 1990. The hand in the web: An interview with Michel Waisvisz. *Computer Music Journal* 14(2), 28–33.

Lewis, George E. 2000. Too many notes: Computers, complexity and culture in Voyager. *Leonardo Music Journal* 10, 33–9.

LeWitt, Sol. 1967. Paragraphs on Conceptual Art. *Artforum* 5(10), 79–83.

Manaris, Bill *et al.* 2005. Zipf's law, music classification, and aesthetics. *Computer Music Journal* 29(1), 55–69.

May, Andrew. 2006. Philippe Manoury's *Jupiter*. In M. Simoni (ed.) *Analytical Methods of Electroacoustic Music*. New York: Routledge, 145–86.

Miranda, Eduardo. 2007. Cellular automata music: From sound synthesis to musical forms. In E. R. Miranda and J. A. Biles (eds.) *Evolutionary Computer Music*. London: Springer-Verlag, 170–93.

Nierhaus, Gerhard. 2009. *Algorithmic Composition: Paradigms of Automated Music Generation*. Wien: Springer-Verlag.

Pachet, Francois. 2003. The continuator: Musical interaction with style. *Journal of New Music Research* 32(3), 333–41.

Plans Casal, David and Morelli, Davide. 2007. Remembering the future: An overview of co-evolution in musical improvisation. *Proceedings of the International Computer Music Conference*, 200–5.

Polli, Andrea. 2004. Modelling storms in sound: The Atmospheric/Weather Works Project. *Organised Sound* 9(2), 175–80.

Pressing, Jeff. 1987. Improvisation: Methods and models. In J. Sloboda (ed.)
    Generative Processes in Music: The Psychology of Performance, Improvisation,
    and Composition. New York: Oxford University Press, 129–78.
    1988. Nonlinear maps as generators of musical design. *Computer Music Journal*
    12(2), 35–46.
Rahn, John. 2004. The swerve and the flow: Music's relation to mathematics.
    Perspectives of New Music 42(1), 130–48.
Stowell, Daniel *et al.* 2009. Evaluation of live human-computer music-making:
    Quantitative and qualitative approaches. *International Journal of Human-*
    Computer Studies 67(11), 960–75.
Todd, Peter M. and Werner, Gregory M. 1999. Frankensteinian methods for
    evolutionary music composition. In N. Griffith and P. M. Todd (eds.) *Musical*
    Networks: Parallel Distributed Perception and Performance. Cambridge, MA:
    MIT Press, 313–39.
Wanderley, Marcelo and Orio, Nicola. 2002. Evaluation of input devices for
    musical expression: Borrowing tools from HCI. *Computer Music Journal*
    26(3), 62–76.
Waschka, Rodney, II. 2007. Composing with genetic algorithms: *GenDash.*
    In E. R. Miranda and J. A. Biles (eds.) *Evolutionary Computer Music.* London:
    Springer-Verlag, 117–36.
Worrall, David. 2009. An introduction to data sonification. In R. Dean (ed.) *The*
    Oxford Handbook of Computer Music. New York: Oxford University Press,
    312–33.
Young, Michael. 2008. NN Music: Improvising with a 'living' computer.
    In R. Kronland-Martinet, S. Ystad and K. Jensen (eds.) *Computer Music*
    Modelling and Retrieval: Sense of Sounds. Berlin: Springer-Verlag, 337–50.
    2010. Identity and intimacy in human-computer improvisation. *Leonardo Music*
    Journal [online] 20. www.mitpressjournals.org/doi/abs/10.1162/LMJ_a_
    00022 (accessed 9 April 2013).
Young, Michael and Blackwell, Tim. 2013. Live algorithms for music: Can
    computers be improvisers? In G. E. Lewis (ed.) *The Oxford Handbook of*
    Critical Improvisation Studies. Oxford University Press.

5 | Some ideas concerning the relationship
between form and texture

RAÚL MINSBURG

Acousmatic music, just like any other kind of music, presents some
difficulties when listening to it, both for a 'non-musician' listener and for
a person who, even with a musical training and education, is not used to
this type of expression. This occurs for a large number of reasons, ranging
from the sound material used in the composition and its organisation to
external reasons such as lack of dissemination and, consequently, lack of
accessibility.

In this chapter we will deal with formal structuring, one of the aspects
that we consider central to music, whether acousmatic or not. It is crucial
when understanding a musical discourse, the art of time by nature, as it
conveys sense to the listener but also to the composer when he gets to
elaborate it. Nevertheless, we will discuss musical form from the point of
view of another musical language feature – *texture*; in other words, the
organisation of *simultaneity*.

In this type of music, there is an indissoluble link between texture and
form: many of the changes produced at a discourse level always cause a
change in texture, generating an indivisible whole; that is why it is often
difficult to determine in which of these aspects a change started. We will
then try to relate these elements – texture and form – in order to attain a
deeper understanding of the complex language of electroacoustic music.

For the sake of clarity, we will first deal with textures in general and then
in acousmatic music in particular.

A first approach to texture

The word 'texture' is well known and widely used among musicians,
especially among those who speak Spanish and English. However, its definition is relatively new. Before 1954, this word did not have an entry in the
Grove Dictionary of Music and Musicians nor did it have a reference in the
1933 edition of the *Oxford English Dictionary* (Dunsby 1989). Things were

English translation of this chapter by Mariela Santoro.

not any better in Spanish: the 1968 voluminous *Diccionario Enciclopédico Quillet* does not provide a musical meaning for this word and the same occurs, for example, in the 1980 edition of the *Enciclopedia Espasa Calpe*.

But beyond the definition itself, as far as we could inquire, we observed that in general music textures are not studied thoroughly, and frequently one finds only a very general description when it comes to explaining the different simultaneity situations. Generally speaking, only four types of textures are discussed: monody, homophony, heterophony and polyphony – all of them linked to instrumental or vocal music.

However, we would like to mention two references which we found interesting and which have driven us to reconsider the traditional categories of texture. Leonard Meyer (1956) makes an important contribution when he decides to apply certain concepts of Gestalt psychology to musical situations. To start with, he defines texture as a *mental association of concurrent musical stimuli*. This is of particular importance for this work since he gives texture an eminently perceptive character. Then, based on a basic principle of visual differentiation, he develops the notion of *figure–ground*, relating figure to melody and ground to accompaniment. He establishes that the musical field can be perceived as one containing only one figure, several figures on their own, one figure (or more) with a ground, similar figures with a ground, or a ground on its own. Undoubtedly, this constitutes a first important step in an attempt to categorise musical simultaneity according to our perceptive experience but, in our opinion, many other key questions are left aside: What is the role of the different lines? Do all the lines have the same importance or is there a hierarchy? What happens to these lines given the substantial musical differences, which have a direct impact on our perception, such as register, instrument or intensity? And, more importantly, can every musical phenomenon be associated to figure and ground? All these questions remain unanswered at this stage, but later we will come back to these concepts developed by Meyer because we believe they may be useful for further discussion.

We will also examine the work of Albert Bregman (1990), who conducted a methodical investigation into sound perception applying Gestalt principles and whose contributions are completely relevant to us. In his chapter on musical perception, Bregman suggests studying the organisational principles of the music perception system. He discusses these principles in connection with melodic organisation, harmony, pitch and counterpoint, but unfortunately does not include texture as such. However, Bregman develops a concept which we find particularly useful: that of the 'auditory stream', which he defines as a perceptual unit grouping together many individual events. For instance, when we say, 'I listened to footsteps in the rain', in fact we are referring to two streams (footsteps and rain), making it obvious that there is a grouping of sounds in each of them. He also argues that the auditory stream is a perceptual association, not something physically measurable.

Following all these considerations, our intention is to develop a proposal to classify musical textures according to our perception. We will develop this proposal in the sphere of electroacoustic music, acousmatic music or, using the broadest terminology established by Leigh Landy (2007a, 2007b), 'sound-based music'. As far as we know, there is no classification of sound simultaneity of its materials. Moreover, this type of music is essentially empirical – however hard one tries to foresee what the meeting between two sounds may produce, one can never be completely certain about the sound result.[1]

Textural complexity

The concept of complexity is widely used in different fields but, in general, there are no adequate definitions. What do we mean when we describe a musical, pictorial or artistic work as *complex*? Furthermore, in the music sphere specifically, one piece may be complex in one aspect (e.g. the harmonic aspect), but very simple in another aspect (e.g. formal organisation).

For the purposes of this work, we will use the term 'complexity' only in relation to simultaneity and will link it to the number of streams. It is obvious that a two-voice polyphonic texture is simpler than one consisting of five voices. In addition, we have confirmed that a more or less trained ear is capable of easily following up to three voices if they are differentiated from a rhythmic and melodic point of view, which is the case with pitched polyphonic music in general. If we bear in mind the concept of 'auditory stream' suggested by Albert Bregman, we can broaden the definition of complex texture as a sound or musical situation in which there are at least three or four voices or streams.

Given this situation, we can put forward the following question: If we find it difficult to listen to a certain level of voice overlapping, what are the strategies we adopt to listen to pieces of high complexity?

When there are three voices or streams as described above, the listener no longer practises a detailed hearing but one which is statistical, global and structural and in which a whole is perceived. What the listener

---

[1] Exchange of ideas via email with composer Francis Dhomont.

privileges is the overall rather than the detailed features, though that whole is composed of individual traits. In this regard, we can bring up the definition of *textural passage* developed by Rosemary Mountain (1998), which develops along the same lines: 'When the listener's attention is drawn to the overall sonic image and the interplay of the component elements rather than on any one individual line, it becomes appropriate to describe the entire passage as *textural*.'

Our proposal

Now we will move towards a proposal for textural organisation in electro-acoustic music, but first we will briefly reconsider what is commonplace in instrumental music. Here we observe that the habitual classification used mainly in music before the twentieth century is founded on two basic criteria: number and functionality of voices. It could be reorganised in the following manner according to the increasing complexity level. Depending on the number of voices, we will talk about monody (one voice), homophony, heterophony and polyphony (two to four voices), and structure, configuration or textural passage (more than four). Depending on functionality, we will talk about homophony, heterophony and polyphony.

This is just a first attempt which serves as a starting point. We can go further and ask ourselves what happens to this classification in electro-acoustic music, or in *sound-based music*, if 'voices' are replaced by 'sounds' or 'sound objects'? We believe that the appropriate approach for this type of music is to replace voices by an auditory stream, following Bregman's theory. In this case, we can talk about a shared classification in terms of number of voices, but not in terms of functionality, because, although each object or stream can have different functions, we would have difficulty using the terms 'homophony' or 'heterophony' exactly as explained above. These categorisations are based on criteria for establishing which is 'the main voice', a situation perfectly applicable to a melody, with prominence to pitch or note, but not applicable to a timbre-based discourse.

We suggest going back to Meyer's proposal (figure and ground), but now linking two types of sound objects, both being very different from a perceptive point of view and also part of a first basic distinction in terms of duration and information: (a) objects of short duration, and variable in terms of morphology (figures); and (b) sustained objects, having a longer duration, which are stable and regular, with little morphological variation (ground). Reducing every sound to the figure/ground couple is somewhat debatable. However, we think that as these are two polarised units, it may prove useful to consider this reduction as a first step, subject to future revision in the event that other units not matching this criterion are observed.

Let us go a bit further: if we combine this first idea with Bregman's auditory stream proposal, we will obtain a preliminary chart comprising the following elements:

- Simple textures
  One or two figures without ground = one or two sounds or streams having short duration (variable or non-redundant).
  Simple ground = one or two sounds or streams having long duration (static or redundant).
  One or two figures with ground = one or two sounds or streams having short duration plus another one which is long (overlapping).
- Complex textures
  Three or more figures without ground = three or more sounds or streams having short duration (variable or non-redundant).
  Compound ground = three or more sounds having long duration (static or redundant).
  Three or more figures with ground = three or more sounds or streams having short duration plus another one which is long (overlapping).

Below are some short examples from different pieces that illustrate the two basic types: simple and complex texture.[2]

Simple textures

Eleazar Garzón: *Marfil y ébano* (2005)

The special feature of this short example of 26 seconds, starting at 3.08 minutes of the piece, is a line formed by several percussive sounds, which occur one after the other practically without generating any overlap at all (Figure 5.1).

Enrique Belloc: *Canto ancestral I – Poieo* (1998)

From the very beginning of this example, lasting 37 seconds starting at second 20 of this movement, we can hear a stream made of singing birds which passes through a reverb that emphasises the higher tones of the spectrum (Figure 5.2). At 0.14 a second stream is added, the sound of the rain. Both are stable and regular and play a role of a ground alone with no figure juxtaposed.

---

[2] Sound examples, EAnalysis movies and colour images are to be found on the website accompanying this book.

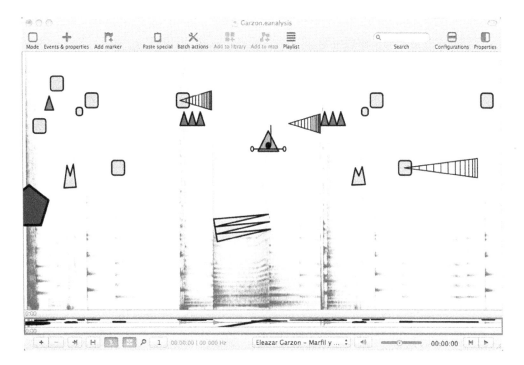

Figure 5.1 Garzón: *Marfil y ébano*

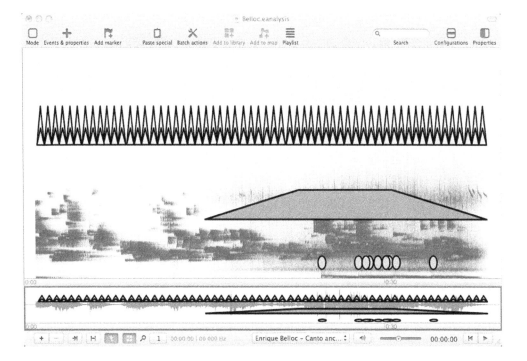

Figure 5.2 Belloc: *Canto ancestral 1 – Poieo*

Bernard Parmegiani: *De natura sonorum – I Incidences/ Resonances* (1974)

In this short example, the first 19 seconds of the well-known work from Bernard Parmegiani, we listen to a simple simultaneity configuration, built up from two basic sounds. They are differentiated by their pitch, duration and timbre: one is higher with a long duration and sounds like a sinusoid, and the other is lower with short attacks and has a metallic sound. This situation makes it easy to identify the figure–ground relationship. After the first attack, where the sustained sound seems to be a resonance of the short sound, other short attacks are heard, at 11, 12 and 14 seconds, starting to function as figures.

Complex textures

Flo Menezes: *Harmonia das Esferas* (2001)

In this one minute and two seconds example, taken from the third section of the work (the section 'C' which starts at the third minute of the whole piece), we can listen to a multiplicity of figures of different sounds perform different rhythmic actions (Figure 5.3). It starts with a kind of

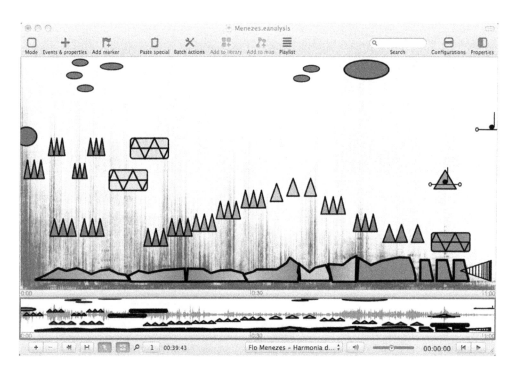

Figure 5.3 Menezes: *Harmonia das Esferas*

'explosion' (in the composer's words) where one figure can be heard in the low register while others are immediately added in the medium/high register, making it difficult to determine how many figures exist due to their timbre similarity in some cases or due to the density in others. The section ends when the global intensity decreases to an almost inaudible level and prominently features percussive timbres but not instrumental actions.

Paul Rudy: *In Lake'ch VIII – a qualing prairie* (2007)

In this short excerpt of 46 seconds, starting at second 50 of the movement, we can hear a percusive and repetitive sound act as ground, while at the same time there are different sounds whose origin seems to be natural, like animals or water, and which are present throughout the excerpt (Figure 5.4). The number of these types of sounds makes it difficult to determine, as in the previous example, how many figures there are.

Now we can try to see how these categorisations can change and evolve in time, and what is their role in the perception of form.

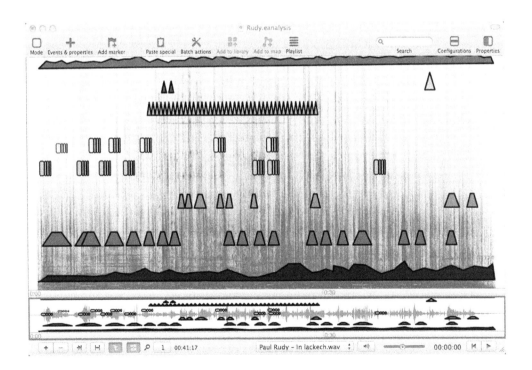

Figure 5.4 Rudy: *In Lake'ch VIII – a qualing prairie*

From texture to form

When defining *texture* as the relations of sound simultaneity, we are placing the emphasis on what is commonly known as 'verticality', which is a kind of opposition to 'horizontality', where form is displayed as such. However, it is necessary to make it clear that these spatial concepts are metaphors reflecting the reduction of the musical phenomenon to the two-dimensionality of musical scores or the reduction of the sound phenomenon to the sonogram, for instance.[3] Nevertheless, this division becomes somehow problematic as soon as we decide to discuss these concepts in depth. What do we specifically mean when we talk about 'verticality'? First, if we ask ourselves what we mean exactly by 'simultaneity', we realise that the answer is not simple. Certainly, the intention or the objective of this work is not reformulating or redefining the concept of simultaneity but challenging the traditional conception and reconsidering its habitual use in music. We could even ask ourselves what the exact difference is from other similar concepts such as 'synchrony' or 'isochrony'. Leaving aside the various definitions of simultaneity within various spheres, we could start by defining it as a 'temporal coincidence of events', following Max Jammer (2006), who truly reviews this concept in depth.

Obviously, this definition does not put an end to the problem; on the contrary, it sparks off the debate even more since we need to define the term 'event', which entails another conceptual limitation due to the various meanings this word also entails. In this regard, we may bring up the work of Gary Kendall who, taking the linguistic concept into account, attempts to apply it to the analysis of electroacoustic music and suggests a model called 'the EVENT schema' (Kendall 2008a, 2008b). In his own words, this is a model 'which is developed through time [. . .] and which captures the essential temporal structure by which auditory experiences may be understood as events'. Consequently, if simultaneity is a coincidence of events and the event is developed through time, it follows that simultaneity is not strictly associated with 'verticality' or with 'instant' (another problematic notion), but it necessarily involves a temporal elapsing as well. As we can see, the subject puts forward a perspective which differs substantially from its practical or habitual use among musicians. In addition, this analysis validates our intention to reconsider the habitual understanding of texture

---

[3] Certainly, this situation is not restricted to music but to any structure itself. It is worth remembering Walter Ong's words: 'writing [. . .] started what print and computers only continue: the reduction of dynamic sound to quiescent space' (1986).

as something separated from the temporal dimension, as a feature independent of the formal structure. It enables us to establish a link between texture and form, especially in electroacoustic music, where neither term is thoroughly defined.

In fact, many analytical works on electroacoustic music focus on the level of units such as 'sound objects' (Schaeffer 1966), or on the level of gesture. This does not occur in discussions on the overlapping of units or gestures – in the case of textures – or applied to the notion of form. Here we can mention two important contributions concerning the analysis of electroacoustic music: the book by Stéphane Roy (2003), where the writer conducts five comparative analyses of a single work, and the work edited by Delmonte and Baroni (1993) following the second European conference on music analysis, where they applied the same idea using a different piece of music. During the conference, several authors dealt with the same piece of music whereas, in the case of Roy, it is the same author that applies different analytical methods. While their perspectives are different, new methods were not applied at the structural level, nor was texture considered a structural factor in the musical discourse.

However, there are two perspectives recently considered in a work by John Young (2010) that may help us understand the creation of forms in electroacoustic music: the notion of 'moment' form (Stockhausen 1991: 63) and the notion of 'morphic' form (Wishart 1994). Although these are interesting approaches, they appear to be personal proposals based on compositional procedures, rather than analytical proposals from a perceptual point of view.

At the time of outlining our textural categorisation proposal, we observed not only that it is not very common to find complete sections of works with only one type of texture, but also that these textures constantly vary depending on the composer's discourse intentions. More specifically, we often find that these texture categories are not steady in time. In fact, on many occasions we perceive a development from one type towards another, not necessarily involving a section change, but certainly involving a textural change that affects an individual's listening, thus capturing his attention and consequently having an impact on the notion of form or on the formal function of a given section.

Let us give examples of what we are talking about in practice in order to illustrate our ideas. For this purpose, and as a first step of research which has among different objectives the aim of including a broader corpus of works, we will examine extracts from two different compositions from Argentinian composers. These works have different types of sounds, characters and aesthetics. But it is interesting for us to discover how each section of these pieces evolves in terms of texture according to their position within the works' discourse.

First, *El sueño de la razón produce monstruos,* by Ricardo de Armas (2011).[4] The source of inspiration of this work is the etching *The Sleep of Reason Produces Monsters* by Goya produced in the late eighteenth century. This etching depicts the artist, collapsed from exhaustion on his worktable, surrounded by several animals (his own monsters). From a sound perspective and in the artist's own words, 'the work seeks to depict the time of Spanish society during the Enlightenment, but also religion and magical thinking. Goya was severely criticized by the Holy Office of the Inquisition, which in those days was still acting with violence and cruelty. But we should not forget that many crimes were also committed in the name of "reason".'[5]

In *El sueño de la razón produce monstruos,* there are five sections based on the type of objects used and the actions performed by such objects. These five sections may be demarcated as follows:

1. 0.00 to 0.49.6
2. 0.49.6 to 1.24.2
3. 1.24.2 to 2.09.8
4. 2.09.8 to 4.24
5. 4.24 to 6.18

Let us now analyse what happens inside one section as far as texture is concerned. The first section is essentially introductory (Figure 5.5). Within a relatively quiescent atmosphere, a characteristic present throughout the piece, the decisive factor that generates an expectation for the listener and reinforces its introductory nature lies in the changes occurring at a textural level. In fact, considering the categories presented above, this section is characterised by a simple ground made up of a sustained pitch in the low register and a stream made up of short and repetitive sounds with a timbre closely linked to noise. Later, two figures are added and presented one after the other, both having a spectrum similar to what was heard as ground, but in a higher register and set the other way round (i.e. first the noisy spectrum and then the sustained note). This setting is repeated, but the

[4] de Armas is an electroacoustic composer who has been awarded for his works and performed worldwide, a sound artist and violoncello player, who often creatively interacts with other aesthetic communication media such as performance, dance, musical theatre, video, photography, installations and interventions in public spaces.
[5] de Armas's own words. https://soundcloud.com/ricardodearmas/el-sue-o-de-la-raz-n-produce

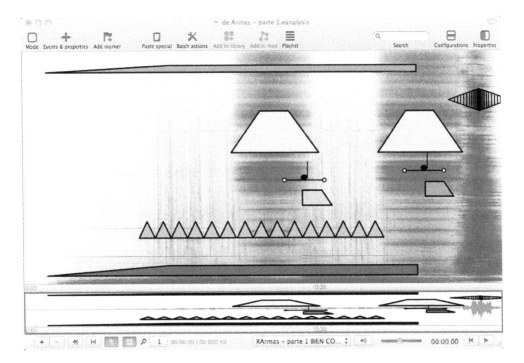

Figure 5.5 de Armas: first section

sustained note changes its frequency and this time it appears with a timbre closer to a vocal one. This whole pattern is interrupted when the sound closing the section appears in a medium register and panned from right to left. In a matter of a few seconds, we get the following sequence: simple ground – figure and ground – figure. The similarity of these materials in terms of spectrum causes continuity, whereas the texture and register changes bring about variation.

If we skip straight to the last (fifth) section (Figure 5.6), we will find a situation different from the first one since this section has a closing nature. To start with, some materials previously used, mainly in the first section, appear again though slightly transformed: the sustained note is now made up of a set of notes in a register closely linked to the stream of short and repetitive sounds with a spectrum similar to noise. Human voices are now added and the three figures mentioned above appear again. From now on, there are two important differences: the panned sound does not serve as a closing feature since the set of sustained notes can still be heard, a set that will be present until the end of the section, having a duration considerably longer than at the beginning. However, the appearance of a sound similar to a small bell, already heard in the second section, which generates some resonance in

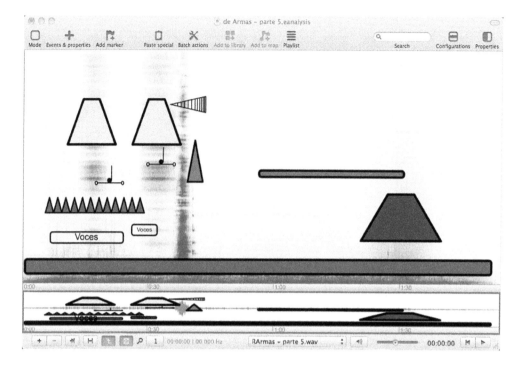

Figure 5.6 de Armas: fifth section

the medium-high register, creates a kind of densification in this set of sounds, which is compensated by a slight intensity decrease. Afterwards, two more streams are successively added. First, one with birds singing or chirping, and then one with a sea sound, while the birds slowly fade out together with the set of sustained notes which disappear little by little. Therefore our conclusion could be that, when perceiving the form, changes in texture are not the only important factor, in this case clearly related to the end of the piece; other factors such as intensity and duration are also relevant, though they are not usually considered when talking about texture.

This can be appreciated in the fourth section of the piece (Figure 5.7), which predominantly features a type of texture, simple ground (basically made up of the two strata mentioned in the previous sections with slight transformations) and a figure (alternatively made up of a clock-like strike, the singing of female voices in unison, mediaeval choral music,[6] and a voice praying in Latin). However, the progressive decrease in intensity is later compensated by its sudden increase. And despite keeping the same sound types, this effectively means that the texture is not perceived as

---

[6] A quotation of the composer Hildegard von Bingen.

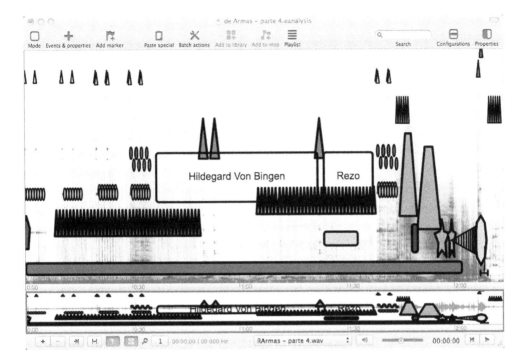

Figure 5.7 de Armas: fourth section

constant, creating a feeling of simplification and lightening. However, these changes made within the section play a clear role to close it, and undoubtedly make sense, creating an expectation for the listener.

Other situations to be considered may be found in the work *Omnipraesentia* by Fabián Esteban Luna (2010).[7] In his own words:[8]

this work explores the figuring out of an acoustic panopticon which is developed on an ambulatory trajectory and, through it, the multiple semantic connections that the listener may make once he is immersed in these environments. Some of them are unmistakeable, others are diffuse while the rest, at most, are imaginary.

Omnipraesentia has four sections with the following timings:

1. 0.00 to 1.32.7
2. 1.32.7 to 4.36.3

---

[7] Luna is a renowned composer, researcher and professor in several institutions in the city of Buenos Aires. His work has a sort of aesthetic closeness to soundscape composition but suggesting a separation from its sound source towards a more musical appreciation of the environment.

[8] Fabián Estaban Luna's own words: https://soundcloud.com/fabianestebanluna/omnipraesentia-2010

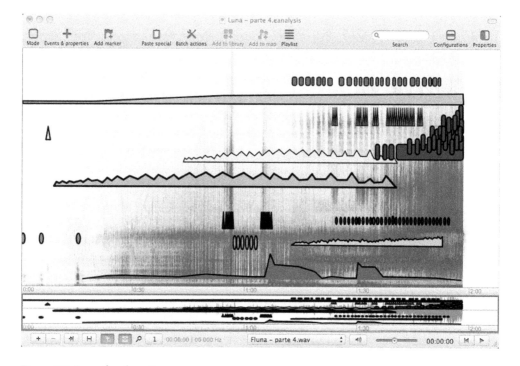

Figure 5.8 Luna: fourth section

3. 4.36.3 to 6.53.2
4. 6.53.2 to 8.53

In the last section (Figure 5.8), we hear a gradual path from simple to complex texture. From the beginning of this section (6.53), a natural environment is presented with a very low intensity and a simple texture, and during the first 20 seconds the prominent figure is a cow mooing together with a ground made up of a stream of birds singing. Slowly cricket sounds together with another sound, apparently a recorded one, with a very regular pulse, are added, while the intensity of all of them grows steadily. From 7.36 more animal sounds are added and now it becomes difficult to perceive each sound individually, a fact we have pointed out as a characteristic of any complex texture. The intensity keeps on increasing until reaching a climax at 8.50 while several sounds follow one another or overlap. By the end, the bird singing is prominent and the section (and the whole work) abruptly concludes. This explains that texture and intensity play a crucial role in this section, and they are determining factors in its conclusive character. The progressive texture complexity, together with an intensity increase, creates an expectation that is surprisingly interrupted to conclude the work.

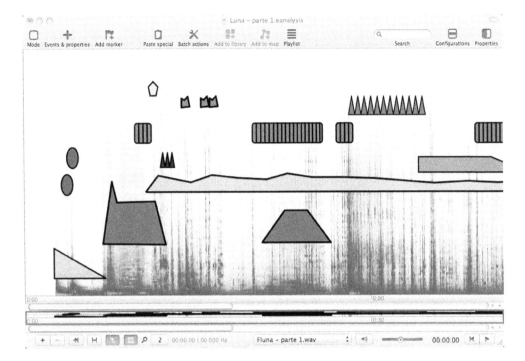

Figure 5.9 Luna: first section

A different situation is presented in the first section (Figure 5.9). Here there is a change at the textural level, which is not related to a change in intensity, where we clearly hear the metallic sound of a door acting as a figure, and then other similar sounds overlap which also act as a figure. Later a ground is added which is made up of low birdsong and finally a stream composed of voices appearing in a theatre hall-like environment. To sum up, we hear a single figure, then several figures, figures with ground, several figures, and then a single figure. We are bound to say that from a textural perspective there is a progressive increase and decrease of complexity, which serves as introduction, development and closure at a structural level.

Towards the end of the piece, in the third section (Figure 5.10), there is a setting we consider worth mentioning. This is the most static of all, which is particularly evidenced in the texture. The objects and streams vary, but they are kept within a combination of one or two figures with one or two streams acting as ground. Beyond the pitch variety, made up of different sounds of doors, voices, atmospheric sounds of different kinds as well as sounds derived from them through very subtle processes, the persistence of the textural setting, together with the prominence of medium amplitude,

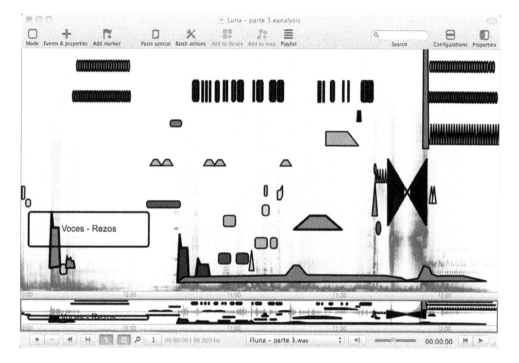

Figure 5.10 Luna: third section

encourages us to perceive this section as quiescent, playing a transition role as regards discourse within the whole work.

A kind of conclusion

The brief comments made on the works mentioned above have led us to reconsider the role of texture in the creation of form. For the time being, we may affirm that this has permitted us to put forward the concept of *textural modulation*, which involves the process of moving from a given textural situation to another one. This concept precisely defines these transitional moments which are characteristic of any modulation. It is in these moments that the most ambiguous situations occur but at the same time the richest ones from an artistic perspective, since the new textural setting is not defined yet nor is the previous one abandoned. As we have commented before, this also means that texture is not something that occurs in a certain moment and that we can measure second by second. Texture needs a minimum time to become established, thus providing the listener with a perceptive pregnancy which may change abruptly or through modulation, according to the musical context.

At this stage, we may still not have enough elements to verify to what extent it may be significant to relate form and texture. But we believe this can provide key findings which have not been considered so far, though there are some immediate questions which are worth answering. For instance, can the gradual construction of a complex texture – something that is common in acousmatic music – be considered a modulation from simple to complex?

However, we consider it necessary to link texture not only to form, but also to amplitude (as commented above), and other parameters such as frequency. We also think it is important to demarcate exactly what kind of relation exists between different types of sound textures.

Surely all these questions can also lead us to reconsider the classification of figure and ground, given the ambiguity (in many cases intentionally caused by the composer) in certain sounds as to their textural setting. While this is attractive and rich from an artistic point of view, it can cause problems when attempting to formulate a classification.

Nevertheless, we believe that these considerations, though provisional at present, can contribute to developing different analytical perspectives if we take into account essential aspects of the musical discourse which have not been considered so far and, above all, we may elaborate a more universal, less fragmented approach to acousmatic music. And perhaps we can also throw light on certain ideas to reconsider music from the past. This is the path we have started to follow.

References

Bregman, Albert S. 1990. *Auditory Scene Analysis*. Cambridge, MA: MIT Press.

Delmonte, R. and Baroni, M. (eds.). 1993. *Atti del Secondo Convegno Europeo di Analisi Musicale*. Universitá di Trento.

Dunsby, Jonathan. 1989. Considerations of texture. *Music & Letters* 70(1), 46–57.

Jammer, Max. 2006. *Concepts of Simultaneity: From Antiquity to Einstein and Beyond*. Baltimore, MD: Johns Hopkins University Press.

Kendall, Gary. 2008a. What is an event? The EVENT schema in relation to listening and electroacoustic cognition. *Proceedings of the Electroacoustic Music Network Conference (EMS08)*, Paris. www.ems-network.org/ems08/papers/kendall.pdf.

　　2008b. What is an event? The EVENT schema, circumstances, metaphor and gist. *Proceedings of the 2008 International Computer Music Conference*, Belfast.

Landy, Leigh. 2007a. *The Music of Sounds*. Série Musique et nouvelles Technologies 3. Paris: Mint/Sorbonne.

2007b. *Understanding the Art of Sound Organization*. Cambridge, MA: MIT Press.

Meyer, Leonard. 1956. *Emotion and Meaning in Music*. University of Chicago Press.

Mountain, Rosemary. 1998. Periodicity and musical texture. http://armchair-researcher.com/Rooms/Research/Rooms/writings/articles/PeriodicityMusical-Texture.pdf (accessed 6 September 2015)

Ong, Walter. 1986. *Oralidad y escrttura*. Mexico: Fondo de Cultura Económica.

Roy, Stéphane. 2003. *L'analyse des musiques électroacoustiques: modèles et propositions*. Paris: L'Harmattan.

Schaeffer, Pierre. 1966. *Traité des objets musicaux*. Paris: du Seuil.

Stockhausen, Karlheinz. 1991. *Stockhausen on Music*. London/NY, Marion Boyars.

Wishart, Trevor. 1994. *Audible Design: A Plain and Easy Introduction to Practical Sound Composition*. York: Orpheus The Pantomime.

Young, John. 2010. Formación de la forma. In R. Minsburg and L. Landy (eds.) *En el límite – Escritos sobre arte y tecnología*. Buenos Aires: Ediciones de la Unla.

Recordings

Belloc, Enrique. 1998. *Canto ancestral I*. Unreleased electroacoustic work.

de Armas, Ricardo. 2011. *El sueño de la razón roduce monstruos*. Electroacoustic work. https://soundcloud.com/ricardodearmas/el-sue-o-de-la-raz-n-produce (accessed 11 April 2015).

Garzón, Eleazar. 2005. *Marfíl y ebano*. Electroacoustic work in *Sonidos en mi laberinto*.

Luna, Fabián Esteban. 2010. *Omnipraesentia*. Electroacoustic work. https://soundcloud.com/fabianestebanluna/omnipraesentia-2010 (accessed 11 April 2015).

Menezes, Flo. 2001. *Harmonia das Esferas*. Electroacoustic work in *Música Maximalista * Maximal Music*, Vol. 7, Studio PANaroma.

Parmegiani, Bernard. 1974. Incidences/Resonances. On *De natura sonorum*. INA/GRM, AM 714.01.

Rudy, Paul. 2007. *In Lake'ch*. Electroacoustic work. https://play.spotify.com/album/1Vp23oIlEAJ0PvmOw6llpp (accessed 11 April 2015).

PART III

Harnessing new forces

| # Exploiting computational paradigms for electroacoustic music analysis

TAE HONG PARK

Introduction

In this chapter we explore electroacoustic music (EAM) analysis approaches that embrace quantitative and systematic analysis strategies through exploitation of digital signal processing and music information retrieval (MIR) practices guided by a methodology called Systematic and Quantitative Electro-Acoustic Music Analysis (SQEMA) (Park *et al.* 2010; Swilley 2014). Our approach to EAM analysis has been motivated in response to the current state of EAM analysis including: (a) a dearth of *quantitative* EAM analysis techniques; (b) difficulty in adjusting to changing technologies and tools for EAM which 'flung these composers squarely back to a period in human creativity that rivals that of the medieval period' (Simoni 2005); (c) lack of analysis software *for* electroacoustic music; (d) importance of timbre (Hirst *et al.* 2002; Dack 1994) rather than pitch and rhythm structures that fit into fixed frequency and time grids; (e) issue of the score as it is typically non-existent or, when present, suffers from idiosyncrasy, crudeness, and sometimes its very usefulness (Stroppa 1984); and (f) rarity of MIR[1] research in the realm of electroacoustic music (Zattra 2005).

The notion of approaching music analysis through electroacoustic means, including through quantitative techniques, is nothing new. It is clearly a technique we employ in the analysis of traditional Western music, folk music, jazz, and popular music. We map the pitches, note durations, segment the music into different temporal divisions and timbrally relevant groups (instrumentation), and conduct various analyses on *quantitative* data while also listening to the music and folding in qualitative observations. We believe that embracing quantitative dimensions for EAM analysis is important in a sense that *both* quantitative and qualitative techniques play a role for all types of music. For tonal music, scores typically exist, or can be straightforwardly created by literate, expert musicians – albeit a potentially time-consuming task to be sure. For EAM, scores are a rarity and oftentimes

---

[1] Music Information Retrieval (MIR) 'is the interdisciplinary science of retrieving information from music' (Wikipedia). This almost always uses computational means.

are neither objective nor reflective of what is measurable in the audio signal. For Western tonal music, MIR has had much success but its application to EAM has been lukewarm at best (as further elaborated in the section "Ground truth' and MIR', pages 143–4). However, as EAM scholars are becoming more familiar with MIR, its utility as a means to address the quantitative side of EAM analysis has in recent years attracted more interest (Swilley 2014; Gulluni *et al.* 2011; Park *et al.* 2009; Dahan 2011; Zattra 2005).

In response to some of the aforementioned issues in EAM analysis, we present some of our approaches by focusing on quantitative and systematic analysis paradigms, which we believe are critical in providing a *balanced* framework for EAM analysis. In particular, we focus on the Electro-Acoustic Music Analysis System (EASY) Toolbox (Park *et al.* 2009) and an accompanying methodology called Systematic and Quantitative Electro-Acoustic Music Analysis (SQEMA) (Park *et al.* 2010). We hope that EASY and SQEMA will contribute to the larger problem of 'partialness' reflective of current EAM practices – that is, contributing and bringing together subjective *and* objective analysis practices, top-down/knowledge-driven and bottom-up/data-driven approaches, as well as utilising perceptual and technological analysis approaches. Furthermore, we also acknowledge the *interpretative* and *non-cochlear* nature of EAM (extrinsic conceptual and contextual elements) (Kim-Cohen 2009), which may lead to idiosyncratic conclusions depending on the analyst. Ultimately, we argue for an analysis approach where interpretation can be made more compelling, more convincing, and more coherent when supported by quantitative musical features that are measurable, consistent, and in fact, present in the music itself, as opposed to being excessively imagined.

The Electro-Acoustic Music Analysis (EASY) Toolbox

A critical component in quantitative analysis is musical feature extraction, which is best accomplished through MIR techniques. The EASY Toolbox (Park *et al.* 2009) was created to take on this role. It was developed through exploration of machine learning and feature extraction techniques (Hirst 2000; Park 2004) for electroacoustic music analysis purposes by embracing quantitative and data-driven analysis strategies.

EASY Toolbox: overview of concepts and features

The EASY Toolbox, implemented in MATLAB, offers standard waveform/spectrogram as well as other visualization formats driven by salient feature extraction techniques for uncovering musical information,[2] especially those that are timbrally and perceptually relevant. Our segmentation algorithms are based on salient feature vector analysis and clustering techniques. The algorithms that are implemented and used for displaying the various visualizations are hidden from the user as much as possible in order to provide an easy-to-use interface. Furthermore, we have attempted to present the feature vectors via intuitive time/frequency-domain interfaces to provide a software-based analysis tool and also encourage users to explore MIR technologies for electroacoustic music analysis. The design ultimately follows a quantitative/data-driven analysis approach to render salient features and measurable sonic elements to facilitate electroacoustic music studies. There are two main display canvases in EASY – the time-domain and frequency-domain canvases as shown in Figure 6.1. Standard functionalities include zoom-in, zoom-out, 3D navigation viewing options, and audio transport control. Other features include modifying the duration of the sound file with or without frequency shifts.

EASY 3D timbre space plots: timbregram

EASY provides 3D, time-variant timbre space displays called *timbregrams* – timbre space visualizations that change as a function of time. Figure 6.2 is an example timbregram that shows a sequence of three sounds – electric bass followed by clarinet and finally a French horn sample. The dimensions may be assigned any feature vector.

The dotted and dashed lines portray the temporal timbre-based trajectory of the audio signal, where the right-pointing triangle refers to the beginning of the audio signal and the left-pointing triangle the end of the audio signal. Each node represents a unit of time equal to the analysis window hop-size. When the audio is played back, the timbregram display, in synchrony with waveform and spectrogram displays, renders timbre-trajectory visualizations.

---

[2] Currently 27 features including: amplitude envelope, AM, attack time, crest factor, dynamic tightness, FM, low energy ratio, noise content, pitch, release time, sound field vector, temporal centroid, ZCR, 3D-spectral envelope, critical band, harmonic compression/expansion, inharmonicity, MFCC, modality/harmonicity/ noisiness, spectral centroid/flux/jitter/roll-off/ shimmer/smoothness, and sensory dissonance.

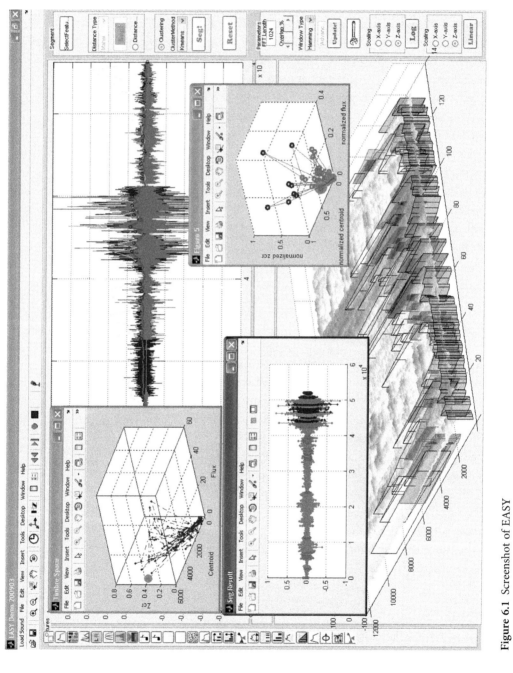

Figure 6.1 Screenshot of EASY

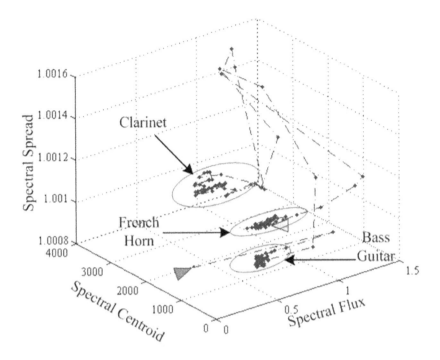

Figure 6.2 Timbre space example

Systematic and Quantitative Electro-Acoustic Music Analysis (SQEMA)

The motivation for developing EASY came from exploring possibilities in using quantitative analysis techniques due to its underemployment in electroacoustic music analysis coupled with MIR research success for Western popular music. Similarly, SQEMA (Park *et al.* 2010) is a response to the lack of agreed-upon basic, standard electroacoustic music analysis methodologies. The primary aim of SQEMA is to work toward creating a comprehensive framework for electroacoustic music analysis employing stepwise segmentation approaches focusing on techniques that yield quantifiable information pertaining to form and content. SQEMA is based on two main analysis strategies: (1) exploitation of MIR and salient feature extraction techniques as addressed in EASY; and (2) employing a systematic analysis paradigm to break down a complex electroacoustic music work into smaller and more manageable parts. Although the literature in electroacoustic music analysis provides an abundance of promising methods and techniques, our review also found a lack of consensus amongst researchers, confusion in nomenclature, and the issue of analysis incompleteness and partiality. The SQEMA methodology in essence attempts to contribute new approaches and ideas, addressing some of the shortcomings found in existing fragmented systems, and also attempts to incorporate useful portions of existing techniques including clarity in nomenclature.

For example, across our readings, we found scarcity of agreement on the definitions of various terminologies and a misuse of others – at times words are attributed multiple meanings, and in other instances, similar words are used to refer to different things. This can be seen in Camilleri (1993), for example, where the goals are 'the creation of an analytical lexicon.' In particular, the essay cites Denis Smalley's *noise-note* continuum – an observation of the perceptual changes that occur when we alter a signal's characteristics from a spectrally random structure to a harmonically organized one. Smalley defines this continuum as being organized into three parts: *noise*, *node*, and *note* and further articulates the node as 'an event having a more complex texture than a single pitch' (Smalley 1986). The word *node*, however, is already clearly defined in acoustics and in fact encompasses the 'note' as part of its definition. David Hirst echoes a similar concern, hoping to 'demystify many of Smalley's concepts since they are shrouded in, sometimes difficult, terminology which is much of his own invention' (Simoni 2005). There are many other examples, especially when 'new' words are introduced, although they already exist in other disciplines. For example, it is not that uncommon to hear composers refer to 'building blocks' of sound simultaneously in a *subtractive* and *additive* context, where a noisy signal and single sinusoid become interchangeable under the same building blocks idea (Holmes 2002). However, we also found certain nomenclature quite valuable and well defined. Some examples are *reduced listening* (Schaeffer 1966), the notion of the *sound object* (Schaeffer 1998), and *source bonding* (Smalley 1986). Thus, the *objective* codification of a lexicon geared toward the particular issues present in electroacoustic music will be important in the development of a comprehensive system for electroacoustic music analysis.

Visual representation examples

One of the important differences between 'note-based music' and electroacoustic music is the lack of standardized scoring techniques in the latter. Waveforms and spectrograms alone do indeed provide valuable and important information in the absence of a score for any music (Cogan 1984). Several extensions for signal analysis, such as David Hirst's use of modified MQ plots (Hirst 2000) and Mara Helmuth's multidimensional analysis method (Simoni 2005), begin to draw correlations across the frequency and time domains. Both of these methods, however, tend to highlight surface layers, and are thus not entirely adequate for exposing spectrally or temporally encoded information. Pierre Couprie presents an insightful discussion of graphical representation, praising the effectiveness of iconic representation where 'the link between graphical qualities and the sound criteria they represent are relatively intuitive' (Couprie 2004). An example of this type of technique can be seen online in Rainer Wehinger's rendering of a visual listening score accompanying György Ligeti's *Artiku-lation* (1958).[3] Couprie hints at future work which would incorporate symbolic and iconic representation into one paradigm (see Chapter 8 in this volume).

Aural perception and partiality

Due to the lack of visualizations and the absence of scores, much of electroacoustic music analysis relies heavily on aural perception. The innate subjectivity of perception and the current difficulty in accurately quantifying perceptual data, however, places severe limitations on this commonly used (although essential) perceptual feedback analysis strategy. This methodology may, however, not necessarily be a matter of preference, but rather due to limitations in alternative analysis strategies. For example, Smalley's spectromorphology builds on Pierre Schaeffer's fundamental concepts based on typomorphology and both rely heavily on *aural perception* – a methodology innately subjective in design, which can lead to great individual variation (Stroppa 1984). This research, of course, plays a necessary role in building the descriptive language of electroacoustic music, and it is indeed critical in addressing the subjective side of music analysis. Listening *alone*, however, is inadequate when viewed from a larger and more comprehensive music analysis model. The objective side of analysis, in combination with the subjective side, is necessary to render a more complete analysis. Moving toward a set of agreed-upon and basic standardized methods for quantitative sound descriptions – while allowing for adaptability to address the changing nature of music – is a necessary step in realising a mature electroacoustic music analysis framework.

One of the biggest issues we noted in our readings was the absence of a reasonably balanced electroacoustic music analysis approach. What we discovered instead were fragmented sets of analysis tools, each of which

---

[3] www.youtube.com/watch?v=71hNl_skTZQ

deals, whether effectively or ineffectively, with only a portion of the analysis process, which in effect only provides a *partial* analysis of any given work. The issue of specificity vs generality also seemed to be a problematic theme in the literature that we examined. For example, techniques such as the MQ plots (Hirst 2000) alone are very *specific*, limiting thorough readings of complex music. Others were more *general*, such as Robert Cogan's theory of oppositions where 13 categories (descriptors) are used to describe a given 'sonic moment' by manually assigning each category with a +, −, +/−, or null (Cogan 1984) label.

SQEMA: methods and procedures

Core SQEMA concepts

The SQEMA analysis approach begins with a less-detail to more-detail methodology employing salient feature extraction techniques whenever possible. Using this methodology, more information is revealed as we step through the various analysis levels as further discussed below. Although our current research is incomplete, we are optimistic of its potential in contributing to electroacoustic music analysis. There is, however, no clear evidence that the proposed method is 'better' than other existing methods, let alone that it will work equally well for every piece. We believe, however, that some type of a less-detail to more-detail model should be employed at some stage of the analysis process. This motivated us to begin drafting a systematic architecture reflecting a procedural analysis model utilizing a feature extraction strategy that loosely adheres to a divide-and-conquer paradigm. In the penultimate phase, which we call *reexamination*, the analyst makes associations, connections, and correlations via an intra/inter-level analysis, combining levels whenever necessary (upper-to-lower, lower-to-upper, diagonally, and side-to-side) for 'omnidirectional' comparisons. These comparisons are, wherever possible, based on subjective, computer-extracted features from previous levels. The machine-based acoustic descriptors are important as they yield consistent results, thus addressing objectivity as well as repeatability. At the final analysis phase, we also take into account the aesthetic aspect of music analysis. This step allows for greater liberty when *interpreting* a composition as we believe that diverse and subjective views are also important in the practice of music analysis. By advocating the use of quantitative features to inform qualitative points of view, however, we hope to promote coherent, consistent, and reasoned interpretations of a given electroacoustic music work.

Implementation and methodology

The entire analysis procedure is divided into six large steps, five of which are shown in Figure 6.3. At levels II, III, and IV, *quantitative* analysis is conducted via salient feature extraction techniques, clustering results from feature vector spaces, and observation of data visualizations.

The Top Level Analysis procedure simply involves multiple listenings to familiarize oneself with the music as further articulated in Park *et al.* (2010).

The aim of the High Level Analysis phase is to segment the piece into formal sections by analyzing salient acoustic features pertinent to energy levels, frequency distribution and flux, texture, and *frequency continuum* (readers are directed to Park *et al.* (2010) for details). We have recently also added an analysis technique we call *companded listening* to this stage which can further be divided into *compressed* and *expanded listening*. Companded listening is a technique that is especially useful and exploits time-compressing or time-expanding (with or without frequency shifts) of a portion of a piece or the entire audio file – this fundamentally differs from Jonty Harrison's *expanded listening*, which is a 'moving on' of Schaeffer's *reduced listening* strategies as per his four listening modes (Harrison 1996).

There is little new about the companded listening technique itself and most digital audio workstations perform these tasks easily. Compressed

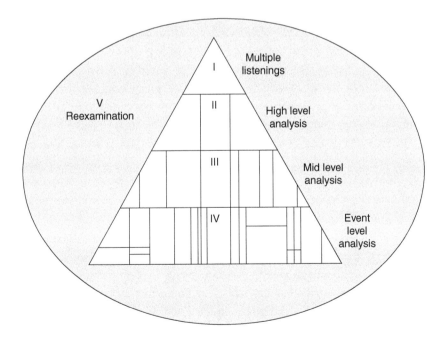

Figure 6.3 SQEMA model

listening has, however, shown promise in providing an 'overview' of a piece by allowing the listener to *perceive* the entire piece in a more 'manageable' time frame. This is particularly useful for long pieces – a technique that would be detrimental to what Morton Feldman tried to achieve in one of his later compositions such as *Piano and String Quartet* (1985). In Feldman's 80-minute work, very soft dynamics with very little variance gently leads the listener to dwell on the current moment and forget the past. Feldman's strategy essentially attempts to erase the past and anticipatory elements of music experience via temporal prolongation. Imagine, however, for analysis purposes, we listen to the piece at one-tenth of its original duration – what results is a *sonic* summary that facilitates the exposure of main musical pillars. Compressed listening provides one way to help us *listen* to form. It augments our understanding of the piece especially when combined with visuals such as waveforms, spectrograms, and feature vectors. We have found companded listening helpful when following level I in clarifying and reinforcing early formal determinations.

The Mid Level Analysis procedure is fundamentally based on similar techniques used in the previous analysis level. In the mid level phase, however, we concentrate on each individual section (e.g. A–B–A) obtained in level II and identify *subsections*, *divisions*, and *events*. In SQEMA, divisions are defined as segments that do not have sufficient saliency or contrasting features to be subsections. Events are defined as salient sonic occurrences that are hierarchically below the section, subsection, and division level such as a staccato wideband percussive sound with modal characteristics. Events, however, do not necessarily have to be limited to 'short' occurrences and can, therefore, take on the role of a division, a subsection, an entire section, or, in extreme cases, even an entire piece. The determination and assignment of labels to extracted sonic occurrences is conducted in phases IV and V.

In level IV, Event Level Analysis, the primary aim is to analyze the identified events using clear nomenclature. For example, when describing an event that elicits a sense of pitch, one can elaborate on its harmonic structure (odd, even, missing fundamental, harmonic expansion/contraction, jitter/shimmer characteristics, etc.) or its modal resonant structure (we use the words *mode* and *modal* to describe sounds that fall between noise and harmonic sounds as articulated in modal synthesis). Other examples include investigating glissando events by determining their rate of change/slope, span in frequency (Hz), frequency continuum between pulse, roughness, pitch, and high frequency sensation.

As in High Level Analysis, companded listening can also be used here: to reveal a sound object's identity that may have previously been unclear.

Simple sample rate conversion can help disambiguate sound source identities allowing the listener to perform source bonding as described in Scheirer (1998). Again, there is very little new about 'resampling' as it has been exploited on countless occasions for *compositional* purposes. For example, in Vladimir Ussachevsky's (1911–90) works, tape speed manipulations were frequently applied to highlight overtones of recorded musical instruments to produce 'an otherwise unheard-of timbre' (Taruskin 2009). In Ussachevsky's case, the slowing down of the recording resulted in lowering of the individually imperceptible overtones to the acute hearing range while pushing the fundamental frequency below the pitch range. Now, when employing this same technique for *analysis* rather than *composition*, the results serve a very different goal. This technique essentially exposes difficult to hear, barely audible, frequency masked, and even imperceptible frequency regions, into the acutely audible frequency range. In addition, time-shifting without frequency modulation allows the listener to monitor fleeting musical passages (via expansion) and structural elements that are difficult to notice at the original playback speed. Beyond its use as a tool for gaining more insights into a musical work, companded listening gives us important information about the composer's methods and tools in a musicological sense. Extrapolating from this idea, we have considered other simple digital signal processing methods, which show potential as tools for music analysis. These include frequency shifting without time companding and time-reversal. Perhaps the most interesting component of companded listening, however, is its implications with respect to musical memory, a topic ripe for further research (we will discuss this briefly in the section 'Companded listening and musical memory', pages 141–2).

The next step in our analysis is level V, Reexamination. Here we take into account all components (sections, subsections, divisions, and events) and analyze them in intra/inter-level cross-examinations. At this stage it is possible to find motifs, streams, and groups of events that have single or repetitive characteristics. This will help us identify developmental ideas, various structures such as retrogrades, inversions, and fragmentations. The final phase of our analysis is level VI: Aesthetic Interpretation. Using all the information from previous analysis levels, one can now interpret the piece and render narrative and aesthetic elaboration. We acknowledge that systematic, data-driven methodologies alone are insufficient for delivering a comprehensive aesthetic interpretation. In order to accomplish a balanced musical analysis, technical detail-oriented analysis techniques should be combined with more subjective approaches. We believe that our methodology, as presented above, offers tools for analysis with the potential to yield the detailed information needed to support coherent connections and articulate aesthetic interpretations about a musical piece.

Electroacoustic music analysis examples

The goal as presented in this section is to show and discuss the potential of quantitative analysis approaches utilizing EASY and SQEMA through analysis excerpts (for additional and more detailed step-by-step analyses results, readers are directed to Park *et al.* 2010, 2009). The results reflect outcomes and insights gained during the development phases of our systems conducted by Tae Hong Park, David Hyman, Peter Leonard, Zhiye Li, Wu Wen, and Phillip Hermans (Park *et al.* 2010, 2009). Included in this section are analysis excerpts of classic compositions from the electroacoustic music canon: *Riverrun* (1986) by Barry Truax, *Stria* (1977) by John Chowning, and *Poème Électronique* (1958) by Edgard Varèse. An exhaustive analysis of Hiller's *Vocalise*, the first movement from *Seven Electronic Studies for Two-Channel Tape Recorder* (1963) can also been found in Daniel Swilley's doctoral dissertation (Swilley 2014). Swilley's analysis of *Vocalize* is 'modeled on the top-down SQEMA methodology, but makes use of other methodologies in the description of sonic characteristics and the functional role of materials' and is 'based on listening, and uses MIR as a tool for confirming the findings of the listening analysis' as a way to address its 'logical process by which a work can be systematically scrutinized, and with a means of "checking" our ears via the quantifiable results of Music Information Retrieval' (Swilley 2014).

Riverrun

In Barry Truax's *Riverrun*, we placed particular emphasis on the timbregram feature to help visualize formal structures and timbral architectures through clustering/segmentation algorithms included in EASY. This was accomplished by running the program using different feature combinations in rendering the timbregrams. What was interesting in the timbregram plot was that the various timbre spaces portrayed a distinct separation of one particular cluster from the rest – the timbral cluster pertaining to the closing section of the piece with high spectral centroid as shown in Figure 6.4. At the same time, Figure 6.4 also shows the

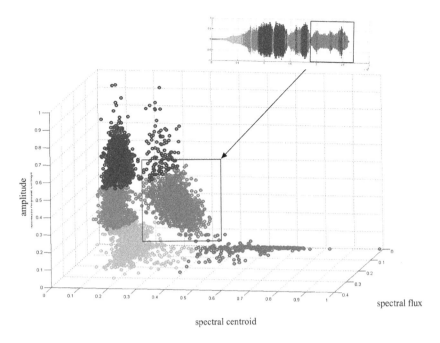

spectral flux

spectral centroid

Figure 6.4 Timbregram and segmentation map of *Riverrun*

metaphorical descriptions of continuous development as described in Simoni 2005 and in Truax's notes:[4]

The corresponding metaphor is that of a river, always moving yet seemingly permanent. From the smallest rivulet to the fullest force of its mass, a river is formed from a collection of countless droplets and sources.

Here we can visualize formal segments, such as the composition's beginnings consisting of sparse and quiet groups of 'droplets' (grains), developing further to 'rivulets,' streams, and finally a massive ocean toward the main part of the piece (high density of grains). The upper right-hand side shows the waveform segmented via timbre clusters and the 3D plot shows the timbregram. In addition to the traditional spectrogram and waveform, we can see that, in this instance, an alternative visualization format can be helpful in not only exposing compositional strategies but also supporting aesthetic and meta-phorical ideas that are addressed in SQEMA's level VI: Aesthetic Interpret-ation (further examples of this approach – using quantitative data to support aesthetic interpretation – are detailed in Park *et al.* 2010).

Although various feature combinations have been employed in generating clusters, segmentation maps, and timbregrams, for the majority of the cases,

---

[4] www.sfu.ca/~truax/river.html

the results have been quite similar even though the timbregram *shapes* were different. The same was also true when using a different number of clusters; in general, more clusters resulted in more detail in the form of subclusters where smaller clusters became part of a larger cluster. This is again shown in Figure 6.4, where the closing section of *Riverrun* becomes one large 'supercluster' consisting of two main subclusters that extend vertically on the normalized amplitude axis. Another interesting observation we found is when applying companded listening to *Riverrun*. We initially time-compressed the piece by 8:1 in order to establish an overall structure of the work. This was done with and without pitch modulation artifacts, where each provided different insights. Using the companded listening technique, we were able to quickly hear *and* see (waveform, amplitude envelope, and spectrogram) global structural points depicting formal segmentation strategies.

The second result was the exposure of 'structural elements' which fall outside of the acutely audible range as articulated in the Fletcher–Munson curve. Using the down-sampling technique for time-compression to shift sensitive frequency regions toward the Nyquist, rendering them into background sound, low frequency components were similarly pushed from the background to the foreground frequency range. This led to exposing a repeating and descending tone pattern, not aurally evident at normal playback speed as it fell in the 20–60 Hz range (11:00–14:10). There are a number of reasons why these types of sonic events are not easily audible without signal processing manipulations. First, the rate of change of this two-minute tone pattern is outside the range of motivic temporality – that is, the notes change too slowly to be perceived as motifs. When we speed up the piece, the long, drawn out section is shifted to a motivically meaningful temporal space. Second, the frequency range of the tone pattern is in the area where our hearing system is 'insensitive.' This situation is made more difficult for the listener as there is a large amount of energy in the acute frequency space, which in turn masks lower frequency spectral content. Companded listening in this example shows that it can be useful in exposing sonic events and organizational properties.

Dissonance curve and *Stria*

A feature vector that we have more recently explored relates to concepts of dissonance as proposed by Plomp (Plomp and Levelt 1965) and extended by Sethares (Sethares 2005). This research is largely based on acoustic roughness and is a dissonance measurement technique previously suggested by Terhardt (Terhardt 1984) and referred to as 'sensory dissonance' by

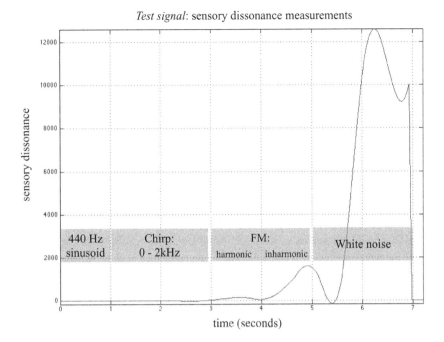

Figure 6.5 Sensory dissonance plot for a test signal

Sethares. Although sensory dissonance can be applied to any type of audio signal, it is particularly well suited to electroacoustic music, as it is not limited to pitch structures/relationships as the algorithm uses frequency differences and critical band relationships to compute dissonance. In essence, sensory dissonance is determined by computing the overall degree of roughness between pairs of spectral peaks. The dissonance for a pair of frequencies is greatest near one quarter of a critical band, which corresponds to approximately a minor second interval in the equal temperament scale. Figure 6.5 shows the progressively increasing dissonance curve for a number of different synthesized signals – a single pure sinusoid followed by a frequency sweep, harmonic and inharmonic FM sounds, and finally pure white noise. As expected, we note the increase in sensory dissonance.

An interesting point to consider from the above is that the dissonance curve approach also takes into account the strength of each peak sinusoid in the spectrum. This is different from traditional music analysis practices: we normally determine 'dissonance' based solely on intervallic pitch relationships between simultaneous notes disregarding the dynamics of each individual note or groups of notes. However, when we *listen* to any music or sound, our perception of dissonance and consonance is at least affected in two ways – (1) the frequency relationships and (2) the energy of the

frequency components (further elaboration on dissonance and its application to EAM can be found in Park *et al.* 2010).

Stria: *dissonance curve*

Here we look at an analysis excerpt of John Chowning's *Stria* (1977) highlighted through the lens of sensory dissonance. We chose *Stria* for the
following reasons: (1) its use of complex sinusoidal synthesis technique; (2)
the utilization of non-traditional scales built on golden mean ratios (Meneghini 2007); and (3) qualities that make it difficult to analyze via traditional
harmonic analysis. We show an examination of the opening section of the
piece as it presents a somewhat flat amplitude envelope, allowing us to see
variations in dissonance relatively unaffected by changes in dynamics.
Figure 6.6 compares the sensory dissonance plot vs the fully rectified waveform from the beginning to 1:40. It is clear that there is correlation between
the two plots. Generally speaking, when the amplitude rises, so does the

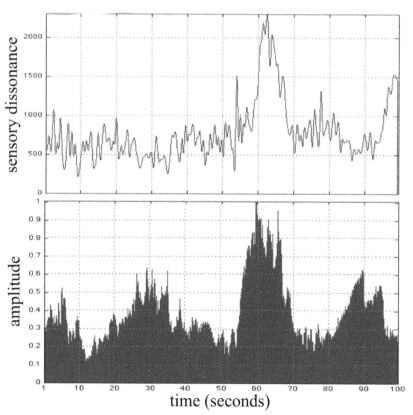

Figure 6.6 Sensory dissonance plot of first 1:40 of *Stria*

dissonance. This is particularly evident between 0:58 and 0:68 where the magnitudes of the waveform and the sensory dissonance both peak. However, greater amplitude does not necessarily result in greater dissonance as both frequency *and* magnitude fair relationships contribute to dissonance.

What we can furthermore infer from the above plots is that the maximum dissonance occurs at the maximum waveform amplitude. This could be suggestive of the composer's strict systematic compositional strategy of highlighting inharmonic frequency ratios 'to re-define the concept of the [equally divided nine-tone] octave' (Meneghini 2007). Chowning further elaborates and states: 'I've never been of the school where the Golden Section is this magical formula, but you find it in nature and it's true. It was a very practical application that generated a sound that I wanted to work with [in *Stria*]. [Because of the golden mean] I understood why I liked that sound' (McGee 2015). The notion of dissonance modulation in *Stria* can also be approached from a compositional context to create subtle textural changes via varying levels of sensory dissonance as the overall timbre stays 'relatively' constant. Perhaps this is what Kevin Dahan refers to as 'surface tension' in his analysis and reconstruction of *Stria* – 'I use this term [surface tension] in a specific sense to refer to points where elements in contact share a number of properties but are still differentiated. This contact between differentiated elements provides musical tension and dynamism without negating an underlying cohesion' (Dahan 2007).

Poème Électronique

Poème Électronique by Edgard Varèse is one of the earliest classic electroacoustic music compositions that include both synthesized and 'natural' sounds. For some of the sounds it is unclear if it is synthetic or a type of natural sound, and for other sounds, like the voice and bell sounds, the identities are clear. A point of interest occurs around 5:00 into the piece. When trying to identify the sound source of this event, we perceived artifacts of tape speed manipulation including filtering effects and temporal distortion. This was one of the instances that lead to the idea of companded listening as previously discussed. Using a time compression ratio of 3:1, we were clearly able to hear the sound of a barking dog and sounds that resembled bird chirps. This was rather surprising and unexpected at first as none of us were previously aware of animal sounds in this piece. Corroborating this finding, these animal sounds are also mentioned in Roger Kamien's listening outline (Kamien and Kamien 1988) of *Poème Électronique*. The result of this finding is interesting and multifaceted as it gives us insight into Varèse's compositional process and also the technologies that were utilized. The ability to perceive the sound of a dog barking is also important in the context of source bonding as introduced by Denis Smalley (1994):

[Source bonding is] the natural tendency to relate sounds to supposed sources and causes, and to relate sounds to each other because they appear to have shared or associated origins.

As another example, the iconic bell sound, which opens the piece, was noticed to sound more 'natural' when time-compressed at approximately 4:1. This would have to be further investigated via more careful analysis of bell sounds in general, but when listening to the modified bell sound, it does seem that Varèse may have applied considerable tape manipulation here as well. Furthermore, it also augments and exposes some of the seemingly 'sloppy' edits when knitting together the various bell recordings at the opening of this classic electroacoustic music work. Interesting questions to pose here are: Does it matter whether we know the identity of the source after the fact? How will it change (if at all) our perception of the piece with this new information?

Discussion

Feature extraction: effectiveness and meaning

Although the EASY system provides 27 feature extraction modules, a number of them proved to be less useful for analysis than we had hoped. This is hardly surprising as not all of the feature vectors will be useful for *every* composition. For example, if we use noise analysis for a piece that is based on harmonically structured sinusoids, not much will be revealed – features such as harmonicity and dissonance will be more apt for this piece. In general, however, we found that one of the greatest challenges in using a data-driven analysis approach was the difficulty in mapping salient features to musically relevant attributes. During the testing phase, we also found that certain attributes such as 'spectral sparseness' and 'spectral fullness' would have been useful in gaining more insights into timbral structures. Our current studies concentrated on timbral feature vectors but showed that other elements such as spatial cues could potentially offer additional analytical insights.

Additional features

A feature that holds promise for music analysis is the *dissonance score* (detailed in the section 'Dissonance curve and *Stria*', pages 136–9). We are considering several modifications to our current implementation of the sensory dissonance algorithm including folding in equal-loudness contours for a more perceptually relevant dissonance model. Also, as this dissonance model is based on non-discrete frequency relationships weighted by amplitude relationships, its application to traditional pitch-based or any other non-timbre-centric music analysis may also hold promise. Specifically, such dissonance analysis models will render a more perceptually accurate representation by considering the individual harmonics and non-harmonic spectral peak contributions to the overall dissonance absent in traditional musical scores, which in turn, can provide further insight into the nuances of 'good' performances (Sethares 2005).

Acoustic features of sounds or groups of sounds are not the only ways to represent musical characteristics. Indeed, the way we 'feel' and experience music is without a doubt very important. One might argue that some of the audience's listening experiences can be described in the context of mood and emotion, while others might go so far as to state that music is the 'language of emotions' (Downie 2008). Mood and emotion detection is a research field that is still in its nascent stages (Kim *et al.* 2010) but has gained interest as a research topic in the MIR community in recent years. It has had some notable advances in Western music based on pitch and rhythm: the annual Music Information Research Evaluation eXchange (MIREX) is a community-based framework for evaluating MIR systems and includes emotion (Downie 2008), introduced to MIREX in 2007 (Hu *et al.* 2008). Mood can often be subjective, especially when considering cultural context and background of the listener; at the same time, however, the existence of universal psychophysical and emotional cues that transcend language and acculturation has also been found (Balkwill and Thompson 1999; Fritz *et al.* 2009). One of our aims in EASY is to develop an emotion feature extractor that will begin to visualize emotional/mood dimensions (e.g. 2D graph depicting 'emotiograms') in addition to waveforms, spectrograms, salient feature vectors, and other visualization formats.

Companded listening and musical memory

Our initial discussion of companded listening found a general agreement that shortening the duration of a piece would provide an acoustic overview and facilitate identification of sonically significant moments of the piece. In effect, compressed listening seems to result in a sort of 'temporal low-pass filtering' effect which subdues details while preserving salient moments such as strong shifts in dynamics, spectral content, and timbre. The result is a rendering that resembles a skeletal representation of the piece, which can be used to elucidate formal compositional designs. Although the signal processing technique is trivial, the resulting phenomenon, especially when considered along with musical memory, can be quite interesting. There are a number of memory recall models including one which uses a schema (Bartlett and Burt 1933) to facilitate remembering via concepts of 'chunking' (Miller 1956). Research shows that musical memory in part relies on 'melody, harmony, meter, and rhythm.' Electroacoustic music, however, is often timbre-centric and includes few instances (or none) of the traditional musical parameters described above. Interestingly enough, some literature in musical memory also suggests that we remember music by recalling the 'gist' and 'generic memories' of a compositional work. Furthermore, memories for events appear to be organized in ways that 'connect temporal series of discrete action through narrative structures' (Hallam *et al.* 2008). Although further research needs to be conducted, it may be that these 'discrete actions' may correspond to salient moments brought to the forefront by the 'temporal low-pass filtering' effect when engaging in compressed listening. Companded listening shows potential in providing insights, which could contribute to issues in musical memory as they relate to the perception of form.

Organizational issues: data and time

Following the steps of the SQEMA methodology, even with a short piece, proved to be a very time-consuming endeavor due to the vast amount of data the methodology yields. The hierarchical nature of the SQEMA methodology prescribes a sequential analysis approach, by which a piece is subsegmented down to the Event Level. Clearly, the longer and more complex a piece is, the longer the process will take. One of the more critical future goals is to realize a more comprehensively automatic data extraction and organization system to include computing and finding associations/connections/correlations between sections, subsections, divisions, and events – ultimately resulting in an interactive mapping interface. An even more difficult task, however, in the quest for creating a comprehensive framework of electroacoustic music is the issue of incorporating the widely ranging, and partially complete, top-down and bottom-up analysis techniques for electroacoustic music from existing literature.

'Ground truth' and MIR

MIR research for electroacoustic music is still in its infancy, as witnessed in the number of research papers presented at the International Society for Music Information Retrieval (ISMIR) conference proceedings database thus far (Gulluni *et al.* 2011; Park *et al.* 2009). Although it is difficult to determine the exact causes for such lack of activity, a number of possible reasons include: (1) the availability of a large *training set* or *ground-truth set* and (2) the financial attractiveness in electroacoustic music MIR research compared to popular music and traditional music. Ground truth as it is used in machine learning refers to human annotations of audio signals – for example, meter, form, melody, chord progression, genre – that are used to develop machine learning algorithms to mimic human listeners. Ground truth in popular music is in abundance when compared to electroacoustic music. When developing MIR algorithms for computational music analysis, the size and accuracy of the ground-truth data set is essential. For electroacoustic music, however, ground truth is close to non-existent. A project that aims to develop such ground truth as part of a larger goal is the Electro-Acoustic Music Mine (EAMM) project. As a comprehensive preservation, 'ground truth' collection, music visualization, and music exploration hub, it essentially aims to facilitate electroacoustic music studies. Music is collected via online submission systems commonly employed by well-established electroacoustic music conferences and festivals such as the International Computer Music Conference (ICMC). The goal of EAMM is also to further develop authorial ground-truth data associated with each work including sectional/subsectional timings, motivic information, salient musical moment labels/tags, and mood/emotional profiles. This will be achieved via web-based user interfaces in the exploration module through authorial and crowd-sourced annotations, tags, and labels, by directly interacting via the waveform/spectrogram graphical user interfaces. Although it remains to be seen how successful a collective 'ground-truth crowd-sourcing' model will be, we are optimistic that composers will in fact find this task worthwhile as the incentives are inherently part of its design: historical preservation of their own work.

From the user's standpoint, having access to authorial ground truth and various visualizations can result in significant services for teachers, students, music enthusiasts, and the general public at large. From a machine learning development perspective, the implications are significant as reliable ground truths are absolutely critical. From the electroacoustic music analysis perspective, the information from EAMM could provide a hub for works that are in the database, as well as the possibility for analyzing 'unknown' compositions (e.g. classic electroacoustic music works) and automatically render musical features, visualizations, and machine-based analyses 'learned' from a giant database of 'significant' electroacoustic music works: instead of the *Million Song Dataset*, 'a freely-available collection of audio features and metadata for a million contemporary popular music tracks' (Bertin-Mahieux 2011), the possibility of a *Million Piece Dataset* is an exciting one.

Summary and conclusion

In this chapter we have discussed our approaches for quantitative/ systematic analysis paradigms motivated by the lack of such techniques in current electroacoustic music analysis practices. There is still much room for improvement as our concepts and systems have not yet been extensively tested on a reasonably large number of electroacoustic music works. However, as our analysis approaches are largely based on exploiting quantitative and data-driven strategies, we are confident that performance consistency will be reflected across the electroacoustic music canon, especially when computing measurable acoustic and musical features. It is also important to note that not all of the extracted information we used for analysis was produced automatically as (1) the EASY Toolbox itself is under development and (2) we found new features for which extraction algorithms do not yet exist. It is not yet possible to do many (let alone every one) of the tasks that humans do with ease.

Although our research heavily relies on data-driven, quantitative analysis strategies, we do not exclusively focus on the 'objective' and quantitative dimensions alone as this impacts the issue of incompleteness and partiality. As such, we include both subjective and qualitative layers, where the aesthetic interpretation layer allows for a more subjective read on the composition as articulated in *Riverrun* and more thoroughly detailed in Park *et al.* (2010). These are not included here. We believe that perceptual approaches hold great value in the aesthetic evaluation and interpretation of a piece. However, we also believe that electroacoustic music analysis as a whole will hold even greater significance when based on accurate, empirical musical data whenever possible, as opposed to excessive reliance on subjective assertions. The result, we hope, will yield more coherent, more consistent, more convincing, and perhaps even more commonly shared musical sentiments. Ultimately, the combination of the subjective and objective, sonic and visual, qualitative and quantitative approaches, timedomain and frequency domain will need to be considered together in moving toward a comprehensive framework for electroacoustic music analysis. At the current juncture, it seems that the quantitative spectrum of analysis is still very much underexplored and much work still needs to be done.

References

Balkwill, L. L. and Thompson, W. F. (1999) A cross-cultural investigation of the perception of emotion in music: Psychophysical and cultural cues. *Music Perception* 71(1), 43–64.

Bartlett, F. C. and Burt, C. (1933) Remembering: A study in experimental and social psychology. *British Journal of Educational Psychology* 3(2), 187–92.

Bertin-Mahieux, T. (2011) The million song dataset. *Proceedings of the 12th International Society for Music Information Retrieval (ISMIR) Conference.* Miami, 591–6.

Camilleri, L. (1993) Electro-acoustic music: Analysis and listening processes. *Sonus Contemporary Music Materials* 1, 37–47.

Cogan, R. (1984) *New Images of Musical Sound.* Cambridge, MA: Harvard University Press.

Couprie, P. (2004) Graphical representation: An analytical and publication tool for electroacoustic music. *Organised Sound* 9(1), 109–13.

Dack, J. (1994) Pierre Schaeffer and the significance of radiophonic art. *Contemporary Music Review* 10(2), 3–11.

Dahan, K. (2007) Surface tensions: Dynamics of stria. *Computer Music Journal* 31(3), 65–74.

  (2011) *Electroacoustic Music: Overcoming Analysis Paralysis.* Ann Arbor, MI: MPublishing, University of Michigan Library.

Downie, J. S. (2008) The Music Information Retrieval Evaluation Exchange (2005–2007): A window into music information retrieval research. *Acoustical Science and Technology* 29(4), 247–55.

Fritz, T., Jentschke, S., Gosselin, N. and Sammler, D. (2009) Universal recognition of three basic emotions in music. *Current Biology* 19(7), 573–6.

Gulluni, S., Essid, S., Buisson, O. and Richard, G. (2011) An interactive system for electro-acoustic music analysis. *Proceedings of the 12th International Society for Music Information Retrieval (ISMIR) Conference*, 145–50.

Hallam, S., Cross, I. and Thaut, M. (eds.) (2008) *Oxford Handbook of Music Psychology.* Oxford University Press.

Harrison, J. (1996) CD liner notes for *Articles indéfinis*, Empreintes DIGITALes IMED 9627.

Hirst, D. (2000) The use of MQ plots in the analysis of electro-acoustic music. Unpublished paper. www.msu.edu/~sullivan/hirst/hirst.html.

Hirst, D. *et al.* (2002) Developing analysis criteria based on Denis Smalley's timbre theories. *Proceedings of the Australasian Computer Music Conference 2002,* 43–52.

Holmes, T. (2002) *Electronic and Experimental Music: Pioneers in Technology and Composition.* New York: Routledge.

Hu, X., Downie, J. S., Laurier, C., Bay, M. and Ehmann, A. F. (2008) The 2007 MIREX audio mood classification task: Lessons learned. *Proceedings of the 9th International Society for Music Information Retrieval (ISMIR) Conference,* 462–7.

Kamien, R. and Kamien, A. (1988) *Music: An Appreciation.* Boston, MA: McGraw-Hill.

Kim, Y., Schmidt, E., Migneco, R., Morton, B. G., Richardson, P., Scott, J., Speck, J. A. and Turnbull, D. (2010) Music emotion recognition: A state of the art review. *Proceedings of the 11th International Society for Music Information Retrieval (ISMIR) Conference,* 255–66.

Kim-Cohen, S. (2009) *In the Blink of an Ear: Toward a Non-Cochlear Sonic Art.* New York: Continuum.

McGee, R. (2015) John Chowning: Overview, techniques, and compositions. Ryanmcgee.net (accessed February 2015).

Meneghini, M. (2007) An analysis of the compositional techniques in John Chowning's Stria. *Computer Music Journal* 31(3), 26–37.

Miller, G. A. (1956) The magical number seven, plus or minus two: Some limits on our capacity for processing information. *Psychological Review* 63(2), 81.

Park, T. H. (2004) Towards automatic musical instrument timbre recognition. Doctoral diss., Princeton University.

Park, T. H., Hyman, D., Leonard, P. and Wu, W. (2010) Systematic and Quantative Electro-Acoustic Music Analysis (SQEMA). *Proceedings of the International Computer Music Conference (ICMC) 2010.* Stony Brook: ICMA.

Park, T. H., Li, Z. and Wu, W. (2009) EASY does it: The Electro-Acoustic Music Analysis Toolbox. *Proceedings of the 10th International Society for Music Information Retrieval (ISMIR) Conference,* 693–8.

Plomp, R. and Levelt, W. J. M. (1965) Tonal consonance and critical bandwidth. *The Journal of the Acoustical Society of America* 28(4), 548–60.

Schaeffer, P. (1966) *Traité des objets musicaux.* Paris: Editions du Seuil.
(1998) Booklet accompanying *Solfège de l'objet sonore.* Paris: INA-GRM.

Scheirer, E. D. (1998) Tempo and beat analysis of acoustic musical signals. *The Journal of the Acoustical Society of America* 103(1), 588–601.

Sethares, W. A. (2005) *Tuning, Timbre, Spectrum, Scale.* London: Springer Verlag.

Simoni, M. (2005) *Analytical Methods of Electroacoustic Music.* Studies on New Music Research. New York: Routledge.

Smalley, D. (1986) Spectro-morphology and structuring processes. In S. Emmerson (ed.), *The Language of Electroacoustic Music*. London: Macmillan, 61–93.

(1994) Defining timbre – refining timbre. *Contemporary Music Review* 10(2), 35–48.

Stroppa, M. (1984) The analysis of electronic music. *Contemporary Music Review* 1(1), 175–80.

Swilley, D. (2014) Problems, current methodologies, and an analytical case study in electro-acoustic music analysis: Lejaren Hiller's *Vocalise* from *Seven Electronic Studies for Two-Channel Tape Recorder* (1963). Doctoral diss., University of Illinois at Urbana-Champaign.

Taruskin, R. (2009) *Music in the Late Twentieth Century: The Oxford History of Western Music*. Oxford University Press,.

Terhardt, E. (1984) The concept of musical consonance: A link between music and psychoacoustics. *Music Perception*, 1(3), 276–95.

Zattra, L. (2005) Analysis and analyses of electroacoustic music. *Proceedings of the Sound and Music Computing Conference (SMC05), Salerno*.

7 | OREMA: an analytical community

MICHAEL GATT

Introduction

This chapter will introduce the concept of an analytical community within electroacoustic music. An analytical community is a collection of practitioners and specialists who work together towards the advancement of electroacoustic music analysis. The format of such collaboration tends to encourage sharing of materials and knowledge; hence, this chapter will be arguing that open access is essential for such endeavours. The OREMA (Online Repository for Electroacoustic Music Analysis) project[1] will be used as an example of such an initiative. It aims to provide an open access knowledge repository and a platform that will facilitate a discourse between creators of original content and its audience.

The term *electroacoustic music* will be defined as 'any music in which electricity has had some involvement in the sound registration and/or production other than that of simple microphone recording or amplification' (Landy 1999: 61). The majority of texts concerning electroacoustic music analysis only consider acousmatic music and not its other categories, such as sound installations and mixed music. This chapter does not profess to rectify these shortcomings, rather it intends to offer a way forward – an analytical community.

The current field of electroacoustic music analysis:
Why is an analytical community needed?

What is interesting about electroacoustic music is that there is no established precedent for analysis. This is not surprising considering that the analysis of instrumental music, as a pursuit in its own right, was only established in the late nineteenth century (Bent 1980: 343). In the last few years there has been an increased number of tools[2] and analyses of

---

[1] www.orema.dmu.ac.uk

[2] The word *tool* in this instance is used to define an analytical methodology and not a software application that analyses sound material.

electroacoustic music, specifically within acousmatic research. However, there is no central consensus on the correct tools or methodologies for the variety of different categories of electroacoustic music. Many prominent publications, such as those on spectromorphology (Smalley 1986, 1997) and typomorphology (Schaeffer 1966), focus on single sound events and not their relations with other sonic materials to create musical structures.[3] Furthermore, these methodologies are intended for acousmatic music.[4] Other publications that do consider musical structure, such as Roy's *Grille Fonctionnelle* (2003), are meant to be used in conjunction with other methodologies that investigate individual sound events. Hence, there is no one explicit 'tool' that can fully analyse a single work.

This lack of a general consensus might be viewed as a negative attribute of electroacoustic music analysis, when in fact it is a positive one. Although it does not provide solid grounding for a singular methodology, it does allow for many different perspectives on a particular work. For example, one analyst might choose to investigate pitch structures within an acousmatic work, whilst another might try to demonstrate how an underlining narrative is communicated to the listener. Both analyses have merits and offer different outlooks on the same work. As Nattiez (1990: 168) states 'there is never only one valid musical analysis for a given work'. The same concept can be applied to the different methodologies of analysis, which inevitably relate to the varying reasons for undertaking one. These varying perspectives provide different insights to an audience and indeed other analysts who might not have noticed aspects of a piece highlighted by another listener. These different insights can lead to disagreements of interpretation and understanding of a work, which can actually be beneficial to a community (this will be investigated in more detail in the section 'Can the electroacoustic community be considered a wise crowd?', pages 155–6). In that respect an analysis can be considered a means of communicating a particular perspective on a work.

Many might question the necessity of such a community and argue that one already exists based on the research so far developed. To some extent this is true; however, it is the contention of this chapter that the current

---

[3] Schaeffer noted this issue at the end of *Traité des Objets Musicaux*. He stated that another book, potentially titled *Traité des Organisations Musicales*, would need to be written to account for this (Schaeffer 1966: 663).

[4] Although Smalley states that spectromorphology is 'intended to account for types of electroacoustic music', he does say that it is really intended for music that is 'partly or wholly acousmatic' (Smalley 1997: 109).

landscape of academia hinders the development of the knowledge base of electroacoustic music analysis. There are a number of factors preventing its advancement, which will be outlined now.

Barriers to the development of electroacoustic music analysis

I. Acquiring knowledge. The first barrier is the cost of acquiring knowledge on this subject. Expert knowledge relating to electroacoustic music is often limited to those who already currently work within an institute that subscribes to the many journal sources, or to those who are willing to pay for either a personal subscription or individually for each article (which can cost in the region of £15 to £25). This causes a barrier of entry for anyone with an interest in learning more about this music, especially for those who might be interested for reasons other than academic research. Ironically, the topic of the accessibility of electroacoustic music has been a subject of investigation for projects such as the Intention/ Reception project (Landy 2006; Weale 2006). The barriers of entry to appreciating electroacoustic music are not just knowledge of the music, but access to this knowledge. If we want electroacoustic music to reach a wider audience, then we do not want the knowledge surrounding it to remain under lock and key.

II. The change of the object of study. The question of what one actually analyses is another potential problem, specifically for cross-media forms of electroacoustic music. Whereas in instrumental music the score was (and in some circles still is) considered the work, the object of study for electroacoustic music, specifically for those forms that rely on fixed media, is also the actual intended musical outcome. Not only does this change the performance practice of the music in comparison to instrumental music, but it also renders many analytical methodologies for score-based music ineffective. A few scholars and methodologies have addressed this change, but more needs to be done to fill the gaps in the field in relation to other electroacoustic musics that incorporate other media within their composition, such as installations or mixed music (live instruments with electroacoustic sounds).

III. Terminology associated with electroacoustic music. The first major milestone for electroacoustic music was to coin a set of terms for the simple purpose of communicating ideas and concepts concerning the new practices and materials of the genre. Many scholars throughout the lifetime of electroacoustic music have tackled this subject. Yet the discussion of terminology surrounding electroacoustic music is still a vehemently contested subject, even to the point where the term *electro-acoustic music* has to be defined within this chapter in order to avoid any confusion with contradictory understandings. Although disagreements regarding methodologies can be healthy, disagreements on terminology mean that discussions do not proceed past the initial semantic meanings of what one is debating.

IV. Emphasis on personal contributions and reputation. The current academic publication system does not encourage collaboration. As researchers we are encouraged to publish our findings within peer-reviewed journals, specifically ones that are considered to be high impact. This is less prevalent within arts and humanities, but there is still a sense that one must publish within a peer-reviewed journal/book in order to advance an academic career.[5] This generates an underlying competitiveness in intellectual property, meaning people are less likely to share their ideas unless there is a perceived personal gain.

V. Lack of interest in musicology. In 1999 Landy wrote 'there still seems to be relatively too little musical analysis of note within the electroacoustic field and, in my view, too few discussions concerning which techniques are appropriate for the analysis of sonic works including those of the popular sorts' (1999: 68). Arguably this has not changed a great deal in the intervening years, as there have only been a few publications that have contributed to the current collection of tools.

VI. The language barrier. Many of the founding research publications, specifically from countries where English in not the first language, is still ignored by countries where English is the first, and generally, the only language. Work has been done to translate Schaeffer's work with a select few scholars assuming this responsibility,[6] yet there is still no translation of Schaeffer's opus *Traité des objets musicaux* (1966).[7] Many English-speaking scholars are isolated from these very important texts and have to depend on English-speaking scholars' summaries to rectify the gaps. This issue of language of course works both ways as many texts written in English create barriers for those who do not speak the language.

Until these issues are addressed in a meaningful way they will continue to hinder the innovation of electroacoustic music analysis. The concept of

---

[5] The phrase 'publish or perish' is often used to describe this ideology.
[6] John Dack and Christine North have made a translation of Chion's book *Guide des objets sonores* (1994), which can be found on the EARS website (www.ears.dmu.ac.uk), as well as Schaeffer's *À la recherche d'une musique concrète* (2012; orig. pub. 1952).
[7] The same team is at work on this text now due for publication 2016.

the analytical community is intended to address all these issues whilst providing potential advantages to the domain. There are two benefits one can foresee from having such an analytical community: open access and wisdom of the crowds.

The analytical community

A community is a group of people who share a similar interest, in this instance electroacoustic music. Many scholars and even organisations use the term *electroacoustic community* to denote this collection of individuals. The proposed analytical community is therefore a subset of individuals within this community who are interested in the analysis of this music. This section will be arguing that a new platform is needed to confront the barriers to development outlined above: one that allows for greater communication and a means to work collaboratively towards a common goal.

The electroacoustic community

The electroacoustic community, although small in comparison to other music communities, is geographically spread across the world providing many different opinions and perspectives on the appropriate approaches to electroacoustic music composition and analysis. Furthermore, the individuals working within this domain often possess a multitude of interdisciplinary traits that range from performers, software developers, sound engineers to scholars. Their focus, however, is on the advancement of electroacoustic music, be it the development of new music, compositional tools/methodologies, analytical tools/methodologies, terminology and so on.

For any community to thrive there needs to be a platform that provides members of the community with the means to communicate with one another and to share ideas. In the case of electroacoustic music, the platform that has satisfied this need up until this point has been the academic music conference/symposium. The concern regarding these forms of communication is that larger international conferences are only held yearly[8] and because of the nature and geographical spread of the

[8] The EMS (Electroacoustic Music Studies Network) and ICMC (International Computer Music Conference) are but two examples of such conferences.

community it can often mean that financial issues prevent some people from attending. Furthermore, there is no specific platform focused on the analysis of electroacoustic music, rather these larger international conferences attempt to cover a wide range of disciplines and studies, which are sometimes focused around a general theme. Smaller regional symposiums allow communities to meet more easily, but these individuals tend to have similar opinions because of their shared interests. Other platforms, such as mailing lists, offer another avenue of communication. However, there is arguably an unspoken hierarchy within such communities, which can hinder independent thought that does not necessarily follow the status quo.

The publication of a paper in an academic journal is another means of communicating concepts and ideas to other likeminded individuals who share the same interest. Concerns have already been raised regarding the limited access for those who are not already part of an organisation or university that subscribes to specific publishers, but this is not the only limitation of this medium. For example, once a paper has been approved and published within an academic journal it cannot be revised. Tapscott and Williams (2006: 152) note that the current archaic peer-review system (specifically within the science domain) cannot keep up with the amount and speed of research currently taking place, meaning that research can often be outdated soon after it is published.[9] This is a major concern for a field that relies heavily on technological advancement, as it can render papers irrelevant within a few years of publication. Another important issue that involves academic journals is the communication between the author and the audience. Unlike an academic conference where an audience member has the option to pose questions to the scholars presenting their research, academic journals only offer one-way communication. If one considers an analysis of a work a means of communicating a perspective, then it would be preferable for readers to be able to have a dialogue with the analyst in order to gain a better understanding of it.

I am not proposing that neither of these avenues work, rather that there are alternatives that could bridge the gap between individuals within a community, whilst tackling the barriers to development of electroacoustic music described in the previous section. With the

---

[9] Although this does not relate directly to arts and humanities subjects, the time needed to review submissions does cause a slow down of information flow, albeit not to the extent it does within the scientific domain.

plethora of possibilities offered through web-based technology, it seems bizarre that the majority of scholarly activity within the electroacoustic community has been through these tried and tested means. The proposed way forward is an amalgamation of community collaboration and open access initiatives.

The proposed way forward: confronting the barriers to development

There are many different avenues one might choose in order to address the development barriers of electroacoustic music analysis. The quickest solution to access is for open access journals[10] to be established or for existing journals to allow for better access (possibly becoming hybrid journals[11]). However, although this does begin to tackle the first of the six development barriers, it does not necessarily address the other five. The other five development barriers are related to semantic and cultural problems that can only be resolved through collaboration and dialogue. The format of peer-reviewed publications, as stated above, does not provide the long-term dialogue needed to address the other five barriers and conferences/symposiums only offer a small window of opportunity to confront these issues.

There is an opportunity to rethink the current academic landscape by expanding it towards collaborative initiatives to harness the untapped potential of the electroacoustic community. The most obvious platform is the Internet, which has already been utilised by other communities, specifically those that work under Creative Commons licences. Such websites provide a platform for practitioners to share and discuss each other's contribution to a knowledge base, which can prove to be very fast and effective. The change in focus can be difficult to grasp for some, as it puts more emphasis on community gain rather than personal gain, hence a change in culture would be necessary. Wikipedia, an online community-created encyclopaedia, is one example of such a site. The question is

---

[10] In Britain there has been a lot of recent activity and recommendations to move from subscription-based journals to open access journals. The reasons are generally financial or to prevent public-funded research being sold by private organisations: some journalists have referred to the current academic model as a 'racket' (Naughton 2012). In June 2012 Dame Janet Finch wrote the report 'Accessibility, sustainability, excellence: how to expand access to research publications', which recommended that journals begin to allow open access to readers by charging the authors of the articles they house.

[11] Hybrid journals allow for the user to access certain articles within a subscription-based structure.

whether or not the electroacoustic community is well suited to work collaboratively towards a particular goal.

Can the electroacoustic community be considered a wise crowd?

In his book *The Wisdom of Crowds* (2004), James Surowiecki outlines four conditions that need to be satisfied in order to facilitate what he terms a 'wise crowd' (2004: 10). The four conditions are:

Diversity of opinion (person should have some private information, even if it's just an eccentric interpretation of known facts), independence (people's opinions are not determined by the opinions of those around them), decentralisation (people are able to specialise and draw on local knowledge), and aggregation (some mechanism exists for turning private judgments into a collective decision).

Although it is clear that the electroacoustic community is diverse, it is important to ensure independence between practitioners in order to prevent homogeneity, which can be commonplace, specifically in small groups.[12] Within the electroacoustic community it could be argued that there exist pockets of small subcommunities (research centres and universities). Even though members within certain subcommunities might have similar opinions, other subcommunities will work independently from them to allow for different perspectives (independence). These subcommunities also ensure that there is no centralised governing body that directs activities, meaning members are able to specialise and build up local knowledge (decentralisation). Bearing all that in mind, the electroacoustic community is a perfect candidate to satisfy three of the four conditions. Satisfying the fourth (aggregation) requires a balance between two imperatives: making individual knowledge globally and collectively useful while still allowing it to remain resolutely specific and local (Surowiecki 2004: 74).

It has already been determined that the electroacoustic community satisfies three of Surowiecki's four conditions of a wise crowd. What is lacking is a platform that could act as an aggregate for the community, one that specifically focuses on addressing the barriers of development in electroacoustic music analysis. A community website that allows for members to share and discuss information could potentially bridge the

---

[12] It is easier to work in groups with other likeminded individuals (also known as cohesive groups) than it is within groups where there are differences of opinion. In cohesive groups decisions can be made because the assumption is that they are right, as there is no one to question the choices (Surowiecki 2004: 36).

gap that both conferences and academic journals miss. There are a few success stories regarding community websites, the most prominent being Wikipedia, which will be discussed now.

Wikipedia: an example of a successful open access community website

Many readers will have come across Wikipedia, as it is ranked as the fifth most popular website in the world (Wikimedia UK 2012: 4).[13] The majority of the content on the website is generated by users, who can apply for an account for free. Articles are added, maintained and cross-referenced with each other, which is all undertaken by what Wikipedia has termed *Wikipedians* (a community of enthusiasts that ensure the quality and relevance of the information being provided by other users). In this instance the community itself, through interaction, peer reviews content on the website. What is also important is that, unlike standard publications, Wikipedia articles can adapt as changes in information occur, meaning information is always relevant at the time of reading an article provided it is being maintained.

There are five main rules (which are referred to as pillars within Wikipedia) for those who wish to contribute to the website. The five pillars of Wikipedia are: Wikipedia is an encyclopaedia; Wikipedia is written from a neutral perspective; Wikipedia is free content that anyone can edit, use, modify and distribute; editors should interact with each other in a respectful and civil manner; and Wikipedia does not have firm rules.[14] Interestingly, the majority of participants that contribute to articles on Wikipedia are approximately aged 25 years old and over 50 per cent of contributors have studied at undergraduate level or higher (Glott *et al.* 2010: 7). What this means is that, in the example of Wikipedia, recent graduates are potentially the biggest demographic that would likely contribute to a community website.

Closing statements

By providing a specific platform for electroacoustic music analysis issues of language (in relation to a taxonomy of terms) and the object of study could

[13] It is important to mention that it is the most visited non-profit site and a great example of an open access initiative that utilises 'wisdom of the crowds' philosophy.
[14] Five pillars taken from www.wikipedia.org/wiki/Wikipedia:Five_pillars

be investigated thoroughly to form a shared understanding of best practice within this field, particularly for other forms of electroacoustic music and not just acousmatic music. This is not to say that there needs to be conformity (as we know homogeneity can stifle progress), far from it. Rather the sharing of different perspectives on issues within this domain might highlight a potential consensus on terminology between practition-ers, whilst providing a platform to undertake applied research on current tools and methodologies.

There are more advantages than just financial benefits to promoting open access initiatives. Open access can broaden the knowledge base of electroacoustic music beyond academia. Although there is diversity within the electroacoustic community, it is made up of specialists and experts. Surowiecki (2004: 30) states that having people within a group who know less, but have different skills, can actually improve a group's performance. There is little incentive for non-experts, at this moment in time, to contrib-ute to the electroacoustic music discussion whilst the barriers of entry are still there. An open access initiative would rectify this. The OREMA project is one example of such an initiative.

The OREMA project

The simplest description of OREMA is that it is a community-based website that functions as a repository for electroacoustic music ana-lyses.[15] All content on the website is user generated (unless referencing external links). It is a non-profit initiative and does not charge users a subscription or submission fee. There is also no peer-reviewed content on the website, instead it permits any user the ability to upload content to the website, provided it is related to the subject of electroacoustic music analysis.[16] All content submitted to the website is maintained under a Creative Commons licence, which allows for adaptations of

---

[15] The OREMA project was part of a three-year funded project titled *New Multimedia Tools for Electroacoustic Music Analysis* (funded by the Arts and Humanities Research Council), which was coordinated by Professor Simon Emmerson and Professor Leigh Landy of De Montfort University, Leicester. The concept of the OREMA project was developed after the funding application and forms part of the original contribution within my PhD research.

[16] The inclusion of a journal section to the website (eOREMA journal) will add the possibility for authors to have their articles peer reviewed by specialists within the field (see section 'Potential changes for the future' (page 167) for more information). Once again this will be free for both authors and readers.

other content as long as it is not for commercial use and the original author is attributed.

Brief history

When first launched in March 2011, the OREMA project existed as a beta website running on MediaWiki,[17] an open source wiki platform. All users of the initial site could edit any page, including the analyses uploaded by others. Although suitable for certain aspects of the OREMA project, most notably the analytical toolbox, it did not lend itself to publishing analyses. It was deemed that a change to a content management system was needed to account for the different areas of the project. In late 2011 the OREMA website changed to Drupal,[18] an open source content management platform.

The original website was a closed beta. Potential participants and universities in the United Kingdom were contacted to invite postgraduate students to be part of the initial testing period.[19] Over 12 participants took part at the beginning of the beta testing whilst other participants joined throughout the rest of the year (these were known as the core participants). Compositions were suggested to the community bimonthly to maintain interest and encourage contributions.[20] After the change in platform to Drupal, the OREMA project opened registration to anyone worldwide and users were encouraged to submit analyses for any electroacoustic composition they wanted.

Ethos and aims

The intention of the OREMA project was to gauge if a community could be formed that would concentrate on the advancement of the analysis of electroacoustic music. Although intended to be open and diverse to allow many different perspectives, five rules were defined to ensure focus and autonomy (much like Wikipedia's five pillars). The rules are as follows:

---

[17] www.mediawiki.org (the most notable website to use this platform is Wikipedia).
[18] www.drupal.org
[19] We chose this demographic as they were the most likely to contribute based on research into other community websites (see section 'Wikipedia', page 156).
[20] A total of four compositions were suggested to the community: *Dripsody* by Hugh Le Caine, *Étude aux chemins de fer* by Pierre Schaeffer, *Presque rien no. 1 C* by Luc Ferrari and *Meattrapezoid* by Merzbow. The reason for the initial choices was to provide a selection of different types of electroacoustic music that were easily found and short in duration.

I. The OREMA project will analyse electroacoustic music in all its guises (acousmatic, sound art, installations, electronica, etc.).

II. There is no one 'true' analysis. The OREMA project encourages the analyst to post analyses of the same composition to show different perspectives.

III. There is no one methodology or strategy for analysis. The analytical toolbox is there for reference and is not a list of the acceptable tools for analysis within the project. Users are allowed to apply their own devised strategies to analyse electroacoustic works.

IV. There is no hierarchy within the OREMA project. All members, regardless of their occupation and status, are equal and share the same rights.

V. All information held on the site is free to access and free for people to reference under the protection of a Creative Commons licence.[21]

Functionality of OREMA

The website is split into three main areas: analyses, the analytical toolbox and a public forum. The analysis section of the website allows users to upload and share analyses of electroacoustic works. There are no rules regarding the type of analysis that is accepted; only that it is an analysis of an electroacoustic work. Only authors and moderators (for administration purposes) have the power to make amendments to an analysis, whilst other users have the option to comment within a comment section on the page. The analytical toolbox is a collection of short articles documenting methodologies and strategies for analysing electroacoustic music. Unlike the analysis section of OREMA, all users have the ability to make amendments to the content, much like Wikipedia articles. The idea is that the entire community will review the information to form a consensus on a shared understanding of each tool. Finally the forum provides a platform for extended discussions beyond the comment section of both analysis and toolbox pages. An image of the current front page of the website can be seen in Figure 7.1.

Drupal allows for administrators of websites to create templates for types of user-generated content. Any content created with these templates by users is automatically sorted into the correct area of the website (something that was not possible with the previous platform, MediaWiki). This means that a user only has to fill out one page of information to upload an analysis or analytical toolbox article.

[21] http://creativecommons.org/

OREMA

Navigation
- Analyses
- Analytical toolbox
- Symposiums
- Forums
- Recent content

User login
Username *

Password *

[Log in]

- Create new account
- Request new password

Information
- About OREMA
- Help
- OREMA googlegroup
- EAnalysis beta
- EARS website
- MTI Research Centre

Quote of the week (week 49)
Tue, 07/24/2012 - 16:50 — mikepatt

Hermeneutic approaches assume that meaning in the larger sense is neither inherent in the object of interpretation nor constructible on the basis of meanings locally encoded in the object; interpretation entails the agency of an interpreter who is more than a decoder, even a creative one (Kramer 2011: 21). KRAMER, L (2011) Interpreting music - California, University of California Press.

Log in or register to post comments

Previous quotes of the week

3rd Symposium videos now online!
Fri, 07/13/2012 - 17:38 — admin

The videos for the 3rd and final analysis symposium held at De Montfort University are now online. You can find them here.

Read more   Log in or register to post comments

Symposium June 20th travel bursaries
Thu, 05/10/2012 - 15:46 — admin

The third Symposium forming part of the AHRC funded project 'New Multimedia Tools for Electroacoustic Music Analysis' (Music, Technology and Innovation Research Centre, De Montfort University, Leicester) takes place on Wednesday 20th June 2012, 10:30am - 5pm. Theme: 'Analysis: application, workshop, discussion'. Included will be a 'hands on' workshop on Pierre Couprie's EAnalysis software as well as analytical presentations. We have up to 6 UK-based train fare bursaries for OREMA participants to come.

[Search]

Recent analyses
- David Hirst's analysis of Smalley's Base Metals
- David Hirst's analysis of Smalley's Wind Chimes
- Robert J. Frank's Étude Aux Chemins De Fer Analysis
- Ben Ramsay's analysis of 'Internal Clock' by Monolake
- Panos Amelides' Meattrapezoid Analysis

New forum threads
- future of OREMA
- SSSP 2012 - 6th and 7th June 2012
- TRAINOFTHOUGHTS
- Logo?
- Visualisation

Who's online
There are currently 0 users online.

Figure 7.1 Front page of the current OREMA website

There are two main templates for the OREMA website: a template for an analysis or an analytical toolbox article. Both operate in a similar manner, but have options specific to that content type. The analysis template grants users the ability to upload files along with a written description. The intention is that this template will account for the vast majority of analyses an analyst can create, from both formalised and non-formalised analyses (Nattiez 1990: 161).[22]

Both analysis pages and analytical toolbox articles record revisions of the content once it has been altered. Users can access this information by clicking the revision tab within the page (see Figure 7.2 for an example). This function allows for two separate actions: authors of content have the ability to revert to a previous version if required and other users, who might not have author rights (this is related to analyses), can view the different versions of a changed document. This highlights the main difference between the analysis section and the analytical toolbox articles. The analysis section is a self-publishing platform in which users can upload an analysis freely for others to see and comment on. The analytical toolbox articles are not intended to be authored in the traditional sense, rather they are collaboratively written by the community. In both cases being able to view past iterations of a publication might offer a great insight into how methodologies are viewed and how understandings change and evolve over time.

Case studies

Since March 2011 to date there has been a total of 12 analyses of seven compositions submitted directly to OREMA with several links to analyses on external websites. The analyses currently hosted on the website range include: graphic transcriptions, typological analyses, spectrogram segmentation using spectromorphological terms (Blackburn 2006) and even a Schenkerian analysis of an acousmatic work (Batchelor 1997). Furthermore, the scope of analysis has not been confined to acousmatic music and has included analyses of electronica (Ramsey 2012) and even an audio-only game (Hugill 2012).

In some instances community interaction has encouraged changes to analyses and allowed others to create analyses that investigate other elements of a

---

[22] Non-formalised analysis can best be described as a written analysis, which Nattiez further divides into three specific styles: impressionistic, paraphrases and hermeneutic readings. Formalised analysis is when one tries to model or simulate the music without using language. This can be achieved by using symbols to illustrate potential schemas within the music.

Revisions for *Michael Gatt's Étude Aux Chemins De Fer Analysis*

View   Edit   Revisions

Revisions allow you to track differences between multiple versions of your content, and revert back to older versions.

Revision	Operations
06/13/2012 - 14:20 by mikegatt	*current revision*
06/13/2012 - 14:19 by mikegatt	revert
06/13/2012 - 14:17 by mikegatt	revert
New version of representation created with EAnalysis.	
02/14/2012 - 14:48 by mikegatt	revert
01/23/2012 - 17:40 by admin	revert
01/23/2012 - 17:39 by admin	revert
12/05/2011 - 12:11 by admin	revert
12/01/2011 - 16:21 by mikegatt	revert

In association with   DE MONTFORT UNIVERSITY LEICESTER   MUSIC, TECHNOLOGY AND INNOVATION RESEARCH CENTRE   and supported by    Arts & Humanities Research Council

Figure 7.2 Example of past revisions of an analysis held on the OREMA website

work. One such example is with my own analysis of *Dripsody* (Gatt 2011a), which was a sound-by-sound aural analysis, and Hill's analysis (Hill 2011) of the same composition, which investigated structural relationships within the piece. *Dripsody* (1955), by Hugh Le Caine, was the first composition to be suggested to the community.[23] To try to encourage others to create an analysis of the work, I submitted an Acousmographe[24] file that visualised individual sounds and their immediate relationships to other events. This meant that the view of the work did not show how these immediate structural relationships affected the larger structure within the piece. Hill commented on this within the comments section of my analysis, stating that it would be beneficial to have an overview of the work as well. Within the month Hill had created another analysis of *Dripsody* that presented an overview of larger structural relationships of the composition. Hill's analysis was not meant to supersede my analysis; rather, it was intended to offer a different perspective. In that respect the two analyses complement each other.

There were a number of assumptions made at the beginning of the project on the types of analyses that would be uploaded. The presumption was that the members would have an understanding of, for example, Denis Smalley's term *spectromorphology* and what it meant. It later transpired that some members had not encountered the terminology and that their expertise was in computer-aided analysis rather than aural analysis (which the majority of analyses on OREMA had been). This meant that some participants did not have the same specialist terminology that we often take for granted, meaning that they needed to borrow terms from other disciplines. Constantinou (2011) offered such an example within his analysis of *Dripsody*. He segmented the work using the drips as a metre. He discovered that the crescendo in the middle of the work coincided with the golden mean ratio. This aspect of the work was not noticed by any other analyst.

There have been two instances where an analyst has made major alterations to an analysis on the website.[25] Figure 7.3 shows two iterations of my analysis (Gatt 2011b) of Pierre Schaeffer's *Étude aux chemins de fer* (1948). I used Schaeffer's typomorphology (Schaeffer 1966) framework to segment sound events by type and to describe their individual morphology.

---

[23] There was no real significance to this choice. However, a conscious decision was made to suggest compositions that were relatively easy to acquire and that were of short duration. This was only within the initial beta stages of the project.

[24] www.inagrm.com/accueil/outils/acousmographe

[25] The other example, which has not been mentioned here, is the change by Hill of his *Dripsody* analysis (Hill 2011). The changes were cosmetic only.

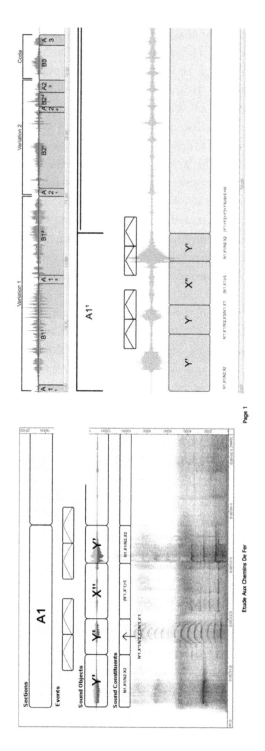

Figure 7.3 An example of the changes of an uploaded analysis on the OREMA website. On the left, the first page of the original analysis and, on the right, the first page of the first major iteration.

The changes made to the analysis were for many reasons, but mainly, in answer to Hill's comment on my *Dripsody* analysis, I decided to present an overview of the piece along with a more detailed view. Furthermore, this allowed me to demonstrate larger structures of the work that previously were not investigated. Colour coding was also added to demonstrate how the typology of sounds, and the changes of this within the piece, affected the overall structure.

Since the OREMA project website functions as a repository of information, it allows analysts to post older analyses of electroacoustic musical works, provided that they are not published anywhere else. If an analysis is published elsewhere, an entry for the analysis with a link to the source can be added to the repository. There are two analyses currently on OREMA that were completed by the analysts initially as part of their undergraduate studies (Batchelor 1997; Blackburn 2006). It just so happens that both the analyses investigate the same composition – Denis Smalley's *Valley Flow* (1992). Each analysis tackles the work in a different way: Batchelor's analysis is a Schenkerian analysis that aims to reduce the work to a fundamental pitch structure, whilst Blackburn's analysis uses Smalley's own spectromorphological terms to describe both foreground and background sounds. These differences in approach inevitably sparked a discussion within the comments section of Blackburn's analysis. Batchelor begun the exchange by saying:

Certainly it draws attention to a great deal of detail which I find myself listening to in a different way when not preoccupied with specific pitch content(!) and the discussion of the interaction between surface and background is useful. The only thing that I remain curious about is how this relates to long-term structure and its perception. I wonder whether some kind of reductive analysis (I suppose I'm bound to propose this since my own was reductive) along these lines would reveal other connections (or consistencies in compositional approach) between foreground and background. (Batchelor quoted from comments section of Blackburn 2006)

Blackburn responded with:

A reductive analysis would be a good idea and natural step forward. This has been the question posed in all the feedback I have received so far on the work and I can see in retrospect how the one-minute segments divert attention away from examining long-term structure. It is interesting that I appear to work in a similar way compositionally – I seem to work more on micro-level detail, leaving larger-scale structuring to a later time. (Blackburn quoted from comments Blackburn 2006)

OREMA is designed to provide not only a means of dialogue between creators of content and readers, but also between analysts that have analysed the same work. Much like the *Dripsody* example above between my analysis (Gatt 2011a) and Hill's (Hill 2011), these two analyses are not meant to be in direct competition, rather they are intended to complement one another and offer different perspectives on the same work.

Another function of a repository, as described by Finch *et al.* (2012: 6), is to provide access to versions of papers either before they are submitted for publication in a journal or at some point after they have been published. Hugill's analysis (Hugill 2012) of the audio-only game *Papa Sangre* (2010) is one example of such an analysis. It was first submitted to the OREMA project, but has since been expanded upon further in this book. It also received praise from one of the creators of the game.[26] The analysis was the first of its kind on OREMA and remains the only analysis that investigates an audio-only game.

What has been learnt?

After an initial flux of activity within the beta stages and the relaunch of the website on a Drupal platform, the frequency of contributions decreased slightly, over the summer of 2012. This is potentially for a multitude of reasons, such as the time of year, but also because many of the core participants were postgraduate students who have since moved on to other projects perhaps more specific to their domain. There was an incentive for some core participants to present their findings at one of the three analysis symposiums,[27] as part of the larger New Multimedia Tools for Electro-acoustic Music Analysis project, but there have not been any opportunities like this since.[28]

The OREMA project is ambitious as, with minimum editorial intervention, it allows any user, who can register for free, the ability to publish their ideas for others to see. The expectation was that the community would act as a peer-review committee by vetting contributions to the site in order to promote excellence. However, not including a recognised peer-review process within the OREMA project has meant that fewer people have been willing to spend their time to contribute to the site. It is particularly hard to galvanise a group of people within academia to work collaboratively towards a common goal without any financial or personal incentive.

---

[26] Discussion between one of the creators of *Papa Sangre* and Hugill outside of the OREMA website: http://allplayall.blogspot.co.uk/2012/02/academic-nightmare.html

[27] Videos of the symposiums can be found on OREMA.

[28] Plans to reignite interest are currently underway, some of which are discussed within the next section.

Unfortunately, the OREMA project exists only as an English website and does not have any translation functionality as of yet. This has inevitably created a barrier to those who perhaps wish to contribute to the project, but are unable to because of language. However, it would be unfeasible to translate all the current content available in English to the many other languages spoken within the electroacoustic community, although there may be a possibility in the future to house content in different languages.

Potential changes for the future

One of the main concerns for OREMA in its current state is the legitimacy of the content submitted. There are no barriers of entry for would-be analysts and scholars. The argument against such initiatives is that they open the floodgates to anyone with an opinion on the subject. Furthermore, the lack of any recognised peer-review group has meant that users have been less willing to spend time on producing content for the website. To rectify this and to add legitimacy to OREMA, a new section of the website was devised to allow for peer-reviewed publications. This new part of OREMA is called the eOREMA journal. A committee of 14 reviewers was assembled and to date two issues of the journal have appeared.

The eOREMA journal is intended to be a biannual publication arm of OREMA that will consist of both peer-reviewed analyses of electroacoustic musical works and peer-reviewed articles on electroacoustic music analysis (something that has not been addressed on the current OREMA website). The hope is not only that this will gain interest from within the electroacoustic community, but also that the interest it gains will filter through to the OREMA website, which will remain the same as detailed above. Users will still have the ability to submit analyses and articles to the toolbox freely without the need of a peer-review committee.

It is imperative that OREMA, including eOREMA, remains as an open access website. Therefore, both OREMA and eOREMA will be freely accessible to all users and there will also be no fee for submitting content.

Conclusion

Electroacoustic music has found a comfortable base within academia and this will continue for the foreseeable future. Advancements will be made, but not at the rate that could conceivably be possible if other alternatives for disseminating information were investigated, such as those that utilise web 2.0 technologies. The OREMA project and similar open access initiatives are not meant to replace the current method, but intend to offer an open access alternative that encourages collaboration. Unless other alternatives are investigated, the barriers to development of electroacoustic music analysis will remain a problem. Furthermore, these new avenues provide more opportunities for collaboration and faster discourse between practitioners, something that is only achieved in conferences and mailing lists.

It is the task of the electroacoustic community to rectify these shortcomings. The only way to address these is to change the culture within electroacoustic music research from publish or perish towards more collaborative ventures. Although OREMA addresses some of the issues raised, it does not consider the entire scope of electroacoustic music research. Other initiatives could conceivably be started that investigate issues concerning composition, programming and cross-art implications, which would ultimately feed specialist knowledge back to the greater community.

References

Batchelor, P. (1997) Peter Batchelor's *Valley Flow* analysis. The OREMA project. www.orema.dmu.ac.uk/?q=content/peter-batchelors-valley-flow-analysis (accessed 27 September 2012).

Bent, I. (1980) Analysis. In S. Sadie (ed.) *The New Grove Dictionary of Music and Musicians Volume 1*. London: Macmillan, 340–88.

Blackburn, M. (2006) Manuella Blackburn's *Valley Flow* analysis. The OREMA project. www.orema.dmu.ac.uk/?q=content/manuella-blackburns-valley-flow-analysis (accessed 27 September 2012).

Chion, M. (1994) *Guide des objets sonores*. Paris: Buchet Chastel.

Constantinou, S. (2011) Stace Constantinou's *Dripsody* analysis. The OREMA project. www.orema.dmu.ac.uk/?q=content/stace-constantinous-dripsody-analysis (accessed 27 September 2012).

Finch, J. *et al.* (2012) Accessibility, sustainability, excellence: How to expand access to research publications. The Research Information Network. www.researchinfonet.org/wp-content/uploads/2012/06/Finch-Group-report-FINAL-VERSION.pdf (accessed 27 September 2012).

Gatt, M. (2011a) Michael Gatt's *Dripsody* analysis. The OREMA project. www.orema.dmu.ac.uk/?q=content/michael-gatts-dripsody-analysis (accessed 27 September 2012).

(2011b) Michael Gatt's *Étude aux chemins de fer* analysis. The OREMA project. www.orema.dmu.ac.uk/?q=content/michael-gatt%E2%80%99s-%C3%A9tude-aux-chemins-de-fer-analysis (accessed 27 September 2012).

Glott, R. *et al.* (2010) Wikipedia survey – overview of results. UNU-MERIT. www.wikipediasurvey.org/docs/Wikipedia_Overview_15March2010-FINAL .pdf (accessed 27 September 2012).

Hill, A. (2011) Andrew Hill's *Dripsody* analysis. The OREMA project. www.orema .dmu.ac.uk/?q=content/andrew-hills-dripsody-analysis (accessed 27 September 2012).

Hugill, A. (2012) Andrew Hugill's *Papa Sangre* analysis. The OREMA project. www.orema.dmu.ac.uk/?q=content/andrew-hugills-papa-sangre-analysis (accessed 27 September 2012).

Landy, L. (1999) Reviewing the musicology of electroacoustic music: A plea for greater triangulation. *Organised Sound*, 4(1), 61–70.

(2006) The Intention/Reception project. In M. Simoni (ed.) *Analytical Methods of Electroacoustic Music.* London: Routledge.

Nattiez, J.-J. (1990) *Music and Discourse: Toward a Semiology of Music.* Princeton University Press.

Naughton, J. (2012) Academic publishing doesn't add up. *Guardian*, 22 April. www.guardian.co.uk/technology/2012/apr/22/academic-publishing-monopoly-challenged (accessed 27 September 2012).

Ramsey, B. (2012) Ben Ramsay's analysis of *Internal Clock* by Monolake. The OREMA project. www.orema.dmu.ac.uk/?q=content/ben-ramsays-analysis-%E2%80%98internal-clock%E2%80%99-monolake (accessed 27 September 2012).

Roy, S. (2003) *L'analyse des musiques életroacoustiques: Modèles et propositions.* Paris: L'Harmattan.

Schaeffer, P. (1966) *Traité des objets musicaux.* Paris: Éditions du Seuil.

(2012) *In Search of a Concrete Music.* Trans. John Dack and Christine North. Los Angeles: University of California Press (orig. pub. *À la recherche d'une musique concrète*, 1952).

Smalley, D. (1986) Spectro-morphology and structuring processes. In S. Emmerson (ed.) *The Language of Electroacoustic Music.* London, Macmillan, 61–93.

(1997) Spectromorphology: Explaining sound-shapes. *Organised Sound*, 2(2), 107–26.

Surowiecki, J. (2004) *The Wisdom of Crowds.* London: Abacus.

Tapscott, D. and Williams, A. (2006) *Wikinomics.* London: Atlantic Books.

Weale, R. (2006). Discovering how accessible electroacoustic music can be: The Intention/Reception project. *Organised Sound*, 11(2), 189–200.

Wikimedia UK (2012) Wikimedia UK annual report 2011–12. Kingston upon Thames: PDC Copyprint. http://upload.wikimedia.org/wikipedia/commons/ b/be/Wikimedia_UK_AR_2012_web.pdf (accessed 10 September 2012).

8 | EAnalysis: developing a sound-based music analytical tool

Introduction

Analysing electroacoustic music is always difficult. Mostly works do not have a visual support or score and when the music has a score (e.g. mixed music), the electronic part is usually written as a form of code and understanding relations between the signs and sound is complex. This is why most musicians use graphic representation to analyse electroacoustic music, to create spatialisation scores, or to transmit knowledge to their students. Also composers use sketches to elaborate forms or structures or to memorise their works during the creative process.

Acousmatic music is not representative of current electroacoustic music. A lot of musicians use live electronics, improvisation, and other arts – such as video, sound sculpture, poetry – where technical means are an important part of the work, and recording these performances is very difficult. A stereophonic sound file alone cannot define the work. Many current electroacoustic works are allographics (Genette 1997), and are defined by different recordings of different performances, multitrack recordings of different instruments/devices, video recordings, scores, data from different devices, and so on. Electroacoustic means and electronic instruments are hybrid and modular. Analysing an electroacoustic performance is a real challenge because you may need to use a range of software to segment sound material, compare various data in different formats, analyse interactions between musicians through movie recordings, and create representations of structures and relations between parts or elements of the performance. Moreover, most software is not compatible – there is no standard exchange format.

Enhancing analytical software is very important but enhancing representation is also essential. To analyse various types of data, we need to create suitable representations: sound representation, line and form/ structure charts, graphic representation of units or moments. These representations also need to integrate images or other representations of performance, even from the creative process itself. Representation in electroacoustic music analysis is not only a graphic representation with beautiful shapes in various colours, each of them representing a sound. Representation can also include sonograms, curve charts of audio descriptors, representation of interaction message lists between musician and computer, tables with time cues, structure representations, space motions, or relations between image and sound in video music.

EAnalysis[1] was created to fill the gaps that exist between various analysis software applications. EAnalysis cannot do everything musicologists, teachers, or musicians want. It is a workspace where the user can create representations, import data from other software or recorded during performance, and analyse them. I did not reinvent the wheel; this piece of software offers the possibility to import data and to export analyses in different formats. It is based on another program, iAnalyse, which was created for written music analysis. But EAnalysis is very different because the main support of iAnalyse is the score and the main support of EAnalysis is the sound.

This chapter presents the development of EAnalysis from three angles. The first is representation and its role in music analysis. The second is new concepts introduced by the software. The final angle presents the most important features of EAnalysis through presenting different examples.

Analysis with graphic representation

Role of graphic representation in musical analysis

Musical analysis generates representations (Chouvel 2011): of form, structures, relations between various elements, representations with or without time, etc. Musicologists need representations to analyse or to present their analyses. Several theories of analysis are also based on representations such as Schenkerian reduction, paradigmatic segmentation, or various representations of harmony. Representation is important for musical analysis because this is a study of a time art. Humans need to write time down to capture the ephemeral moment and study it. For example a representation of structural segmentation in a formal diagram can reveal new points of view on musical structures. Analytical representation is always a reduction of the musical process. It focuses on one or several musical parameters to reveal internal or external relationships between them. In a pedagogical field, analytical representation can also reveal implicit relations or structural processes.

---

[1] EAnalysis is available from http://eanalysis.pierrecouprie.fr.

One of the particularities of electroacoustic music is to have no (or to have incomplete) visual support. Mixed music uses a score with various symbols or graphic shapes to represent the electronic part. These symbols can represent a number of preset, simple text indications of sound transformation, or graphic shapes representing a reduction of the electroacoustic part. All these have great importance for the musician and/or technical assistant. Musicologists and musicians can also use them to analyse the work, to understand the musical ideas of the composer, or to reconstruct the creative process. Teachers can use them to understand the work and to prepare presentations for their students. But these texts, symbols, or graphic reductions are limited to what the composer wants to give you, to what he thinks important to perform his work. These indications are important for analysing the work but they are not in themselves an analysis.

Analysing a work means understanding complex relations between parts/moments/units and revealing something difficult to perceive through simple listening. The most important goal of analysis is to give you keys to understand music. Students need these keys to understand how the composer works or to create their own music. Teachers need these keys to present work to their students and to move their ears to what they need to hear. Musicologists need these keys to develop their own theory of music, to create links between different works, or simply to understand aspects of a work. These keys cannot exist only in thought: you have to record them through text, simple graphics, or more elaborated graphic representations. Moreover, these records are also very important for memory. With them, you can memorise, anticipate, link moments of a work even if they are not close, and navigate inside one or several works.

Graphic or text representations are important to study and understand electroacoustic music (Couprie 2009). But there is also another aspect, the transmission of knowledge: how a teacher can transmit to his students an analysis of electroacoustic music; how a researcher can transmit his analysis or his music theory; how a student can share experiences of listening to a work. For many different reasons, graphic/text representations are a good solution to sharing and publishing analysis. Interactive examples of electroacoustic music created with sonogram/waveforms and graphic/text representations are more efficient at communication than a simple reference to an extract of an audio track.

How to create a graphical representation

How to create a graphic/text representation depends on what you want to do with it (Couprie 2006). If you need to guide your students inside a work,

Figure 8.1 Iconic versus symbolic graphic representation

maybe it is better to use iconic graphics. Links between music properties and iconic graphics are easier to understand. Listeners will not need any explanation or key to associate particular aspects of music and graphic shapes. Figure 8.1 shows two types of representation: an iconic shape that represents the dynamic part of the sound and a symbolic shape that represents the sound type. I used the second in a representation of a work by Alain Savouret (Couprie 2000). The colour of the shape represented the level of sound transformation and the form of the shape represented the sound type. I decided to use symbolic rather than iconic representations because the structure of the work is very formal, a theme and variations. Demonstrating how the composer used sound transformations to structure his work seemed to be easier using symbolic representation.

If you need to communicate complex analysis with a number of different parameters, you need to associate iconic and symbolic representations. The iconic part allows the representation of significant moments or saliences of musical flow. With the symbolic part (text or graphics), you can represent numerous sonic properties, structural layers, musical functions, or very detailed analysis of moments. This takes more time but a key to understand it is a good complement to the iconic part.

The symbolic part also allows the analyst to represent several points of view. Placing side-by-side different interpretations of structure or different segmentations of musical flow is a good way to transmit complex relationships or indeterminate aspects of analysis (Roy 2003).

One last point I want to make concerns the aesthetic aspect of graphic representation. Do we need to be neutral or do we authorise an aesthetic look to the graphics without links with the music? Once again, this aspect depends on what you want to do with your graphic representation. If representation is only to analyse or is only a part of your research process, you do not need to consider this question. But if you have to communicate your analysis to a range of different people, maybe you have to consider further the communicational aspect of your work. For a paper on Luc Ferrari, I realised graphic representations (Teruggi and Couprie 2001) that are very close to artistic or pedagogical realisations. These representations were an experiment to extend the borders of analysis by representation.

EAnalysis: new concepts for analysis and graphic representation

Applications and limitations of current software

As I have developed in several papers, creating a graphic representation of electroacoustic music is complex. Complex because analysis is complex: you have to determine a point of view, you have to learn the work in depth, you have to extract significant aspects and link them to others in the work or in other works. The process of analysis of electroacoustic music is like discovering a new landscape without knowing the right way forward – and there is no right way. Very often, you have to change direction or to start again in a different direction. Knowing the final direction when you start the analysis is very rare.

Using software to analyse electroacoustic music is important because you need to learn about properties of sounds, to validate your listening or to help your listening when the musical flow is too complex. Maybe it will be useful to mask some sounds or to change the gain of other sounds to understand the different layers of the music. Several software programs are very useful for this. There are four categories:

1. Software to manipulate audio by filtering, changing gain, or changing pitch: Audiosculpt[2] and SPEAR[3] are perfect examples for that. Both of

---

[2] Audiosculpt is developed by IRCAM and is available through the Forum: http://forumnet.ircam.fr.
[3] SPEAR is free software developed by Michael Klingbeil: www.klingbeil.com/spear/.

them are analysis/synthesis software. Audiosculpt was developed for composers to sculpt the sound. With SPEAR, you can extract formants and manipulate them individually. These programs are complex to use but very important for musicologists who want to work on sound. They can extract parts of a complex spectrum and thus focus their analysis on specific sound properties.

2. Software to extract data from sound: Audiosculpt and Sonic Visualiser[4] (with Vamp plug-ins) are good examples. Sonic Visualiser uses the Vamp plug-ins to extract audio descriptors such as spectral centroid, inharmonicity, energy, etc. These descriptors help researchers to isolate individual sound characteristics as clues for musical analysis.

3. Software to annotate or to create graphic representations: Sonic Visualiser, ASAnnotation,[5] MetaScore,[6] Acousmographe,[7] or Flash/Multimedia sketches. Creating Flash or HTML5 animation is a good option for multimedia publications but this needs coding and complex development. Then, other software such as Acousmographe or MetaScore are good compromises. Unfortunately, MetaScore is not publicly available: this software was developed for the library of Cité de la Musique (Paris) and is only used for internal publications. If you only need to annotate (e.g. to add small texts (markers) to a sound), then you can also use Sonic Visualiser or ASAnnotation.

4. Software-oriented musical analysis: Acousmographe with the Aural Sonology Plug-In,[8] Acousmoscribe,[9] and TIAALS.[10] The first two packages contain tools to describe and represent sounds with an augmented version of Pierre Schaeffer's sound object theory (Thoresen 2007; Di Santo 2009). TIAALS focuses on sound material analysis and realisation of typological, paradigmatical or other analytical charts.

---

[4] Sonic Visualiser is developed by the Centre for Digital Music at Queen Mary University of London: www.sonicvisualiser.org. Sonic Visualiser uses Vamp plug-ins: www.vamp-plugins.org.

[5] ASAnnotation is a free software based on Audiosculpt and developed by IRCAM: http://recherche.ircam.fr/anasyn/ASAnnotation/.

[6] MetaScore is developed by Olivier Koechlin (2011).

[7] Acousmographe is developed by INA-GRM: www.inagrm.com/accueil/outils/ acousmographe.

[8] Aural Sonology Plug-In is developed by INA-GRM from Lasse Thoresen's research: www.inagrm.com/aural-sonology-plugin-0.

[9] Acousmoscribe is developed by SCRIME from ideas by Jean-Louis Di Santo: http://scrime.labri.fr.

[10] TIAALS is developed by the University of Huddersfield and Durham University: www.hud.ac.uk/research/researchcentres/tacem/.

These categories are of course not limited to these specific software packages. I only presented here the most advanced or useful software to analyse electroacoustic music.

Unfortunately, these software packages have limitations:

- They cannot analyse audio-visual files, they only use sound files, and most of them only stereophonic files. Video music and multitrack works are very common in electroacoustic music. Moreover, video is a good support to analyse performance.
- Several of them cannot export their data to readable files or import data from other software. There is no format to exchange analysis data between them but nevertheless, analysing electroacoustic music requires the use of several software applications from the extraction of data to creating representations.
- The interface is often limited and not adapted for musical studies. For example, there is no possibility to navigate inside a file and to compare different moments of a work or of different works.
- While they have interesting features (such as the Timbre Scope of Acousmographe or drawing of audio descriptor values on the sonogram with Sonic Visualiser), most of them are difficult to use in some contexts (e.g. with a long work, without the possibility to filter data, or to synchronise with a graphic representation).

To this list of software, I have to add programs for interactive analysis. Several musicologists have published realisations that are closed software, proposing interactive experiences or musical material for the reader. Michael Clarke has published several analyses as standalone software applications (Clarke 2012). Even if these realisations are not exactly software because the user cannot use them to analyse other pieces, the interactive parts are very complex and seem to consist of small applications to explore the composer's musical researches. In the field of creative process analysis, IRCAM has published several CD-ROMs such as those on Philippe Manoury (Battier *et al.* 2003) and Roger Reynolds (McAdams and Battier 2005). These CD-ROMs contain analysis and musical material from the specific work. Readers can use them to create their own analysis.

This short presentation of the most common software used in analytical research demonstrates that current packages offer a huge array of possibilities to the researcher. Each software application is focused on very specific and powerful features. Unfortunately, most of them were not developed by or with musicologists. They are not the result of the study of musical analysis workflow. Analysing music requires some useful features that these software packages do not integrate.

EAnalysis: towards a new tool for electroacoustic music analysis

If these limitations were not so important 15 or 20 years ago, they are more problematic to study more recent electroacoustic music. This is why I decided to reverse the method and to develop EAnalysis in a different way:

- To develop software suitable for musicologists and musicians – while not only for them they are the primary targets.
- Not to reinvent the wheel – for example, there already exists good software to realise data extraction from sound, so use their results but do not redevelop them.
- To develop a useful player for electroacoustic music – to navigate and compare different moments of a work or of different works, to play different tracks of a multitrack work, to use audio-visual or image files.
- To create analytic/text/graphic tools for the study of music. Simply to create software with beautiful graphic tools to draw anything you want may not be useful to realise a graphic representation. Musicologists, students, teachers, even children need very specific tools to create a music representation during the time of listening or very quickly after.
- To develop specific analytic tools using analytic tags or an interface to compare analyses. Moreover, analytic tools have to be linked to graphic tools.
- To analyse, we need to present and manipulate various values. This is not always possible with a simple two-dimensional view; we need to use them in different kinds of view to create augmented representations.
- Finally, I wanted to create a laboratory to experiment with new types of representation, and new tools without any limits.[11]

Various limitations of other software had to be resolved with EAnalysis:

- Projects in EAnalysis would be able to use one or several audio-visual files.
- EAnalysis would interact with other software through import/export features.
- The interface would be developed to study sound and music, not only to play a sound file like a very simple player.
- Each feature would be well configured not to be limited to a specific context.

This list of goals is the result of several years of research. I have used various software packages in my papers and experimented with them for

---

[11] This is why several of them are not finalised and need further research to be accomplished.

musical analysis. Unfortunately, musicology rarely integrates digital developments but nevertheless to study recent electroacoustic composition and to go beyond common representation/analysis are very important goals for research.

Inside the development of EAnalysis

From iAnalyse Studio to EAnalysis

The development of EAnalysis was a long process. The project 'New Multimedia Tools for Electroacoustic Music Analysis' started in October 2010 but EAnalysis is in part the result of my previous research. Over several years around 2006, I developed a first piece of software, iAnalyse,[12] which was a presentation application for musicians. It contained slides and graphic shapes much like PowerPoint but each of them could be synchronised to an audio-visual file. iAnalyse was perfectly adapted to the presentation of written music. The user could annotate a score, create a playhead to help the following of the score and create simple animations for musicologists or teachers. Around 2008, I imagined a development of this idea to extend it with analytical tools. In 2008, I presented new features to the EMS Conference that included possibilities to analyse electroacoustic music. Annotations were based on Lasse Thoresen's system (Thoresen 2007) and were used with a sonogram. This first presentation was very incomplete and worked only as a simulated part of iAnalyse. Then, I started research to create a system of annotation that was more open and that included other analytical theories. Indeed, soundscape analysis (Schafer 1994), spectromophology (Smalley 1997), Temporal Semiotic Units (Hautbois 2013), functions (Roy 2003), or language grid (Emmerson 1986) are good examples of what an analytical software package must include. Finally the 'New Multimedia Tools for Electroacoustic Music Analysis' project started and we decided to create a separate piece of software instead to include the electroacoustic analytic tools already inside iAnalyse.

During these years of research, I realised that to create tools for electroacoustic music analysis needs very specific thought and solutions for analysis. Then, I needed to re-think the current tools. I followed three main ideas:

[12] iAnalyse Studio is available as free software: http://ianalyse.pierrecouprie.fr.

- Analysis of electroacoustic music involves starting with analysis, not with drawing. Drawing is the final step and it should be possible to automate the mapping between analytic and graphical parameters.
- Analysis is a great tool to understand music and concerns not only musicologists. One of the aims of the 'New Multimedia Tools for Electroacoustic Music Analysis' project was to create a toolbox for different types of users. The software must offer a range of strategies adapted to very different types of music, users and habits.
- Analysis means to use and to link various different research and results, so the software must be able to import and export data from and to other software. Moreover, users must be able to exchange part of a work, and develop libraries or a whole analysis.

Some of these ideas have been realised in EAnalysis as it exists at the time of writing, others have yet to be developed to be more efficient. But research has been started and if EAnalysis is only a laboratory for these ideas, it is a substantial laboratory for future developments.

Associating various points of view

One of the most important goals of EAnalysis is to represent several parameters or values at the same time. In previous research, I demonstrated the difficulty of representing more than four analytic parameters in the same representation (Couprie 2009). Common graphic representation uses x/y-axes and shapes to represent sound parameters:

- X-axis usually represents time position and time duration.
- Y-axis usually represents a pitch or frequency range.
- Morphology of shape is used to represent amplitude of the sound.
- The analyst can also use colour and texture to represent frequency range, grain, or structural level.

Figure 8.2 represents the beginning of a piece by Alain Savouret. I worked on a graphical representation of this piece for the CD-ROM *La musique électroacoustique* by INA-GRM (Couprie 2000) and this new representation is based on it. The space of Figure 8.2 allows the representation of several parameters of sound:

- X-axis – time position and time duration.
- Y-axis – panoramic position indicated by letters R, C, L for right, centre and left.

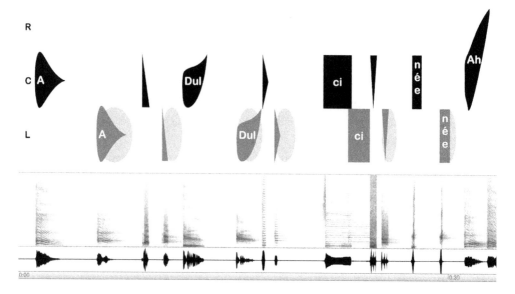

Figure 8.2 Graphic representation of the beginning of *Dulcinea*, extract from *Don Quichotte Corporation* by Alain Savouret

- The morphology of shape is used to represent type of sound and/or amplitude morphology.
- Colour represents sound transformation – black is original sound, grey is original sound with filter processing, and the light grey ellipse is reverberation.

This graphic representation is very simple but we can observe an important point. Graphic representation is a good tool to represent listening characteristics of sound (type, space position, transformation) and implicit musical aspects (rhythm and duration, structural construction). Moreover, associated graphics, waveform and sonogram allow us to represent more parameters (pitches, range of spectrum, intensity variations).

Is it possible to create a complex graphic representation that will associate the information of these three representations?

Adding more parameters demands more dimensions to extend the graphic representation. Use of 3D causes two important problems:

- The listener misses precision. Distinguishing exact positions between different shapes becomes complex.
- 3D adds only one further dimension for one parameter. How can we add more parameters?

Another issue is to create different kinds of representations within only one analysis. Musicologists need to change their point of view without recreating their graphic representation. Current software is limited because analysis is created through drawing: you segment sound material and analyse structure by drawing shapes. Changing point of view or creating another representation with time and frequency positions of shape you have already created demands a redraw, a new representation. This limitation can be removed by disconnecting analysis from drawing. EAnalysis offers the possibility to create analytic events with time and frequency positions. The analytic part of the event consists of several analytic properties that you have created for your analysis. After you analyse, you decide how shapes are drawn. A system of rules, such as in style sheets, allows associating analytic properties to graphic properties. Events contain three types of properties: bound, that is, the global frame properties; graphic, that contain all properties for drawing; and analytic, that are optional properties to list any kind of analytic description of sound. These events are drawn in a time view from bound and graphic properties. But the user has the possibility to change any bound and graphic properties from graphic, or analytic properties.

This system is powerful and allows working with several strategies:

- Creating a common graphic representation without analytic properties and without rules.
- Creating a common graphic representation with analytic properties and drawing different types of representation, different types of analysis.
- Focusing on analysis by working with analytic properties – drawing simple shapes (e.g. a rectangle), adding analytic properties and deciding afterwards how they will be drawn.

Tools for different types of users

Working with different types of users at different levels is one of the aims of the project 'New Multimedia Tools for Electroacoustic Music Analysis'. EAnalysis integrates this possibility in three parts: modes, types of view, and types of event.

Modes

EAnalysis integrates three modes: normal, add text and drawing. These modes allow the user to create events with different tools. Normal mode is the default mode. The user adds an event by 'drag and drop' from a preformatted list or from his own library to the view. With add text mode, the user enters text during playback and can annotate audio-visual files with words or sentences. Each part of the text is an event and the user can switch to normal mode to change its graphic properties. This mode is realised for analysts who prefer to work with text or for simple annotations of ideas during the first listening. Drawing mode is for users who prefer to draw with mouse, graphic tablet, or interactive whiteboard. This mode is very useful to create very simple annotations on a white page, to highlight a sonogram, or to work on a whiteboard while listening with children. Moreover, if the user uses a graphic tablet, pressure is detected and might be used to create artistic drawing like calligraphy.

These three modes were the first features that were developed to respond to various users and were not created as individual elements but as part of a global architecture.

Views

The user can create several types of view. These are used to edit and/or show events, images or other data:

- *Time view* is the most important view. The background contains waveform, linear or logarithmic sonogram, layers of sonograms, differential sonogram (Chouvel *et al.* 2007), image, or colour. The middleground shows imported data from other software such as audio descriptors with curve charts. The foreground shows markers and graphic events. The user creates graphic representations with this view.
- *Image view* displays slideshows of images. For example, pictures taken during a performance or a soundwalk can be synchronised with the sound recording.
- *Map view* is used to create a chart from extracts of audio files. These extracts are represented by sonogram, waveform, events or colour and can be linked with lines like a mind map.
- *Structure view* shows linear structures with different representations – linear, formal diagram, arc diagram to display patterns, similarity matrix.
- *Video view* displays the image of movie files.

Views are stacked in a vertical axis. Time position can be synchronised or not. Unsynchronised time allows the comparing of different time positions or different track positions in the same piece, or in different pieces.

With EAnalysis, the user can associate different types of view. Figure 8.3 displays two types of view (from bottom to top):

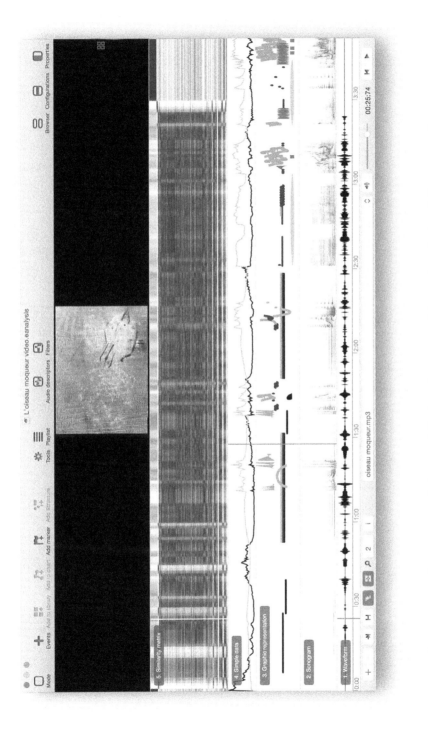

Figure 8.3 *L'oiseau moqueur* by François Bayle (animated film by Robert Lapoujade). EAnalysis displays different types of view: five time views, and video view.

1. Five time views – waveform of the whole piece, sonogram, graphic representation, chart with data (audio descriptors), similarity matrix from audio descriptors.
2. A video view with animated film by Robert Lapoujade (Bayle 2013).

Associating different views creates a complex representation to study or present results of an analysis.

Figure 8.4 displays another example of complex representation. The piece *NoaNoa* by Kaija Saariaho for flute and electronics is structured around a root cell of two notes. All other segmented micro-structures can be analysed with a paradigmatic chart. This figure represents three views (from bottom to top):

1. The sonogram.
2. The paradigmatic chart of the opening with three units (y-axis) displayed in time (x-axis).
3. The score of this opening extract.

The chart view allows the creation of any kind of chart from extracts of audio files. Blocks of colour, waveform, sonogram, or graphic events represent these extracts. Blocks can be linked and positioned on a white view. In this example, positions represent units and time, but blocks are movable in any direction. The user can select a block and play the corresponding extract or visualise what block is under the playhead when playing the whole piece.

Figure 8.5 shows different types of structure representations (from bottom to top):

1. *Linear structure* shows segmentation in a classical manner but colours can be mapped to time duration or title of units.
2. *Formal diagram* highlights novelty and repetitions of units.
3. *Arc diagram* represents patterns by linking similar sets of units.
4. *Similarity matrix* is computed from titles of units and reveals similarity between different parts of the structure.

Figure 8.6 uses a chart and similarity matrix to represent data imported from Sonic Visualiser. Because visualisation of data is important to extract similarity and singularities for musical analysis, EAnalysis also offers other possibilities to create representations from data. Figure 8.6 presents five types of graphs (from bottom to top):

1. A *similarity matrix* does not show values but similarities between values (black represents similarities and white non-similarities).

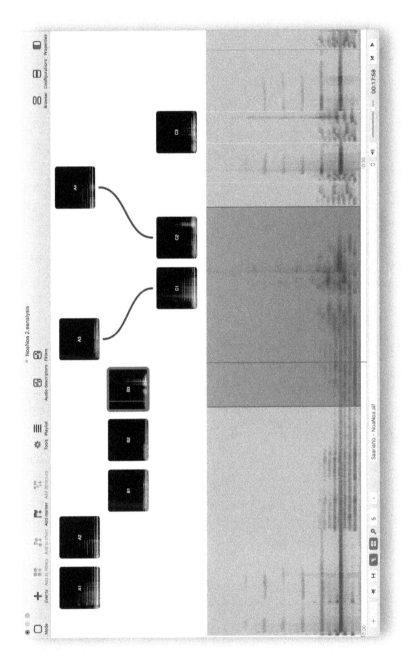

Figure 8.4 Sonogram and paradigmatic chart of beginning of *NoaNoa* by Kaija Saariaho

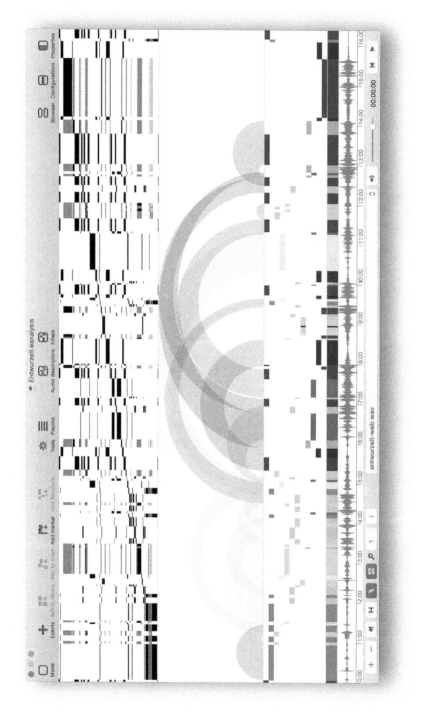

Figure 8.5 Different types of structure representations (from bottom to top:) linear, formal diagram, arc diagram, similarity matrix

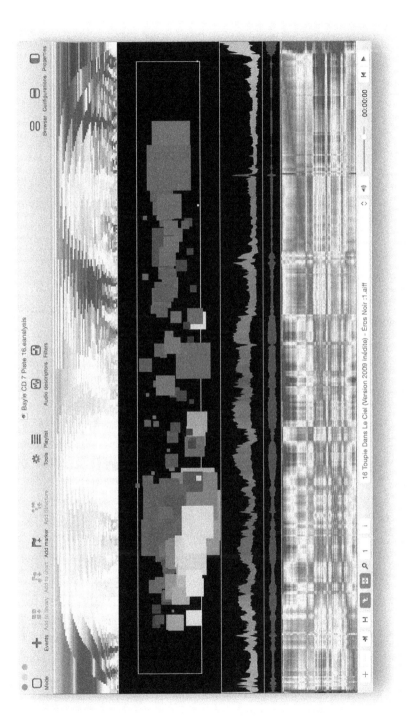

Figure 8.6 Different types of representation of data (from bottom to top:) similarity matrix, simple chart (mirrored line), BStD chart, point cloud chart, hierarchical correlation plot

2. Simple chart to represent data in a very simple way.
3. A BStD chart (Malt and Jourdan 2015) represents evolution of timbre from three audio descriptors in only one line: spectral centroid (Y), spectral variance (height) and intensity (gradient of colours).
4. A cloud of points can represent five data (X, Y, size, colour, opacity). EAnalysis uses one or more charts in cloud point to represent data from different tracks to help in comparative analysis.
5. A *hierarchical correlation plot* (Collective 2009) represents correlation between two sets of data from different levels of structure.

These four examples demonstrate possibilities in terms of analysing, teaching, or communicating with EAnalysis. Different configurations of view can also be saved in the same project.

Events

Because events contain three types of property, they can be used for different strategies and with different levels of complexity:

1. Graphic events are very simple shapes such as are available in every drawing software application: rectangle, ellipse, text, polygon, image, etc. This level is adapted to first annotations of the piece before analysis, working at listening with children, or creating beautiful graphic representations.
2. Analytic events are preformatted shapes for analysis. Each event contains a graphic shape and one or more analytic parameters. Working with preformatted analytic events is a good starting point for students to learn musical analysis or specialists to apply existing theories.
3. Users can also create their own analytic events with personalised analytic parameters. This level is highly flexible, allowing the user to adapt representation and analytic segmentation to the analysed work or to a personalised analytical theory.

Figure 8.7 is three extracts of an EAnalysis interface: an example of a selected event and its graphical and analytical properties. Graphical properties contain three groups of parameters (graphic, text and advanced) and are very close to graphic software. Analytical properties are key-value pairs of parameters.

EAnalysis contains fifteen preformatted analytic parameters (sound objects, spectromorphologies, language grid, space, etc.) and users can add their own parameters and group them into a list and library to share

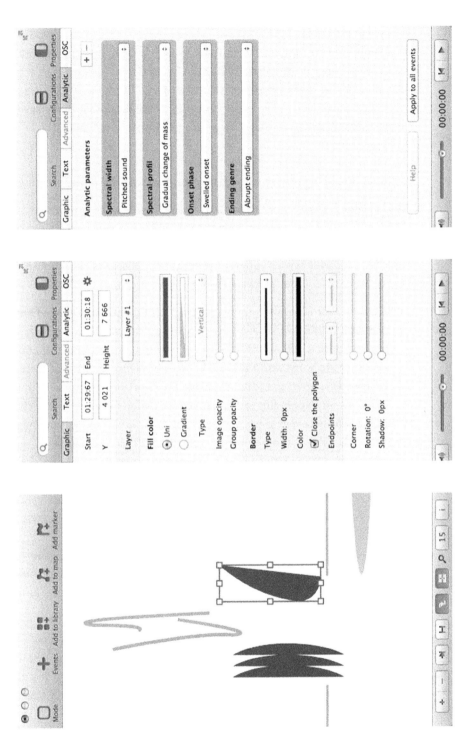

Figure 8.7 A selected event (left) and its graphical (centre) and analytical (right) properties

with other users. The interface to edit events and manage their properties is simple and flexible.

Events are also completed with markers. Markers are only time positions with simple graphic properties. They can be used to annotate ideas on first listening, or to mark breaks or structure parts. Events and markers are editable in time view. This is why time view is the default view to visualise, listen and edit analyses. Other views are to display other data.

Import, export, share works with communities, and communicate

As explained above, modern software must be able to communicate with other software. Musicologists do not work with only one application, they use different software to prepare audio files, to create representations, or to analyse data with several different procedures. EAnalysis can import and export data from other software through four categories of files:

1. **Audio-visual file** is the root file from which the project is created and a common export format. EAnalysis creates a project from a monophonic or stereophonic audio or video file. The user can also import other audio-visual files to work with multitrack pieces or compare different pieces.
2. **Image file** is used to create an image event or slideshow inside image view. As an export file format, image is useful to create a key (with export selected event as image feature) or to export an analysis to images.
3. **Text file** is a common format to exchange various types of data. EAnalysis uses this to import a list of time cues (to create markers), time value pairs (to create curves in data view), or graphic representations (from ProTools information sessions or Acousmographe XML export). It can also export lists of events and markers to analyse or use in other software such as Open Music, Max, Excel.
4. EAnalysis has also two types of format: **eanalysis** project and **ealibrary**. Both of them allow the user to share analyses with or without media files (if copyright does not allow that) as well as an event library including personalised analytic parameters.

The fourth point is very important for the 'New Multimedia Tools for Electroacoustic Music Analysis' project. To share their work or research with other communities is the main activity of the musicologist or musician. With the OREMA website,[13] Michael Gatt aims to enhance sharing

[13] Online Repository for Electroacoustic Music Analysis: www.orema.dmu.ac.uk.

works and tools, and to develop theory discussion around musical analysis of electroacoustic music. EAnalysis offers two formats to share projects (with or without media) and theoretical research (analytical event library).

In parallel with file exchange data, the current version of EAnalysis can also use the LibXtract plug-in and SuperVP[14] to compute audio descriptors and modification of gain. The workflow (export from one application to import in EAnalysis) is reduced to some actions inside EAnalysis that use command line tools to communicate with both technologies. The LibXtract plug-in offers the computation of about 40 audio descriptors and SuperVP allows us to transform the gain within spectrum areas drawn with graphical events.

Perspectives

With import/export data, EAnalysis can be defined as a workspace. Because it is difficult to create a real synergy between different software applications, allowing the user to exchange data is essential. It increases research in musicology and the power of each piece of software. The first step of development was to offer a large range of possibilities; the second step will be demonstrating them through the realisation of different examples and increasing them by adding new features.

One part of the perspective of EAnalysis development is to show how to use it with other software such as in Figure 8.3, which uses data from Sonic Visualiser. Visualisation of data is a powerful feature of EAnalysis – any kind of lists that contain time-value pairs of data may be visualised.

The second part of the perspective will be adding new software compatibilities. The list presented in the section 'Applications and limitations of current software' (pages 174–6) contains common software used in musical analysis but musicologists use also other software such as statistical applications or software used in musical production. EAnalysis needs to integrate these other applications and maybe new types of view to represent their data. These perspectives are very exciting but also very complex, indeed not possible in several cases, because some software uses a specific format with particular representations. As I mentioned, there does not exist a compatible format to exchange data: only software that uses text formats (text, XML, JSON) can currently be used in EAnalysis. EAnalysis was developed to facilitate adding new types of view. But as discussed in

---

[14] SuperVP is a technology developed at IRCAM to compute spectrum and time transformation. Audiosculpt is based on SuperVP.

the section 'Associating various points of view' (pages 179–181), new types of representation have to emerge from needs.

EAnalysis answers to the need for a multipurpose tool for electroacoustic music analysis. Of course, this workspace gives new possibilities by working with many types of data and creating representations with them, but EAnalysis is also a classical piece of software because it works with historical theories of analysis. Musicology needs also to go beyond these simple perspectives. During the development of EAnalysis, some decisions were difficult because I realised that several steps were important but the method appeared outdated and there was a need to restart and go beyond the original aim. The best example is events. In EAnalysis, events are objects with a border (e.g. time and frequency) but are adapted to specific analytical strategies. A lot of recent electroacoustic music works are very complex in terms of media or musical realisation and cannot be analysed with bordered or static objects. Another example of an EAnalysis limitation is the representation of sound. The software proposes different representations from waveform or sonogram. One of them, the similarity matrix, allows us to research singularities inside spectromorphologies but realisation of the matrix from data of different tracks or different pieces needs to be improved with the dynamic time warping (DTW) algorithm (Zattra and Orio 2009). Finally, some researchers are exploring new forms of analytical representation: the MaMux seminar at IRCAM presented some of them.[15] The emergence of researches in this field is evidence that musicologists need new kinds of representation for complex musical relationships.

Conclusion

This chapter presents an account of the development of the EAnalysis software. EAnalysis, as a sound-based music (Landy 2007) analytical software, is created for the study of music based on sound, not only electroacoustic music but also other non-written music. Choices I made to create two or more possibilities to achieve the same result, or different interface parts for the same feature are going in the same direction: to respond to different types of user and to allow analysis of different genres and categories of music. This chapter has presented theoretical origins and

[15] MaMux: Mathematics and Music research seminar (IRCAM). Several sessions presented mathematical representations of musical, and one session explored analytical, representation: http://repmus.ircam.fr/mamux/saisons/saison12–2012–2013/2013–02–01.

technical choices to propose a software package that is more adapted to musical analysis than other software. As I mentioned, above all other goals, EAnalysis is an experimental laboratory.[16] Realisations by Michael Clarke in the field of aural analysis, research on archive preservations (Barkati *et al.* 2012), or new representations of sound (differential sonogram or similarity matrix of sonograms) demonstrate the importance of software development in the analysis of electroacoustic music.

Most of the current graphical representations used for the analysis of electroacoustic music are based on the same paradigm: a 2D representation of time and frequency with some annotations. EAnalysis offers other possibilities but this is probably only a first step in a different direction. In the field of electroacoustic music, analytical researches are in their teenage years. Computer science and multimedia possibilities have been developed significantly in recent years. Musicologists have now more keys to explore new paradigms of representation.

References

Barkati, K., Bonardi, A., Vincent, A. and Rousseaux, F. 2012. GAMELAN: A knowledge approach for digital audio production workflows. *Artificial Intelligence for Knowledge Management.* Montpellier: ECAI/IFIP.

Battier, M., Cheret, B., Lemouton, S. and Manoury, P. 2003. *PMA LIB: The Electronic Music of Philippe Manoury.* Paris: IRCAM.

Bayle, F. 2013. *L'expérience acoustique.* Paris: Magison.

Chouvel, J. M. 2011. Musical analysis and the representation. *7th European Music Analysis Conference.* Rome. http://jeanmarc.chouvel.3.free.fr/textes/English/ AnalysisAndRepresentationMTO.pdf.

Chouvel, J. M., Bresson, J. and Agon, C. 2007. L'analyse musicale différentielle: principes, représentation et application à l'analyse de l'interprétation. *EMS Conference.* Leicester: De Montfort University. http://jeanmarc.chouvel.3.free .fr/Flash/ArticleTFDHTML/index.html.

Clarke, M. 2012. Analysing electroacoustic music: An interactive aural approach. *Music Analysis* 31(3), 347–80.

Collective. 2009. *Hierarchical Correlation Plots.* www.mazurka.org.uk/ana/ timescape/.

Couprie, P. 2000. Transformation/transmutation. Analyse d'un extrait de Don Quichotte Corporation d'Alain Savouret. *La musique électroacoustique.* Paris: INA-GRM/Hyptique.

---

[16] It appears also to be an important step for my research. In this software, I have realised and experimented with some of the research ideas I have developed in several papers since 2005.

2006. (Re)Presenting electroacoustic music. *Organised Sound* 11(2), 119–23.

2009. La representación gráfica: una herramienta de análisis y de publicación de la música. *Doce Notas, El análisis de la música* 19–20, 172–80.

Di Santo, J. L. 2009. L'acousmoscribe, un éditeur de partitions acousmatiques. *EMS Conference.* Buenos Aires: UNTREF. www.ems-network.org/ems09/papers/disanto.pdf.

Emmerson, S. 1986. The Relation of Language to Materials. In S. Emmerson (ed.) *The Language of Electroacoustic Music.* Houndmills: Palgrave Macmillan.

Genette, G. 1997. *L'œuvre de l'art.* Paris: Seuil.

Hautbois, X. 2013. Temporal Semiotic Units (TSUs), a very short introduction. www.labo-mim.org/site/index.php?2013/03/29/225-temporal-semiotic-units-tsus-a-very-short-introduction.

Koechlin, O. 2011. De l'influence des outils numériques interactifs sur le temps musical. *Musimédiane* 6. www.musimediane.com.

Landy, L. 2007. *Understanding the Art of Sound Organization.* Cambridge, MA: MIT Press.

Malt, M. and Jourdan, E. 2015. *Le BStD – Une représentation graphique de la brillance et de l'écart type spectral, comme possible représentation de l'évolution du timbre sonore.*

McAdams, S. and Battier, M. 2005. *Creation and Perception of a Contemporary Musical Work: The Angel of Death by Roger Reynolds.* Paris: IRCAM.

Roy, S. 2003. *L'analyse des musiques électroacoustiques: modèles et propositions.* Paris: L'Harmattan.

Schafer, M. 1994. *The Soundscape.* Rochester, VT: Destiny Books.

Smalley, D. 1997. Spectromorphology: Explaining sound-shapes. *Organised Sound* 2(2), 107–26.

Teruggi, D. and Couprie, P. 2001. *Hétérozygote et les Presque rien. Portrait Polychromes Luc Ferrari.* Paris: INA-GRM.

Thoresen. L. 2007. Spectromorphological analysis of sound objects: An adaptation of Pierre Schaeffer's typomorphology. *Organised Sound* 12(2), 129–41.

Zattra, L. and Orio, N. 2009. ACAME – Analyse comparative automatique de la musique électroacoustique. *Musimédiane* 4. www.musimediane.com/spip.php?article87.

Analyses of key works

9 | Trevor Wishart's *Children's Stories II* from *Encounters in the Republic of Heaven*: an analysis for children of a sample-based composition

LEIGH LANDY

General introduction

This analysis differs from the others in this Part IV due to the fact that it addresses a specific user group. The answers to the four-part question introduced in Part I are:

- For which users? – For teachers, particularly those instructing children aged 11–14 (Key Stage 3 in the UK) utilising a language that is appropriate for their students.
- For which works/genres? – The short 'portrait' *Children's Stories II* from Act 2 of Trevor Wishart's 2010 composition, *Encounters in the Republic of Heaven*.
- With what intentions and with which tools? – Using EAnalysis software to find appropriate representations for the meaningful (more comprehensible word-based) and musical (more abstract sound-based) aspects of the movement with the intention of making the work both accessible and comprehensible to young listeners.

The book's analysis template will be integrated into the discussion wherever relevant as well as those elements proposed in Part I specific to *sample-based music*. Given the users' group for which this is intended, the tone of the analysis has been adapted. For example, anecdotes not directly related to the analysis, yet directly related to the piece's sonic universe, are included to offer the teachers' students a context that is familiar to them already.

Introduction to the analysis

The intention of this analysis is to introduce a piece of music made with sounds, in this case the speaking voice, as opposed to musical notes. This type of music, which you may have heard before but didn't know what to call it, is known as electroacoustic or sound-based music. Sound-based music can be quite innovative and it often does not have terribly much in common with other types of music; therefore, the intention of this analysis

197

is to help you discover what the piece involves, what the composer's goals were as well as how to listen to and, ideally, appreciate a piece of music like this one. A movement from a longer work has been chosen due to its specific content and its relatively short duration. Before we talk about and hear the piece, let's introduce sound-based music and the chosen composer briefly to provide you with the context of *Children's Stories II*.

Making music with sounds

In music history some unusual sounds have been used such as cuckoo clocks in symphonies as well as typewriters and even airplane propellers. These are most often used as 'new' instruments to make unusual melodies and percussive rhythms. In the last century a novel type of music was born that allows a musician to use any sound. There are two main types of sounds that can be used in this music: those that already exist, we normally call them samples, that can be recorded and later modified in many ways, such as speeding them up, playing them backwards and much more; and those that are generated electronically. In the latter we speak of sound generation or synthesis. Today these two approaches are often combined; in fact, this type of music is made virtually everywhere as current digital processing tools can transform sound quite radically. In our case, we are only dealing with recordings of the human voice, so we will not pursue the subject of sound synthesis any further.

Making music with the spoken voice

As radical as the idea of making music with any sounds may appear, making music just with sounds of the spoken voice may seem equally odd. In fact, since the early twentieth century fascinating creative works have been made with the speaking voice and the voice producing utterances beyond speech. This type of work has been known by a number of names including phonetic poetry, text-sound poetry – think of poetry to be heard, but not necessarily read, and when the intention is clearly music, text-sound composition.

Many of you will be familiar with rap, but where might this fit in? Rap is performed normally with traditional instruments, sometimes with turntables. The beat and, when used, the underlying melody of the voice are combined with the instruments. The speaking voice may be the main part in the music, but it is generally combined with traditional musical aspects such as normal notes, harmony, rhythm, etc.

There are also notated pieces of music made solely of the speaking voice. When I was a child, I performed a choral composition called *The Geographical Fugue* by a composer named Ernst Toch, which was first performed in 1930. Four parts were written out mainly with names of places and rivers and the structure of the piece was like a fugue, a form that evolved in the Baroque era.

There is something very interesting to discover about the voice that you might not know. In classes I have taught I have asked students: 'Do you think the speaking voice is chromatic, speaking mainly on pitches with intervals similar to those between the keys on the piano?' Most people have no idea what the answer is. When listening to someone, it's hard to tell. However, if someone is speaking a language you don't know, it's easier. I can record my voice and play it backwards to take out the language to which most people's attention is drawn. I then add reverberation to extend the sounds (think of any sound made in a large space like a church; it lasts longer as the space allows it to 'sound out'). When people experience the voice under these conditions, it is easy to hear that the speaking voice is indeed more or less chromatic. This fact is important, as we shall discover when we investigate our piece.

Listening to various forms of speaking in music led us, like Wishart, to experiment musically with the speaking voice. Our experiments would end up taking us well beyond the traditional musical aspects referred to above. Using the speaking voice and then manipulating it using tools for sound processing allows a musician to treat the information in a text, in a word or syllable and the individual sound in a multiplicity of ways. In fact the sound of the voice can be manipulated beyond the comprehension of its contents. Therefore there is plenty to choose from when making a piece in this manner.

Who is Trevor Wishart?

The composer chosen for this analysis is the British musician Trevor Wishart. Almost all of his pieces are sound based (as opposed to note based), using any sound as potential material in his music. Still, he has a huge interest in the voice, often saying that, after the computer, the voice is the instrument that can produce the most types of sound. Therefore, some of his works have involved live vocalists, too. However, the type of composition we shall be discussing is not one performed live; instead, it has been pre-recorded and is played back from a sound file.

Wishart is well known internationally as a composer, writer and software developer. He has also won many awards for his work, including the most important prize in his field, the Ars Electronica prize. As said, he is fascinated by the human voice and can produce hundreds of different types of vocal utterances (see Wishart 1985). A few of these sounds are quite normal and many are very odd indeed. His belief is that these sounds can all be used musically. Sonic art is his name for this type of music. As it is relatively young, compared with many traditional forms of music, many names for more or less the same thing are in circulation! Another thing he is very well known for is what is called sound transformations. Imagine the sound of a human voice turning into the sound of bees 'naturally'. It is like magic. We sometimes call this morphing. Sound transformations are similar to visual ones you will have seen on the television, at the movies or on computer games. We won't be returning to this as sounds range from the comprehensible spoken word to more abstract ones, that is, without meaning related to language, in our piece. What is important here is that Wishart likes to treat his sounds as a sculptor treats clay. It is about moulding a sound until it sounds just the way he wants, one of the most exciting things one can discover when making sound-based music.

Another thing that Wishart is known for, and that is one of the reasons why he has been chosen here, is that he is very interested in introducing this type of music to people who don't know about it, in particular young people. He has worked in schools often throughout his career and, in the 1970s, put together two books called *Sounds Fun* (1977, 1990) that are filled with interesting sound-based 'musical games' for young people. In fact, his work inspired me to write a book introducing this type of music to younger people called *Making Music with Sounds* (Landy 2012). If you are interested in this type of work, you can look at the book and go to its educational website (ears2.dmu.ac.uk) known by its abbreviation EARS 2 (ElectroAcoustic Resource Site). It is with Wishart's educational interest in mind as well as his desire that as many people enjoy this type of music as possible that it comes as no surprise that two of the movements of his concert-length piece involve children's voices.

About the piece and how the movement fits within it

The composer has always identified himself as a composer from the north of England. He claims in his CD text and in the work's description in his book *Sound Composition* that he originally wanted to make a work focusing on the sounds of Yorkshire, where he lives. However, as fortune would have it, he was awarded a three-year Artist in Residence grant at Durham University, further north in England, and used this opportunity to celebrate the unique dialect that can be found in the country's north-east corner.

Wishart has written the following about the work:

Encounters is an exploration of the music inherent in everyday speech. . . . [T]he aim of this project was to capture the musical features of speech at the level of the spoken phrase, its melody and rhythm, and the sonority of individual speaking voices, that indefinable yet recognisable something that enables us to distinguish one person from another. I especially wanted to capture both the diversity of human expression, and the sense of an entire community of speakers, a poetic snapshot of the diversity of human life (Wishart 2012: 131)

Elsewhere Wishart also mentions combining voices or a single voice's sounds to create harmonies. Therefore, the musical aspects we know from instrumental music, melody, rhythm, harmony and spectral sonic qualities (such as the rasp of a bowed violin or the plucking sound of a guitar) are also being investigated in this speech-based piece. He uses surround sound in many of the piece's movements (but not ours) and offered a lovely thought regarding placing the voices around a performance space:

As the piece would attempt to encapsulate this community of speech, I decided to work in 8-channel sound-surround, so that the audience would be embraced within this community. (Wishart 2012: 132)[1]

His aim was to capture people talking naturally as they would to each other. Therefore, he did not ask people to read any texts he had prepared beforehand; instead, he wanted people to act as normally as possible, telling stories. He said to me that sometimes children were a bit shy, but by putting two or three together and letting them speak amongst themselves, it was easy to record very special stories.

As you can see from his remarks, he was looking for interesting stories, different vocal sounds and musical aspects of the speaking voice. After making a large number of recordings, he classified them, cleaned them (taking away any sounds beyond the speaker and any unwanted sounds, such as someone clearing his or her throat), and tried to structure the sounds into themes and sound types on long lists. This was a huge undertaking as he had recorded up to two hours of each person talking!

[1] In some sections, not the one we are going to look into, he gets some sounds to rotate around the room.

With the children, he sometimes found a sentence and had them repeat it to different rhythms so that he could use the rhythms musically. In our movement, the rhythms are already in the sentences as we can hear.

It is important to know that Wishart asked all of the people he recorded whether they wouldn't mind his using their voices to make a piece about the north-east of England. He told me he even played back the relevant parts of the piece to those who had their voices recorded to see whether they were happy with the result and didn't mind the recording being used in his composition. He never intended to make fun of any person or the accent, but instead wanted to celebrate the dialect from the region and the diversity of voices and people he had found. It was his goal that these voices and their stories play a central role throughout this piece.

Many works of this type are of a particular length; most are longer than many pop songs, but hardly ever longer than a half hour. This one, however, is similar to an opera as it is in four acts, each act consisting of several movements, in fact 25 in all. It lasts well over one hour. There are different themes given to the movements. The two *Children's Stories* movements belong to what he calls portraits. The first one in Act 1 consists mainly of boys' voices; in Act 2, ours consists mainly of girl's voices (except the voice in the hamster story that we shall be looking at).

To summarise what has been introduced, the composer has recorded many voices telling stories or in a normal setting (e.g. someone at a marketplace) and chosen only certain extracts – sentences, phrases, words and syllables – as samples and has made music based on these samples. How the music has been put together and what you can listen for in such a speech sample-based piece is the subject of our next section.

Children's Stories II

This portrait that lasts about 2½ minutes is not a single story, but consists of several, even though a number of sounds from some of these, like the first one, reappear at the end. It consists of a number of children, mainly girls, telling stories. The composer then takes some of the musical characteristics of the words and emphasises them as the texts are modified and sometimes combined.

There are two important things for us to think about when learning about this piece. The first thing is that as sounds move from their original appearance to their modified form, our listening changes. When we are clearly following words, we are listening to what might be called the *meaningful* side of the content.[2] As the words are modified and become more abstract, we tend to focus on their sonic qualities and thus we are more aware of the *musical* side of the content. The second thing is that some of the materials appear again and again, but change slightly every time they appear. This is traditionally known as *theme and variations*. Normally that means listening to a passage of music that changes every time it recurs. Here it means that a text is presented or treated differently every time it recurs; so it is the same approach, but the specific means of composition and what it is combined with are quite different.

The composer cleverly starts the movement introducing something with which all of you will be acquainted, namely the nursery rhyme *Humpty Dumpty*. The child speaking it not only has a lovely accent, she also charmingly swallows some of her sounds. And, at the end, it appears as if she forgets the end of the nursery rhyme when she says, 'And you know I don'.' Wishart apparently liked this sentence because he found other ones that are similar, such as: 'Do you know what it was?' and 'And do you know what I done?' So we already have two things that are going to reappear in this piece: the two words, Humpty and Dumpty and sentences including 'you know'. As innovative as this music is, he is already providing us with two things to hold on to as we listen to the work. In the case of *Humpty Dumpty* we do get the other lines about putting him together again, so there is another link.

Regularly these two words are chopped up and played back to us again and again, gradually modified until they become just a flow of sound. Because we have been able to follow this change from real to abstract, we are therefore aware that the sounds in the middle and at the end are all to do with Humpty Dumpty. This is what was meant when we spoke of moulding sounds and it has a magical quality to it as well.

Let's take a look at this when it first happens in the piece (***Sound example 1 from EAnalysis file: 0–21”***).[3] You will probably have noticed that paying attention to the melody or rhythm whilst the girl was speaking is not the first thing that came to mind, but once the words Humpty and Dumpty start appearing on their own or even part of the words, things start getting more musical, in the traditional sense, and thus we can hear pitches (like in a tune) and a funny rhythmical combination more clearly.

---

[2] If the sounds are, for example, from a city or a forest, we speak of the *contextual* side of the content.

[3] The sound examples and EAnalysis movies with a key to the symbols used are to be found on the website accompanying this book.

Finally out of this comes a sound as if shot into the mixture that then fades away. Although it is not entirely apparent that this flowing sound is the same voice, it is clear that its sonic quality is the same and so we move from real to cut up to unrecognisable in just 21 seconds. Wishart is gradually transforming the sound and then uses a treatment that sustains it to create that sound flow.

In the analysis score that is provided, you will notice that the text is in a blue box. There is more information provided, too. The capital **A** in the yellow box represents the first story (A) and the little **a** represents modifications made to words and sounds from story A. The blue arrows represent recurring sounds of either word Humpty or Dumpty and, when there is a dotted outline around the arrow, it means there are multiple sounds in rapid succession. The descending blue line represents the flowing sound taken from the voice and how it gets quieter. The three letters in the green box, **R+M+S** represent the fact that we've heard rhythm, melody and spectral (in the sense of the sonic quality) treatment of the sounds after the initial story is heard: rhythm particularly once the words have been chopped out; melody because the girl's voice is quite melodic already and the fact that there are only a few pitches in the chopped-up sounds; and spectral because of the sound qualities that evolve once the sounds are fragmented and, in particular, the sound flow commences at the end.

The second half of the nursery rhyme is identified as **A'** because it is part of the same story, but different from **A**. Similarly when you read small letters with one or more inverted commas after them, this means that the modifications have to do with that story and are the second, third (and so on) appearance of those sounds. The fact that it is another voice that replies with 'Do you know what it was?' has been represented in a different letter colour in the blue box. In this case, the letter **H** has been added to the **R+M+S** as the sounds are also treated harmonically in what is indicated as **a'**, especially once the sound flow gets louder and combines with the second group of fragmented Humpty Dumpty's. Again, here we have the two types of blue arrows and the blue line that, this time, rises before it falls again. This is a variation of what we heard in **a**. The blue line also continues throughout the entire **B** story and is even on its own for a while when the story ends. The blue arrows appear again and even continue throughout **C** and the beginning of **D**. In this way we have something we recognise from our first story whilst others are introduced. The directions of the blue arrows have to do with how loud they are just like the blue lines.

The **B** hamster story, the one with the only boy's voice, is the longest in terms of its text. It is not modified when we hear it and a separate girl's voice ends it by answering 'Yeah' after he suggests that his hamsters 'couldn't have been hungry'. But that boy's voice does reappear in **D** as we shall discover shortly. Similarly the **C** wishing star story is accompanied by the Humpty Dumpty sounds. Take note, the **B** and **C** voices will return and will be varied later in the piece so that we are not always encountering new materials and voices. This **B** section does not have much of a melody between the original text and what follows, but once the repeated 'Yeah' sound appears combined with the chopped-up and flowing Humpty Dumpty sounds, it becomes rhythmical in terms of the discrete sounds in time, spectral in terms of sound qualities as well as harmonic in terms of the pitch combinations which evolve.

Section **D** is the most dense section aurally in the sense that there are voices to the left and different voices to the right and this short passage becomes difficult to follow in terms of meaning at times. Recognisable words flow into sounds due to information overload. Still, if you listen carefully, you can hear the reappearance of the hamster story voice. So it is primarily rhythmical, not in the sense of wanting to tap your foot to the beat – although if you listen carefully, there is a beat as well as an ever-alternating melody – but instead in terms of creating a pattern, be it a more complex one than what we've heard thus far. It becomes even more melodic when the composer adds some reverberation to sustain the sounds so that we can perceive pitch better than we did at the beginning. Towards the end of **D**, there is a canon just like 'Row your Boat' using familiar material from **B** which evolves into a fragmented sound that seems to have been derived from it that fades out quickly and will reappear once again at the very end of the piece. Let's listen to the piece between **B** and **D** to follow this entire sequence. (***Sound example 2 from EAnalysis file: 21"–1'25"***).

The following section, **E** starts with that familiar sentence, 'And do you know wha' I don'?' and continues with the same voice as 'wishing star' but with an entirely different story about getting 'soakin' wet'. This is followed by the reappearance of the 'Yeah' from **B** processed and repeated rapidly and 'Humpty' from **A** treated similarly as before, leading to the flowing sound that is related to it that carries on to the next part of the story. In this part, rhythm does not play much of a role, but the other three factors do. This sequence follows into what might be a related sequence as the same voice continues with a story, **E'**, that took place in a pushchair. This little story leads to the girl enthusiastically ending her story with a loud 'I went out' which is manipulated and rapidly repeated as well as the 'Yeah!' that is treated the same as it was at the end of the last story. Harmony doesn't really feature here although there is an interval between the two repeated sounds; rhythm and melody appear as before and the spectral quality becomes a focus once the repeated sounds have commenced. One can identify the new and existent materials by listening to this combined **E** and **E'** sequence (***Sound example 3 from EAnalysis file: 1'25"–1'55"***).

As we approach the end, things move on to a climax in which much of what we have already been introduced to reappears. I have called this section **F–Mix** because it contains so many things. We start off by clearly hearing the words 'My cousin', which will continue to be present in a manipulated form until shortly before the end of the piece. Here, again, the manipulation makes the original sound become increasingly abstract; it also becomes fragmented towards the end, producing a sound quality as if it were plucked. Other words and phrases from **A** to **E** appear, but, similar to **D**, it is not the goal that these words and phrases be clearly understood, but, instead, only partially perceived so that the fine line between meaning related to the text and musical listening seems to get crossed now and then. Along with the flowing 'my cousin' sound, the one associated with Humpty Dumpty reappears for the last time. Where it launched after the chopped-up Humpty Dumpty words and syllables previously, it appears first here and then the fragments follow in two bunches. In this way it is quite symmetric with the beginning of the movement. All four factors – melody, rhythm, harmony and spectral qualities – can easily be identified here and it is not surprising that they're all combined for this final mix.

The very end of this final section consists of the final seconds of the plucked sound and reappearances of three texts we've encountered several times: first 'And do you know what I done' appearing in canon, thus featuring rhythm and melody, 'So he couldn't have been hungry' from the hamster story and that often recurring 'Yeah!' again manipulated and rapidly repeated until it has been faded out. The fragmented sound that we heard at the end of **C** related to the hamsters not being hungry is the final sound in this movement and appears like a cadence in traditional music. Let's listen to this conclusion before making some general remarks and listening to the entire piece. (***Sound example 4 from EAnalysis file: 1'55"–2'34"***).

I sometimes wonder whether Humpty Dumpty is being broken into pieces in many ways throughout the piece and, perhaps, with everything coming together at the end, he might be put together again. Or, perhaps it's the opposite: so many things become fragmented and mixed together (mixed up) at the end, maybe that's when Humpty Dumpty really does fall to pieces. Who knows?

The nice thing about music is that it does not need to be about something specific and is open to interpretation. This means that not only the composer, but also the listener, can use his or her imagination to think about what is going on and make up the music's story. Consider which things in your life you might connect anything in the piece with. You might also explore which emotional responses are triggered and share and compare these thoughts with your friends.

For anyone who understands English, you get a chance to mix the meaning of the words with the sounds of the music. Everyone loves the sounds of children telling stories and, as the composer says, you get a real taste of the accents of that part of England to enjoy. And then there are the various remarkable manipulated sounds as well!

To conclude

To return to where we started, this discussion is about a piece of music made out of spoken word sounds. Many of you will have thought at the beginning, 'Can you really make music from any sounds? Can you really make music from speech?' It is clear that *Children's Stories II* doesn't sound like pop music, classical or folk music. It sounds like something new and different. But wait. We could have looked at the pitches in greater detail or even made a score of some of this; or the rhythms; or the harmonies; or even those spectral sonic qualities. In other movements of this work, Wishart does make sound-based music with clear harmonies, rhythms and pitches, some that those with popular or classical tastes will recognise. The fun challenge with this music is that we can use both traditional techniques and new ones, too. There are infinite choices, especially with those magical means of moulding sounds and combining them. Too many choices may be confusing, but if you know what kinds of sounds you like or like to make and the types of manipulation that work for you, it isn't that difficult at all! The limitations are determined according to your imagination.

Let's now look one last time at some of the things that we discovered here. There are a number of stories told by a few main voices. All the stories reappear in one form or another after they have been introduced. So we have an unusual form of theme and variations with several things to hold on to. We can follow the voices and how they appear and reappear in the stories. We can also hear some words and phrases and their manipulated versions that evolve throughout the movement. Note that the main sounds that are manipulated all reappear at one point. The flowing sounds tend to grow and fade away. The words, such as Humpty and Dumpty that come back again and again, tend to reappear in the same ways as their original appearance so that you never get lost.

Although the stories evolve from **A** to **F**, there are many things that appear and reappear so that the listener is not constantly encountering something new. We are guided through one story as if it were made of many little mini-stories evolving at the same time. And then there are all of those musical qualities to take in as well. This keeps our ears and our minds very busy and it takes us from familiar stories to funny stories to gory ones to ridiculous ones. It may be quite a bit to take in but we don't need to listen to this piece only once. Listen again and again and you will discover more each time as I have whilst preparing this for you. In any case, listen to the entire movement now and discuss what you hear with someone else listening to it with you. And, above all, have fun with it (***Sound example 5 from EAnalysis file: the entire piece***).

References

EARS 2 (the ElectroAcoustic Resource Site pedagogical project). ears2.dmu.ac.uk (accessed 30 October 2012).

Landy, L. 2012. *Making Music with Sounds*. New York: Routledge.

Wishart, T. 1977. *Sounds Fun 2: A Book of Musical Games*. London: Universal Edition.

　　1985. *On Sonic Art*. York: Imagineering Press (2nd edn, 1996, ed. Simon Emmerson, Amsterdam: Harwood Academic).

　　1990. *Sounds Fun: A Book of Musical Games*. London: Universal Edition (reprint, orig. 1975, Schools Council).

　　2010. Encounters in the Republic of Heaven. . . . All the Colours of Speech . . . CD. York: Orpheus The Pantomime.

　　2012. *Sound Composition*. York: Orpheus The Pantomime.

10 | Analysis of *Foil* by Autechre (from *Amber* (1994))

BEN RAMSAY

Introduction

The late 1980s and early 1990s marked a significant development in techno music as composers began experimenting with sound and composition using the tools and instruments that became available during this period. Through this experimentation, techno found a new sound, initially in the UK, which the music press of the time labelled 'intelligent dance music' or IDM. This analysis will deliberately avoid using the IDM classification in favour of the term electronica.[1] Composers of this music sought to challenge some of the conventions of electronic dance music (EDM) composition by exploring irregular time signatures, virtual synthesised spaces, and sound itself. During the very early part of the 1990s, electronic music record labels such as Warp Records from the UK found a growing audience for this new music. Warp Records continue to release music from many of the established names in the genre, including Autechre, who remain at the forefront of the movement some 20 years on. This analysis will explore a piece by Autechre entitled *Foil* from their 1994 album *Amber*. The track has been chosen for two reasons. First, *Foil* is an excellent example of the sound of mid-1990s electronica and demonstrates where the sound of the genre has grown from, in particular its timbral and compositional links with techno from the late 1980s and early 1990s. Second, *Foil* contains a collection of examples which show where electronica composition strategies began to become more defined against the techno backdrop of the music. This is further highlighted when comparing *Amber* with Autechre's first album *Incunabula*, from 1993, which contained much closer compositional and timbral ties with early techno.

---

[1] The term 'IDM' was not widely adopted by the artists or the enthusiasts of the music, primarily because of the elitist connotations of the word 'intelligent'. In the UK, the preferred term was 'electronica', which will be the term used in this chapter.

Analytical tools and electronica

There are two existing analytical theories that are of particular relevance to the listening and appreciation of electronica. The first of these is reduced listening, a mode of listening that focuses on the sound itself, disregarding any recognition of source or cause. This listening mode relates to electronica in particular for two key reasons. First, electronica largely exists on a fixed medium; the method by which the audience hears the music remains the same every time they hear it. This affords the audience the ability to listen to the same work, or section of a work, a number of times without change in the sounding flow. This simple 'fixing' process allows for deeper analysis of the nuances in the music through repeated listening, examples of which are discussed later in this chapter. The listener can gain a great deal from listening in a reduced way to electronica, and quite often any message that the music may contain is either not relevant or imagined,[2] making the listening mode all the more relevant.

Much of the soundworld in electronica is either synthetically produced using various synthesis methods, or is made up of a combination of synthesised sounds and processed field recordings. It is rarely the case that the listener will hear a timbre that is recognisable as a real-world sound, and the general ethos in the composition of the music backs this idea up. Most composers of the music are seeking to extend sounds and timbres of the sounds they use through processing and sound transformation. The fact that many of the sounds are non-representational further enhances their ability to be appreciated in a reduced listening manner.

Second, it is useful to explore the sounds of electronica in terms of their internal behaviours and associated motion and growth processes. The term *spectromorphology* was coined by Denis Smalley in 1986[3] and addresses this examination of internal sonic behaviour, and seeks to describe what we are listening to when we engage in reduced listening. Electronica is constructed from structures that are familiar to the Western musical tradition, notably beats and pitched sounds. However, there is another layer of composition in the music that cannot be adequately explained by Western musical theory, and it is this group of sounds that this analysis will explore. Many of these ideas are based around reduced listening and a spectromorphological approach to listening and analysis.

---

[2] Richard James (aka Aphex Twin) discussed this idea in an interview from 1995, where he suggested that electronic music did not contain any lyrics or meanings because in his words the music is '*more abstract*' (James 1995).

[3] And later refined in Smalley 1997.

Dynamic range

One of the most distinctive aspects of electronica is the preservation of dynamic range, which gives listeners a clear indication as to the purpose of the music which Warp themselves describe as 'listening music'. Between 1992 and 1994 Warp Records released the well-documented *Artificial Intelligence* series of albums, bookended by the compilation albums *Artificial Intelligence* and *Artificial Intelligence II*. The front covers of both of these albums display the title of the album and the phrase 'Electronic Listening Music From Warp' on *Artificial Intelligence* and 'More Electronic Listening Music From Warp' on *Artificial Intelligence II*. The artwork on the front cover of the first CD also includes a futuristic-looking android relaxing in front of the hi-fi, alone, listening to the music without any distractions. Interestingly the interview with The Black Dog inside asks, 'Why did you contribute to (A.I)?' To which they answer, 'So that maybe people will SIT DOWN and listen' (Various artists 1994).

When listening to *Foil*, the preservation of dynamic range and detail is initially clear. Figure 10.1 shows a waveform view of *Foil* illustrating the dynamic range of the work and its highly transient content. This audible and visible dynamic range suggests that the preservation of

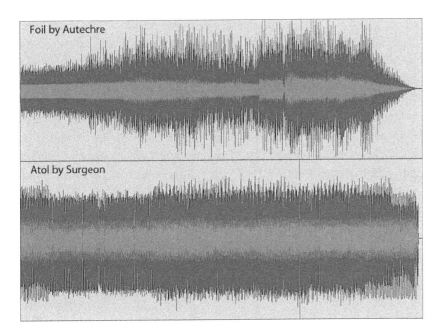

Figure 10.1 Comparing the waveform displays from *Foil* by Autechre with *Atol* by Surgeon

dynamics and detail in the piece are more important than its suitability for the dance floor.

Contrast this with a more heavily compressed techno piece from the same era – a piece entitled *Atol* from Surgeon's *Magneze EP* (Child 1995) (also Figure 10.1). The track sounds much less detailed but, of course, detail and intricacy are not necessarily the focal point of this kind of music. *Atol* relies entirely on the interrelationships of the sounding elements and on how these elements work together to create the 'soul' of the track. In this kind of techno music it is not important to maintain a wide dynamic range, and in fact the sounding elements in the track benefit from being at a similar perceived loudness to ensure the track works in environments with a high background noise floor, such as the dance music club where clubbers will be chatting and socialising with friends. The trade-off with this mastering approach, of course, is that the dynamic range is reduced, creating a less intricate piece of music and the listener potentially being led away from a deep listening approach to less conscious listening. Undertaking amplitude analysis in these two pieces indicated that the average in *Foil* was a little over – 15d BFS and *Atol* was around – 10 dBFS. This 5 dB difference is significant and apparent both in listening and in looking at the waveform views of the pieces.

The waveform view of *Atol* illustrates more consistency in the amplitude of the percussive content, as well a greater overall loudness and less dynamic range. This would lead us to surmise that the composer of *Atol* wants us to focus less on the depth of detail in the piece, and more on the arrangement of the sounds themselves and in particular the continuity of beat. *Atol* was clearly designed to be listened to in a location with a higher noise floor than the Autechre piece, and across a wider range of loudspeaker systems.

The evidence to support the claim that *Foil* is a piece of listening music is apparent, both from the label's comments about the genre and from considering some of the aspects of the music's composition. However, in live performance this music can be at odds with itself as the listening attention that the music demands is often in conflict with the more social aspects associated with a gig of this kind.[4] To attempt to resolve this, Autechre often perform without any lights or visuals to reduce distraction and to encourage more detailed listening in their audience. Their recent live performances have also been sonically very different from their studio work, often adopting a musical style that is much more dance floor

---

[4] Gigs are often set in pubs or clubs and other venues which are associated with consumption of alcohol and other drugs. These venues also have a high social noise floor resulting in a partial loss of sonic detail of certain elements of the performance.

oriented. Another group from the Warp roster, Plaid, performed in the Queen Elizabeth Hall in London at the 2004 Ether Festival and have performed in similar sit-down concert halls in the past. This type of concert, in a seated-only venue, seems to reinforce the idea established by the *Artificial Intelligence* albums some 12 years previously that this is 'music for listening'. However, the gig in the Queen Elizabeth Hall also featured large visual projections which accompanied the audio, making it more of a multimedia experience. Other artists such as Tim Exile and Mouse On Mars have explored more 'performative' aspects of the live music setting including alternative control methods and the use of more traditional instrumentation.

The problems that this music faces in live performance can be attributed to the aesthetic and social aspects that influence electronica composition and performance practice. It can be difficult to combine dance floor and art music practices in a single space that is both socially and sonically rewarding to the audience. However, rather than detracting from the music, this combination of contrasting compositional disciplines and associated listening methods adds to the value of this form of music and is at the very centre of this analysis.

Subjective and objective groupings

In 1959 the psychologist Ernest Schachtel documented his studies of human development and the psychology of creativity in a book entitled *Metamorphosis* (Schachtel 1959). The book distinguished between two kinds of human perceptions: those which are largely subjective, relating to human emotion and feelings, and those which are objective in nature and disregard subjective distractions. Schachtel defined these two types as *autocentric*, relating to subject-centred perception, and *allocentric*, relating to object-centred perception. Denis Smalley argues that when listening to Western art music, such as acousmatic music, there should ideally be a partnership between both allocentric and autocentric modes (Smalley 1996).[5] Further to this, psychologists generally acknowledge that there is no such ideal as 'pure' objectivity or subjectivity, but rather a continuing discourse between our feelings about the world and the reality of what we perceive (Chandler and Munday 2011). If the ideas of allocentric and autocentric perception are

---

[5] Smalley actually addresses this concept in relation to Pierre Schaeffer's listening modes and their relationship to Schachtel's work.

mapped onto the sounds we hear in electronica, then it is possible to begin describing two distinct sound groups within the music which are directly aligned with some of the issues discussed previously.

The first of these two sound groups is affiliated with our autocentric perception and contains emotive, subjective content. In this grouping are sounds and sound arrangements that lead to a physical or emotional response in the listener,[6] such as beats, and arrangement of pitched material. This grouping plays a vital role within electronica; it is imbued with the cultural memes[7] of techno and is a fundamental part of the popular appeal and accessibility of the music. The rest of this analysis will refer to this collection of sounds as the *subjective* grouping. Pinpointing the subjective content in an analysis of this kind will help to uncover the vestiges of the language of techno, including the sonic memes that are responsible for certain structures within the music, and which explain why certain sounds are selected based on their affiliation with the sound of techno; for example, the Roland TR-909 kick drum.

The second sound grouping is affiliated with our allocentric perception, our intellectualisation of the world, and describes sounds which contain real-world objective references. This group of sounds includes aspects such as the movement of sounds in space or their physical shape and composition. Timbre plays a more pivotal role with this sound group and suggests movement, spatialisation and various other transformations and change processes with which we might be familiar from our experiences of the natural world. This categorisation will be referred to as the *objective* grouping. By exploring the objective features of *Foil* it will be possible to begin to see how the piece dovetails into the compositional strategies used within acousmatic music.

Electronica straddles the divide between the avant-garde and club scenes and is a symbiosis of both objective and subjective sound groupings. The music is able to engage a dance music audience with a subjective group of sounds with which they will be familiar, such as the use of beats and pitched material and the associated memes from other forms of dance music. This collection of sounds can be seen as '*something to hold on to*' (Landy 1994) and a way to ease the new listener into the objective content in the music, such as space, movement and location. The music is potentially a useful tool to connect the study of acousmatic sound with students

[6] This might be described as a Dionysian response to the music as discussed in *Living Electronic Music* (Emmerson 2007).
[7] As discussed by Richard Dawkins in *The Selfish Gene* (Dawkins 1989). The term 'meme' describes the existence and transmission of cultural ideas through society.

from dance music backgrounds as a way to discuss composing with space and energy as central compositional tools, and moving away from traditional beat and pitch-based structures.

Subjective sounds within *Foil*

Foil is constructed from numerous emotive sounds which speak to our autocentric perception, beginning with the elongated drones and pads at the start of the track, suggesting an ominous and oppressive atmosphere whilst setting up a sense of tension and apprehension in the listener. The percussive elements are programmed around a tempo of 124 bpm outlining the groove and time signature, and are sparse enough to make the track feel slow paced and relaxed. At around 00m 16s the first bass drum sounds begin building the main rhythm of the track to which other layers are added. The structuring process of adding layers of sound on top of one another in sequence, gradually building and revealing the structure of the track, is an arrangement method transplanted directly from techno, which will be discussed in more detail later. There is no set order in which sounds are introduced in techno, but the bass drum is arguably the dominant element and is often introduced early on in a work. The bass drum in *Foil* is also the first rhythmic sound to be introduced but unlike a typical bass drum sound used in techno the sound is lighter, more subdued and quieter than some of the other percussive elements in the track. Techno music would normally feature a compressed Roland TR-808 or TR-909 bass drum with a longer release and larger bass extension arranged on each beat in the bar. *Foil*, however, uses a less regular, more delicate bass drum sound with a short burst of delayed white noise. The bass drum is also much more muted in the mix than would be heard in a dance floor techno track. This is a good indication of how closely electronica is related to techno, but also begins to pinpoint where the two forms of music diverge. To contrast this, early Aphex Twin and Polygon Window albums such as *Selected Ambient Works 85–92* and *Surfing On Sine Waves* (James 1993) use TR-808 and TR-909 bass drum sounds much more overtly, often on the down beat, which indicates a much closer tie with the techno roots of the albums.[8]

---

[8] The term 'electronica' can only ever be applied loosely to an artist, label or compositional ethos as electronica is often nothing more than an alternative take on techno. These two Aphex Twin albums are excellent examples of this.

At around 00m 24s a burst of shaped white noise programmed percussively around the bass drum is introduced. This sound becomes the focal element of the piece and can be described in terms of its subjective qualities, as it adds to the 'feeling' of the track, but its objective significance within the context of the work plays a much more pivotal role which will be discussed later. There is an important subjective shift at 1m 25s as the discordant drone of the pads that have been a static presence since the beginning of the track shift into an alternating pattern which repeats every eight bars. This subtle shift could be described as intensifying the already sinister feel of the track as well as adding a sense of movement to the other elements that are present. At 1m 40s and 1m 56s more percussive sounds build in that are programmed around the bass drum. These sounds gradually build tension until 2m 04s when a highly detailed, fast-paced percussive element is introduced and adds to the intricacy of the rhythm before the middle breakdown section. During this middle section, the remaining elements suggest a more desolate landscape and are further thinned out to reveal more of the intricacy in the remaining sounding elements. During this section, the gently undulating bass pad that formed part of the discordant drone is revealed further, maintaining the feeling that this track is dark and oppressive. From 3m 37s the subjective features of the track mentioned previously are reintroduced together at the track's fullest section. The bass drum, drone pads, reverberant snare and intricate percussive sounds all produce a punchy energetic reintroduction of the main rhythmical elements which are maintained for around 20 seconds until there is a drop-out of the main driving elements of the music a little later. This is a classic call-back to the language of techno where layers are built up and drop out creating the structure and building tension and excitement.

From 4m 37s the track begins to fall apart and, from a subjective viewpoint, the listener might get the sense that the main elements of the piece are losing their power as they stutter and falter and appear to try, in vain, to cling on to life. At the same time the main elements of the piece drift off into the distance, indicating that the track is moving away from the listener. This last section is discussed in more detail later as the sonic characteristics lend themselves to a more objective viewpoint.

Overall the track is slow paced and calm in structure and timbre. Sounds are clean, rounded and distortion free, which further emphasise the overall smoothness of the work. There are periods where the piece becomes a little more intense but the 'feel' of the track remains gentle and lethargic, certainly not energetic and exciting; this is not music to excite a dance floor. The dynamic range discussed earlier tends to drag the listener into the work, certainly in the section between 2m 40s and 3m 36s where the track becomes quieter in amplitude and further subdued through the use of low-pass filtering. There are no surprise gestures or restless juxtapositions to break the laid-back listening situation.

Objective sounds within *Foil*

As discussed previously, an additional understanding and appreciation of electronica can be found by exploring its objective soundworld. The term 'IDM' is not an especially useful one but it might be possible to suggest that, when coining the term in the 1990s, the music press were, in some ways, pointing out that the 'intelligent' or objective aspects of the music carry significance. Appreciation of the objective elements in the music requires a more considered listening approach. This process is not an entirely unnatural one but requires a shift in listening attention from the subjective sound objects inside the composition that give us more immediate pleasure (beats, melody) to the intrinsic properties of the objective sounds and how they are shaped over time.[9] It is dangerous territory to label a certain form of music as 'intelligent' but there is undoubtedly a link between a more interactive, engaged listening approach and the appreciation of the nuances of certain aspects of the music in question. Whether this appreciation requires more or less intellect on the part of the listener is outside the scope of this analysis, but it is true to say that appreciation of electronica requires closer listening attention, reduction of external sonic or visual stimuli and the time and space to listen.

As with many works within this genre, the use of space, spatialisation and movement in *Foil* are treated as primary compositional elements and are among the pivotal allocentric aspects of the work. The use of delay and reverberation is widespread throughout the track and gives sounds a sense of depth and sonic density that is generally not present in more dance floor oriented techno. A good example of this use of space is at 1m 40s when a hollow wooden sound is first introduced. This sound is panned hard left and is distinctly reverberant, which pushes it back in the mix and away from the upfront compressed sound of techno mentioned earlier. The stereo space of the sound is emphasised further as the signal in the right channel contains only reverberant signal, whereas the left channel contains the original dry input signal as well as the processed sound. Figure 10.2

---

[9] Which is described in Smalley's notion of spectromorphology (Smalley 1986).

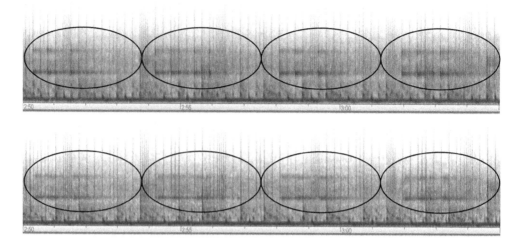

Figure 10.2 *Foil.* Left (upper) channel: the darker colour of the events illustrates increased amplitude. The higher frequency content and attack transients are also visible. Right (lower) channel: shows lower amplitude, diminished transient content and less high frequencies.

shows the left and right channel spectrograms (using EAnalysis) illustrating the variations across both channels in the hollow wooden sound event during the breakdown section at 2m 50s. This section was chosen as it is sonically less dense and illustrates the differing amplitudes and spectral content of each of the channels. The dry sound in the left (upper) channel can be seen as having a more defined transient at the beginning of the sound event, whereas in the right (lower) channel the transient is not present.

A similar use of reverberation can also be heard at 1m 56s when the snare is first introduced. The timbre and length of the reverb on this sound is entering into the realms of science fiction as it is so long and bright it contradicts what might be possible in the real world. Both the wooden sound and the snare remain fixed in their respective locations throughout the track but each spatial location is distinct from the other. The balance between the dry, unprocessed snare and the wet reverberant signal makes it sit in a very close local space frame[10] but inside a very reverberant space, whereas the hollow wooden percussive sound sits in a much more distant frame and generally sounds more natural. The detailed percussive sound first heard at 2m 04s also has some reverberation applied to it and in terms of its location in the mix is static, even though it does have some abstract

---

[10] As defined by Emmerson in 'Aural landscape: Musical space' (Emmerson 1999).

movement implied with the accented hits and automated delay which add to the detail and intricacy of its programming.

The focal sound of the work, and the one that illustrates the objective aspects of this piece very well, is the sound first introduced at 00m 24s which was discussed earlier in terms of its subjective qualities. This sound grows and evolves over time through the variation of four sonic parameters that give movement and meaning to this sound object. These four parameters are *loudness*, *spatial distance*, *spectral density* and a term I label *cohesion*. Each of these parameters is discussed in turn.

Loudness is the most simple to identify within a work. Loudness relates not just to perceived volume of the audio but also to the amount of energy being used to bring the sound into life. Whilst this can be a useful parameter in isolation, it becomes more effective at conveying localisation and spatial messages when augmented with the additional parameters discussed here.[11]

The second parameter is *spatial distance*. This parameter is best understood and recognised by taking a combined Gestalt[12] view of loudness, panning, reverb and filtering/EQ. Combining these four elements gives additional information that forms an understanding of spatial location. Electronica regularly uses this parameter to place or move sounds from an intimate space to a more environmentally distant space.[13]

Spectral density is the third parameter and relates to the richness of the sound or abundance of frequencies contained within it. A sound which contains a wide range of closely packed frequencies could be described as spectrally dense (e.g. white noise), whilst a sound with fewer more widely spaced frequencies could be described as spectrally thin or sparse (e.g. at its most extreme a pure sine tone). This parameter relates to a continuum of sonic growth and decline and can suggest the physical size or intensity of a

---

[11] For example, we can easily tell the difference between a loud sound far away and a quiet sound at close proximity by their different spectral content even though they might be the same perceived loudness.

[12] Gestalt theory suggests that the whole is not the same as the sum of its individual parts. In this example, the 'whole' will give the listener a single parameter, *spatial distance*, with which to judge apparent distance from sound source.

[13] A good example of this can be heard in the 1994 Autechre remix of *Like a Motorway* by the group Saint Etienne. The track is called *Skin Up You're Already Dead* and features a processed, nonsensical female vocal at 3m 55s which moves towards the listener in a rather unnerving manner over the course of around a minute and a half. Interestingly *Skin Up You're Already Dead* was released just six months prior to *Amber*, the album which features *Foil*, and compositionally speaking bears many stylistic similarities to those discussed in this analysis, including a focus on sonic evolution and spatial movement.

sound and is sometimes used as a focal compositional construct in electro-nica. Spectral density is associated to loudness; however, a sound object can be sonically dense but quiet at the same time, indicating that spectral density can also be understood separately from loudness. The spectral density of an object can be automated and controlled through the use of EQ and filters and can be observed and analysed using a spectrogram.[14]

The final parameter is *cohesion*. Cohesion relates directly to the structure of the sound and how bonded a sonic object is to itself and other sounds that make up the object. This term can also relate to a group of sound objects that form a cohesive whole or phrase. It is often the case with music in this genre that sounds are destroyed through various automated processes such as bitcrushing, distortion, granulation and other sonic decimation tools. The term *cohesion* defines this bonding and describes the 'togetherness' of the sound over time. Like spatial distance, cohesion is best understood by taking a Gestalt view of the sound, or collection of sounds, and how they are constructed and deconstructed over time. Towards the end of *Foil* the cohesion of the track gradually declines as elements trip over themselves and become sonically fractured, bitcrushed and rearranged, suggesting the sound is coming apart.

These four parameters relate to many other works in the genre. In fact, the concept of sounds evolving over time forms a central part of electronica composition, and most artists have engaged with these ideas at one time or another, some more than others. Early forms of the music from 1990 to 1994 generally did not employ these compositional ideas as fully as later examples of the genre, and it was not until *Amber* that Autechre really exploited this compositional method to its fullest. By the late 1990s and early 2000s this kind of processing was commonplace and now forms the foundation of many electronica works. Berlin's Monolake is an especially good example of an artist who regularly explores these kinds of compos-itional developments in his more recent albums *Silence* (Henke 2009) and *Ghosts* (Henke 2012).

Taking a sectional approach, eight distinct phases of growth and deple-tion can be identified in *Foil* by using these four parameters to analyse the shaped white noise that begins at 00m 24s. These phases see the sound transform from a relatively insignificant object in the composition to a sound that sits at the forefront of the piece before eventually being destroyed. These eight phases are listed in Table 10.1 along with the time

---

[14] A spectrally dense sound will appear full on a spectrogram and vice versa.

Table 10.1 The eight phases of *Foil* by Autechre and their associated motion

Phase	Time stamp	Motion	Motion graphic
Introduction	00m 24s	Growth	
Phase 1	00m 43s	Growth	
Phase 2	01m 25s	Growth	
Phase 3	02m 20s	Depletion	
Termination	03m 21s	Termination	
Phase 4	03m 37s	Static	
Phase 5	04m 00s	Growth	
Phase 6	04m 37s	Depletion	
Phase 7	05m 00s	Depletion	
Phase 8	05m 25s	Depletion	
Termination	End	Termination	

of occurrence and dominant motion within the phase as well as a graphical representation of this motion.

By exploring each of these phases individually in relation to the four parameters discussed above, it is possible to gain a more thorough understanding of the sound being analysed. After examining each of these phases, the analysis will turn its attention to the micro-level sounds and how these are constructed to form larger meso- and macro-level objects.

Between 00m 24s and 00m 43s the sound rises gently in spectral density as the pulse of the sound becomes slightly more elongated with each sound event. Loudness remains constant, as does the sound's spatial distance. Phase 1 begins at 00m 43s, at which point there is a perceivable jump in spectral density as the pulses of the sound become more elongated, adding to the tension of this section. Spatial distance increases here also as the delay becomes more prominent, indicating that the object is growing more remote from the listener. At around 1 minute the sound goes through the first of several spatial transformations as the sound object appears to undergo a shift in location through the use of a flange effect. This shift occurs at intervals of roughly 46 seconds. Throughout Phase 1, perceived loudness increases but spatial location is kept relatively consistent throughout, as if the sound object is not moving but growing in size and power. Spectral density also increases through this section, reinforcing this growth.

Phase 2 begins as another shift in spectral density occurs. As in Phase 1 previously, the growth that takes place is an elongation of a collection of sound events that form this phase, resulting in a perceptible presence of the sound. Loudness increases here also, adding to the tension of this section and reflecting the size and physical presence of the sound object. Comparing the significance and presence of the sound at 00m 34s with 01m 40s, where the sound is fully formed and coherent, demonstrates how much the sound has evolved over the course of Phase 1 and the beginning of Phase 2. Phase 2 also contains a similar spatial transformation to Phase 1 at 01m 46s as the sound object undergoes a shift in spatial location through the use of a flange effect, emulating sound behaviour in the physical world.

The beginning of Phase 3 marks the first point of depletion for this sound layer. The sound maintains its cohesion as it is still bonded together. However, this bonded object makes a 30 second transition from being in close proximity to the listening position to being very distant. The flange effect that is applied to the sound at this location adds to the sense of movement in space as it pushes and pulls the phase relationships creating a sound which behaves in a way similar to a real-world object in air. The reverberation that is applied in this section gives the impression that the sound is travelling upwards away from the listening position, as there do not seem to be any other reflective objects between the object itself and the listening position. To further enhance this view, the delay that is related to this sound is panned hard left and right, indicating that the listener is surrounded by objects, presumably on the landscape around the listening position. This all adds up to the impression that the object that is creating the sound is taking off and disappearing upwards and eventually out of earshot by 03m 21s.

Phase 4 is a short section that begins abruptly at 03m 37s as the object suddenly returns without warning, as if its journey from its lofty position back to earth has been concealed, to sit in close proximity and to the front of the listener once more. By the end of Phase 4 the sound appears not to have the power to continue and has to take a pause, as if to gather energy.

During Phase 5 the object attempts to make another journey skyward as spatial distance begins to increase. However, the sound object does not make it as high as it did in Phase 3 and the listener gets the sense that the energy required to make the ascent is no longer present in the sound-emitting object. By the middle section of Phase 5, additional sounds appear to emanate from the object at 04m 23s and 04m 28s, which mark the beginning of the breakdown of this sound as it begins to falter and come to pieces.

Phase 6 begins at 04m 37s and marks the first point at which the sound completely trips over itself as the lack of cohesion begins to take over. At 04m 44s there is another moment of hesitation and clawing for form as cohesion breaks down further. During this brief phase the sound is constantly attempting to climb away from the listener as it did in Phase 3 but with much less success; the listener gets the impression that rather than efficiently and forcefully powering upwards as the sound did in Phase 3, the object is now wearily limping away from the listener, barely able to support itself.

Phase 7 begins at 05m 00s and marks another drop in cohesion as the sound falters once more, this time shifting in timbre and becoming much less bonded to the original. The sound appears to try to maintain its integrity but falters once more at 05m 12s and is seemingly unable to get back to its original, coherent, powerful self. Loudness begins to drop off significantly during Phase 7 and it becomes clear by the end of this section that the end of the piece is approaching.

Phase 8 marks the final shift in cohesion as the sound transforms into its final state at 05m 25s. At this point loudness and spectral density are decreasing and the spatial distance is increasing as the sound is faded out over a duration of around 40 seconds. The deconstruction brings about the conclusion of the piece at 06m 04s.

Figure 10.3 maps the four parameters *cohesion, spectral density, spatial distance* and *loudness,* and their continuous change over time. The diagram also includes the first ten time markers from Table 10.1 indicating the beginning of each phase along with two other significant events, 'Introduction' at 00m 24s and 'Termination' at 03m 21s.

Micro-, meso- and macro-level structures

The final aspect of this analysis will explore *Foil* on three levels of magnification: micro, meso and macro. These three levels describe the individual building blocks of *Foil* and how they are constructed to define the overall shape of the composition. These three levels begin with the micro-level.

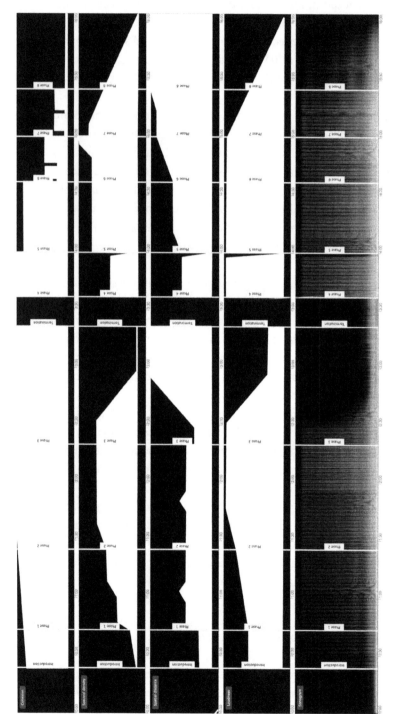

Figure 10.3 Map of *Foil* by Autechre denoting the eight phases and associated parameters

This level is formed from the individual sounds that create the phrases and loops in the work such as bass drum sounds, snares and various pitched material. The phrases and loops reside in the meso-level and are formed from clusters of sound from the micro-level. The meso-level units then group to form the macro-level and describe the shape of the composition.

As with many works in this genre, the micro-level of *Foil* contains both percussive and textural sounds. This is not always the case within electronica as the genre itself is created as a product of individual experimentation and 'play'. Making a generalisation about what is heard at the micro-level across the genre is not possible as each artist, and each individual track, will contain different collections of sound. Some pieces might favour elongated and textural sounds, and others might favour gestural and percussive ones. Equally, these sounds might be synthetic or synthesised, and others might be organic, sampled or constructed from field recordings. What can be said about *Foil* is that its micro-level soundworld is highly synthetic in nature. The majority of the percussive sounds appear to be from a drum machine and whilst they do not all have a synthetic timbre, the wood block being an example, they are evidently programmed and quantised at the meso-level, indicating that a synthetic process has been employed in their structuring. The percussive noise that was discussed in depth previously is a good example of the synthetic soundworld. Whilst this sound contains movement and a growth/depletion cycle reminiscent of the physical world, the timbre of the sound is highly synthetic in nature.

An important factor at the micro-level of this track is that many of the sound events that form the micro-level are constantly shifting in terms of their timbre to create an additional layer of structure on the meso-level that is concerned with change and flux. This flux is no more evident than in the bass drum that is illustrated in Figure 10.4 which shows a 12 second period from 01m 25s to 01m 37s, during which time the attack of the bass drum and the spectral content dynamically morph. At the beginning of this section, the bass drum has a slower attack phase and diminished spectral content resulting in a weaker sound. The timbre then morphs to create a more punctuating attack phase with richer spectral content, resulting in a deeper, punchier bass drum sound. This can clearly be heard in the track and is represented in the spectrogram in Figure 10.4. The initial bass drum sounds on the left of Figure 10.4 are lighter in colour and gradually become darker as the piece progresses, indicating a fuller sound in this range of the spectrum.

Many of the other sonic materials in *Foil* incorporate this gradual and subtle shifting of timbre over time. Whilst this gradual flux has significance

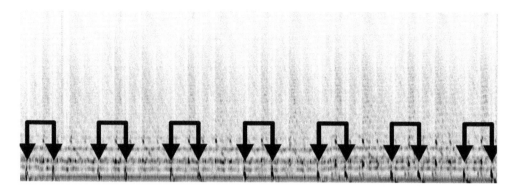

Figure 10.4 Bass drum hits in *Foil* indicated by the arrows in a section between 01m 25s and 01m 37s

at the micro-level, which can be analysed and discussed using various graphical representations, its significance at the meso-level is more pronounced. This gradual shifting and morphing adds depth and detail to the work and is both objectively and subjectively significant.

The pitched material in the piece plays a significant role but is so elongated that its significance is more related to the meso-level structuring of the track rather than at the micro-level. This pitched material gives the track a very drone-based feel that would have been familiar from other music in the underground electronic music scene around the time that *Amber* was released. The meso-level also contains loops that are formed from sounds that exist at the micro-level. These loops are constructed in a 4/4 time signature but, as discussed previously, are in a constant state of flux. Unlike a standard dance floor techno track, no phrase or looped section is identical to any other. This fact further enhances the view that the music is designed for listening and will benefit from a more attentive, objective listening approach.

As with techno and other forms of electronic dance music, *Foil* is constructed using layers of meso-level sound that are either built into the track gradually or are introduced abruptly creating the macro-level structure of the work. As well as gradually revealing the overall structure to the work, this compositional process is used to build tension within various types of dance music, including electronica. *Foil* can be broken down into eight distinct layers of sound at the meso level, which are represented graphically in Figure 10.5.

The eight layers listed in Figure 10.5 were identified and categorised in the following way. For a sound or collection of sounds to be grouped as a single layer, they need to be introduced together, work together and be brought to a conclusion together. An example would be the percussive

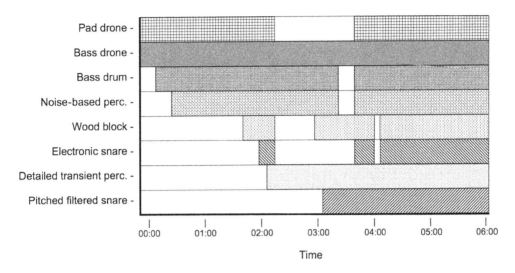

Figure 10.5 Graphical representation of *Foil* depicting the macro-structure of the piece

sounds in this piece which are clearly programmed and sequenced individually. The *bass drum, snare, wood block* and *detailed transient percussion* in Figure 10.5 all add to the rhythmical flow of the track, but must be dealt with as individual layers as they are introduced and drop out at different times to create structure. This would be in contrast to a sampled drum loop for example, which should be dealt with as a single layer as the sequence of drum hits would remain fixed in terms of their timing and timbral relationships. For the purposes of this analysis, as soon as sounds worked in a discrete manner, in isolation from other sounds or groups of sound, they were categorised as an individual layer. Without adopting this categorisation method, any analysis undertaken of the work would not have been an accurate account of structure at the macro level.

Table 10.2 lists the same eight events in *Foil* and their associated time stamps. This table is included for accuracy as the graphical representation above is only useful as an overview.

Summary

Foil is a classic example of early electronica and features many composition techniques that can be heard in more contemporary forms of the genre. Electronica contains a mix of influences and compositional approaches which range from established dance music practice and a soundworld

Table 10.2 The various sound events and their associated time stamps

Time stamp	Sound event
00:00	Introduction of pad drone
00:00	Introduction of bass drone
00:15	Introduction of bass drum
00:24	Introduction of noise-based percussion
01:40	Introduction of wood block
01:56	Introduction of electronic snare
02:04	Introduction of detailed transient percussion
02:19	Drop-out of pad drone, hollow wooden sound, electronic snare
02:50	Reintroduction of hollow wooden sound
03:05	Introduction of pitched filtered snare
03:21	Drop-out of bass drum and noise-based percussion
03:37	Reintroduction of pad drone, bass drum, noise-based percussion, electronic snare
03:58	Drop-out of electronic snare and wood block
04:08	Reintroduction of electronic snare and wood block
05:02	Deconstruction of all elements

which is entirely subjective, appealing to our autocentric perception, to a soundworld which speaks directly to our allocentric perception and can be best understood and analysed by taking a more objective and analytical approach to listening. This would suggest that the music is written with the discerning listener in mind and for a listening environment that supports close attention and deep listening.[15] However, at the same time the music often includes materials which are arranged using conventional Western musical structures such as a rhythmic grid and more traditional pitch structures. This suggests a more 'commercial' audience and a listening approach that favours an emotional response to music. Of course many types of music can be discussed, analysed and understood in terms of their ability to promote both intellectual and emotional responses to the sounds. However, electronica is of particular interest as it sits centrally between avant-garde music practices and the compositional ideas and soundworlds that are associated with other forms of electronic dance music, especially techno.

There are tangible problems with blending such diverse compositional ideas, some of which have been discussed here with respect to the performance situation. However, this coming together of two quite different

---

[15] As defined by Pauline Oliveros (2005).

compositional ideologies is something to celebrate and nurture as it will only serve to broaden access to electronic music. Rather than being something to shy away from, this fusion of genres is a rich area for further study and most certainly an area to watch for contemporary and future innovation in electronic music making.

The analysis of electronica gives composers and listeners a new set of tools with which to appreciate the music and to understand where it fits within the social context of electronic music making and listening in general. Electronica can be seen as a fundamental 'missing link' between what some might call 'academic' music and a musical form which is made in a more commercial setting. Of course, these two categorisations are, in reality, a plastic notion, but to some they can be fixed barriers to appreciation, understanding or learning. It is envisaged that, by analysing and describing the arrangement, shape and timbre of the sounds in electronica, any future analyses will further inform practices on both sides of the academic and commercial continuum.

References

Chandler, D. and Munday, R. (2011) *A Dictionary of Media and Communication*. Oxford University Press.

Dawkins, R. (1989) *The Selfish Gene*, 2nd rev. edn. Oxford Paperbacks.

Emmerson, S. (1999) Aural landscape: Musical space. *Organised Sound*, 3(2), 135–40.

(2007) *Living Electronic Music*. Aldershot: Ashgate.

James, R. (1995) *Aphex Twin – Rich talk about himself (1995)*. www.youtube.com/watch?v=i-fYouVrIWo.

Landy, L. (1994) The 'something to hold on to factor' in timbral composition. *Contemporary Music Review*, 10(2), 49–60.

Oliveros, P. (2005) *Deep Listening: A Composer's Sound Practice*. New York: iUniverse.

Schachtel, E. G. (1959) *Metamorphosis: On the Conflict of Human Development and the Development of Creativity*. New York: Basic Books.

Smalley, D. (1986) Spectro-morphology and structural processes. In S. Emmerson (ed.) *The Language of Electroacoustic Music*. London: Palgrave Macmillan, 61–93.

(1996) The listening imagination: Listening in the electroacoustic era. *Contemporary Music Review*, 13(2), 77–107.

(1997) Spectromorphology: Explaining sound-shapes. *Organised Sound*, 2(2), 107–26.

Recordings

Child, A. (1995) *Magneze EP*. Downwards Records.
Henke, R. (2009) *Silence*. Monolake/Imbalance Computer Music.
  (2012) *Ghosts*. Monolake/Imbalance Computer Music.
James, R. (1993) *Surfing On Sine Waves*. Warp Records.
Various artists (1994) *Artificial Intelligence II*. Warp Records.

11 | Temporal recurrence in Andrew Lewis's *Penmon Point*

AMBROSE SEDDON

INTRODUCTION

This analysis considers Andrew Lewis's acousmatic work *Penmon Point* (2002–3) in terms of recurrent phenomena occurring over a number of different timescales. Investigating a work from this viewpoint involves considering the various kinds and types of sound materials present, assessing aspects of similarity or difference among them, noting how they function when they recur, and contemplating why they are significant.[1] Before embarking on the analytical discussion, a brief clarification of the idea of recurrence, as it relates to acousmatic music, is necessary.

BACKGROUND TO THE ADOPTED ANALYTICAL APPROACH

Notions of recurrence extend beyond pure repetition, and hints, glimpses or vestiges of earlier material may be sufficient to remind the listener of preceding events, even though the original material has not reappeared explicitly. Such referrals among sound materials might be founded on different degrees of similarity, ranging from apparent sameness to just residual resemblance. Thus, recurrent phenomena might include returning states, types of sounds and sound sources, or derivations produced through transformation processes. Naturally, sound material must be lodged in memory to some degree for a recurrence to be perceived; it must be memorable. Furthermore, the sound material must be striking and differentiable from its surroundings in the first instance, and have a clearly discernible identity. If sound material appears among other similar sounds, or if it is masked in some way, its potential to make an impact may be reduced.

A recurrence-based approach to analysis concerns the ways in which sound materials correspond and might be related, particularly when they exhibit variability, or only traces of earlier events. Correspondences among

---

[1] This approach was initially formulated with acousmatic works in mind (Seddon 2013), but can potentially be applied to many other genres such as (but not restricted to) instrument with electronic sound, IDM, or contemporary instrumental and vocal composition.

sound identities may be perceived and usefully described in terms of shared spectromorphological[2] attributes and/or shared source associations. Furthermore, corresponding sounds will invariably recur over different timescales, so the temporal relationships among them must be considered in order to better understand how recurrent phenomena operate at different levels of structure. Discrete sound events arranged over relatively short timescales may establish lower-level relationships, and these can be broadly thought of in terms of repetition and identity variation. These can often be considered to be operating at the gestural level. However, this analysis of *Penmon Point* will focus on the higher-level relationships at play, that is, the relationships among recurrent phenomena that provide a more global sense of structure. These may occur among discrete identities or events, as well as spatial environments or *settings*,[3] and are founded on the notion of return, implying that an earlier instance has been 'left behind' in some way.

The musical significance of recurrent sound material is also defined by the contextual role it fulfils when it returns, along with any expectations that it evokes based on the preceding instance(s). As such, the structural function of the recurrent material, and its degree of interaction with other sound materials present, must also be considered as these factors inform the observed temporal relationship. This analysis will draw upon the ideas of Smalley (1997) and Roy (1996, 1998, 2003) in the description of structural functions and the behavioural relationships observed among the sound identities within a particular context.[4]

ANALYSIS[5]

Penmon Point (2002–3) features a variety of higher-level relationships established by the recurrences of a limited number of sound types. These

---

[2] 'Spectromorphology is concerned with perceiving and thinking in terms of spectral energies and shapes in space, their behaviour, their motion and growth processes, and their relative functions in a musical context' (Smalley 1997: 124).

[3] The *Oxford English Dictionary* defines a 'setting' as 'the place or type of surroundings where something is positioned or where an event takes place', emphasising both configuration and location. In musical contexts, acousmatic images (a term used by Smalley (2007)) will appear both fleetingly as well as existing for more extended durations, so the concept of the setting as used here includes not just configuration and location, but a sense of temporal permanence and, in turn, the establishment of a spatial feel. It is not possible to define the setting in terms of a minimum duration, but rather its existence is rooted in a state of perceived permanence.

[4] This analysis will also refer to concepts that have been developed as part of the author's doctoral research (Seddon 2013) to help describe a variety of recurrence-based higher-level relationships. Terms have been selected to be (as far as possible) self-explanatory.

[5] Higher-level relationship-types will appear in **bold italics**. Terminology referring to structural function and behavioural relationships will appear in *italics*.

are often characterised by distinct source bondings[6] and spectromorphological details, and can be summarised as:

- fast attack, slowly decaying inharmonic sounds, possessing bell-like
  source bondings to varying degrees;
- environmental seascapes, suggested by distant surf and bird cries;
- various proximate sounds, such as pebbles or stones rolling and collid-
  ing, wave-like noise-based morphologies, water trickling/flowing, snapping and breaking sounds;
- vocal utterances.

The following discussion will outline some of the different relationships at play,
assessing their musical significance and how they contribute to the perceived
structural organisation and the interpretation of the work as a whole.

Bell identities

Various bell sounds occur. These are all connected by the impression of a
metallic, fast attack, slowly decaying resonance, whilst also sharing distinctive spectral characteristics based around a G♯ pitch. Although the recurrences of these sounds might be grouped because they are 'bell-like', forming
a typological 'bell' grouping based upon that types of sound source,[7] more
specific subgroups become apparent, largely defined by distinct source
bondings. Indeed, the various bell types are distinguished by a number of
sound qualities, such as: the impressions of space that they convey, their
differing durations and their more specific spectromorphological details.

The recurrent bell identities act as ***markers***, particularly when the piece is
considered as a whole (see Figure 11.1) delineating the unfolding sections.[8]
However, within the local contexts they function in further capacities.

---

[6] Smalley's concept of *source bonding* highlights 'the *natural* tendency to relate sounds to
supposed sources and causes, and to relate sounds to each other because they appear to have
shared or associated origins' (1997: 110). Such bonding will influence the perception of a sound's
identity and its musical significance.

[7] Correspondences among sounds can be established according to *types* of source and cause,
resulting in 'typological' groupings and recurrences. This can be the case even if the individual
sounds are perceived to be different, assuming that they are somehow similar in the kind or type
of source–cause activity. A sound archetype founded on a particular sound source stimulates
expectation and comparison based on the listener's real-world experience of that source. For
example, an archetype described as 'wave-like' will consist of particular characteristics which
must be shared by the sounds that are part of the archetypal grouping.

[8] Markers are often similar sounds that draw attention to temporal position, marking sections
or particular points within a work. Their recurrence jogs memory and creates a sense of
temporal perspective, encouraging the appraisal of what has happened in between. Thus,
markers might be considered recurrent musical landmarks.

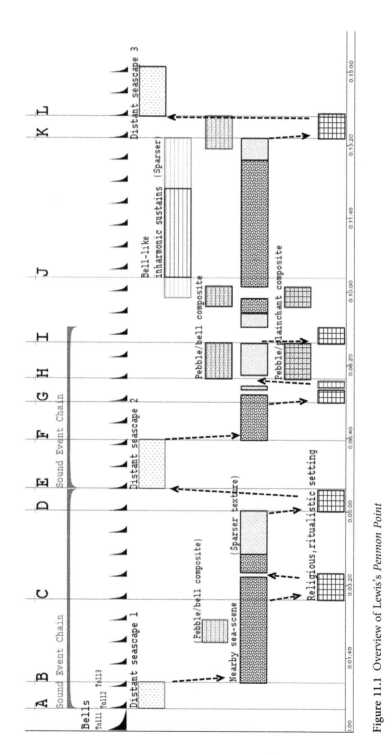

Figure 11.1 Overview of Lewis's *Penmon Point*

Illustrative bell recurrences

Toll 1 0'00

The spectromorphologically complex sound at the opening of the work commands attention much as a ringing bell might in everyday experience, and might be considered bell-like in broad terms. However, it exhibits some notable sound qualities. The extended resonance becomes partly absorbed by the additional layers of spectral swells and descending spectral contours (some emerging with accelerating and decelerating iterations). However, these subsequently withdraw, allowing the bell-like resonance to re-emerge and decay (audio ex. 1, 0'00–0'28).[9] Due to the various layers, this sound might be described as a third-order surrogate (Smalley 1997: 111–12), and its source-bonded spatiality is more remote from reality compared to many of the subsequent bells.[10]

Toll 2 0'30

In contrast, the source-bonded lighthouse bell at 0'30 is much shorter in duration, sounding distant due to the spectral restriction in both higher and lower frequency ranges (audio ex. 2, 0'28–0'38).[11] It is the second bell type, and as well as performing a marker function it *signals* the entry of a 'real-world' seascape environment, which *coexists* with the remaining continuant spectral residues of toll 1, resulting in two layered or superimposed spaces. It also reminds of toll 1 since its fundamental pitch is the same. Contextual elements become significant; in retrospect, this bell instance is part of the newly introduced distant seascape setting due to the source-bonded spatial and contextual congruency between it and the seascape.[12]

Toll 3 1'00

The recurrence of the lighthouse bell at 1'00 **reinforces** that sound in our perception: it is embedded within the ongoing seascape environment

---

[9] The sound examples are to be found on the website accompanying this book.

[10] *'Third-order surrogacy* is where a gesture is inferred or imagined in the music. The nature of the spectromorphology makes us unsure about the reality of either the source or the cause, or both. We may not be sure about how the sound was made to behave as it does, what the sounding material might be, or perhaps about the energy–motion trajectory involved' (Smalley 1997: 112).

[11] The subsequent presence of source-bonded seascape sound material reinforces this sense of space, which in turn strengthens the impression of this bell identity. The programme note accompanying the DVD-Audio reveals that the bell is actually that of Penmon Point lighthouse.

[12] The idea of contextual congruence concerns whether sound material appears to be congruent with the current context, either in terms of its spectromorphology or source associations.

and the sense of contextual congruency is strengthened (audio ex. 3, 0'54–1'04). Additionally, it creates a *marker* relationship (which extends as the piece unfolds) by delineating this local distant seascape passage, and provoking the expectation that it could ring a third time. It also *terminates* the continuing spectral residues of toll 1, an action that connects the two superimposed spaces, yet does not instigate or signal any new material.

Aspects of correspondence among subsequent bell tolls

The subsequent bell instances exhibit different kinds of correspondence with tolls 1, 2 and 3. For example, the bell at 1'30 is spectrally brighter than tolls 2 and 3, and sounds to be more proximate (audio ex. 4, 1'28–1'34). The external lighthouse bell sound at 2'00 is synchronous with descending, pulsed, inharmonic spectral figurations reminiscent of toll 1 (audio ex. 5, 1'58–2'10). At 2'30, similar figurations *coexist* with a spectrally brighter and nearer bell toll, recalling that of 1'30 but appearing to be a composite of layered bell-like sounds (audio ex. 6, 2'27–2'51). And the instance at 3'00 features the lower-frequency spectral material of toll 1, simultaneous with the nearer bell-like material (audio ex. 7, 2'58–3'10). Thus the linear separation and recurrence of different elements of the initial bell sounds allows attention to focus on particular aspects of correspondence. It also stimulates a process of comparison between them and the subsequent instances, resulting in networks of correspondence that establish some striking layered combinations based upon distinct sound qualities and the impressions of space evoked by the original tolls.

Issues of function

Following tolls 1, 2 and 3, the bell identities continue to fulfil the marker role, but they perform additional structural functions as indicated in Table 11.1 (audio ex. 8, 0'00–5'50).

An *instigative* function increasingly becomes associated with the bell sounds, and accordingly this passage conveys a considerable sense of forward motion. However, this impression changes at other points in the work. For example, between 10'00 and 12'30, the bell tolls largely *coexist* with the more slowly evolving sustain texture, wave and pebble sounds, and the sense of forward motion driven by the bell tolls is reduced; any expectations of instigative change are unfulfilled (J[13] audio ex. 9, 9'58–12'30). Similarly,

---

[13] Capital letters refer to locations indicated on Figure 1.

Table 11.1 Functions attributed to bell sounds in *Penmon Point* 0'00–5'50

Time	Functions attributed to bell recurrences
0'00	• First occurrence
0'30	• *Signal*: signals entry of 'real-world' seascape
1'00	• *Termination*: terminates continuant spectral residues
1'30	• *Interruption*: briefly interrupts/halts the pebble-based texture, which then returns at 1'35
2'00	• *Termination*: appears to terminate the proximate, pebble-based activity
2'30	• *Signal*: synchronous with climax of pebble-based *intensification/ accumulation/release* pattern at 2'28; increases in motion, density and amplitude of the pebble-like granular material create a sense of tension, which is released by the bell strike
	• Specific context recurs at 7'00
3'00	• *Signal*: signals spatial shift; ritualistic utterance space emerges out of the bell resonance
3'30	• *Instigation*: instigates crescendo of the vocal-like graduated continuant, itself leading to the return of the pebble/waves texture
	• *Termination*: terminates the ritualistic utterance space
4'00	• *Termination*: terminates the pebble/waves activity (more quickly than at 2'00)
	• *Deflection*: initiates change in textural emphasis
4'30	• *Instigation*: instigates new continuant spectra (related to bell); instigates iterative descents
5'00	• *Termination*: terminates continuant bell-like spectral residues
	• *Instigation*: instigates change to ritualistic utterance space
5'30	• *Termination*: terminates ritualistic utterance space
	• *Instigation*: instigates recurrence of environmental seascape

when the bell and seascape combination recurs at 5'30 (E), the bell acts as a sectional **marker** whilst also temporally dividing the seascape passage (at 6'00 and **reinforced** at 6'30). However, within this context the bell becomes established as an environmental feature, contributing to the evocation of the seascape (audio ex. 10, 5'25–6'48). When the tolls are embedded within the realistic sea setting, the notion of energetic forward motion is reduced.

Ritualistic, possibly religious, bells are the third distinct bell-type to occur (e.g. at 5'15), and their source bonding conveys a particular internal spatiality (audio ex. 11, 5'12–5'34).[14] They are higher in register compared to the work's opening bell-like sound and the lighthouse bells, yet they share the same pitch-centre (approximately G♯), as is evident at 5'30 (E). At this point, the ritualistic bell fulfils the sectional **marker** function,

---

[14] Additional source-bonded sounds again reinforce the sense of space, in this case, plainchant utterances, bringing internal, ritualistic and religious associations.

terminates the sense of religious/ritualistic space (see section 'Recurrent settings', pages 240–2), and *instigates* textural and spatial change.[15]

Each bell recurrence **reinforces** our awareness of the bell archetype. Even the opening sound (0'00) conforms to this archetype in broad terms (overall morphology and core spectral content), yet it might be best described as a 'hyper-bell'. It is bell-like when compared to the following lighthouse tolls and ritualistic bell sounds, yet the extended resonance, expanded spectral range and additional spectral figurations suggest that it is highly transformed. Thus, the hyper-bell attains **significance in retrospect** due to the subsequent occurrence of more strongly source-bonded bells. (Of course, the recurrence of separate elements of the hyper-bell contributes to this impression.) This also suggests that groupings based upon sound-type can occur retrospectively.

However, while the various bell sound identities manifest typological similarities, they convey contrasting cultural associations and meanings that establish subgroups. For example, the ritualistic, ceremonial bell identities act as religious signifiers representative of cultural/spiritual ritual, while the external lighthouse bells could be associated with warning and danger. Of course, such interpretations are the products of culturally learned contexts, and the degree of significance to the listener will depend on familiarity with the relevant cultural cues.

Temporal distribution of bell recurrences

One remains aware of the recurring bell tolls throughout, but they are sufficiently spaced in time not to be perceived as temporally regular (although they actually occur every 30 seconds, often delineating sections at the sequence level), and are largely perceived as sectional **markers** and landmarks.[16] Impressions of regularity and temporal flow are influenced by the intervening sound materials and their source associations. Snyder suggests that the speed at which time is perceived to pass is related to familiarity with, and density of, sound events (2000: 213–15). In *Penmon Point*, the densely populated, active sections (e.g. B, audio ex. 12, 1'05–2'10, and audio ex. 13, 2'25–3'10) give the impression of time passing rapidly between the bell tolls. However, the calmer distant seascape setting (see next section) conveys continuity, regularity and a recognisably expansive sound source (the ocean),

---

[15] The coincidence of the ritualistic bell with the lighthouse bell underlines their pitch correspondence.

[16] The liner notes to the DVD-A indicate that the Penmon Point lighthouse bell actually tolls every 30 seconds.

alluding to a sense of permanence and even stasis, particularly at 5'30–6'30 (E, audio ex. 10, 5'25–6'48). At this point the bell's marker role is less overt, and it fulfils an additional function by helping to maintain the setting and the section. This passage may also be perceived to take longer to unfold 'in the moment' because less seems to happen, and there is also a natural expectation for the setting to continue.

Spatial perspectives

The recurrence of source-bonded settings is a defining characteristic of *Penmon Point*, and the piece features three distinct setting-types.

Distant seascape. The distant seascape (initially appearing at A, 0'30) is a strongly source-bonded, and largely unaltered, environmental phenomenon observed at a distance (audio ex. 14, 0'28–1'15). The distant perspective is suggested by its restricted spectral resolution, and this setting conveys a sense of permanence both spectromorphologically (by remaining consistent and unaltered) and through the source bondings that it evokes – the sea is expected to continue making sound even when not heard.

Nearby sea-scene. The nearby sea-scene first appears at 1'10 (B), and features source-bonded sounds of: pebbles rolling and pounding together; wave-like noise structures; water trickling/flowing; snapping and breaking sounds (audio ex. 15, 1'05–1'59). These source associations in combination create a context suggesting a coastal location and experience. A sense of heightened activity, mobility and energy is conveyed, and these presumed details of the distant seascape suggest the energy of breaking waves on a pebble beach when close at hand. Both the distant seascape and the proximate sea-scene potentially allude to the same source (the sea experienced at a coastal location) but perceived from very different spatial perspectives. Accordingly, there is a generalised source association common among these sounds even though the specific sound sources themselves are actually different.[17]

Ritualistic/religious spaces. The recordings of plainchant, first emerging at around 3'00 (C) but most clearly apparent at 5'00 (D, audio ex. 16, 4'59–5'32), bring with them impressions of human presence within a religious or ritualistic context. Reverberation reinforces the sense of an internal location, possibly suggesting a monastery or church, yet the concurrent

---

[17] High- and low-register inharmonic sustains (presumably abstracted from the bell sound material) appear concurrently with the sea-scene sounds. This results in a mix of sound-types, spatial perspectives and locations, yet the spatially proximate, sea-related sounds remain the dominant feature.

internal resonance of the bell might also suggest that the voices are contained within the resonance. Potentially affective (depending on one's previous experience of plainchant), the recordings suggest a particular social and cultural scenario, conveying a contemplative, inward-looking emotional state.

Recurrent settings

The distant seascape, nearby sea-scene and ritualistic, religious space are encountered under different circumstances. Recurrent *shifts* and *ruptures*, as well as the recurrent settings in themselves, establish higher-level relationships that contribute to the structure of the piece.[18] The recurrent settings are indicated in Figure 11.1 with the shifts between them shown by arrows.

Distant seascape

Occurring at 0'30, 5'30 and 14'00 (A, E and L), the distant seascape delineates the higher-level structure by providing three setting-based, environmental **markers** or landmarks. The recurrences **reinforce** the seascape setting, and all the instances feature similar onset functions, but with different durations and terminations.

Instigated by the lighthouse bell, each instance of the distant seascape contrasts strongly with the preceding material in spatial, spectral and source-bonded terms. The first seascape occurrence at 0'30 instils this setting in our perception, masking (although not eradicating) the spectral and spatial impression of the opening 'hyper-bell' (audio ex. 17, 0'00–0'42). This masking is striking and creates a partial *rupture*, with the seascape now the dominant element within the music. The two recurrences (5'30 (E) and 14'00 (L)) categorically *rupture* ritualistic, religious settings, the rupture process enhancing the impact of the seascape on both occasions and establishing a distinct spatiomorphological trajectory (audio ex. 18, 5'25–5'40, and audio ex. 19, 13'50–14'15).[19] These later *ruptures* feature changes from pitch-based to noise-based texture, intimacy to remoteness,

---

[18] *Ruptures* of, and *shifts* between, particular spaces, contexts and ongoing sounds can become significant recurrent features. Rupture implies suddenness, as if the existing impression is instantaneously shattered by a change to a new state or context, while shift involves a less sudden change, or a less overt contrast between what is shifted from and what is shifted to.

[19] The sense of the ritualistic space is enhanced on both occasions by the high-pitched bells, which stimulate further religious connotations. In retrospect, these bells function by anticipating and marking the terminating rupture and change to the distal seascape, and this recurrent process suggests that the music is nearing the end of a larger-scale section.

internal to external space, and social/cultural human presence to solitude in an outside environment. Accordingly, the listening perspective changes from intimate engagement to more remote observation, resulting in recurrent processes of withdrawal in spatial terms, and *termination* of the preceding setting/section in functional terms.

The distant seascapes are longer in duration when they recur, spanning three of the regular bell tolls instead of two. This creates an increased sense of stability and permanence from 5'30 (E) while also thwarting the expectation of an imminent setting shift. The sense of permanence is **reinforced** at 14'00 (L). However, the methods of *termination* change. The distal seascapes at 0'30 (A) and 5'30 (E) are terminated by *shifts* to the next sea-scene (audio ex. 14, 0'28–1'15, and audio ex. 10, 5'25–6'48). This **reinforces** a spatiomorphological process that results in increased energy, mobility, proximate spatial focus, and a sense of forward motion. The music 'zooms in' to the details of the seascape, offering a new, immersive perspective on the distantly observed, source-bonded phenomenon. However, the final distant seascape (14'00–15'00, L) is *terminated* by the third lighthouse toll, whose elongation and gradually dissipating energy, along with the subsequent bass sound, conveys a sense of closure. This subverts any expectation of a return to the proximate sea-scene (audio ex. 20, 13'50–15'25). Thus, while the three distant seascape sections sound similar and evoke common source bondings, they feature changing structural functions, fulfilling different roles within the music.

The distant seascape attains particular significance when it recurs. The instance at 5'30 (E) becomes a notable point of energetic calm and stability relative to the more active preceding sections. Additionally, it helps define the spatial bounds of the piece so far by returning to the earlier distant location, instilling a sense of closure to the sequence of contrasting settings. These musical attributes are not apparent until the seascape recurs; they are largely determined by the nature of the intervening sound material, and the significance of the seascape is **delayed** until this point.

Ritualistic settings

Recurrences of the religious, ritualistic setting are also the result of *shift* and *rupture*. It initially *emerges* at 3'00–3'30 (C) amid nearby wave sounds, yet the potential *shift* to this new space is not completed, the music soon returning to the nearby sea-scene (audio ex. 21, 2'55–3'45). However, this initial instance *anticipates* the more explicit recurrence at 5'00 (D), which **reinforces** and **elaborates** the setting through clearer human utterances and human-caused bell strikes.[20] Instigated by a bell toll, this instance of the religious, ritualistic setting definitively *ruptures* the sparser preceding bell-like spectral residues and pebble-like gestures to become the dominant element, emphasising its musical significance (audio ex. 22, 4'50–5'35).[21] Furthermore, although less marked than the earlier ruptures (A and B), the recurrent rupture function is now conveyed by different sound materials, suggesting structural functions can noticeably recur even if the sounds themselves are different.[22]

Sound-event chains

The pattern of settings and transitions from 0'30 to 5'30 largely recurs in a similar order from 6'30 to 9'00, forming a recurrent, setting-based *sound-event chain* but of shorter duration.[23] Recurrences of both the settings, their sequential arrangement, and the shift/rupture types remind of the earlier instances, *reinforcing* them while featuring local variations, changes in gestural pacing and *elaborations*. Indeed, additional material is featured at 8'00–8'30.

However, at 9'10, instead of returning to the distant seascape after the plainchant recurrence (as occurred at 5'30), the music moves, via the sparser proximate sea-scene, to a new section (J, 10'20–12'30) dominated by sustaining sounds that correspond spectrally with the bell (audio ex. 9, 9'58–12'30). Any expectation of a return to the distant seascape is unfulfilled. The eventual *recession* of the bell-related sustains allows attention to focus on the sparser proximate sea-scene. The subsequent *shift* from the sea-scene to the returning religious, ritualistic space at 13'30 (K; now existing alongside a low amplitude, 'pebble/bell' composite sound, discussed below) *reinforces* this particular setting transition whilst creating an impression of partial closure. The music is back in familiar territory following the more 'abstracted' setting. Significantly, the ruptural return of the wave sounds at 14'00 (L) completes the closure sequence, with the sense of sectional termination largely conditioned by the similar (and similarly closural)

---

[20] These two instances might also be considered as an *announcement/reminder* pair, in Roy's sense. 'An *announcement* states a fragment of the *reminder* in order to prepare for, and to increase the perceptual importance of, the complete event that will appear later. The *announcement* and the *reminder* may be separated by a long time span; an *announcement* can have many *reminders* but a *reminder* has only one *announcement*' (1998).

[21] The bell at 5'00 could now be seen to possess religious connotations (a church or monastery bell) due to the context suggested by the plainchant. Its decay becomes part of the ensuing setting.

[22] Later recurrences of the ritualistic, religious setting exhibit similar emergent and ruptural structural functions.

[23] Recurrent linear arrangements of sounds can establish sound-event sequences, or *chains*. The identity of such a chain will be determined by the sounds present, their sequential occurrence, their structural function and the nature of the temporal relationships among them.

spatial movement at 5'30. Additionally, the waves and distant seascape at 14'00 (L) seem nearer than in the earlier distant seascapes (increased high-frequency resolution and greater definition in the wave sounds) yet the appearance on its own, and the low degree of volatility, reminds of the distant seascape rather than the more energetic nearby sea-scene.

Covert correspondences

Covert correspondences, in terms of specific sound qualities, exist among certain sustaining sounds and the bell spectra, connecting apparently novel material to identities that are central to the work. For example, the proximate sea-scene at 1'10–2'00 (B) features inharmonic sustains that create a spectral *covert correspondence* (of fixed pitch-centre) with the bell sound heard at the end of the passage (audio ex. 12, 1'05–2'10). The texture of inharmonic sustains at 10'20–12'30 (J) exhibits a similar *covert correspondence*; the metallic, inharmonic sound quality suggests a generic spectral connection to the bell sounds, which are the other significant 'metallic' materials of the piece (audio ex. 9, 9'58–12'30).

Some identities exhibit multiple *covert correspondences*.[24] A recurrence of the plainchant at 7'30 (G) appears over two simultaneous pitch-centres (audio ex. 23, 7'27–7'45). The higher pitch-centre recalls the plainchant material of 5'00 (itself spectrally corresponding with the recurring bell sounds), while the lower instance sounds more 'naturally' vocal and untransformed. A similar spectral duality occurs in the subsequent passage from 8'00 to 8'50 (H). This features pebble-like sounds exhibiting bell-like and vocal-like spectra, forming 'pebble/bell' and 'pebble/vocal' composites that enmesh the two 'parent' sounds' identities. (The original pebble-like sounds can be heard in audio ex. 24, 1'33–1'44.[25]) The 'pebble/bell' and 'pebble/vocal' composites thus feature multiple *covert correspondences* with various parent identities. While their spectra are not exactly the same as the bell and plainchant material, the sense of correspondence is palpable, in effect blending together or enmeshing the contrasting parent sound materials (e.g. at 8'01–8'05, 8'11–8'16 and 8'25–8'32, all passages heard in audio ex. 25).[26]

---

[24] These composites *remind* of a similar type of identity at 2'00–2'30.

[25] The pebble-like spectromorphologies appear in this extract amid inharmonic graduated continuants and breaking/snapping sounds.

[26] Identities featuring pebble-like morphologies and resonant-pitch spectra are heard earlier at 2'00–2'30, yet they do not spectrally correspond with the bell or vocal material. However, these identities do correlate with the 'pebble/bell' and pebble/vocal' composites in broad terms due to their similar morphology and generally pitch-focused spectral character, potentially preparing the listener for these kinds of sound materials.

These composites privilege particular sound qualities while remaining rooted in the existing soundworld; they remind of the bell-like spectra and the pebble-like activity, yet move away from the parent sounds by defining their own identity and spatiality. Of course, such conclusions are conditional on heaving heart the parent material already.[27]

REFLECTION

Lewis's *Penmon Point* is a compelling evocation of place conveyed by a finely balanced musical structure. The recurrent sounds operate to present and reinforce the different aspects of that location, providing a clear impression of its fundamental characteristics. Higher-level relationships are formed throughout the work in a variety of ways, and returning impressions of space significantly contribute to the evolving sense of form.

The recurring bells delineate the work, marking section boundaries and sectional progression. Although regular in 'clock time' (as is the actual bell of the Penmon Point lighthouse), the bells' precise division of time is not immediately apparent. Lewis manipulates the listener's different experiences of time through the various kinds of intervening sound materials, be they the close-up, energetic sea-scene, the distant seascape, the 'indoors' religious/ritualistic settings, or the more abstracted bell-like sustains. Each of these conveys a specific notion of time unfolding, and, in sequence, results in a sense of ebb and flow that affects the temporal experience of the work as a whole.[28] Rather than experiencing rigid '30-second' blocks, one encounters a variety of rates of activity, which shape our experience of time.

The idea of 'the bell' provides a fundamental unifying strand in the music, reflecting a sound that occurs in, and defines, the actual location of Penmon Point. Although the bell sound-type accounts for a number of distinct sound identities, the notion of 'bellness' is the central element around which the various environments of the composition are situated. The different kinds of bells complement the various sea-related sounds and vocal material to evoke coastal environmental and ritualistic/religious associations, resulting in a very specific sense of location. In a sense, the various bells together create a metaphorical vantage point from which the

[27] These composites recur again at 13'30, but with more stable morphological activity and spectral content, and the reduced energy instils a sense of imminent closure.
[28] It is acknowledged that while the diagrammatic representation is useful in discussing or pinpointing certain features, it is more of an architectural overview, and cannot be considered a true representation of temporal experience.

different scenarios are encountered; the bell is never 'far away', and each passage is experienced with reference to a bell of some sort.

Over longer timescales, the distant seascapes delineate a two-part structure in which materials and settings in the first section are revisited, reinforced and elaborated in the second. Accordingly, the form evolves in a loosely cyclical way based upon the recurrent chain of sound events and settings, yet elaborations are explored in the latter stages of the second cycle. The significance of these later passages depends on the earlier prevalence and reinforcement of source-bonded sounds, the soundworld becoming perceivably 'abstracted'. Indeed, an important feature of the work is that sounds that are potentially evocative of different lived, bodily experiences (i.e. 'I can see/hear the distant sea; I am near/in the surf; I am in a church or monastery') are the basis of the more abstracted passages. Lewis enmeshes many of the sounds (pebbles, bell resonances, voices) to create new hybrids, fusing specific sound qualities and source associations, and stimulating the reappraisal of the preceding material. The **covert correspondences** (including the fused identities, but also the bell-like spectral sustains) create correspondences with remembered scenarios, but also define new perspectives on them. From a formal perspective, the abstracted sounds provide considerable elaborations within the soundworld, taking the music to new territories, yet paving the way for the eventual return of more familiar material. They are sufficiently remote from the original sounds to make the final recurrences of the nearby sea-scene, religious setting and distant seascape notable, creating a sense of wholeness and resolution by returning to those familiar scenarios. Perhaps the listener attends more fully to those corresponding qualities in the earlier sounds when hearing the work again, being more 'tuned in' to those aspects of the sounds' identities. Furthermore, the abstracted sounds are poetically significant, existing in and defining new spaces, intimately mixing and blurring the boundaries between the 'parents' to create an environment derived from the originally distinct sources: bells, sea sounds and vocal utterances. In a sense, these sounds embody a particular view of what Penmon Point is – the confluence of cultural/ritualistic spaces, human presence and environmental phenomena.

CLOSING REMARKS

In considering what we want from the analysis of electroacoustic music and how might we get it, this book proposes a four-part question: Which tools/ approaches? For which works/genres? For which users? With what intentions?

Regarding tools/approaches, this analysis has illustrated some of the ways in which recurrent phenomena can be considered within an acousmatic composition. Whilst the underlying concepts have been developed through the consideration of acousmatic music more generally, they can potentially be applied to other genres including (but not restricted to) instrument(s) with electronics, IDM, or contemporary instrumental and vocal composition. Indeed, the ideas of recurrence as demonstrated here may provide useful approaches to the analysis of works in which a solid pitch language is not clearly evident, and works that depend on other criteria for form to cohere.

Considering which users, whilst it is hoped that music analysts will find the concepts illuminating and usable, these ideas can be adopted in less-formal, real-time listening contexts, for example, concert performances and private listening. In this sense, the consideration of recurrent phenomena provides a listening strategy, which can help to articulate and to make sense of particular aspects of listening experience. Furthermore, the ideas are equally valuable to composers, potentially stimulating new approaches to sound organisation and transformation in terms of correspondences among sounds, and the deployment of those materials over different timescales.

What is the intention of such an analysis? What might be achieved? By adopting a recurrence-based listening strategy, listeners, analysts and composers are engaged with the sound materials from which the work has been composed and how these have been organised. This approach heightens awareness of the sounds present, their distinctive sound qualities and aspects of correspondence, and the temporal relationships at play. Whether considering covert correspondences or more overt recurrences, sensitivity to recurrent phenomena offers an essential way to consider and understand this fundamental aspect of musical organisation.

References

Lewis, A. 2002–3. *Penmon Point.* Miroirs obscurs. Empreintes Digitales. IMED 0789. DVD-Audio.

Roy, S. 1996. Form and referential citation in a work by Francis Dhomont. *Organised Sound* 1(1), 29–41.

1998. Functional and implicative analysis of *Ombres Blanches. Journal of New Music Research* 27(1–2), 165–84.

2003. *L'analyse des musiques électroacoustiques: modèles et propositions.* Paris: L'Harmattan.

Seddon, A. 2013. Recurrence in acousmatic music. Unpublished doctoral thesis, City University, London.

Smalley, D. 1997. Spectromorphology: Explaining sound-shapes. *Organised Sound* 2(2), 107–26.

2007. Space-form and the acousmatic image. *Organised Sound* 12 (1), 35–58.

Snyder, B. 2000. *Music and Memory: An Introduction.* Cambridge, MA: MIT Press.

12 | Michel Waisvisz: *No Backup / Hyper Instruments*

JOHN ROBERT FERGUSON

Introduction

Focusing on Michel Waisvisz's *No Backup* (2004) and *Hyper Instruments* (ca. 1999), this chapter draws upon a range of examples relevant to a discussion around electroacoustic improvisation with new instruments and technologies. The approach to 'analysis' I shall take is in many ways a critique of some of the more traditional methods. The open-ended, inter-active structures characteristic of digital media are not wholly compatible with conventional conceptualisations of music where 'performers' play 'compositions'. Improvisation offers a distinctive mode of engagement, in that it not only challenges the separability of performance from compos-ition, but also emphasises process over product, and is therefore more compatible with the interactive capabilities of new technologies. The impact of these issues on what we, as a culture, imagine musicians to be, and the interrogation of received notions of authorship and creativity, is an important undercurrent that shapes the discussion within this chapter. To unpick some ideas around new instruments and technologies I would like, initially, to consider Kaffe Matthews's (1999) work *Call Me,* which raises interesting questions of agency and presence, and highlights 'new' roles for what a musician might be:

kaffe walked the city with local resident Lia Gasch searching out the varying sonic nooks and crannies containing a public phone box. with a map of the area, the chosen call boxes were then marked, a route decided, and during the performance time, Lia walked this route, calling kaffe in the gallery...

in the gallery, kaffe was working with her violin and gallery sounds, building and sculpting a piece, the phone beside her, which would then ring and interrupt her playing at some point. the rule was that she had to answer the phone, but did not necessarily have to use its sound. Lia at the other end, would not chat, but hold the phone out to the surrounding sounds of that location.[1]

---

[1] Unpublished description previously available on www.annetteworks.com (non-capitalisation in original text).

In *Call Me*, as well as importing external sound, the telephone is utilised for performative interruption and sonic fracture, indicating a desire for unpredictable events and moment-to-moment negotiation, and in this way seems to me to build upon and further previous artistic strategies.[2] By incorporating sounds from her immediate field or environment, with those received from a distance via a low-fidelity connection,[3] the application of technological flair and expertise may be less legible than previous understandings of instrumental virtuosity. However, this process-based approach, focused not on the representation of a finished or fixed composition/work, is clearly not a problem for this musician; expertise is legible in Matthews's familiarity with a variety of tools and her flexible multitasking (digital processing of sound from violin/gallery/telephone). In relocating some creative agency to remote places, via Lia, Matthews must anticipate and interact with fracture, but to what extent is Lia's role as interrupter compatible with traditional conceptualisations of musicianship? Although she may appear to be passive and disconnected from the 'on stage' actions of Matthews, the theatricality of the telephone ringing means that Lia does, to some extent, represent the combination of sound and performance that is often expected of a live musician, that is, she has easily decipherable agency, albeit without physical presence in the same space as the audience. Although there is a cultural expectation that a musician authors sound, as this example shows, there is actually ambiguity and indeterminacy to take account of. From an audience's perspective a laptop computer is potentially ambiguous,[4] whereas the use of the telephone in *Call Me* is consistent with the historical expectations of this tool, that is, both the possibilities of the technology and the application within the musical work are familiar. It seems that Matthews's creative relations with the world are less predicated upon the production of an aesthetic product than upon a need to negotiate with the present conditions and with the affordances and possibilities of the

---

[2] The creative application of the telephone has a rich history, from Marinetti's (1914) *Dynamic and Synoptic Declaration*, which was the first telephone-mediated distributed art event, to Kaprow's (1965) *Calling* or Cage's (1966) *Variations VII*.

[3] Introducing the lo-fi environment of the city soundscape via the limited frequency bandwidth of a telephone into a hi-fi concert-like environment is an interesting environmental juxtaposition which foregrounds the creative potential of the telephone (utilising lo-fi and hi-fi in the same sense as R. Murray Schafer: '[a] hi-fi system is one possessing a favorable signal-to-noise ratio. The hi-fi soundscape is one in which discrete sounds can be heard clearly because of the low ambient noise level. The country is generally more hi-fi than the city; night more than day; ancient times more than modern. In the hi-fi soundscape, sounds overlap less frequently; there is perspective – foreground and background' (Schafer 1977: 43)).

[4] For a more detailed discussion see Ferguson and Bell (2007).

contemporary cultural situation; is this a new role for the live musician? Not necessarily: *Call Me* pushes beyond conventional conceptualisations of music where 'performers' play 'compositions', and both Lia and Matthews represent (in different ways) the *combination* of sound and performance. However, the extent to which these roles are regarded as 'new' or 'established' depends largely on audience expectation. Atau Tanaka (2000: 402) has asked 'What are the keys to understanding unfamiliar instruments?' and suggests the 'most straightforward answer is history, consistency, and repetition'. *Call Me* foregrounds ways of working with the resistances and challenges that are offered by various technologies, and these issues are highlighted in a visible and easily decipherable manner, thanks to a very familiar technology: the telephone. *Call Me* illustrates questions around agency, presence, ephemeral events and co-authorship rather than individual control, and I believe these are vital themes when considering new instruments/improvisation. I have argued elsewhere in a discussion around 'prior knowledge and expectation of instrumental capability' that in comparison to traditional acoustic/electronic instruments, a musician 'working with electronic or digital technologies "benefits" from a more open-ended expectation of sound production' (Ferguson 2013: 138). However, *Call Me* benefits from the history and recognisability of the telephone, and this helps make underlying themes apparent. With digital and electronic tools the transparency of technical function is often quite opaque, and discussion can be shrouded by technical information; the telephone, in contrast, offers a clear and obvious function. Considering the possibility that geographic distance may be perceived, perhaps metaphorically, between a musician and their instrument, and that remote agencies may not be other musicians, but imagined presences conjured through various forms of automation, or technologic (dis)functionalities, I hope to now locate and further similar themes to those identified within *Call Me*, in the work of an inventor of some rather unfamiliar instruments, the late Michel Waisvisz.[5]

Michel Waisvisz

Waisvisz (1949–2008) was a Dutch composer-improviser, and founder of the legendary Studio for Electro-Instrumental Music (STEIM) in

---

[5] Although I visited STEIM on several occasions, I met Michel Waisvisz only once at an orientation session, where he presented his ideas and demonstrated his practice. This was a hugely influential experience that marked a turning point in my work and I departed the orientation with renewed enthusiasm for live electronic music.

Amsterdam. Widely regarded as a virtuoso performer of new instruments including 'the hands'[6] and the 'crackle synthesiser', Waisvisz was also responsible for the co-development of 'live sampling' (LiSa)[7] software as used by Matthews in *Call Me*. LiSa combines the 'precision of studio practice with the liveliness of the stage' offering 'live recording, gestural controlled playback, and immediate use and reshaping of other musicians' live sound', thus a performer is able to sample a snippet of live sound and then immediately touch, navigate and manipulate it (STEIM 2009). Documentation of Waisvisz using LiSa with 'the hands', which consist of two wooden brackets with multiple switches, movement/infrared sensors, and a microphone attached, is relatively scarce. However, a studio album recorded with alto saxophonist Christine Sehnaoui called *Shortwave* was released via the Lebanese label Al Maslakh in 2008; this was only Waisvisz's second studio album since the 1970s, and was the first where he performed entirely with 'the hands'.[8] In this recording, music emerges through real-time collaborative interaction between two musicians, who each negotiate the sound palette of their chosen instrument with familiarity and expertise, and although in one sense *Shortwave* may be regarded as a 'fixed' or 'complete' artistic work, the accompanying text notes that:

Selecting the music that you will hear on this CD has surely been the hardest part of the entire process. There was so much interesting and different material available that narrowing them down to an hour seemed an impossible task. There have been as much as 6 different versions of the recording, many of them with no single track in common, and all of them seemed perfect in the moment. The final decision was made after the artists gave the label this responsibility. We hope to have made the most out of the material at hand. (Waisvisz and Sehnaoui 2008)

---

[6] See Waisvisz 2006a.
[7] '[LiSa] contains one big stereo Sample Buffer ... and the user defines so called "Zones" which have access to some part of the sample buffer ... One of the more important features of LiSa is that at all times the user is able to record new samples in the Sample buffer, not only while other Zones are playing, using this part of the Sample buffer, but more than one recording Zone may be active, meaning that the samples can be recorded in different parts of the Sample buffer simultaneously! ... LiSa gives you the possibility to control more than thirty parameters in real-time, such as Zone start point and length, filters, playback behaviour, time stretching, pitch shifting, etc.' (STEIM 2009).
[8] Much of the documentation that does exist of Waisvisz performing is of relatively low sonic quality, whereas this recording, made at GRM (Groupe de Recherches Musicales), wears its electroacoustic credentials on its sleeves, so via the close/detailed saxophone capture and careful mixing of the performance, an interpretation very suitable for concentrated listening has emerged.

As 'complete' as the recordings of these improvisations may therefore appear, the aesthetics behind this artistic work are not fully represented by the recording. What I mean by this is that music is so much more than the sound it makes. If the music is but one document of the various materials that emerged during the recording sessions, and if the decisions regarding which materials to include were not made by the musicians, then what can we learn about the practice of these musicians by just analysing the recorded sound? As hinted at in the quote above, and evidenced by the relative scarcity of documentation, Waisvisz's main agenda was live performance not studio recording: 'composers must go back on the stage and listen and think; they must work and perform where the music actually reigns' (Krefeld 1990: 28). It is therefore the performance strategies and instrumental ecologies that I have chosen to foreground in this text, as the interactive characteristics of the instruments used to make this music are at least as important as the underlying structures of that music.

The question of analysis

Of course the listener does not only perceive 'the music' in an abstracted way. In many cultures, it is the musical apparatus and performance practice that is central.[9] My intention in this text is to highlight the importance of artistic research, which involves broad analytical processes, but focuses on immersion within and interpretative development of artistic practice. If I want anything from analysis, it is greater exploration and acknowledgement of the relationship between artistic research and analytical method. In support of this I point to Borgdorff's (2006: 23) articulations of research in the arts, Nyrnes's (2006: 7) portrayal of arts research as idiosyncratic topological manoeuvring, Sennett's (2008: 1) '[m]aking is thinking', Fiske's (1992) '[t]hinking is for doing', Doruff's 'urgent need for folding theory back through practice',[10] and Gadamer's disavowal of methodology in favour of rigorous but idiosyncratic method (Dostal 2002: 2).

---

[9] Rock and roll was not just listening to the radio or consuming records, the commercial production of the electric guitar created an interactive scenario; the culture surrounding the music, the way the music is produced, disseminated and interpreted is at least as relevant to its understanding as the sound of the music.

[10] During her keynote presentation at DRHA08 (Digital Research in the Humanities and Arts 2008 at Cambridge University), Doruff highlighted a lack of artistic practice in theorising, and suggested an urgent need for folding theory back through practice, asserting that for the reflexive practitioner, the practice is always moving on and becoming something else.

Functioning as a reflection on research in the arts, the following discussion is based around video documentation of *No Backup* and *Hyper Instruments*, as well as a variety of other examples. The main aim, as I see it, is to unpick the relationship between Waisvisz, his instruments and the resultant artistic practice.

Connectivity(?)

The second half (6'34"–9'39") of Waisvisz's (2004) *No Backup* concert at STEIM features a solo performance of the crackle synthesiser. Like the cracklebox,[11] the metallic body contacts of the crackle synthesiser allow a performer to 'control' parameters by changing the area of skin placed in contact with the circuit. Although a performer of this technology may feel like the sound is directly affected by pressure, the technical situation is actually rather more complex, as this apparatus is not pressure sensitive, at least not directly. However, the extent to which the curves of the flesh are squashed against the body contacts does affect the amount of electricity that leaves the circuit and flows through the skin, and this is what most directly affects the resultant sound. So, the human body becomes a circuit board component, like a variable resistor or capacitor, which results in an unpredictable but nevertheless tactile system that greatly amplifies any variation in touch, so very small movements can have a radical impact on sound.

The Crackle Synthesizer consisted of the components of 3 Crackleboxes. These could be linked by touching special conductive pads. Potentiometers were used to control the amount of controllability of this instrument. 'Minimum control' meant that the Crackle Synthesizer would easily play on its own for hours. (Waisvisz 2007)

Although the specifics of how Waisvisz is coaxing sound from the crackle synthesiser may not be immediately clear to the casual perceiver, I think the liveness of this performance is well conveyed. As the quote above shows, and although varying degrees of responsiveness are possible, the crackle synthesiser is capable of playing on its own, autonomously. This offers a clear challenge to the instrument's performer, which is quite obvious in this video. The initial state of responsiveness at 6'34" seems to involve this apparatus being almost, but not quite, on the threshold of

---

[11] More information on the history of the cracklebox can be found at Waisvisz 2004. A new version of the cracklebox has been available since 2004; see STEIM 2004.

playing itself, which means that it is also sensitive to Waisvisz, who is able to interact with what appears to be a mixture of regularly timed and random variations from the circuitry. Aside from a slight adjustment to volume/timbre at 7'12", the performance continues until 7'56" with Waisvisz exploring a variety of body contact combinations and direct manipulations to the upturned loudspeaker. From 7'56" to 8'36" the relationship between Waisvisz's physical actions and the resultant sound becomes more causal and direct; rather than interacting with an 'on the verge of playing itself' agency within the instrument, each of Waisvisz's hands now seems to be directly authoring sound in a search for interesting sonic results. At times both hands appear to sculpt one unified sonic outcome, but there is also some parallel and discreet activity, which I guess is down to the crackle synthesiser being made up of three cracklebox circuits. There appears to be no 'backup' or supporting contribution from the circuitry during this section. It is a little difficult to decipher at 8'36" to 8'51"; although the crackle synthesiser seems quite responsive, Waisvisz finds a sensitive combination that appears in some way to trouble, worry, or threaten this responsiveness, which sounds to me like a meeting point or co-authored moment of struggle. This is abandoned at 8'51" in favour of more simplistic and direct interaction; the autonomy of the circuitry is briefly exposed at 9'10" and quickly restrained at 9'12"; after a short section of interplay reminiscent of the introduction but more aggressive and gestural, the instrument appears to withdraw its cooperation at 9'24".

Waisvisz utilises the various levels of responsiveness and apparent agencies available through the crackle synthesiser to form this performance into something beyond a series of ephemeral moments. Although I believe he is as 'in control' as he wants to be, some elements of this control are occasionally relinquished and an alternative form of agency exposed (albeit within the limited capabilities of the instrument). We can see and hear that he is open to surprise, that he is experimenting with the possibility of the instrument, and delegating/filtering/restraining accordingly. The interruptions and challenges to his perceived autonomy may not be as obvious as a telephone ringing 'off the hook' in *Call Me*. However, like Matthews, Waisvisz must anticipate and interact with the potential fracture of the emergent musical structures, and here develops a rather theatrical strategy in order to deal with this. Also, in terms of the themes that were identified in *Call Me*, I think it is clear that amplifying the micro-potential of touch/physical proximity can be as productive as geographical separation in conjuring an apparent agency from technological tools, that is, extreme closeness and extreme distance offer productive creative potentials.

In this video Waisvisz does embody the *combination* of sound and performance, rather like any other musician. However, although improvisation may appear to challenge the separability of performance from composition, the compositional process can be said to exist in the design and craft of this idiosyncratic and unfamiliar instrument, as much as within the underlying structures of the music. So perhaps the most relevant questions are not to do with the relationship between performance and composition, but between composition and instrument design. However, when asked if he considered himself 'in the first place: an inventor of musical instruments, a composer, or a performer?', Waisvisz discussed the various issues in some detail, but then summarised with:

> Your question suggests divisions that don't exist for me; I cannot see a personal involvement in the technical functionality of the instruments and performance as separate from the work of composing, so simply consider me a composer. (Krefeld 1990: 28)

New instruments, like the crackle synthesiser, are lacking historical codes and established modes of performance practice, which makes them difficult to comprehend, and this can lead to the musical qualities of new instruments and technologies being considered via previous instrumental paradigms. In an article entitled 'Riding the Sphinx – Lines about "Live"', which appears to focus on an early version of the 'Crackle Synthesiser', Waisvisz puts forward some ideas on audience perception in electronic music, which are useful to consider here:

> The audience asked: 'Are these sounds really electronic? They sound like scratching on wood, like human voices.'

> The audience of the day could only interpret the system in terms of playing mechanical sound objects such as traditional instruments and extended instrumental techniques.

> So when human curves were applied to electronics, it made those people believe that what they were listening to wasn't electronics at all. They use the information of these movements as a way to (mis)judge the timbral information.

> To a great extent, the expression of music is influenced by the listener's mental reconstruction of the performer's efforts. (Waisvisz 1999: 120)

It is interesting to note Waisvisz's use of 'timbral information' and the 'performers efforts', because what I think most fascinating about both the cracklebox and the crackle synthesiser is the lack of haptic feedback. When performing with these instruments, unlike many traditional instruments, the primary mode of feedback is auditory; there is no cymbal to strike, string to pluck or bow, or key to press. In terms of gestural interaction the entire expressive range is found somewhere between a gentle poke and not touching it at all. Some of the most interesting sounds are elicited by barely touching the instrument, and a physical strike can often result in silence. As Nic Collins (2009) has pointed out in a tutorial on how to turn a portable radio into a pseudo-cracklebox, getting any sound out of circuits of this nature can be difficult.[12] This lack of both haptic and visual feedback does two very useful things: (1) force the performer to focus on the timbral information, so the intuitive act of listening and adjusting is privileged above the negotiation of electronic or computationally complex interfaces/parameters; (2) the electronic and expressive potential of touch is foreground at an almost unimaginable microscopic level, this allows incredibly expressive and intimate relationships between musician and machine.

Touch

Waisvsz has stated 'I see the hand as part of the brain, not as a lower instrument of the brain' (Krefeld 1990: 28), which would seem to foreground his belief in the importance of touch and embodied musical activity; I would like to unpick some background around this:

Modern technology is frequently developed in order to bridge great distances, as evidenced by today's abundant use of the 'tele-' prefix. But while many cybernauts show a chronic propensity for thinking big, for acclaiming the remote reach of their often vacuous cyberchat, recent technologies also constitute an excellent means for enhancing and appreciating extreme proximity. Touch is interested in giganauts and nanonauts, in the full gamut of up and down-scaled representations afforded by electronic and digital tools, in all things and events made manifest by signal detectors and amplifiers operating beyond the range of normal human perception. (Norman *et al.* 1998)

In terms of digital technologies, this can be considered in light of what physical computing expert Dan O'Sullivan (2004: xviii) terms 'Intelligence Amplification'; this idea involves a specific focus on the importance of human agency for creative spark, and utilises computers to capture and convey expression. So, rather than mimicking the autonomy of humans, this approach aims to support and facilitate; the computer is

---

[12] See chapter 11 of the DVD that accompanies Collins 2009.

foreground only as a medium of communication. O'Sullivan suggests that whilst computing is not directly analogous to human thought, artificial intelligence and the use of computing to imitate and replace human beings is often at the heart of computer science. The physical manifestation of this is found in robotics, where robots attempt to imitate the autonomy of their human counterparts, whereas a focus on supporting human autonomy rather than mimicking it is, according to O'Sullivan, the difference between physical computing and computer science. Beyond 'supporting' human autonomy, Waisvisz undoubtedly recognised that a challenge to human autonomy could make for exciting performance practice; his belief that digital/electronic instruments should be as challenging as their acoustic counterparts was ingrained in his inventions and articulated in various publications, but I most enjoy his metaphorical reference to performing with technology as being akin to a struggle with a mythical creature.[13]

The Sphinx is known for its riddles and its hunger for losers. Personally I prefer to view this fabulous creature as being the unification of challenges both physical (animalistic) and mental (feminine). For that reason, I envisage that creating and performing electronic music on 'The Sphinx', the new instrument of my dreams, will be like riding in a rodeo . . . *but* on the back of a sphinx. (Waisvisz 1999: 119)

This acceptance of risk and failure, often inherent when improvising with new instruments, can be considered in terms of post-digital performance practice, a notion informed by Kim Cascone (2002), in particular the ways in which post-digital creative practices reintroduce notions of physicality into digital arts. Also, what Steve Anderson (2007: 4) terms '"digital analogue", a mode of representation that foregrounds material aspects of production seemingly in defiance of the conventional wisdom that digital media are characterized by dematerialization and disconnection from the physical world', which might also be considered in the light of what Joel Ryan (1991: 145) has termed the placing of '[p]hysical handles on phantom models [where] [t]he image with which the artist works to realize his or her idea is no longer a phantom, it can be touched, navigated and negotiated with'. So, although post-digital practices often remain heavily oriented towards recording technologies, their animation relies on human presence to bring them to life; they are not autonomously 'performing' (except, perhaps, for the cracklebox/synthesiser). In grappling with his instruments Waisvisz attempts to embody a broader understanding of 'play' than the

---

[13] This is similar to my conceptualisation of 'imagined agency': see Ferguson 2013.

linear reproductive connotations of 'playback', and perhaps this can be best illustrated by returning to the Sphinx:

Audiences would come to hear whether the composer/performer can hold his/her own against the experience and qualities of **The Sphinx** ... an instrumental compositional system, and simultaneously a performance vehicle with history and an automation that throws down the gauntlet. Who is more 'alive': The Sphinx or the average composer/performers of **the future?** History could overpower these composer/performers, they could 'lose' in new and unimaginable ways. At the beginning of these future concerts, no one will yet know the final outcome. Music becomes an art of the **arena.** (Waisvisz 1999: 125)

Whilst this rather combative portrayal of future performance practice with new instruments and technologies is quite idiosyncratic, it is not without precedent. Simon Waters has discussed the ways that composer, player, performer and audience have emerged in response to 'quantum shifts in music's storage – from the body, to the text, to the recording'. He also states that these 'separations and distinctions [are] essentially symptomatic of a very short period of musical history in a fairly localised geographical area' and proposes that 'current developments (DJ culture, turntablism, downloading, sampling, real-time composition & improvisation, laptop performance etc)' can be seen 'as part of a socially self-regulatory negative feedback process returning us to a "joined-up" situation of music as practice' (Waters 2007: 20). This is analogous to what Christopher Small (1994) defines as 'music making', which is dependent upon process, action and a participative agenda of doing.[14] The notion of music making also questions the separability of performance from composition, resists commodity exploitation, and foregrounds the practice of real-time (re)negotiation.[15] By 'returning us to a "joined-up" situation of music as practice', Waters seems to be critical of traditional conceptualisations of music, where performers play compositions, within an (often) inherently compartmentalised practice. What he conceives as 'current developments' seem to offer the possibility to move beyond the traditional reliance on the fixity of the musical text, but perhaps – in current times – this fixity has already been devoured by the Sphinx.

---

[14] Small sees 'music making' as characteristic of African musical practices, and he explicitly opposes such practices with those of Western art music. This is a complex set of assertions to argue, and – although relevant – lies well outside of the scope of the present discussion.

[15] Also usefully negating 'free improvisation', a term which I consider to explicitly reference a genre that emerged in parallel on both sides of the Atlantic in the 1960s that is now adopted by its principal parents.

Effort/struggle

By Waisvisz's own admission 'there is still some way to go before the Sphinx can invite us to take up the challenge' (1999: 125). However, in *Hyper Instruments Part I* (ca. 1999), a performance from STEIM's VHS archive (now featured on YouTube), this 'arena' mentality is made very clear. The performance begins with Waisvisz initiating applause with a nod to the audience, he samples this using LiSa via 'the hands' and begins playback of the applause at 09". However, he appears to struggle with the material he has captured; I suspect that the initial applause was not loud enough to be effective, but perhaps he was hoping to capture a more complex overall timbre. He pauses at 16" and encourages the audience to applaud further and louder, this he recaptures from 20–30" and launches straight into a flowing 'almost out of control' texture that increases in intensity until 37", where a 'pitched' harmonic gesture challenges this textural development, and a variation at 39" appears to cause a fracture at 41". Following this fracture Waisvisz explores the possibility of engaging a more stilted version of the applause and the pitched material in interplay, the applause now has more pronounced low/mid frequency content, but the 'pitched' material dominates and it is difficult to imagine how this could be moulded into dialogue; this leads to another fracture at 50". At 51" Waisvisz reverts to manipulations of just the applause sample, this is reminiscent of 09", but he appears to be grasping at something that is just out of reach, and these materials do not allow sufficient traction for his inspiration to hold, and – as before – this section fails to develop.

At 56" Waisvisz appears unsatisfied, and visibly focuses his efforts. When he re-engages with the sampled applause at 57" the whole performance seems slower, less dense, and less layered. Initially the sample is largely untouched by the speed of playback or spectral shaping capabilities of LiSa, that is, this is no longer the 'almost out of control' texture of 30". At this point I imagine Waisvisz 'taking a moment' to listen to the material itself, to be subject to it, to appreciate it for what it is. Then, rather than (metaphorically) 'riding the Sphinx', he appears to 'tweak' its tail or otherwise provide a stimulus that holds its attention in a non-combative manner; this seems a more domestic 'cat and mouse' antagonism than an imagined 'life or death' scenario. Perhaps the previous false starts can be attributed to a nervousness caused by having to prompt and recapture the applause? This might account for the second introduction at 30", which is a convincing dramatic statement on the one hand, but could perhaps be considered an ill-conceived jump into a blind alley on the other, that is, Waisvisz does not leave himself much sonic space to develop this material. That said, the open-endedness of this section suitably emphasises process, struggle and the interactive potentials of new technologies, and perhaps Waisvisz's intention during the first minute of this piece is to measure the capabilities of this particular incarnation of the Sphinx before fully engaging with it. This also makes clear to an audience the resistances and challenges with which he has chosen to grapple.

From 56" to 1'07" features delicate and refined interactions with both auditory and physical gestures having a more measured feel than previously. I particularly enjoy the short stabs of 'sped-up' clapping that begin around 1'07", these have an engaging texture and set the scene for similar but more flowing textures that evolve as physical and auditory gesture becomes wild and ambiguous at 1'09". The pause at 1'15" seems, for the first time, to have a calculated quality, that is, it conveys confidence and suspense, rather than struggle or fracture. Then, at 1'22", whilst outputting a medium density of sampled applause, Waisvisz captures the sound[16] of tapping 'the hands' on a microphone stand and layers this with itself from 1'28" to 1'32", which results in an off-kilter rhythm. The density of this rhythm increases from 1'32" to 1'52", this could be due to speed of sample playback, but I suspect it was achieved by resampling the applause recording using an 'overdub' mode so that this material builds up on top of itself (difficult to be sure as this section is accompanied by further loud manipulations of previous elements). There is a 5" pause at 1'52" where Waisvisz makes some adjustments to 'the hands', but – again – this pause has a calculated feel as it functions as a termination of and release from the previous section, and is convincingly situated within the overall flow of the performance. Overall, this section steps away from the previous jarring challenges to Waisvisz's autonomy, and there appears to be more cooperation from the instrument, which allows him to negotiate longer and more complex passages, with a greater emphasis on the development of musical narrative and overall flow.

---

[16] There appears to be a sprung-mounted block of wood with a piezo contact attached, that is, pressure piezometers, like microphones, translate vibration into an electronic impulse, in which the variance in voltage is directly proportional to the sound pressure oscillation, and can thus be re-rendered as sound. Unlike microphones, which are sensitive to airborne oscillation, pressure piezometers are sensitive only to tactile physical vibration, hence their name in common usage 'contact microphone'.

After brief adjustments to the hands at 1'58" we hear, perhaps for the first time,[17] the introduction of new material that sounds like it was recorded ahead of the performance, this is clearer at 2'05" where Waisvisz works it into dialogue with the previous tapping samples using infrared sensors that measure distance between each of 'the hands'. This move away from the obvious manipulation of 'real-world' sounds is counterbalanced by a vocal sample that is captured at 2'09" and amalgamated within a glitchy pulse-based rhythmic section, which is enriched from 2'18" with the addition of splattery concrete sounds and pitched manipulations of a playful electronic tone with a very vocal quality. Despite the obvious sonority between this tone and the underlying textures (derived from the vocal sample), the music at this point is lively and mimetic, and the new materials tend to very much 'jump out of the mix'. Then 2'28" pre-empts the loud swooping gesture at 2'30', at which point the physical and auditory gesture appears synchronous, this appears to signpost a shift in the flow of the work. The synthetic and bouncy playfulness from 2'36' onwards suggests an almost cartoon-like soundworld, which is very different to the previous section. From 2'51' to 4'14' sees a return to more obvious manipulation of real-world sounds, and develops in a similar fashion to 2'18' except a new theme is hinted at between 3'28' and 3'38', and this also foregrounds a playful and synthetic quality similar to 2'36". Both of these sections are quintessentially LiSa, that is, the ability to simultaneously play back multiple zones within the same audio buffer is a recognisable hallmark of this software, and we hear Waisvisz scrubbing through audio buffers, landing on and reacting to various pre-recorded samples. At times the relationship between Waisvisz's gestures and the pre-recorded material acquires exciting fluidity and complexity, with shifts in steer ranging from synchronised dramaturgical gesture to outright fracture of the physical and auditory.

4'15' marks a shift in the harmonic texture, with what sounds like one sample accessed via two different playback zones running out of synchronisation. From 4'48' to 5'11' introduces a sparse and distorted version of the theme that was briefly present at 3'28', the slowed-down-karate-chop like activity makes this section quite theatrical, and points

---

[17] Although I **think** this is the first time that we hear a sound that is not live sampled during the course of the performance, I am unsure of the source of the pitched material at 37" and 39", that is, this could well be extreme processing of the applause sample, and the sample seems to dissolve into the pitched material rather than run in parallel with it, so I believe this to be most likely. However, I'm not entirely sure and it may be that the first pre-recorded sample is introduced at 37".

towards a conclusion. The final minute of this performance returns to subtle negotiations of the original applause sample, which Waisvisz punctuates with a series of noisy outbursts, ending with rippling manipulations of the audience sample, bookended by live applause from the audience.

This is an engaging performance, but what is expressed? Fundamentally, I think Phil Archer (2004: 43) has summed up something close in a discussion about his own work: '[r]ather than saying "look at me", the performer says "look at this" – he assumes a position not dissimilar to that of the audience, surprised at and responsive'. This is a key difference in role between performers of new instruments/technologies and more traditional modes of performance. Thinking about this a rather blunt question emerges: Does decipherability of physical gesture actually matter? And perhaps more reasonably: What forms of effort are decipherable? One answer might be that the relationship between 'live' human agency and the agency embodied within pre-existing musical materials is complex, relatively new and constantly evolving. A more detailed discussion would require a broad survey of artists and works, including the DJ practice of Jeff Mills and Richie Hawtin.[18] However, this is something that Waisvisz (2006b) has also identified in a panel discussion on virtuosity in live electronic music titled 'Manager or musician?'. He asks: Do we operate our electronic systems or do we play them? This might be considered the difference between learning to play an instrument and learning to map software parameters to physical controllers, that is, the latter does not necessarily equate to an instrument or a performance strategy. Perhaps

---

[18] For example, Mills (2004) can be configured as an expert instrumentalist. The delicacy and effort through which he keeps his three turntables running 'in time' while almost constantly changing vinyl is very impressive. The 'struggle' in this performance seems to be with the possibility that the various elements in the mix may become unsynchronised. This is a stark contrast to Hawtin's effortless approach using a computerised 'virtual deck' set-up (2008). To my way of thinking, Hawtin foregrounds compositional selection and decision, above improvised performative display. Whereas Mills is all about the live performance; small adjustments are constantly required, mistakes part of the performance, but mistakes have to be rectified and much of his effort goes into the utility of keeping things synchronised. Although I perceive Mills as virtuosic, his fast and rapid movements often seem to have little in the way of dramaturgical consequence within the music. Hawtin, however, allows the computer to do more of the utilitarian work, and he is able to make short loops and let them fall apart in the mix in the sure certainty that a press of one button will bring everything 'back in' on the beat, effortlessly. These videos represent quite different approaches to the performance practice of not dissimilar beat-based musics, but it is interesting to perceive the different sorts of effort that these musicians display, some of which is recognisable within the music, some of which is not; perhaps it's this tension which makes their music so interesting. (Readers interested in detailed comparison should consult Vandemast-Bell 2013: 245.)

the ways in which a musician working with new instruments/technologies manages their instrument/materials is akin to how a guitarist tunes their instrument or chooses one chord shape over the other due to favourable intonation. What I mean by this is that there are often activities in any musical performance that have no audible or dramaturgical consequence, but whether or not an audience can relate to this depends on their familiarity with the instrument. One reading of 'Manager or musician' could continue the idea that new instruments should equate to new musics, but bypass any apparent focus on physical human agency in favour of freeing the musician from the mechanics of their body or the mechanics of the instrumental technology. This, of course, is what the cracklebox/synthesiser achieves: the expressiveness of touch is celebrated and extended. I have suggested that in regard to the cracklebox the primary mode of feedback is auditory. During *Hyper Instruments Part I*, 'the hands' demand a similar focus on auditory feedback, although the keypads offer some degree of direct access to the musical materials, and relative movement in space/angle of rotation remains an ambiguous form of control, which is lacking in tactile feedback. As already discussed: there is an expectation that a musician authors sound. However, although Waisvisz represents the *combination* of sound and performance, there is actually ambiguity and indeterminacy to take account of, and this is often evident as resistance or struggle. In searching for the untouchable thresholds at which the Sphinx might engage Waisvisz seems to be chasing an infinitely variable presence, which makes any performance with 'the hands' feel co-authored and ephemeral. Like *Call Me* and *No Backup*, the artistic strategies within *Hyper Instruments Part I* are predicated on the negotiation of performative rupture and sonic fracture; sometimes challenging the performer's autonomy, as well as challenging the very notion of what a live musician might be.

Conclusion

In regard to improvisation with new instruments and technologies, I believe that analysis should focus as much on the interactive activities of music making as the audio documentation of that activity. In support of this I point to Simon Waters's (2007: 20) 'joined-up situation of music as practice' and suggest that in the field of improvisation with new instruments and technologies a very productive form of analysis is often already embedded in the process of research intensive and reflexive practice.

This text foregrounds questions around agency, presence and ephemerality, and attempts to locate and discuss these notions from a variety of perspectives. My overarching belief is that the freedom offered by new instruments and technologies has resulted in a multiplicity of traditions, and that this multiplicity is hugely beneficial and should be celebrated (as it very often is). However, the relationship between freedom and tradition is tricky, in terms of an audience being able to decipher the relationship between performer(s) and instrument(s), but also from the musician's perspective of what a new instrument might be. Some musicians choose to assemble instruments that require huge amounts of 'effort' and energy to master or 'control', others utilise technology to free musical expression from the constrains of the human body. Alternative approaches focus on music making with a participatory or interactive agenda, and therefore the notions of musician or instrument can be seen to all but disappear. This chapter focuses on Michel Waisvisz, a hugely influential musician who has worked across and inspired many others throughout these areas and beyond; I write as a practitioner who is influenced by, and in awe of, his ability to reach out and touch us with sound.

References

Anderson, S. F. 2007. Aporias of the digital avant-garde. *Digital Humanities Quarterly*, 1(2). http://digitalhumanities.org/dhq/vol/1/2/000011.html

Archer, P. 2004. *Intervention and Appropriation: Studies in the Aesthetics of the Homemade in Real-Time Electroacoustic Composition*. Norwich: ARiADA texts. www.ariada.uea.ac.uk/ariadatexts/5/1/index.html

Borgdorff, H. 2006. *The Debate on Research in the Arts*. Bergen National Academy of the Arts.

Cascone, K. 2002. The aesthetics of failure: 'Post-digital' tendencies in contemporary computer music. *Computer Music Journal*, 24(4), 12–18.

Collins, N. 2009. *Handmade Electronic Music: The Art of Hardware Hacking*. New York: Routledge. An alternative version can be found at www.youtube.com/watch?v=-l5EhwsXUGg

Dostal, R. J. (ed.) 2002. *The Cambridge Companion to Gadamer*. Cambridge University Press.

Ferguson, J. R. 2013. Imagined agency: Technology, unpredictability, and ambiguity. *Contemporary Music Review*, 32(2), 131–45.

Ferguson, J. R. and Bell, P. 2007. The role of ambiguity within musical creativity. *Leonardo Electronic Almanac*, 15(11–12). www.leoalmanac.org/wp-content/uploads/2012/09/03_JFerguson.pdf

Fiske, S. T. 1992. Thinking is for doing: Portraits of social cognition from daguerreotype to laserphoto. *Journal of Personality and Social Psychology*, 63, 877–89.

Krefeld, V. 1990. The hand in the web: An interview with Michel Waisvisz. *Computer Music Journal*, 14(2), 28–33.

Norman, S. J., Waisvisz, M. and Ryan, J. 1998. *Touchstone*. Amsterdam: STEIM. http://crackle.org/touch.htm

Nyrnes, A. 2006. *Lighting from the Side*. Bergen National Academy of the Arts.

O'Sullivan, D. 2004. *Physical Computing: Sensing and Controlling the Physical World with Computers*. Droitwich, UK: Premier Press.

Ryan, J. 1991. Some remarks on musical instrument design at STEIM. *Contemporary Music Review*, 6(1), 131–45.

Schafer, R. M. 1977. *The Soundscape: Our Sonic Environment and the Tuning of the World*. Rochester, VT: Destiny Books.

Sennett, R. 2008. *The Craftsman*. London: Penguin Books.

Small, C. 1994. *Music of the Common Tongue*. London: Calder Publishing.

STEIM. 2004. *Cracklebox*. Amsterdam: STEIM. www.steim.org/steim/cracklebox.php

2009. *LiSa*. http://steim.org/2012/01/lisa-x-v1–25/ (Also see: http://steim.org/product/rosa/).

Tanaka, A. 2000. Musical performance practice on sensor-based instruments. www.music.mcgill.ca/~mwanderley/MUMT-615/Papers/Class02/P.Tan.pdf

Vandemast-Bell, P. 2013. Rethinking live electronic music: A DJ perspective. *Contemporary Music Review*, 32(2), 239–48.

Waisvisz, M. 1999. Riding the Sphinx – Lines about 'live'. *Contemporary Music Review*, 18, part 3, 119–26.

2004. *The CrackleBox*. Amsterdam: STEIM. http://crackle.org/CrackleBox.htm

2006a. *The Hands*. www.crackle.org/TheHands.htm

2006b. Manager or musician? *Proceedings of the 2006 International Conference on New Interfaces for Musical Expression (NIME06)*. Paris: NIME. http://recherche.ircam.fr/equipes/temps-reel/nime06/proc/nime2006_415.pdf

2007. *1976–1983 The Crackle Synthesizer*. www.crackle.org/Crackle%20Synth.htm

Waters, S. (2007) Performance ecosystems: Ecological approaches to musical interaction. *EMS-07 Proceedings*. www.ems-network.org/spip.php?article278

Recordings

Hawtin, R. 2008. Richie Hawtin on his Traktor Scratch DJ setup – Pt 1. Berlin: Native Instruments. www.youtube.com/watch?v=J1H9W_iLff0

Matthews, K. 1999. *Call Me*. Barcelona: Metronom Gallery.

Mills, J. 2004. *Purpose Maker Mix. Exhibitionist* [Digital Video Disk]. London: React.

Waisvisz, M. ca. 1999. *Hyper Instruments* [video recording]. Amsterdam: STEIM. www.youtube.com/watch?v=pYfRORkuPX8

2004. *No Backup* [video recording]. Amsterdam: STEIM. www.youtube.com/watch?v=U1L-mVGqug4

Waisvisz, M. and Sehnaoui, C. 2008. *Shortwave* [CD Audio]. Lebanon: Al Maslakh.

Analysing Sound Art: Douglas Henderson's
Fadensonnen (2009)

KERSTEN GLANDIEN

The analysis of a Sound Art work confronts us with problems and conditions fundamentally different from those of musical analysis as we know it.
This applies both to the properties of the work itself and to the kinds of
perception it calls for. We will need to take into account the special
character of this relatively new art form and, in the context of this book
on electroacoustic music, the important ways in which it differs from what
we usually file under the heading of music. The following text looks at a
sound sculpture by the American Sound Art artist Douglas Henderson.
The field of Sound Art is populated by hybrid artworks that combine
sound with non-sounding components. This chapter provides a short
introduction into the nature of Sound Art, stressing its particular engagement with space, followed by an investigation of the synergetic workings of
Henderson's *Fadensonnen*. It aims to give an impression of the work's
experiential dimensions by leading the reader through its spatial, sculptural
and sonic features, underpinning this with analytical detail. Because of the
hybrid nature of the topic, theoretical ideas from a variety of disciplines
have been drawn upon, including aesthetics, psychology, musicology,
architecture, philosophy, media theory and cultural theory.[1]

Sound Art

Sound Art is one of several new art forms to have evolved in response to
fundamental changes in Western culture in the course of the twentieth
century. Many of those new forms do not conform to the traditional
division between time-based and space-based arts and reject the allocation
of individual senses to particular art forms as for instance in conventional
visual or audio arts. In the last 60 years artists have challenged the limitations intrinsic to traditional genres and crossed into other art disciplines,
or have rejected the domains of conventional art altogether, shifting their

---

[1] Such as Henri Bergson, Edgard Varèse, James Gibson, Nicolas Bourriaud, Peter Weibel, John
Dewey, Lev Manovich.

field of action into everyday life. The result has been an unprecedented diversification in the arts with their practices becoming ever more hybrid and fluid and the art discourse, including its terminology, ever more tortured.

Sound Art emerged in the second half of the twentieth century as one of these hybrid art forms. Beneath its umbrella, artists from different backgrounds began to work with sound in a physical and *relational* way (Neuhaus 2000), not treating it as autonomous and self-referential in the manner of a musical composition that relates sound solely to itself and to the logic and consistency of a finished and self-contained work, but rather combining sound with elements drawn in from other fields of human activity, whether artistic or not. The resulting synergies varied greatly, according to their protagonists' specific interests, and merged sound variously with architecture, sculpture, design, ecology, instrument building, engineering, still and moving images, poetry, experimental performance and even radio (Glandien 2000, 2007). Such hybrid fusions of sound with elements from other disciplines were both experimental and challenging, and called for a fundamentally new kind of perception on the part of the public. As individual encounterers[2] came into contact with such works, they had to engage not a single designated sense – their hearing – but their entire sensorium. The multisensory, synaesthetic perception that hybrid Sound Art works require is of a piece with the new aesthetics that slowly gained currency in the course of the second half of the twentieth century, and that is now characteristic of today's contemporary art.

Space

Sound Art is also deeply implicated in another aspect of twentieth-century art: the discovery of space. While some art forms, such as ballet or theatre, had always worked with three-dimensional space, the visual arts only burst out of their spatial confinements – the picture plane and compact sculptural form – in the first half of the twentieth century.[3] At around the same time, music also developed an interest in spatial effects, initially by simply

---

[2] I am using the terms 'encounterer', suggested by Arthur Danto (1996: 16), or 'experiencer', in order to avoid the determination of the perceptive process through a single sense – such as viewer, listener, audience.

[3] Kurt Schwitters: *Merz-Bau* (1924–48), El Lissitzki: *Proun Room* (1923), Marcel Duchamp: *Mile of String* (New York City 1942) and *1,200 Bags of Coal* (Galerie Beaux Arts, New York 1938).

separating the performers in space.[4] But as technology developed, the possibilities for spatialisation grew more complex and sophisticated, allowing visual artists and musicians to devise *installational* configurations. In any installation, space is a crucial feature, since it connects the multiple constituent parts in a very distinctive way. These parts may be of the same kind (e.g. loudspeakers or screens), or of different kinds (e.g. objects or screens combined with loudspeakers). In either case, space is the decisive factor, determining how the parts will relate both to one another and to their respective surroundings. This also applies when visitors are not just facing a space, but are able to enter it, since they become part of the installation, constantly shifting their audio and visual perspectives as they move between the components. The disposition of these components might relate to a number of different aspects of the space it occupies: its size, its form, its surface material, its environmental qualities, or the cultural or social significance of its location.

Along with the incorporation of space into the artwork came the abolition of established presentation spaces – both in art and in music. Traditionally, 'closed' works were presented in 'neutral' spaces – such as galleries and concert halls designed to accommodate a range of different works. But in the 1960s, art practitioners looking for a less exclusive and more 'lifelike' (Kaprow 2003a: 204) context for their work took to the streets or searched for unconventional spaces. Composers, too, demanded 'new spaces for new music' (Stockhausen 1963) and – in rare cases – found an opportunity to realise this dream.[5] With the progression of technology, composers began to think differently about performance spaces and to devise new kinds of musical spatialisation.[6]

Space in Sound Art

Space was the place in which art and music met, and in which Sound Art was first conceived.[7] It became both medium and environment for the

---

[4] Erik Satie: musique d'ameublement (1917), Charles Ives: *Unanswered Question* (1906), Arseny Avraamov: *Symphony of Sirens* (Baku 1922).

[5] Edgard Varèse and Iannis Xenakis: *Philips Pavilion* (Brussels 1958), Karlheinz Stockhausen: *German Pavilion* (Osaka 1970), Iannis Xenakis *Polytopes* (Montreal 1967, Persépolis 1971, Cluny 1972; Mycènes 1978) and *Diatope* (Paris 1978), La Monte Young and Marian Zazeela: *Dream House* (New York City 1962–present).

[6] *Acousmonium* (Bayle, GRM 1974), *Klangdom* (ZKM Institute for Music and Acoustics 2006), *BEAST* (Birmingham Electroacoustic Sound Theatre 1982), *Espace de Projection* (IRCAM 1977).

[7] cf. Sound Art practices of Max Neuhaus and Bernhard Leitner in the 1960s.

new art form. Artists began to work with the physical properties of spaces in their specific relation to sound – as well as with the psychological connotations that those spaces invoke. Finding interesting and unusual spaces, such as vacant industrial buildings, warehouses, underground car parks, fields, derelict swimming pools, disused gasometers, prisons or churches, became a vital part of artistic practice, since artists conceived works for such spaces *in situ*, investing them with a site-specific or site-dependent character. Beside indoor spaces, Sound Art artists became equally intrigued by the infinite variety of natural or cultivated outdoor spaces: environments invested with their own distinctive sonic character, or exhibiting a significant natural or cultural identity, offering intriguing sound material with which to work,[8] as well as the compelling possibility of acoustic intervention.[9] Such spaces not only informed the acoustic detail, aesthetics and cultural character of a work, but also often *became* the work itself.

Today, spatial Sound Art works span a wide range, from free-standing, autonomous, still or kinetic works in enclosed spaces – such as sound sculptures,[10] sculptural or installational instruments,[11] site-specific sculptural installations,[12] spatial conditionings and room-frequency works,[13] spatial articulations,[14] newly built or altered autonomous sound spaces,[15] topophonies,[16] sound-induced shape-shifting architecture[17] – to works in outdoor spaces, including autonomous sound sculptures or installations,[18] listening posts in city spaces,[19] soundwalks,[20] sound interventions in public spaces[21] and – not to forget them – Sound Art in *virtual* spaces (radio and internet).[22]

The extraordinary variety of sound-space work undertaken by Sound Art artists is indicative of the creative potential of the new field, which offers practitioners new challenges and an opportunity to explore and discover possibilities that more traditional genres, including music, lack.

---

[8] cf. R. Murray Schafer and The World Soundscape Project.
[9] cf. Janet Cardiff, Akio Suzuki.
[10] cf. Douglas Henderson, Bernhard Leitner, Javier Pérez, Jean Tinguely, Ray Lee.
[11] cf. Trimpin, Tim Hawkinson.   [12] cf. Andreas Oldörp.
[13] cf. Robin Minard, Alvin Lucier.
[14] cf. Christina Kubisch, Bernhard Leitner, Hans Peter Kuhn, Robin Minard.
[15] cf. Bernhard Leitner, Carsten Nicolai.   [16] cf. Sabine Schäfer, Dieter Krebs.
[17] cf. Liminal.   [18] cf. Paul Fuchs, Lutz Glandien and Malte Lüders, Andres Bosshard.
[19] cf. Akio Suzuki.   [20] cf. Janet Cardiff, John Drever, Lavinia Greenlaw.
[21] cf. Peter Cusack, Sam Auinger and Bruce Odland, Hans Peter Kuhn.
[22] Many more artists could be named.

Sound-space perception

The variety of spatialised Sound Art works is matched by the range of encounters they facilitate. Unlike musical perception, which calls for focused, attentive and directional listening – a mono-sensory perception undertaken from a fixed position (Blauert 1983: 13) – sound-space works afford multisensory experiences, simultaneously engaging the eyes, body and other senses, in addition to the ears. Such site-specific or space-dependent works must be experienced first hand and *in situ* – and cannot be captured by recorded media. While this is arguably also true for music – particularly of the spatially diffused kind – most Sound Art works are conceived as 'open' constellations that need to be completed, in fact *performed* (Glandien 2012), by their encounterers as they construct the work through their immediate and individual exploration of its given time-space continuum. In such sound-space works, sound enters into a synergetic relationship with other components in which none dominates and all are given sufficient room to influence the others. The sound part of an inclusive Sound Art work therefore answers to other than musical criteria, and through-composed components that assert their own internal progression, displaying inner coherence and calling solely on audio perception, are by their nature exclusive and in Sound Art as a consequence rather the exception.

All these qualities, which are native to and irreducible in Sound Art, present critical problems both for the publication of Sound Art works and for their analysis. The need for first-hand, multisensory experience and a dependence on individual and immediate engagement with a work make sound-space works elusive if approached through the linear and mono-sensory modes of perception associated with printed or recorded publications.[23] In order to advance an academic discourse on Sound Art and raise awareness about it, concessions will have to be made – so long as we remain aware of the situation, and do not take the recording for the actual work.

In the context of this publication, then, I have chosen to examine a sound sculpture rather than a sound installation. The difference lies in the spatialisation. While installations consist of multiple components connected by space, often large enough to allow visitors to enter, sculptural

---

[23] 'Acoustics can not be published. They need to be experienced *in situ*. The passing-on of acoustic experience (*Erfahrung*) can actually only happen through *direct* experience (*Erleben*)' (Leitner 2008: 179, trans. KG).

components form a more compact unit, which is surrounded by space and can only be approached from the outside. Both spatial forms need to be experienced directly. Sound sculptures seem to be more conducive to written analysis since their spatial features are simpler to comprehend, and the exploratory actions of encounterers easier to imagine. The spatial effects characteristic of such works still point to the more complex situations found in sound-space installations.

The reference material for my analysis consists: (1) of a 16'43" edited stereo reduction made from the original 26-minute eight-channel audio track, which is diffused in the work through a vertical 16-speaker matrix; and (2) a series of still images of the sculpture.[24] These, together with a description of the work and how it functions, will hopefully aid the reader-listener to imagine the missing spatial and exploratory dimensions.

Fadensonnen

The set-up

The American Sound Art artist Douglas Henderson[25] constructed the vertical sound sculpture *Fadensonnen* in 2009.[26] It is the third of a series of six vertical sound sculptures he has made in the past few years,[27] in which he explores the confined sound space around a compact vertical core. *Fadensonnen* consists of 16 loudspeakers arranged in a 3.5 metre high vertical helix, designed so that the sound radiates out in different directions as the speakers spiral around the central core in two full circles (Figure 13.1). This core is made from thick rope, casually bound to a shackle attached to a hook and fixed to the ceiling. The speaker cables are invisibly embedded in the rope, the bottom end of which is tied to a heavy trapezoid block of concrete and then trails loosely to the ground. All the cables and amplification equipment are concealed, so that the impression given is that the 16 speakers are floating on a hanging rope. The speaker diaphragms are painted bright orange, with black accents,

---

[24] The stereo recording and colour versions of the figures are to be found on the website accompanying this book. Timings given subsequently in this chapter refer to this recording.

[25] Since March 2007 Henderson has lived in Berlin.

[26] Fibreglass, wood, concrete, loudspeakers, 350cm high x 42cm in diameter, eight-channel audio, 26 min.

[27] See, *we rise* (2008), *Dukatenscheißer* (2009), *Babel III: Language Angel* (2010), *Royal Flush* (2011), *Babel V: Dream Man* (2012).

Figure 13.1 Douglas Henderson: *Fadensonnen*

while the drivers and cones are set in transparent, sky-blue, fibreglass moulds (Figure 13.2). All the elements of the work are derived from a short poem by Paul Celan, written in 1968, from which the work also takes its title: *Fadensonnen*.[28] Henderson aims to give Celan's refined

---

[28] cf. www.douglashenderson.org/Fadensonnen1.html. First published in Paul Celan: *Fadensonnen Gedichte*. Suhrkamp Verlag, Frankfurt am Main, 1968. English translation by Pierre Joris in Celan, Paul. *Threadsun*. København and Los Angeles: Green Integer 112, 2005.

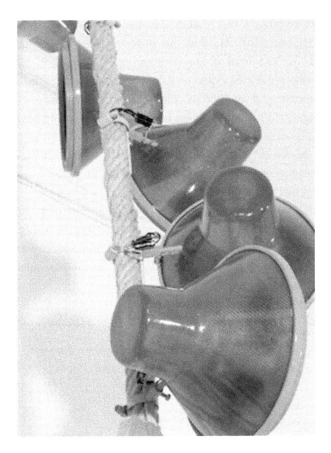

Figure 13.2 *Fadensonnen* (detail)

text composition, in all its dense fusion of melancholy and hope, a physical acoustical form.

The symbolism of the sculptural elements is direct: 'blue – sky, orange – sun, concrete – wasteland' (Henderson 2009). The sound material is anecdotal and follows the general mood of the poem in which over barren land, heavy footsteps fall, where the handling of countless books, accompanied by restrained breathing, connotes the encounter of ideas, and thoughts rise in fluttering motion out of human reach and 'when coloured with the light of the sound . . . develop . . . a kind of sublimity' (Henderson 2009).

The sound material

Henderson works with recognisable sounds whose familiarity contributes to the accessibility of the work: 'It is in the sounds nearest to us, the ordinary events that we process daily, that the heaviest psychological power is harnessed' (Henderson 2010). He finds his material in environmental sounds and sounds elicited from objects and physical materials in his workshop in a lengthy process of experimentation. Then he collects these sounds through elaborate and multiple recordings: 'I cannot imagine' – he says – 'using existing sound material by other people' (Henderson 2009). He prefers to use 'simple sounds that are familiar to the listener' (Henderson 2009). Building on this closeness, he leads these familiar sounds into abstraction through digital processing, while carefully attempting to preserve distinctive residual imprints of the original material.

For *Fadensonnen*, Henderson selected sounds bearing an interpretative significance in relation to the content of the poem. And since he always records his own sounds, he looked for sound with qualities conducive to the kinds of sound processing he intended to do – and to the particular spatialisation he wished to achieve in the final sculpture.

The initial material of *Fadensonnen* was limited to:

- the sound of footsteps on gravel;
- page-sounds using different books, with a variety of paper thicknesses and page sizes – rustled, snapped, fluttered, stroked, rubbed and leafed-through;
- the whooshing of large sheets of cloth;
- body sound – breathing sounds;
- the jingling of keys;
- sounds of Berlin S-Bahn trains;
- birdsong;
- the beeping sounds generated by a 'magic brush', a children's toy which translates painting gestures – such as the pressure, thickness and length of brush strokes – into ascending pitches (Figure 13.3).

The sound processing

At the processing stage, Henderson is drawn to multiple structures, seeking sounds that already naturally appear as multiples and are therefore sonically suited to further multiplication, such as splintering glass, dripping water, rustling leaves, crackling ice, popping corn, ringing coins or, in the case of *Fadensonnen*, leafing through books and snapping pages. He relies on analogue granulation, which – very different from uniform digital granular synthesis – assigns a slightly different sound character to each individual fragment. It is the sonic characteristics that shine through from the original

Figure 13.3 'Magic brush' translates painting gestures to pitch

material – frequency configurations, which Bill Viola once called the 'second shadow existence' (Viola 1990: 43) of the object – that endow Henderson's compositional stratifications, sequencings and convolutions with their multivariant, lively textures. These can only be realised through meticulous and detailed work. In addition to these multiplication procedures, Henderson also – and distinctively – uses convolution as 'a way of imprinting the frequency characteristics of one sound onto another in order to make two dissimilar things occupy the same spectral space/time' (Henderson 2010). These morphed sound-figures and precisely superimposed layerings act not only as the source of sound textures, but also provide the building blocks for the various spatialisation techniques Henderson uses throughout the piece. For *Fadensonnen*, the sounds of hundreds of pages were sourced from books of different sizes and various paper thickness – flipped, snapped, rustled, fluttered, rubbed and stroked. The sounds were then collected in dozens of recordings, which constitute the base material for further granulation and layering. Page-sounds appear as single events as well as being multiplied into sound clouds of varying density and intensity (2:50–6:00). Convolution is used selectively, for instance to process S-Bahn sounds (7:33; 9:08–10:00) or to link sounds that occupy opposing frequency ranges: when low frequency walking-sounds reach a certain amplitude, a gate opens, directing this source to a bank of convolvers, which use the high-frequency sounds of keys jingling for their convolution impulses. Each convolver has a different key jingle, and the footsteps are rotated through the convolvers by a panning device to create a very rich hybrid sound. Flutter sounds, however, are modulated through equalisation, allowing them to spread across the entire frequency range and mediate between the upper, middle and lower bands. Simple mixing techniques, as well as various forms of distortion, equalisation and alterations of speed, complete Henderson's processing toolbox.

The sound organisation

The organisation of sound in Sound Art rarely takes a linear form, since a perceptual situation of a very different kind pertains. The perception of a Sound Art work does not relate to the internal coherence of a composition or the dramatic course of a musical progression – or affect common to linear musical works with their definite endings and beginnings. Perceptual conventions established in the concert hall do not apply here, i.e. sitting with other listeners in neat rows in a designated listening area facing a defined performance space and following a presentation from begining to end with high concentration, immobile and silent. In Sound Art, the organisation of sounds has rather to accommodate an open situation in which individual encounterers address the work in their own way, entering the sound space at their own volition – which could be at any point in its temporal flow. The public moves around in the space, either with no path to observe or guided by cues and features of the installation or sculpture itself. Such open works (cf. Eco 1989) do not present encounterers with any unfolding linear meaning, but rather suggest fields of possibilities (Eco 1989: 44), which are at once *in movement*, involving, relational and performative (Eco 1989: 21) – with each work *affording* (cf. Gibson 1977) multiple perspectives. This perceptual situation must be heeded when sound is organised in a Sound Art work, since orchestrated effects, compositional arches, or coherent developmental expositions are lost on a visitor randomly arriving and dipping in and out at will.

A note on the stereo reduction

These Sound Art specifics need to be borne in mind when listening to the stereo reduction of Henderson's *Fadensonnen* accompanying this publication, since the recording cannot convey the condition of its sculptural context.[29] The recording here is a 16'43" edited stereo version of an eight-channel sculptural matrix which, in its spatial setting repeats every 26 minutes and is diffused across 16 speakers.[30]

Where the recording gives the impression of a linear, musical composition, the sound *in situ* may be experienced beginning from any point in the composition, considerably changing the impression received of the structure.

In an effective sound-space work, the organisation of the sound has to take into account the experiential situation generated by the work as a whole, as well as the perceptual habits of its visitors. Here, the entire sensorium is activated and all senses work together, none suppressed through ceremonial conventions or formal rules – the creative engagement of the visitor being an indispensable aspect of the work. To achieve this, an artist needs a good understanding of the intermodal mechanisms of human perception. Such considerations stand at the beginning of all sound organisation in any Sound Art practice.

Sound Art artists will trace the different psychological aspects of listening in relation to other senses, and devise set-ups that explore the properties of sound in all its different facets – considering in particular how we relate to sounds in ways that are not musical. Their work is to create aesthetic situations in which encounterers become involved with their own capacity for sensory response and are enabled to challenge their sensuality. Since at present the field of intersensorial research is still wide open, due in particular to the complexity of cross-modal perception (see Filk and Lommel 2004), contemporary artists working in hybrid media such as Sound Art are contributing both to a greater awareness of these issues and to the general pool of empirical research.

These are the perceptual conditions that need to be considered when creating or analysing the compositional dimension of any Sound Art work. In *Fadensonnen*, we observe two perceptual aspects that are particularly pertinent to Henderson's organisation of the sound – one of which is

---

[29] The eight-channel copy of the sound files is in private hands. The accompanying stereo version was made by the artist for study purposes only.

[30] All time designations in the paragraph relate to the stereo recording and serve as indication for the reader/listener to imagine the spatialisation.

temporal, working with the shortened attention span of today's media-conditioned listener, and the other spatial, relating to the perceptual dimensions of *vertical space*. Both have a considerable bearing on the sound organisation of the overall work.

In the stereo mix we can make out a general rhythm running throughout the piece, which is composed of contiguous 20-second sections. This length is derived from studies of today's reduced attention span and is adopted with the intention of capturing the visitors' attention, holding it and then luring them into the work. Such techniques have proven vital for Sound Art works in general, since the boredom threshold of today's public seems very short. Twenty seconds, however, is a duration long enough to create a phrase sufficiently coherent to induce closer engagement with the work. In *Fadensonnen*, these 20-second passages are occasionally doubled in length with the intention (Henderson 2012) of stretching the visitors' attention. These longer passages feature more ear-catching and complex sound structures, designed to bind the encounterer's curiosity, or less animated sections, such as various kinds of drone, that induce an 'attentive listening to the passing of time itself' (Hanssen 2009: 135).

Another general organisational feature clear in the stereo reduction is the division of the sound material into three frequency bands, which play an important part in the vertical spatialisation of the sound across the sculpture: in the lower range fall the gravel footsteps, associated with the barren, stony wasteland; in the middle we find page-sounds, as well as closely related breathing sounds, which invoke near and intimate human activities associated with the encounter of thoughts and ideas. In the upper range we find the sounds of fluttering pages and spacious rustling, whooshing paper sounds, high jingling linked to the footsteps in the low range, and the beeping of the magic brush that refers to 'the light-tone' mentioned in the poem.

Close-up

The recording begins with footsteps on gravel, moving from one side to the other attended by high whooshing noises, mid- and high-frequency jingling sounds and light breathing. As the walking sounds recede (1:07), closer and softer sounds of rubbing, page-turning and a spacious whooshing are established, followed at 1:43 by the sound of pages swiftly leafed through and page-rubbing. At 1:53 sharp page-snapping appears, initially as unevenly spaced single events, though still close-to and accompanied by occasional soft breathing, then slowly increasing in frequency and intensity (2:50), growing distant for a moment and then accelerating at around 3:40 into an abstract, dense structure that gradually becomes a vehement, intense pattering at around 4:40. Widening and narrowing in wavelike sequences, this pattering persists until 6:00, making it one of three event planes in the piece. After this, the atmosphere calms again – returning to low footsteps and high key sounds, occasionally accompanied by breathing and followed by spacious whooshing and page-turning sounds. At 7:40, out of the whooshing a soft drone emerges, growing more intense as page-rubbing and flutter sounds are added along with intermittent birdsong. At 8:20, a short interlude of footsteps on gravel and modulated key sounds emerges and grows, fading into soft reverberation at 9:08. Thereafter the sound becomes more intense again, with convolved S-Bahn drones increasing in volume and intensity to form the second event plane, which eventually fades at 10:00.

The last part of the mix emphasises movements between all three levels, focusing on mid-range sounds between 10:00 and 14:00. A longer passage of flutter sounds with some key noises and whooshing accents follows in waves of fluctuating intensity and volume; growing particularly intense at 12:00, then softer and more calm at 12:20, before taking off again at 12:40 when the 'light-tone' of the magic brush finally surfaces as an ascending beeping at 13:26, to perform a serene two-minute solo, constituting the third event plane. At the end of this section, the soft whooshing sounds return until at 15:16 footsteps and breathing mark the turn into the final stretch. Accompanied by jingling, whooshing, fluttering and breathing, the footsteps come steadily closer until at 15:50 a stick falls and the footsteps instantly recede, leaving only close-up sounds of page-rubbing and leafing. A thunder of whooshing draws the recording to a close at 16:43. The longer section at the end of the recording indicates another mode of listening, induced by an overall less animated and more regular sonic flow that directs the listening towards the passing of time and allows the 'experience of duration' (Block 1990: 10; 2001: 64). This short stereo reduction, however, can give only a vague impression of the longer, looped vertical sound diffusion of the sculpture itself.

Vertical sound space

Here the vertical sound spatialisation takes the form of an eight-channel sound diffusion relayed through 16 speakers. These speakers are positioned above one another to form a 3.5 metre vertical helix that accommodates two full 360° rotations. All 16 of the 12 cm speakers are attached by their bases to a thick rope – facing outward (Figure 13.1). This arrangement provides a distinct spatial sound experience that is essentially different in kind from the linear sound progression we perceive in the stereo reduction, not least because of its synaesthetic relation to the visual and corporeal aspects of the sculpture.

The sound diffusion devised in the *Fadensonnen* sculpture works with our learned metaphorical associations of low-, middle- and high-frequency sound as they correlate to the low, middle and high spatial location of the sound sources. The three frequency ranges compressed together in the stereo mix are now distributed around and from bottom to top of a three-dimensional speaker array, consisting of 16 speakers organised in pairs: two pairs on the lower level, where walking sounds describe a semi-circle moving around, both towards and away from the visitor as well as upwards, reaching waist height (Figure 13.1). Four pairs make up the larger middle section, which features mid-range sounds relating to upper body activities, page-handling and breathing. These are sounds we associate as being 'directly in front of us' – level with the ear, close and intimate. This middle area is where most of the compositional details are set, since it is where human aural perception is clearest. The last four speakers comprise the upper level, just below the ceiling and well above head height and out of reach. They project high-frequency sounds: spacious page-fluttering, rustling, jingling, ringing and the beeping sounds of the magic brush.

All sounds move constantly upward, relating metaphorically to Celan's poetic idea of high-flying thoughts and morphologically to the vertical up-thrusting structure of the sculpture. Flutter sounds, transposed into different frequency ranges, negotiate the different vertical strata, appearing fatter in the lower speakers and thinner in the higher. Their sonic likeness facilitates easy movement across the speaker array seamlessly binding the levels together and rising without changing character, thus aiding perceptual transition from one level to another.

Oftentimes sound multiples, created by means of analogue granulation, are projected from the speakers with a high intensity, density and volume – as in the page-snapping section (2:50–6:00). A compact sound cloud grows out of the spiral-shaped speaker column, which 'stiffens the air' around it. Sonic energy generates fluctuations in the air pressure that spread latently around the speaker helix giving it a palpable presence, as of an 'invisible physical object made entirely of vibrating air' (Henderson 2010).[31] Here

---

[31] cf. also Glandien, 'sound's dreams of us' in *Doug Henderson. Poets and Superheroes. Works 2010–2012* (Galerie Mazzoli, Berlin, 2012).

sound becomes a sculptural body, a delimited spatial compactness: tangible, palpable – almost visible.

As mentioned earlier, the problems of sound spatialisation in sound sculptures differ from those found in sound installations, since the constitutive components are not spatially dispersed but confined to a single sculptural form. In *Fadensonnen*, sound does not pass through an encounterer's body – as it does in Bernhard Leitner's installations *Tuba Architecture* (1999), *Pulsation Silence* (2007)[32] or *Sound Dome* (1996),[33] nor does it immerse the body in the way of Robin Minard's spatial conditioning in *Music for Quiet Spaces* (1999),[34] but rather it presents itself to the encounterer as a physical entity. And although, just as in sound installations, the loudspeakers project sound into space, radiating outward and, inevitably, reflecting back from any hard surface, the sculptural configuration of *Fadensonnen* tends to hold the sound together, forming a compact though invisible physical space around its visible armature.

In *Fadensonnen*, sound alters between different degrees of compactness. By muting different speakers in turn, Henderson causes the work to move and shift shape. Visitors are drawn towards and around it as the ascending sequences of sound are mediated through direct physical contact – as ear, eye and body follow the sounds involuntarily. On other occasions, we experience intense high-volume bursts of similar (3:40–6:00) or different (9:08–10:00) sound material out of all the speakers at once, turning the fluctuating shape of the helix into a solid, massive column of sound. This sound mass disrupts the encounterers' meanderings around the sculpture and induces a distancing effect. Detailed sound exploration is prevented while loud sound-surges trigger an instinctive corporeal withdrawal. The short, loud bursts also function as an event plane, standing out against the more even-keeled flow of sound that follows. This extended passage (10:00–16:43) is mainly built from rising mid-range page-sounds that are diffused through the entire speaker array from bottom to top. Shorter event passages are nested within the fluctuating intensity of this section, affording a closer, more intimate and detailed encounter with the work – as well as the experience of durational flow.

---

[32] Bernhard Leitner: *Pulsierende Stille* (2007) and *Tuba Architecture* (Klangkunstforum Berlin, 1999) documented in Leitner 2008.

[33] Leitner: *Ton-Höhe (Sound Dome)* (Kollegienkirche, Salzburg, 1996), documented in Leitner 2008.

[34] Robin Minard: *Music for Quiet Spaces* (City Gallery Saarbrücken, 1999), documented in Schulz 1999.

The vertical experience of sound

Since all sounds in *Fadensonnen*'s sound space are constantly rising, there is a distinct directionality to the sculpture, imparting a general lifting impression.[35] The vertical sound movements are always exaggerated, the location of the sound being emphasised through sound calibration – making sound have more bass at the bottom and more treble at the top. Such spatial considerations must stand at the very beginning of the work, when sounds appropriate to the representation of the poem and for the low-, middle- and high-frequency ranges are chosen.

Although the effect of sound rising is achieved by projecting sounds through one speaker after another, '*the listening process* does not suggest abrupt switches but rather relatively slow perceptual transitions' (Rebelo 2002–3). We perceive sound as seamlessly rising. It grows from the lower and middle levels of the sculpture – where our audio perception is well defined – to well over our heads where our audio location is weak (cf. Blauert 1983, 1985) (Figure 13.4). Because vertical audio localisation in humans is poorly developed, and much of it learnt in childhood, vertical listening is more effective when combined with other senses. By supporting the upward directionality of sound through the helical positioning of speakers, and the affordance (cf. Gibson 1977) of body movement around the sculpture, the sensorial impression of a rising circular sound motion is reinforced.

In Henderson's sound sculptures, speakers are rarely just the inevitable source of sound projection – as is so often the case in Sound Art works. The artist treats them as distinct visual components of the sculptural body, giving them distinct forms and functions, which vary from work to work, as well as using them as perceptual indicators for specific encounters. Colourful, unusually designed speakers adopt a multitude of shapes reminiscent of space helmets, water bowls, brassieres; they are inserted into drainpipes, little houses or giant flowers. In Henderson's kinetic sculptures,[36] sound is not only audible but also a source of motion. Projected through speakers, sound can animate not only air but also any liquids or solids placed inside them, and can set speaker bodies themselves into motion.[37] In *Fadensonnen*, both the ascending spiral positioning and the

---

[35] Henderson also created downward-directed vertical sculptures like the *Dukatenscheißer* (2009), made of drainpipe segments containing speakers that projected the sounds of spinning coins; a metaphorical comment on the global financial crisis.

[36] Super Hero Series: *Flash Gordon* (2009), *Wonder Woman* (2011), *Silver Surfer* (2011 and 2012), *Gagarin* (2012) and *In Order* (2012); *Untitled (Water Speakers)* (2006).

[37] *Gagarin* (2012), *Wonder Woman* (2011), *Flash Gordon* (2009), *Silver Surfer* (2011).

Figure 13.4 *Fadensonnen* and human scale

vibrant blue moulding and orange-black cones of the speakers – radiating out like little suns – carry not only a poetic significance, but also prompt spontaneous spatial behaviour in their encounterers, inviting them to move around the sculpture as they follow the upward path of the loud-speakers. Even for the contained spatialisation of sound sculptures, 'the most important thing for spatial listening is to move around' (Leitner 2010), since only then can sound movements work their magic.

Since artists cannot predict the exact navigational path encounterers will choose, or the explorative activity they might perform – how they move their bodies and heads, whether they bend, even kneel, which way they tilt their heads while circling the sculpture, taking one direction or another and each at their own pace – they need to accommodate all possible actions. The particularity of a sculptural design taken together with its sound organisation and diffusion constitute an *open work*, intended to capture the encounterers' attention, draw them into spatial exploration and suggest certain performative actions. When successful, 'a dynamic field is generated between sound and listener' (Weibel 2008: 100).

Dynamic and engaging, open works afford multiple perspectives of perception. Here the traditional roles of artist-producer and audience-receiver blur. Artists would rather share experiences than hand out messages or finished products. As they devise interactive dispositions, such artists act simultaneously as creators and audience, having particular experiences with the materials and passing them on. When relating to the arranged material, encounterers in their turn make their own experiences and become both audience and creator-performers of the piece. And while, in the process of production, an artist constantly checks the effectiveness of her or his decisions from an experiential perspective, so, in the process of perception, the experiencer completes the production through creative, performative actions. The final impression that the encounterer draws from the work will depend on her or his unique sensorial make-up – a combination of individual psychophysical dispositions and specific cultural conditioning acquired over a lifetime. In this respect, every encounter is de facto unique, making life-experience an indispensible condition for art-experience (cf. Dewey 1980). Although this applies, to a certain degree, to every perceptual process, and is true for the perception of art in general, the scope for flexibility and non-regimentation in an open work delegates more of the performative action to the encounterers, who use their own unique senses to execute the work. This process generates a greater tolerance towards the way a work is approached and allows us to move away from a judgemental culture of connoisseurship and exclusive specialism in the arts. In this respect, Sound Art has a great potential to overcome the division between high and low art, achieving wide accessibility through its open character. By generating fields of possibilities, Sound Art works offer experiences on different levels and of different forms 'according to our talents for "engagement"' (Kaprow 2003b: 11). And since individual experience depends on personal disposition and circumstance, perceptive abilities vary. For some, Sound Art encounters will always be meaningless and boring while, for others, they will be exciting and deep. The same goes for the expectations with which encounterers approach works of Sound

Art. Such open and hybrid creations will not satisfy expectations harboured for closed musical compositions.

Building work on experiences – which artists share with their public through exposure to their common cultural conditions – connects art with life on an *aesthetic* level.[38] In *Fadensonnen*, Henderson addresses modern society's short attention span and aims to stimulate our vertical sound perception through a synergetic fusion of sonic, spatial, visual and corporeal components, affording synaesthetic experiences through intersensory perception. In the face of an unexpected form, the encounterer rises above habitual quotidian perception. The sharing of experiences between artist-facilitator and encounterer-co-producer is extended in experiential exchanges that take place between encounterers. The communicative processes we find at the heart of contemporary art perform a vital function in a culture of increasing isolation, dispersed communities and loss of immediacy. In this wider cultural context, Sound Art's self-proclaimed role as an expander of awareness and enabler of experiences offers a counterweight to the ubiquitous perceptual conditioning driven on by the fast-moving mass-entertainment and virtual media culture we experience daily. By providing direct, first-hand experiences Sound Art challenges the mediated and indirect second-hand experiences promulgated by light entertainment and mass media. And by stimulating creative and immediate activities in which the unique faculties of each individual encounterer are called into play, it opposes the perceptual patterns of a culture characterised by operational conditioning, technocratic obedience and heightened self-referentiality.

As art becomes an immediate, involving and synaesthetic experience, embedded in a process of exchange, it not only changes its character, but also establishes a new purpose for itself in the context of a fundamentally transformed culture. Artists like Douglas Henderson are acutely aware of this.

References

Blauert, J. 1983. *Spatial Hearing*. Cambridge, MA/London: MIT Press (original *Räumliches Hören*, 1974. Stuttgart: S Hirzel Verlag).
    1985. *Räumliches Hören. Nachschrift. Neue Ergebnisse und Trends seit 1972.* Stuttgart: S Hirzel Verlag.

---

[38] Aesthetics from Greek *aisthētikos*, from *aisthēta 'perceptible things'*, from *aisthesthai 'perceive'*.

Block, R. 1990. Models of psychological time. In R. Block (ed.), *Cognitive Models of Psychological Time*. Hillsdale: Lawrence Erlbaum Associates, 1–35.

2001. Retrospective and prospective timing: Memory, attention and consciousness. In C. Hoerl and T. McCormack (eds.), *Time and Memory: Issues in Philosophy and Psychology*. Oxford: Clarendon Press, 59–76.

Danto, A. C. 1996. Hegel, Biedermeier and the intractable avant-garde. In L. Weintraub (ed.), *Art on the Edge and Over: Searching for Art's Meaning in Contemporary Society 1970s–1990s*. Litchfield, CT: Art Insights, 12–31.

Dewey, J. 1980. *Art as Experience*. New York: Perigee Books (original 1934).

Eco, U. 1989. *The Open Work*, trans Anna Cangogni. Cambridge, MA: Harvard University Press (original *Opera aperta*, 1962, rev. 1976).

Filk, C. and Lommel, M. 2004. Media synaesthetics – eine Einleitung. In C. Filk, M. Lommel and M. Sandbothe (eds.), *Media Synaesthetics: Konturen einer physiologischen Medienästhetik*. Cologne: Herbert von Halem, 9–21.

Gibson, J. J. 1977. The theory of affordances. In R. Shaw and J. Bransford (eds.), *Perceiving, Acting, and Knowing: Toward an Ecological Psychology*. Hillsdale, NJ: Lawrence Erlbaum, 67–82.

Glandien, K. 2000. Art on air. A profile of new radio art. In S. Emmerson (ed.), *Music, Electronic Media and Culture*. Aldershot: Ashgate, 167–93.

2007. Art on and off air. Post scriptum 2007: Mostly Europe. www .kerstenglandien.com

2012. SoundArt and performativity. In A. R. Brown (ed.), *Sound Musicianship: Understanding the Crafts of Music*. Newcastle upon Tyne: Cambridge Scholars Press, 264–76.

Hanssen, T. R. 2009. The omnipresent soundscape of drones: Reflections on Bill Viola's sound design in *Five Angels for the Millennium*. *The Soundtrack*, 2(2), 127–41.

Henderson, D. 2009. Henderson in conversation with the author.

2010. Gilding the Dukatenscheißer. Objects in sound and sound in objects. Unpublished lecture manuscript, HBKsaar, 21 June.

2012. Henderson in conversation with the author.

Kaprow, A. 2003a. The real experiment. In Allan Kaprow, ed. J. Kelly, *Essays on the Blurring of Art and Life*. Berkeley: University of California Press, 201–8.

2003b. Notes on the creation of a total art. In Allan Kaprow, ed. J. Kelly, *Essays on the Blurring of Art and Life*. Berkeley: University of California Press, 10–12.

Leitner, B. 2008. I hear with my knee better than with my calf. Stefan Fricke and Bernhard Leitner. A dialog. In B. Leitner (ed.), *.P.U.L.S.E.* Ostfildern/ Karlsruhe: Hatje Cantz/ZKM, 171–85.

2010. Leitner in conversation with the author. Vienna, 12 December.

Neuhaus, M. 2000. Sound art? Volume: Bed of sound. Introduction to the *Exhibition, P.S.1 Contemporary Art Center*. www.max-neuhaus.info/ soundworks/Sound Art/ (accessed August 2012).

Rebelo, P. 2002–3. Fragment and overlay. http://ddm.ace.ed.ac.uk/2002–03/pages/cources/vcm/1_webdesign/fragmentoverlay.html (accessed 4 September 2012).

Schulz, B. (ed.) 1999. *Robin Minard: Silent Music*. Heidelberg: Kehrer.

Stockhausen, K. 1963. Music in space. In D. Schnebel (ed.), *Texte zur Musik*, vol. I. Cologne: M. DuMont Schauberg, 152–75.

Viola, B. 1990. The sound of one line scanning. In D. Lander and M. Lexier (eds.), *Sound by Artists*. Toronto and Banff: Art Metropole and Walter Philips Gallery, 39–54.

Weibel, P. 2008. On the *Moving Heads*. Beue Galerie Graz, 2007/2008. In B. Leitner (ed.), *.P.U.L.S.E.* Ostfildern/Karlsruhe: Hatje Cantz/ZKM, 98–101.

14 | Analysing the identifiable: cultural borrowing
in Diana Salazar's *La voz del fuelle*

MANUELLA BLACKBURN

Introduction

What do we want from analysis of electroacoustic music?

Carrying out an analysis of Diana Salazar's acousmatic music work *La voz del fuelle* (2011) is an attempt to identify the various compositional strategies involved when cultural sounds become source material for creative work. An analysis of where this iconic sound material appears may help shed light on how a composer can both borrow and embed culturally identifable sound material within the more abstract sonic *milieu* most typical to the acousmatic genre. Understanding how a composer has placed cultural symbols, well-known motifs and sometimes whole passages of existing music into a new piece of sonic art is a worthy subject for analysis so as to demonstrate the evolution of existing musical ideas as well as the composer's prowess in gaining ownership over something borrowed.

Salazar's *La voz del fuelle* engages with the concept of the 'sonic souvenir',[1] integrating many musical samples borrowed from a foreign culture. Analysing the work's intricate integration of identifiable cultural material (traditional Argentine instruments and tango recordings) with sound materials of a more *culture neutral*[2] nature reveals how one as a listener might re-imagine 'the stylistic, cultural and performative qualities that characterise the music of Tango'[3] within a new context. I aim to convey the importance of causality in establishing plausible (although entirely

---

[1] 'I have coined the phrase "sonic souvenir" to encompass culturally tied sounds/sound objects that are not common or familiar to one's own cultural heritage or immediate surroundings' (Blackburn 2011).

[2] It may be claimed that all sounds suggest a cultural base or origin, however, I use the term 'culture neutral' to differentiate between sound materials that are highly referential or attached to a given culture. Sounds more universal in terms of their cultural background – for example, footsteps, kettle boiling or car engine – demonstrate a level of 'culture neutrality'. The same cannot be said for bagpipes, cicadas, a koto, or the sound of someone speaking Cantonese. Sound transformations that eliminate any trace of the sound's origin may also lead to achieving a more culture neutral status.

[3] Diana Salazar, programme note for *La voz del fuelle*.

fabricated) connections between the recognisable and the abstract and how the listener's acceptance of these impossible, causally triggered events rests entirely upon the precise placements of sound chosen by the composer. Cultural borrowing within electroacoustic music can occur in many different formats and guises and by analysing this work I aim to illuminate a more comprehensive perspective from an outsider's use of an Argentine music tradition and its transference to the acousmatic medium.

About the piece

La voz del fuelle is an acousmatic work that incorporates recognisable samples of existing tango music amid swathes of textural and gestural sound material of a more culture-neutral status. These somewhat 'iconic'[4] music samples make many brief appearances, along with individual instrumental recordings collected as either 'found sound' or originating from tango music performances. These cultural references frequently poke through the work's sonic structure in an identifiable fashion. Salazar corroborates this observation:

The work presents some unmistakable musical quotations from the Tango tradition such as the opening theme of Astor Piazzolla's *Fugata No.2* in order to evoke the cultural associations which are so closely tied to the bandoneón. Recordings of this instrument are woven in amongst other typical instruments of the style, as well as extended and electronically manipulated material from bandoneón, piano, violin, and cello.[5]

The title, translating as *'the voice of the bellows'*, suggests a programmatic theme and provides a means for interpreting the many breath-like sighs, gasps and expulsions emerging from the bandoneón at key structural points within the work.

This work finds itself within a growing trend of acousmatic pieces that import outside influences and sampled sounds from foreign cultures. Rationales for this popular activity of sourcing sound materials vary across cultures, ranging from sociopolitical reasons to more common situations of personal taste, where a composer may become inspired after experiencing new sounds in unfamiliar or exotic places. This appears to be the case with Salazar's work, which transpired from a composition residency at the Fundacion Destellos Studios, Argentina, after Salazar was awarded first

---

[4] 'For a sound to be iconic it must somehow be a part of mass media' (D'Escriván and Jackson 2008: 4).
[5] Email correspondence with Diana Salazar, July 2012.

prize in the Destellos Electroacoustic Music Competition, 2009 for her work *Papyrus* (2014; comp. 2008–9). Salazar confirms an encounter with the unfamiliar as the starting point for her creative work: 'In 2010 I witnessed a performance by a young *Orquesta Typica* in Buenos Aires, and was stunned to experience such expressive performances of Tango music.'[6] This cross-cultural sound-seeking activity most notably widens the available sound palette to composers, providing fresh inspiration for new works.

Which tools and approaches?

It seems necessary to begin an analysis of acousmatic music with an aural approach since *La voz del fuelle*, like many others in the genre, lacks a visual score and comes accompanied with no more than a programme note. Observations through listening enable the initial identification of borrowed tango fragments.

For which users?

Conducting an analysis of integration methods for cultural sound use is particularly beneficial for composers interested in pursuing similar activity, since through analysis it is possible to both identify and learn from the techniques of others. This type of analysis enables a closer study of what has been 'taken' and how this has been transferred and embedded within a new compositional context. Figure 14.1 demonstrates a brief summary of what may be considered as cross-cultural borrowing and inconclusively gives examples typical to each category.

With what intentions?

For a listener, the perceived strength or presence of cultural material within an acousmatic work depends on a network of complex factors. Amongst many, these include its links with the culture of origin, the length of the sample, methods of integration, and any editing or processing applied. All these factors have an impact upon how 'explicit' borrowed material is perceived to be in an acousmatic work. Whilst this experience is unique to each listener, the significance and implications resulting from identifiable cultural material use within an acousmatic setting is an attractive area of analysis.

---

[6] Email correspondence with Diana Salazar, July 2012.

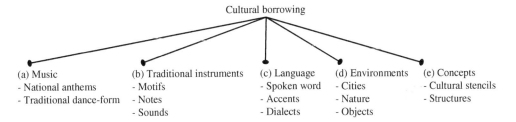

Figure 14.1 Summary of cross-cultural borrowings[7]

When faced with recognisable and often symbolic material in a concert situation, it is often impossible not to question the presence of cultural borrowing, and in particular, the connection the composer might have with the material presented.[8] It is this aspect that particularly interests me, along with the steps a composer may take to 'personalise' borrowed material.

Methodology and tools for analysis

To support what is experienced exclusively through listening, existing typologies dealing with musical quotation have been consulted as a way of applying conventional and current terminology within a wider musical context; for example, as found in instrumental music analyses. In light of the observable musical samples (which may also be described as 'plunderphones'[9]) appearing within *La voz del fuelle*, Peter J. Burkholder's typology (1994: 854) of using existing music in new works provides a useful method of analysing appearances of tango music recordings found within Salazar's acousmatic work. In addition to a typology, Burkholder lists six questions (Table 14.1) constructed to explore a wider understanding of the word 'quotation' and its various re-inventions, manipulations, alterations and evolutions when a composer borrows existing music for use within a new composition.

---

[7] My term 'cultural stencil' (from Figure 14.1) refers to the process of using a cultural sound as an imprint around which other non-cultural-specific sound can be arranged in a sequencer. Salazar admits to using this concept in her work: 'One technique I do distinctly remember using was to set a section of an existing Tango down in Pro Tools, and basically recreate it using samples over the top. I then removed the original recording and was left with a reconstruction using odd samples' (email correspondence with Salazar, July 2012).

[8] 'In principle, the incorporation of borrowed material can take place anywhere along a continuum: at the one hypothetical extreme, the original meaning of the quotation can be unimpaired; at the other, the quotation can be totally stripped of its original meaning' (Ballantine 1984: 73).

[9] John Oswald: 'A plunderphone is a recognizable sonic quote, using the actual sound of something familiar which has already been recorded' (Igma n.d.).

Table 14.1 Notes towards a typology of musical borrowing
(after Burkholder 1994: 867–9)

---

1. What is the relationship of the existing piece to the new work that borrows from it?
2. What element or elements of the existing piece are incorporated into or alluded to by the new work, in whole or part?
3. How does the borrowed material relate to the shape of the new work?
4. How is the borrowed material altered in the new work?
5. What is the function of the borrowed material within the new work in musical terms?
6. What is the function or meaning of the borrowed material within the new work in associative or extra-musical terms, if any?

These questions appear particularly relevant to acousmatic works involving cultural borrowings, such as *La voz del fuelle*, where the use of tango music is explicit. Through the analysis I endeavour to respond to these lines of inquiry which will, in turn, offer a speculative assessment of the composer's intentions as she looks back to works from another culture and era for new inspiration. The mechanisms of how Salazar integrates such borrowed material also come under scrutiny with these questions, probing why the composer may have enhanced or disguised cultural imports.

While Burkholder's experiences of borrowed music have likely involved score studying (most notably in the music of Charles Ives (Burkholder 1995)), my approach will differ by conducting an aurally led analysis of Salazar's use of existing music in order to answer these questions. Burkholder's identification of 14 types of quotation within his typology demonstrates the many incarnations of the term, effectively showing how a single word in this instance is insufficient in connoting the great variety of actions a composer may consider within the domain of musical borrowing.[10] It is anticipated that through this analysis this list may be addressed and possibly expanded to specifically deal with musical quotation use within acousmatic music, since the possibilities of transformational development for borrowed materials in the studio are incredibly vast, and therefore require their own means of classification. It is thus the aim of the analysis to identify the various types of borrowed material and the methods of integration employed by the composer.

---

[10] 'I began to see, first, that the word "quotation" did not begin to account for the variety of ways Ives used existing music, nor to describe the extent of the dependence of many of this works on their sources; second, that many of his procedures resembled those of earlier nineteenth-century composers; and therefore, third, that Ives was not as unique in his borrowing practices as his reputation and previous scholarship had led me to believe' (Burkholder 1994: 853).

My analysis will employ illustrative diagrams as a tool to support and consolidate the findings from the aural analysis. These visual representations will attempt to capture significant moments featuring cultural borrowing. Summarising the entrance and termination of such borrowings through visual means within the EAnalysis sonogram will also direct attention towards these carefully constructed moments, providing an insight into the handling of cultural references, and the imagery and evocation created through causality.

Sources of sound: quotation and sampling

Before beginning the analysis, a few points should be made regarding the use of the term 'quotation'. Quotation is defined as 'reproducing a melodic, stylistic or timbral excerpt of a pre-existing musical work in the new context of another musical work' (Holm-Hudson 1997: 17). This common practice has a long and broad history, one that was and still is essential to the development and progression of many types/genres of music. It may be considered that 'there is an element of borrowing . . . in every successful instance of musical communication' (Holm-Hudson 1997: 17). While reproduction of musical quotes via score transcription for instrumental music typifies the definition of quotation given above, I believe a line may be drawn between this definition and the one given for sampling. In acousmatic music, the act of sampling captures more than a melody, harmony, motif or sound, it also captures (in some cases) the time, space and technology involved in the recording. The sound quality of raw samples presents a further challenge for the composer interested in integrating musical samples into their work. A noisy performance hall or a soundproofed live room are two extreme opposites of the spectrum, both telling of their space. An old recording sampled from an LP record will indicate its age and media. The raw *Caballo Negro* samples within Javier Alvarez's *Mambo à la Braque* (1996) and the *Cha cha cha* and *Mambo* samples found in Michel Chion's *Credo Mambo* (1992) are examples that exhibit the 'time and space-stamped' sample phenomenon.

In terms of *La voz del fuelle*, it is possible to glean some useful information regarding the cultural borrowing via the programme note. The listener is informed that samples of existing music are used, as are recordings of instruments associated with tango music. Further dialogue with the composer reveals how and where these materials were initially

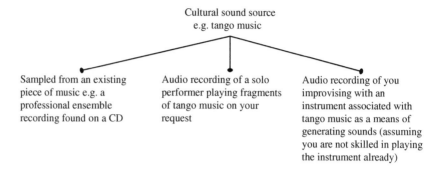

Figure 14.2 Pathway of choices when engaging with cultural sound

captured.[11] Two traditional Tango recordings (now out of copyright) were sourced along with several traditional Argentine instruments as a means of 'reinforcing pulse and attack'.[12] When viewed more closely, these aspects indicate a pathway of choices a composer is faced with when engaging with culturally sourced sounds. An important distinction can be made between the possibilities of sourcing cultural material. Figure 14.2 outlines three possible sources which will undoubtedly produce differing aural results.

Aural analysis

An aural analysis will first isolate key appearances of recognisable tango music and will then examine the means of integration within the work. Information provided on the sonogram will be structured mainly around these focal points.[13] An assessment of further cultural references will be made and identified to demonstrate how their inclusion is negotiated amidst material considered to be more culture-neutral.

Tango extract 1: 0'15"–0'19"

The bandoneón appears to exhale (Figure 14.3), pushing air out along with a tango extract at 0'16". This short melodic figure is distant, taking a less foreground position. This brief musical borrowing is terminated by a foreground attack, leading to two further causal events before resting on a sustained bandoneón pitch (E).

---

[11] Email correspondence with Diana Salazar, July 2012: 'The work contains a brief reference to Astor Piazzolla's *Fugata* (No.2 from *Silfio y Ondina*).'

[12] Email correspondence with Diana Salazar, July 2012.

[13] The sound examples and colour sonogram created with EAnalysis is to be found on the website accompanying this book.

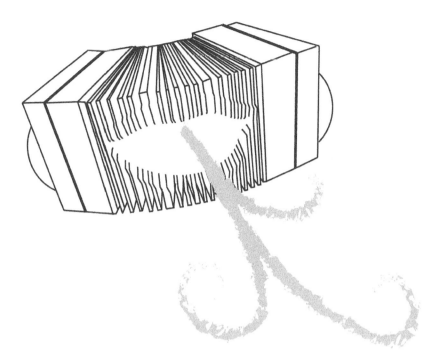

Figure 14.3 The bandoneón exhales

Tango extract 2: 0'33"–0'47"

At 0'33" the bandoneón bellows appear to 'exhale' and, with this, release upward directional textures that transition into a sustained pitch on E. This pitch is significant since it is the starting pitch of the *Fugata* quote (Figure 14.4). The entry of this tango sample is prepared and anticipated by introducing the starting pitch earlier, enabling the melody to appear as a natural progression of the sonic material. This preparation starts at 0'37" where the sustained E merges seamlessly into the starting pitch for the *Fugata* sample. Figure 14.4 demonstrates the perceived imagery resulting from the integration of this cultural reference.

The careful construction of causality has an interesting effect on the resulting imagery: 'in acousmatic concerts we are asked to suspend *this* [impossible pairing of sounds not found in the real world] cynical disbelief and to allow our imaginations to reinstate the magic' (Emmerson 2007: 18), as demonstrated in Figure 14.4. The acousmatic music practice, by its very nature, facilitates juxtapositions and causalities impossible in the real world – the *onset continuation* pairing of a bandoneón's bellows (onset) opening up to release more abstract (culture neutral) directional textures

Figure 14.4 Bandoneón bellows open up, allowing sound materials to flow upwards from its interior, settling on E which links to opening three bars of Astor Piazzolla's *Fugata* (No. 2 from *Silfo y Ondina*)

Figure 14.5 Bars 4–5 from Astor Piazzolla's *Fugata* (No. 2 from *Silfo y Ondina*) appearing in *La voz del fuelle*

(continuation) produces a make-believe situation unachievable in reality. Careful synchronisation in the studio fuses the real object (bandoneón) with the unreal (abstract sound), with the latter now appearing to emanate from the instrument's interior. The final pitch of the sample (G♯) is prolonged from 0'42" to 0'51". The sample has ended but remnants from its appearance remain as a means of transitioning away from the quotation material and back to Salazar's material.

Tango extract 3: 0'47"–0'51"

The music sample at 0'47" is a repeat of extract 1 in its appearance, preparation and termination.

Tango extract 4: 0'51"–0'55"

A two-bar quote from the *Fugata* in an unaltered form (bars 4–5, Figure 14.5) appears at 0'51". This sample interrupts the sustained bandoneón pitch (E) from the previous quotation termination, displaying no preparation for its entry.

Tango extract 5: 0'55"–1'05"

Non-pitched bandoneón sounds (fingers striking bellows and mechanical cluncks) accumulate in preparation for a *Fugata* melody entry at 0'57". The causal relationship between these sound sources is clear, leading to the imagery of the melody and pitches arising and almost 'leaping' out of this percussive activity. The quotation is less explicit as the melody is fragmented and possibly pitch-shifted. A bandoneón pitch (D♯) at 1'01" is sustained as a means of transitioning away from the tango material and on to the next idea. The bandoneón melody is observable but altered through processing so that it is less explicit/identifiable as a sort of 'blurred' version of the original.

Tango extract 6: 1'05"–1'15"

The quotations at 1'08" appeares to float above a sustained drone (on B) from the previous quotation's termination. This quotation is more distant sounding and less pronounced, sounding similar to the effect achieved in extracts 1 and 3.

Tango extract 7: 2'16"–2'24"

The entry of a tango melody at 2'16" is prepared through the sound of a rapid finger scrape across the bandoneón's concertina bellows (Figure 14.6). This directional sound is ideal leading material – expectation of cause and effect is increased with directional sounds with defined motion. The final pitch of the quotation (B) at 2'19" is prolonged as a means of transitioning out of this quotation material and back into the piece. This pitch is held until 2'24" where a transposition to D (up a minor third) is made, accompanied by an accumulating (reversed) decay, further solidifying the transition away from the melodic material.

Tango extract 8: 2'29"–2'38"

Bars 2 and 3 from the *Fugata* appear at 2'29". The bandoneón bellows sound, sculpted as an attack, causally initiates the appearance of the tango quote exhibiting finely timed synchronicity. Instead of prolonging the final pitch (G♯) of the quotation at 2'31", the phrase develops into a series of lungeing pulses typically associated with tango music (creating a sort of mini-mashup of tango fragments). This series of ideas (including piano

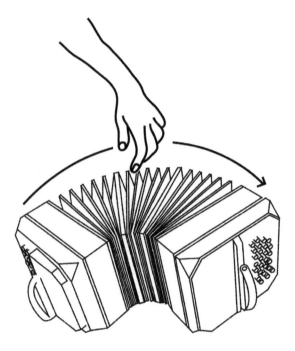

Figure 14.6 Rapid finger scrape across the bandoneón

and bandoneón pitches) acts as a transitioning path between a direct unaltered borrowing and the acousmatic realm.

Tango extract 9 and 10: 3'14"–3'26" and 3'28"–3'40"

This segment contains two similar extracts at 3'19" and 3'28". This ascending melody line first appears after a series of non-pitched bandoneón sounds in close succession, which establishes a causal relationship with the subsequent quotation that appears to emanate from this turbulent activity. The quotation is altered to appear distant and its dynamic level is relatively low. The final pitch of extract 10 (G♯) reached at 3'22" dissolves into the surrounding drone. The second appearance of the same quotation at 3'28" (transposed up) occurs over this sustained drone. The final pitch of the quotation (B) transforms into a sustain drone at 3'32" to transition out of the quotation material.

Tango extract 11: 3'41"–3'49"

The borrowed material at 3'42" is a repeat of extract 6. The preparation of this extract is different as it is introduced by pitched material (G♯). The termination via a descending high pitch is the same as in 7.

Tango extract 12: 4'48"–5'02"

It is difficult to pinpoint the exact moment of preparation for extract 12 (at 4'59"), since it acts as a termination and release for the tension accumulated back at 3'52". The iterative material triggering the extract appears most prominent from around 4'48", where this material begins to crescendo directionally towards the climax. The extract appears to comprise an ascending figure from the opening three bars of the *Fugata*, time compressed to fit into this moment of shifting textures. The final pitch of the quotation is used dramatically to terminate the turbulence of previous texture. This moment also functions as an arrival point to trigger 'calmer' material comprising a looping piano motif and violin drone.

Tango extract 13: 5'25"–5'31"

Extract 13 appearing at 5'26" is a variation of quotation 12. Whilst the borrowed material is similar, its presentation is quite different. The outline of the ascending motif is recognisable, but its presence is more muted as a result of frequency filtering. Its ascending motion triggers a bandoneón bellow exhale of a similar muted quality as a means of terminating the quotation appearance within the piece.

Tango extract 14: 6'14"–6'22"

Bars 2–3 from the *Fugata* return at 6'19". The entry of this extract is preceded by repeated rhythmic piano stabs. The extract interrupts the continuity of the piano motif briefly before it returns at 6'21".

Tango extract 15: 6'49"–6'56"

Preparation for the appearance of extract 15 begins early, as material emerges at 6'49", appearing to be a pitch-shifted version of bellow tension, which resolves through a pop-like attack, causing a quick succession of pitches from assorted instrumentation. This energetic release opens up into the extract at 6'52" (an ascending melodic figure), which is a variation of extracts 12 and 13. The termination is hidden by a pulsing bandoneón iteration in a very foreground position.

Tango extract 16: 7'02"–7'06"

The borrowed material occuring at 7'02" does not have an observable preparation as such. Instead it subtly overlaps with the disappearance of the previous event, moving from the heavy textural material to a thinner single-line moment. This extract is quite brief, and an accompaniment of fast-paced accumulating materials soon joins in. The final pitch from the extract is held (B) forming a short drone to transition away and into new material. Bandoneón march-like stabs emerge from this drone reminiscent of the famous material from Gerardo Matos Rodríguez's *La Cumparsita* (1916).

Discussion: forms of integration and quotation types

My analysis revealed 16 instances of explicit borrowed tango music extracts. These instances were selected on the basis of their identity being recognisable to their original source (as derived from tango music). Some instances were repeats or variations upon previously stated material.

The methods of integration (focusing on preparation and termination) for these borrowed fragments are summarised in Tables 14.2 and 14.3.

The tables indicate favoured approaches for introducing and terminating borrowed material into the acousmatic work. Salazar appears to rely upon causality when introducing the tango extracts and opts for pitch matching for terminating extracts so as to avoid blunt cuts that might otherwise indicate the end of the borrowed material. What this analysis shows is that the borrowed extracts are not dropped into the

Table 14.2 Quotation entry types

Extract entry	Sample no.
Pitch matching (anticipating the starting pitch of the extract)	2
Causal triggering	1, 3, 5, 7, 8, 9, 12, 15
Dovetailing/overlapping	6, 10, 11, 13
Interruption to previous material	4, 14, 16

Table 14.3 Quotation termination types

Extract termination	Sample no.
Pitch matching/sustaining (prolonging the final pitch from the extract)	2, 4, 5, 6, 7, 10, 15, 16
Dovetailing/overlapping	8, 9, 11
Interruption by subsequent materials	1, 3, 12, 13, 14

composition, but instead are carefully woven and fit seamlessly into the fabric of the composition.

The types of borrowed material isolated in the analysis included:

- direct extracts (no alteration) with no additional sound material, usually a one to three bar fragment;
- direct extracts (no alteration) accompanied with additional sound material;
- direct extracts (minor alteration through frequency filtering);
- extracts with unrecognisable source.

Hierarchy

The analysis revealed a hierarchy (Figure 14.7) which demonstrates the types of sampling available when dealing with traditional instruments of a given culture, where the vertical axis suggests a gradual move away from idiomatic sound. The further one descends through the hierarchy for sourcing and using sound, the less likely the finished composition is to point specifically at cultural borrowing as a defining feature. A piece focusing on the lower levels of this hierarchy becomes less *about* the cultural import and more to do with sonic or abstract properties. For example, the use of bandoneón button clicks within a work is less likely to conjure the same associations that the use of a tango melody line might, since the button clicks alone do not possess the weighty cultural baggage of a national, historic dance-form. In some instances, depending on their use, the button clicks may not be perceived to be derived from a bandoneón at all, thus taking on a more culture neutral status.

La voz del fuelle incorporates all samples types belonging to the hierarchy, with the exception of the first type (whole piece of music). The acousmatic piece is outwardly about tango music, but engagement with the lower levels of the sampling hierarchy remind the listener that this is an

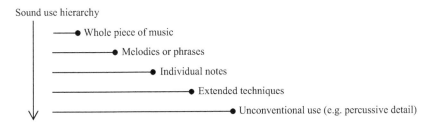

Sound use hierarchy

- Whole piece of music
- Melodies or phrases
- Individual notes
- Extended techniques
- Unconventional use (e.g. percussive detail)

Figure 14.7 Hierarchy of sampling from a bandoneón

Figure 14.8 Visual metaphor for a bandoneón sound in its raw state (left) and four subsequent transformations displaying increasing degrees of identity removal

acousmatic work where the composer's voice in reworking sounds and timbres may also be experienced.

Levels of surrogacy

The use of transformational tools in *La voz del fuelle* dislocates some materials from their original sources[14] and as a result it becomes challenging and often impossible to identify these materials with certainty when processing has removed these sounds to third and remote levels of surrogacy (Smalley 1997: 112). This process is a further nuance belonging to the hierarchy in Figure 14.7 and is presented metaphorically in Figure 14.8.

My analysis has sought out materials of first and second orders of surrogacy where identity has been preserved. The first (untransformed) bandoneón from Figure 14.8 visually represents these identifiable sound materials (e.g. tango extract 2: 0'33"–0'47"), while the two further images suggest increasingly destructive forms of processing, where only vestiges of the original may remain. Extending the processing chain continues to remove all semblance of the original source so that they become 'untraceable'.[15] Editing a sound into a grain-sized fragment (Figure 14.8 last two images) is an example of how original source material may move further and further away, stripping the sound of its cultural identity and reference.

La voz del fuelle engages with these processing tools, often depriving the sound of its original recognisibility, giving rise to the perception of further culture neutral sound material. The iterative pulses at 2'46" and the granular eruption at 4'15" provide two examples where source of origin cannot be pinpointed due to processing undertaken.

[14] Denis Smalley calls this removal 'surrogacy': 'It is particularly important for acousmatic music where the sources and causes of sound-making become remote or detached from known, directly experienced physical gesture and sounding sources' (Smalley 1997: 112).
[15] 'Sources untraceable . . . These are manipulations which take the sounds plundered and stretch and treat them so radically that it is impossible to divine their source at all' (Cutler 2000: 109).

Levels of certainty

If stripped of its identity through processing, speculation may lead a listener to source-bond a sound to an imagined cause or action. *La voz del fuelle* explores the third and remote levels of surrogacy with the presence of more abstract and culture neutral sound materials. These gestures and textures may have started life as cultural borrowings – for example, a bandoneón melody or air sound – although it is impossible to say with certainty where these materials were derived from. Figure 14.9 demonstrates a generalised table of how the type of sample taken from a traditional instrument (vertical) along with the application of processing (horizontal) can affect the identification of cultural borrowing. With certainty, it would be possible to identify the presence of a whole piece of music in its raw and recognisable state in an acousmatic work. The same could not be said if the piece were to be heavily processed (e.g. granulated, reversed, pitch shifted). Broadly speaking, certainty wanes when processing is involved.

There has, of course, been a degree of restraint when making conclusions regarding the origins of cultural borrowings in their processed or edited versions in *La voz del fuelle*. For example, it is observable that extracts 1 and 7 originate from tango music but it has not been possible to identify the source or piece of music they were taken from. Without being the composer, it is difficult to mark out these evolutions since these processes are truly acousmatic and concealed from the listener.

Certainty and meaning

The more certainty a listener has in recognising a cultural reference within an acousmatic work, the more likely meaning and significance from the original source will also be communicated. This undoubtedly relies upon a previous understanding of the original source and how well known the material is emblematically.[16] In key places, Salazar has resisted the need to dismantle and reconfigure the identifiable borrowed material. The maintenance of pitches, intervallic relationships and rhythms as found in the original music in a number of instances (e.g. tango extracts 2 and 8) provides evidence for retaining identity and subsequently suggesting

---

[16] 'This subdivision of sonic souvenirs, leading to the category labeled cultural emblems accounts for sounds that tend to be highly loaded and culture-associative often exhibiting strong sacred, religious, musical, political or geographic connections' (Blackburn 2011: 5).

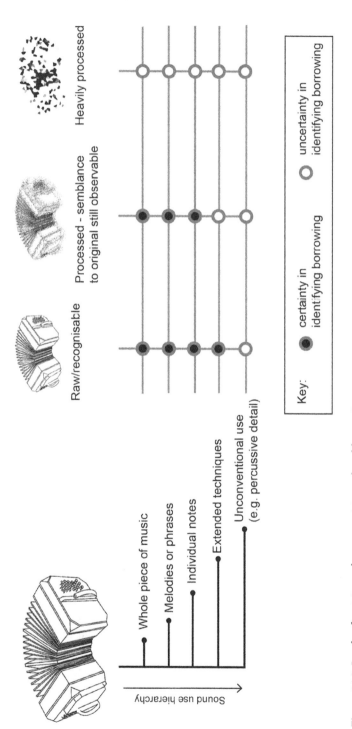

Figure 14.9 Levels of certainty when recognising cultural borrowings

meaning and referential weight associated with the original musical source. Conveyance of the extracts as recognisable entities is clearly important in this work.

Salazar mentions the use of two further tango recordings used within *La voz del fuelle*: 'They were really terrible quality (think hiss, crackles and pops) and in the end the samples I used from them were very short, often typical flourishes and anacruses that could embellish the rhythmic elements built from higher-quality samples.'[17] It is difficult to isolate moments featuring these two recordings with certainty. Their involvement is deeply embedded and more fragmented, possibly as a means of disguising the reduced quality of the recordings, thus negating the conflicting effect of mixing the 'old' nostaglic sound with the new cleaner and polished sound. A sample communicating its age – for example, a raw historical recording – would have stood out in relief, and may not have been the best candidate for alluding to seamless integration or behaving as a natural component of the piece.

Evocation

The analysis has encountered a number of significant evocations of imagery connected to the programmatic title '*The voice of the bellows*'. Imagery perceived in accordance with the programmatic theme has been particularly strong as demonstrated in the analysis and illustrations. The extending and contracting mechanism of the bandoneón's concertina can be personified as 'breathing' – the instrument appears to 'inhale' and 'exhale'. The frequency of breath-like appearances (marked on the EAnalysis sonogram) is a constant reminder that the sonic content playing out in the piece originates from the bandoneón's interior. The 'exhales' of air play an important role as preparatory material for the appearances of tango music extracts. Exhales act as onsets, initiating the materials that appear to cascade out. The variation of bandoneón 'breaths' contributes to the different intensities (powerful exhale at 1'34") and moments of passiveness (longer, slower exhale at 5'17") throughout the work.

Finally, in completing the analysis of cultural samples within *La voz del fuelle*, I have returned to the initial line of inquiry in Salazar's work and responded to Burkholder's questions (below). Due to the variety of borrowings, multiple answers have been selected from Burkholder's publication.

---

[17] Email correspondence with Diana Salazar, July 2012.

Responses to Burkholder's questions

1. **What is the relationship of the existing piece to the new work that borrows from it?**

   - It is of a different genre, medium and style
   - It is of a different musical tradition
   - It is a single-line melody used within a new polyphonic work
   - It is from a distant place and earlier time
   - It is likely to be familiar to most listeners at the time and place where the new work is created

2. **What elements or elements of the existing piece are incorporated into or alluded to by the new work, in whole or part?**

   - A melodic line
   - An aspect of harmony and striking sonorities
   - An instrumental colour

3. **How does the borrowed material relate to the shape of the new work?**

   - It is part of a collage
   - It is used as a motif
   - It provides material (motives, structural ideas, contrapuntal combinations etc.), that is, freely reworked

4. **How is the borrowed material altered in the new work?**

   - In some instances it is not altered
   - In some instances it is minimally altered
   - It appears only in fragments (up to three bars in length max)
   - It is used as a theme, perhaps not significantly altered when it appears as a theme but is elsewhere developed and fragmented as themes
   - It is placed in a new context, changing its effect
   - It is disguised
   - It is subjected to processing: frequency filtering, EQ-ing, time stretching etc.

5. **What is the function of the borrowed material within the new work in musical terms?**

   - It serves as a theme
   - It serves as a motif
   - It provides melodic and harmonic content

6. What is the function or meaning of the borrowed material within the new work in associative or extra-musical terms, if any?

- Its appearance is a central component within the creation of impossible imagery. The musical quotes spring out of the bandoneón fumblings
- Its appearance symbolises something or someone associated with it or with pieces of its general type
- It pays homage to its source.

Conclusions

An aural and sonogram analysis has identified the care and attention directed towards the integration of cultural material within *La voz del fuelle* as a means of fusing the soundworlds (cultural borrowings and culture neutral material) together. This is most notably achieved through the preparation of musical samples in advance of their appearance. Their termination is also prioritised and often prolonged through pitch sustains as a means of creating seamless transitions between the borrowed and the new.

The analysis encouraged the development of a hierarchy to gauge the categorisation of traditional instrumental samples. This hierarchy presents a variable scale of idiomatic sound, estimating the reception of cultural import within a given work. Combining this hierarchy with a scale of transformation (from raw to heavily processed), it becomes possible to assess the perceived strength of the cultural import within its new context based on the idea of certainty of recognition. Cultural borrowings that are less idiomatic and have undergone heavy processing are more challenging to recognise and thus do not carry the cultural weight of their source as they might do in their raw format. It was revealed that *La voz del fuelle* engages with a number of different borrowings and degrees of transformation as a means of both highlighting and disguising particular cultural material. Sound materials of third and remote levels of surrogacy become regarded as culture neutral, since their identity (whether or not from a cultural source) could not be recognised.

A number of tango music samples from Piazzolla's *Fugata* interestingly maintained the original pitches and intervallic relationships. Staying faithful to the original in these instances may be an indication of the composer's intentions to pay *homage* to the historical work. It is important that the samples are recognisable to the audience for meaning to be communicated. The use of recognisable cultural borrowings within acousmatic music can also force audiences to question why borrowing has taken place and what this material means in its new context.[18] The decision to incorporate such explicit samples is often motivated by a programmatic or underlying rationale. In this case, Salazar's inspiring encounter with a tango orchestra in a foreign context is transformed as she presents her personal take on this iconic material, communicating the vibrancy and energy of this music still within the confines of her individual compositional voice.

References

Ballantine, Christopher. 1984. *Music and its Social Meanings*. New York: Gordon and Breach.

Blackburn, Manuella. 2011. Importing the sonic souvenir: Issues of cross-cultural composition. *Proceedings of the Electroacoustic Music Studies Network Conference,* New York. www.ems-network.org/IMG/pdf_EMS11_Blackburn.pdf.

Burkholder, Peter J. 1994. The uses of existing music. *Music Library Association Notes*, 50(3), 851–70.

   1995. *All Made of Tunes: Charles Ives and the Uses of Musical Borrowing*. New Haven: Yale University Press.

Cutler, Chris. 2000. Plunderphonics. In Simon Emmerson (ed.), *Music, Electronic Media and Culture*. Aldershot: Ashgate, 87–115.

d'Escriván, Julio and Jackson, Paul. 2008. Applied Plunderphonia: tagging electronic music with electronic music. Proceedings of the Electroacoustic Music Studies Network Conference, Paris. www.ems-network.org/ems08/papers/escrivan.pdf.

Emmerson, Simon. 2007. *Living Electronic Music*. Aldershot: Ashgate.

Holm-Hudson, Kevin. 1997. Quotation and context: Sampling and John Oswald's plunderphonics. *Leonardo Music Journal*, 7, 17–25.

Igma, Norman. n.d. Plunderphonics: an interview with transproducer John Oswald. www.plunderphonics.com/xhtml/xinterviews.html (accessed 11 July 2012).

Smalley, Denis. 1997. Explaining sound shapes. *Organised Sound*, 2(2), 107–26.

---

[18] '[T]he unheralded appearance of atavistic or exogeneous traits as part of a new art work, that dramatically attract attention to themselves and raise questions that call for a systematic answer. The simplest and most basic of these questions is: What does the incorporation of these foreign elements mean?' (Ballantine 1984: 72).

Recordings

Alvarez, Javier. 1996. *Mambo à la Braque*, empreintes DIGITALes, IMED 9604.
Chion, Michel. 1992. *Credo Mambo*, Metamkine MKCD004.
Matos, Gerardo. 1916. Rodríguez's *La Cumparsita*.
Salazar, Diana. 2011. *La voz del fuelle*, Elektramusic CD Volume III.
    2014. *Papyrus* (2008–9), CMMAS CD020.

15 | *Kireek* 2011 Championship routine analysis

SOPHY SMITH

This analysis focuses on the turntable routine created by the turntable team Kireek (DJ-HI-C and DJ YASA) for the DMC World Team Championships 2011.[1] In 2004, DJs Yasa and Hi-C combined to form Kireek and, according to Elisabeth Lambert (2006), developed a new style of scratch-based turntablism that showcased the skill and technique of scratch in such a way as to 'move the masses'. Three years later in 2007, these two world-class DJs were the first Asian team to be winners of the DMC World DJ Championships and went on to be the first ever team to win five years in a row. The routine is accessible on DMC TV (online) as well as on the commercially available DVD *World Team + Battle For Supremacy 2011* (DMC 2011). This routine is a strong example of team turntablism, the team winning the competition with the unanimous agreement of the eight judges.[2] The DMC competitions are an opportunity for teams to perform rehearsed set routines, and these filmed routines provide a static document of a turntable performance that it is possible to analyse.

The techniques and processes of hip-hop turntablism are not widely known outside the hip-hop community and so for a full appreciation it is important that listeners unfamiliar with the genre have an understanding of how the music is composed and performed. Those familiar with hip-hop turntable composition are able to hear and recognise the performance techniques as they are played out and so have a deep understanding of the sound manipulation happening in real time. For those new to the genre, it may be difficult to fully appreciate and comprehend what is being heard and I hope that this analysis might offer a way in. For this reason, this analysis will use a framework that encompasses sound

---

[1] Founded as a DJ-only record subscription club in 1983, DMC was at the forefront of the DJ Culture movement which began in the 1980s. In 1985 DMC launched the DMC World DJ Championships and remains committed to exposing and inspiring DJ art and talent. For further details see www.dmcworld.com.

[2] Whilst the judging criteria of the DMC World Team Championship is not in the public domain, DJ Yasa explains that there are usually five judging criteria in competitions: technique, audience reaction, track selection, DJ performance or showmanship, and rhythm and tempo control (in Lambert 2006).

sources, sound synthesis, sound quality, order and organisation, drama-turgic information and performative aspects. This is not intended as a definitive analysis however – there is so much to draw out of a turntable team routine – but hopefully it provides a starting point for a deeper understanding of turntable team routines and how they are created and performed.

BACKGROUND TO TURNTABLISM

In 1995, the term 'turntablism' emerged to reflect the artistic practices of the hip-hop DJ. The term was first used by DJ Babu of the Beat Junkies crew who stated, 'My definition of a Turntablist is a person who uses the turntables not to play music, but to manipulate sound and create music' (Gragg 1999). Although the term is not embraced by all hip-hop DJs and musicians, it is generally recognised and used within hip-hop culture. Within this context, a turntable team is a group of turntable musicians who come together to collectively compose and perform original music through the manipulation of records on turntables. Turntable musicians use a variety of manipulation techniques to create original sound material from records, including structural techniques (e.g. the breakbeat, general mixing, punchphasing and backspinning), rhythmic techniques (e.g. scratching and beatjuggling) and melodic techniques (e.g. the creation of melodies via the turntables' bass, tone and pitch controls). The three main manipulation techniques mentioned in this analysis and depicted in the notation are punchphasing, scratching and beatjuggling. Each of these techniques has complicated variations but, simply put, punch-phasing is a technique whereby the turntablist incorporates shorter stabs of sound from one record over the breakbeat from another record, scratching is a technique where the turntablist moves the record back and forth against the stylus with one hand (often whilst using the cross-fade of the mixing desk) and beatjuggling is a technique where the turntablist alternates between two records on two separate turntables to create original patterns.[3] Team members may refer to the finished com-position as a 'routine'.

---

[3] More detailed information about the various DJ techniques are available in a wide range of instructional DJ books and DVDs including Broughton and Brewster's *How to DJ (Properly)* (2006) and DVDs including Stephen Webber's *Turntable Technique – The Art Of The DJ* (2003).

THE TECHNOLOGY

To perform their 2011 DMC Team Championship routine, Kireek use four turntables, three mixers, two controllers and two laptops running Digital Vinyl Systems (DVS)[4] (see Figure 15.1).

THE NOTATION

To allow a closer look at the relationships between the parts played by the two performers, I have used my own system of turntable notation, developed from the Turntable Transcription Methodology (TTM) of Carluccio, Imboden and Pirtle (2000). For the purposes of my analysis I have adapted the score used for TTM, adding to it a coding system to highlight the types of sound manipulation used. The pairs of turntables are designated a stave upon which the parts are notated (Figure 15.2). The main manipulation techniques used in this routine are depicted on the staff and these are shown in a key to the right of the stave. To assist the analysis and for overall clarity these techniques have been shaded and patterned to increase their visibility.

The stave is derived from a graph of the rotation of the record versus time and runs from left to right. The vertical axis of the stave represents the rotation of the record and the horizontal axis represents time, subdivided into bars and beats. The basic stave is in 4/4 time, reflecting the time signature of the routine. Each stave has an area added to its left, the 'sample bank', to provide room for noting the origin (or other description) of the samples to be manipulated. Samples are written and numbered in the order they appear during the section notated. The numbers are then used on the stave to indicate a change in the sample being manipulated, though I shall also opt to write the sample next to the notation for ease of use during analysis. A sample is drawn as a diagonal line on the staff, indicating when the sound starts and continuing to the point in the bar or phrase that the sound ends (Figure 15.3).

---

[4] Digital Vinyl Systems (DVS) are hardware and software-based systems that allow music on a computer to be controlled by vinyl, CD, MIDI or supported USB controllers. By doing so, they integrate the traditional analogue DJ set-up of turntables and a mixer with digital audio files stored and accessed via a computer. A more in-depth discussion about DVS and their implications for turntablism can be found in my book *Hip-Hop Turntablism, Creativity and Collaboration* (Smith 2013).

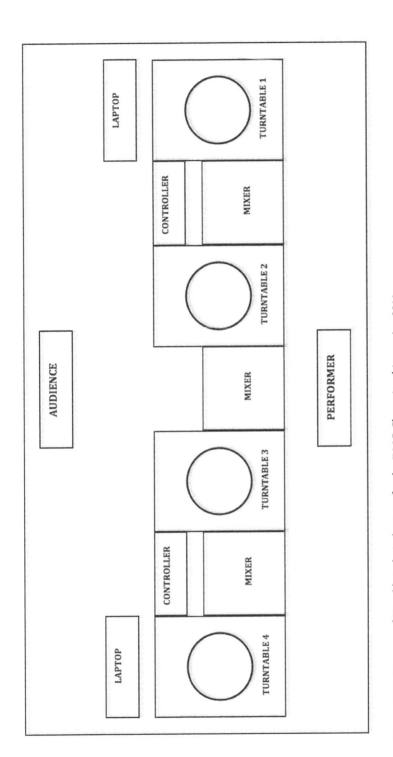

Figure 15.1 Diagram of Kireek's technical set-up for the DMC Championship routine 2011

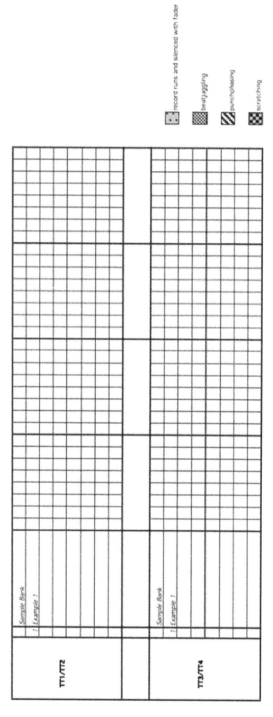

record runs and silenced with fader

beatjuggling

punchphasing

scratching

Figure 15.2 Template of stave for turntable notation

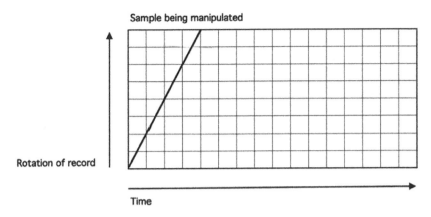

Figure 15.3 Rotation of record versus time

THE ROUTINE

Kireek's championship-winning routine of 2011 combines technical excellence and creative flair to create a unique sound, blending a range of different music genres into a cohesive composition, including traditional Japanese music, rock, hip-hop, breakbeat, jungle and drum'n'bass. Kireek describe how the individual components are carefully selected and combined to create a cohesive routine:

All songs combine a lot of individual sounds, and when we play we basically use some of those individual sounds to create a brand new track. What you hear is still a song, not a nonsensical mess. Anyone can let a record play, but when you are a DJ, and especially a turntablist, you definitely want to create something more. (Gaskin 2011)

The turntable routine was created by using a range of samples and sonic material including vocal samples (sung and spoken), instrumental samples, textural samples and sound effects. The two performers manipulate these samples through a variety of techniques including punchphasing, scratching and beatjuggling. Whilst the two performers tend to work from one set of turntables, they also move between turntables, partly for theatrical effect. This routine fuses contemporary issues with recognisable musical references from popular culture. Throughout the routine, specific reference is made to the Japanese tsunami and Fukushima disaster of 2011; both performers wear T-shirts with 'Spin for Japan' slogans (Spin for Japan was a combination of charitable events to support the disaster relief efforts) and political comment is made through the selection and use of spoken voice samples. The structure of the routine takes the listener on a musical and emotional journey, beginning and ending with reference to the Japanese tsunami of 2011. This

Table 15.1 General information about Kireek's DMC Championship Routine 2011

No.	Section Name	Duration	Tempo	Component Parts
1	*I Hate*	90 seconds	91 bpm	A1, B, A2, C D
2	*Article I. Witness the Fitness*	70 seconds	91 bpm	E, F, G
3	*Article II. It's Like This Y'All*	76 seconds	91 bpm	H, I
4	*Article III. Spin for Japan*	125 seconds	69–73 bpm	J, K

is a clearly personal composition, Kireek reflecting, 'We found that the only way to create was to play from the bottom of our heart' (Kireek 2012). The routine has a clear structure. It lasts for just over six minutes and for the purpose of this analysis I have divided it into four sections named *I Hate*, *Witness the Fitness*, *It's Like This Y'All* and *Spin for Japan*. I have chosen to divide the routine in this way as the different sections are characterised by clear changes in musical style and new sets of samples being used. Table 15.1 gives general information about each section.

The routine has a clear beginning, middle and end, with the two longest sections (*I Hate* and *Spin for Japan*) either side of the two shorter middle sections (*It's Like This Y'All* and *Witness the Fitness*). This structure is also reflected in the narrative shape of the routine, created by two main thematic focuses: the communication of the team's personal viewpoint on the Fukushima disaster and the competitive nature of the environment for which the routine was created, where Kireek were aiming to create history by becoming the first team to win the team title at the DMC Team Championship for five consecutive years. Sections 1 and 4 both refer to the aftermath of the Fukushima disaster and sections 2 and 3 focus on the musical expertise and prowess of Kireek themselves. This is communicated both thematically through the choice of spoken samples (in section 1, for example, 'We are here to make history', 'To inspire the people of Japan', in sections 2 and 3, 'Witness the fitness', 'Intergalactic' and 'The game is not over' and in section 4 'hope that everyone can live freely, harmoniously and joyfully') and also through the energy curve of the routine. Section 1 of the routine is high energy, which drops in *Witness the Fitness* before building through the second half of *It's Like This Y'All* to a high-energy end to *Spin for Japan*.

AN ANALYSIS

In the analysis below I will discuss each of the sections in turn, focusing on sound sources, sound synthesis, sound quality, order and organisation and

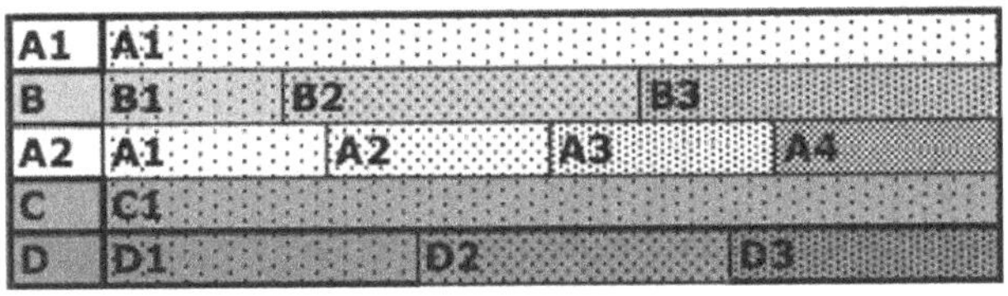

Figure 15.4 Structure of section 1 of *I Hate*

performative aspects. At the beginning of the discussion about each
section, I will provide a diagram of its structure, and the related parts
and subsections. Each part of the section is labelled with a letter and shade,
subsequent parts appearing horizontally. To the right of the part name are
the subsections of the part. The length of each part represents the whole
part, and the subsections have been shown in proportion to the whole. The
subsections are numbered and patterned, relating to their number, making
it easier to see correlations between parts. This notation will also enable
comparisons between sections to be made later in the analysis. These
diagrams do not include the short transition phrases between sections
but do show the internal transitions between subsections in sections 3
and 4 (shown as a chequered pattern in Figures 15.10 and 15.11). In
Figure 15.4, sections are numbered above and each square represents one
bar. The sections are made up of a number of different parts and each is
labelled with a letter and shade.

Section 1: *I Hate*

Types of sound sources, sound synthesis, sound quality

The samples and sound effects used in this section are recognisable.
Samples are instrumental and vocal in nature, including drums, guitars
and the spoken voice and other miscellaneous samples including sounds
and textures. The relationship between the samples changes throughout the
section – at times the vocal and instrumental sounds are of equal importance, and at other times the vocal sounds have precedence and the guitar
and drum sounds are used as accompaniment. Where spoken word is used,
it is used to convey a clear message to the audience about the composers'/
performers' feelings relating to the Japanese tsunami and Fukushima disaster of 2011. The sound quality of this section retains that of the original
samples – drums, guitars and vocals. The texture of this section is very
dense, partly due to the layering of the different sample types and partly due

to the hard aggressive nature of the drum and guitar samples selected. The dynamic is loud and remains consistent throughout the section.

Order and organisation

The samples are manipulated using a mixture of punchphasing, beatjuggling and scratching techniques. Drum samples are beatjuggled and specific vocal samples are punchphased in. There is some scratching of the vocal samples, accentuating the word through repetition. This opening section lasts for one and a half minutes at 91 bpm in 4/4 time and is very ordered with a clear structure. The section has a structure of A1, B, A2, C, D followed by a four-bar transition to the next section. It is performed with both musicians using all four turntables (1, 2 and 3 until Part C, where 4 is also used).

Part A1

The section opens with a four-bar introduction consisting of vocal samples – one spoken word ('I hate') and the other one textural, 'I hate' sounding for one crotchet beat for each word, repeated four times. This is followed by the same spoken sample timestretched over six beats, and a vocal shout for the last two beats of the four-bar phrase.

Part B

In bar 5 a different ten-bar phrase begins, the last bar of which is in 2/4 time dividing into one two-bar phrase followed by two four-bar phrases (B1, B2 and B3). A new vocal sample is used in this section, and this vocal line is joined by a drum line that develops throughout the section. In B1, the drum part begins as an off-beat bar-long motif consisting of high-hat and snare, lasting for a bar and half after which another drum motif in double time is added. Four into B2 (bar 10), a snare rhythm is added on top and this drum part continues throughout B3, until the end of the 2/4 bar in bar 14. The two performers create the rhythm by beatjuggling two records across turntables 2 and 3, changing places as they do so adding to the performative aspect of the routine.

Part A2

In bar 15 the final eight-bar phrase of the section begins, which is a development of the opening four bars. This breaks down into a two-bar phrase repeated three times (with variation), followed by a two-bar end (A1, A2, A3, A4). The vocal sample 'I hate' is used in the same way as in the opening of the section, a beat for each word. However, here it is repeated three times and in the second half of the last bar of the phrase it is replaced with another spoken word sample which changes each time the phrase is repeated and each time creates a different sentence (Figure 15.5). The first time (A1) the sample is 'nuclear powerplants', the second time (A2) the sample is 'government' and the third time (A3) it is 'capitalism'. Each of these individual samples is punchphased into the composition from turntable 1.

In this section, the drums also revert back to those used in the opening four bars. The off-beat bar-long motif is repeated 1½ times, silenced in the second half of the second bar so that the spoken vocal sample sounds without accompaniment. This drum phrase repeats three times, mirroring the structure of the vocal sample. In the final two bars of the section (A4), the 'I hate' sample is used again as in the introduction but here it is used for eight full beats – held for four beats and then the sample is sped up to create a dotted rhythmic motif. The textural vocal sample from the opening can be heard again.

Part C

From this part to the end of the section, all four turntables are used, primarily with one musician performing the vocal parts from turntables 3 and 4 and the other performing the drum parts from turntables 1 and 2. This four-bar section from bars 23 to 26 (Figure 15.6) takes the form of two two-bar phrases. It introduces new vocal samples that are punchphased into the composition and also scratched, in a kind of short call-and-response with the drum part. The vocal sample 'We are here to make history' plays for the first four beats accompanied by short drum motifs (kick and snare) on the first and last beats of the bar.

This is the same sample as used in sections B and A2. In the first half of the second bar of the phrase, the vocal sample is scratched until the third beat where the word 'history' repeats, followed by 'war' on the fourth. The kick and snare drum part plays whilst the vocal sample is scratched but is silent during the third beat when 'history' sounds before returning on the last beat of the phrase. By comparing the two notated passages from this section, it is possible to see how this part of section C mirrors section A2 – the fluid spoken text precedes the rhythmic part of the phrase, whereas in section A2 the fluid spoken part comes at the end. Also, in section

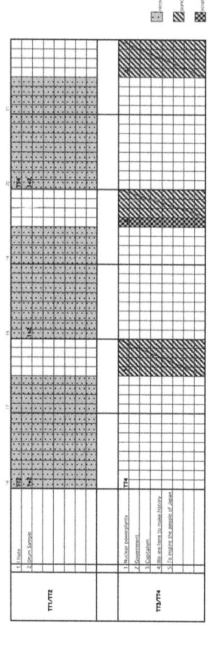

Figure 15.5 Notation of section 1, bars 16–21

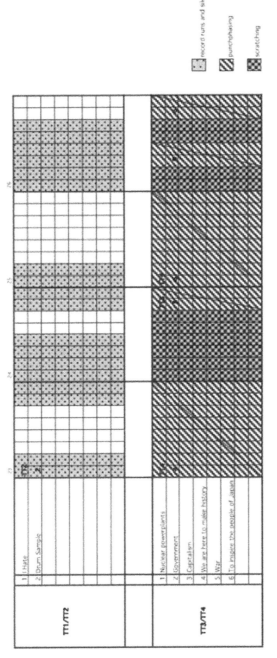

Figure 15.6 Notation of section 1, bars 23–6

C scratching is used to add rhythmic detail to the vocal line, which does not happen in A2.

A similar pattern is followed for the next two-bar phrase, but with key differences. This time, the vocal sample in the first bar of the phrase is changed to 'To inspire the people of Japan' and although the sample is again scratched in the second bar of the phrase, the scratched motif occurs on beats 1 and 3, with the vocal sample 'Japan' repeated on beats 2 and 4. Again, the drum pattern sounds on the first beat of the first half of the phrase, but it plays through the first three beats of the second bar and is silent on the last beat of the phrase.

Part D

This part of the section lasts for six bars, from bars 27 to 32, and again is constructed through the manipulation of vocal samples and drum samples. Here, the vocal sample used is 'We will, we will rock you'. The section is broken down into three smaller two-bar phrases (D1, D2, D3), the first is repeated, followed by the third that ends the section. The first phrase (D1) consists of the vocal sample manipulated to sound as 'We will, we will' as four beats of the first bar, followed by 'rock, rock, rock you, rock, rock, rock you' as equal quaver beats throughout the second bar of the phrase. This crotchet motif of vocal line 'We will' mirrors the crotchet motif 'I Hate' in sections D1 and D2, providing a through-line between sections. The rhythm part consists of a kick and snare motif for the first bar of each two-bar phrase (the same sample as used in the other sections), layered with a motif in double time in the second bar. This is repeated (D2). The 'We will rock you' vocal sample is used again in bars 31 and 32, but is drawn out in duration, drawing the section to a close (D3). 'We' is held for the four beats of the first bar of the phrase and in the final bar 'will' is drawn out for three beats, followed by a two-quaver rhythm for 'rock you' on the final beat. This vocal line is punctuated by a horn-like sample sounding as syncopated quavers after the vocal interjections and a sample of a scream which sounds on the third beat of the first bar of the phrase and fades out during the second.

Transition

Bars 33–6 are a transition to the next section. It begins on the upbeat to bar 33 with beatjuggled drums performed on turntables 3 and 4, which continues throughout the four-bar section again breaking down into two

two-bar phrases. Vocals are manipulated by scratching from turntable 2. In bars 33 and 34 the vocal sample 'kick' sounds as a syncopated quaver motif and in bar 36 the vocal 'like' is scratched, to sound the word on the second and fourth beat of the final bar.

Performative aspects

The performative element is very important in this section, and the performers use physical gesture to accentuate their opinions reflected in the vocal samples. In the first half of the section, the team gesticulate to the crowd, shaking their heads and making dismissive arm gestures. On the key punchphased vocal sample 'nuclear powerplant' and 'government', they shake their heads and hold their hands over their eyes, and then hold their noses on the vocal sample 'capitalism'. The second half of the section is more positive in tone and this is also reflected in the performative aspects. The performers make thumbs up signs and nod their heads, pointing at the crowd and the 'Spin for Japan' phrase on the front of their T-shirts.

Section 2: *Witness the Fitness*

Types of sound sources/sound synthesis/sound quality

The samples and sound effects used in this section are again recognisable. Sounds are instrumental and vocal in nature, including drums, bass and a number of spoken voice samples. Where they are included, the vocal samples take precedence over the other sounds, as the words are used to convey a message of positivity to the audience relating to the crew, and possibly Japan. The sound quality of this section retains that of the original samples – drums, bass and vocals – but they are manipulated using different techniques that help create a range of textures and timbres. The overall texture of this section is dense – whilst there are only a few samples played at once, the nature of the sounds selected is quite thick. The dynamic is loud and remains consistent throughout the section.

Order and organisation

The first half of the section primarily uses beatjuggling, whereas in the middle scratching is used to manipulate the vocal sample 'witness the

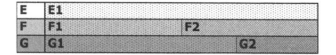

Figure 15.7 Structure of section 2 of *Witness the Fitness*

fitness', which alters the sound of the sample as well as adding rhythmic interest. Following this, the 'witness the fitness' sample is left to run and is accompanied by the bass and drum patterns. This second section lasts for approximately 1 minute and 10 seconds. It is in 4/4 time, again at 91 bpm. The section breaks down into three shorter sections, each one characterised by a different vocal sample (Figure 15.7). The section has a three-part structure (E, F and G), each four bars longer than the one it precedes, plus a two-bar transition. The section consists of vocal samples (sung and spoken word) and drum samples, and is performed with musicians using all four turntables.

Part E

Part E lasts for four bars. Turntable 2 plays a vocal sample 'Like Da-da', which lasts for the four bars. Alongside this, the beatjuggled drums continue on from the previous section (turntables 1 and 2), though they are broken into two smaller phrases. In bars 37–8 the kick and snare sample repeats a one-bar crotchet and quaver pattern, which in bars 39–40 is developed into a semiquaver pattern.

Part F

Part F lasts for eight bars and divides into two smaller four-bar sections (F1 and F2). The vocal sample changes to 'Keep your hands clapping', played from turntable 3. The treatment of this vocal motif develops throughout the section. In F1 (bars 41–4) the phrase lasts for one bar and is repeated four times. However, from F2 (bars 45–8) the motif is developed into a more syncopated rhythm, using both turntables 3 and 4. Again, the rhythm part (i.e. drums) is performed from turntables 1 and 2 and mirrors the structure of turntables 3 and 4. From bars 41 to 44 the beatjuggled drum pattern plays a one-bar phrase, which is repeated four times, using the motif from the previous section. In bars 45–8 this rhythmic motif is developed into a more syncopated rhythm, to complement that in the vocal line played by turntables 3 and 4. The use of the same rhythmic motif (though developed throughout the parts) provides consistency, when the vocal line changes frequently.

Part G

This final part lasts for 12 bars, from bars 49 to 60, and utilises the sample 'Witness the fitness'. This part divides into two smaller sections, G1 (eight bars long) and G2 (four bars long). In this section the performers change roles, with turntables 1 and 2 working with the vocal sample, and turntables 3 and 4 providing the rhythm line. The first eight bars (G1) follow a similar two-bar pattern, repeated four times (Figure 15.8). In the vocal line, the sample 'witness the fitness' (turntable 1) plays for the first two counts, and is then scratched for six counts – the final two counts of the bar, and the entire next bar. This pattern is repeated three more times. There is slight variation the second time the pattern is performed, where following the sample being played for the first two counts of the phrase, the platter of turntable 1 is stopped, silencing the sample abruptly for the second half of the bar, until the scratching resumes on the other turntable (2) for the second half of the bar and continues on this turntable until the end of the section. The rhythm line for this part is performed on turntables 3 and 4, which plays a syncopated pattern through beatjuggling and scratching a kick and snare motif. Variation is provided the third time that the two-bar vocal phrase repeats, by the rhythm line dropping out in bar 53, before returning on the upbeat to bar 54. This creates a mirror structure to this first eight bars of the part – the final time the two-bar phrase is heard it follows a similar pattern to the first time it is played, but in the second and third repetitions, variation is provided first by the dropping out of the melody line (bar 51) and then by the dropping out of the rhythm line (bar 53).

The part ends with a four-bar phrase (G2) where the vocal sample plays on turntable 2 without any rhythm line from turntables 3 and 4. Here the record is left to play the vocal sample, 'Witness the fitness, the cruffatin liveth, one hope, one quest', which is repeated twice. The section ends with a small transition lasting two bars (bars 61–2), beginning with a blend of melodic and vocal samples, and ending with the scratched sample 'The game is not over'.

Performative aspects

The performative element is important in this section, though due to the complexity of the manipulation techniques there is not so much as in the

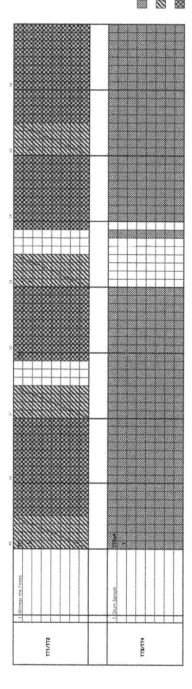

Figure 15.8 Notation of section 2, bars 49–56

previous section. Again, the performers engage with the audience through physical gesture; for example, hand gestures and clapping to the crowd to encourage their participation.

Section 3: *It's Like This Y'All*

Sound sources/sound synthesis/sound quality

The team uses a range of recognisable instrumental sounds again, including drum, instrumental and vocal samples. As the samples are primarily manipulated through beatjuggling techniques, the pitch of the original samples is not radically altered. In this section sustained vocal tones are used as well as spoken word, adding depth to the vocal texture. The samples are treated equally in the first part of the section, but as the words are recognisable, the listener is drawn to hearing those at the forefront. The vocal and instrumental samples move together rhythmically, giving a much more homophonic texture than the previous sections. However, in final part of the section, the relationship reverts to the drum and bass samples as accompaniment to the vocal sample.

Order and organisation

This section lasts for approximately 1 minute 16 seconds over 25 bars (bars 63–87) plus a two-bar transition at the end (bars 88–9). It is in 4/4 time, again at 91 bpm. The section breaks down into two parts: part H lasting for 17 bars and part I for eight bars. All four turntables are used during the section, and although scratching is used, the primary manipulation technique is beatjuggling. The section ends with a two-bar transition to the next section.

Part H

Part H lasts for 17 bars – four four-bar phrases (H1, H2, H3, H4) and a one-bar transition to Part I (Figure 15.9). This part is constructed from both vocal and rhythmic samples, primarily beatjuggled, across the two

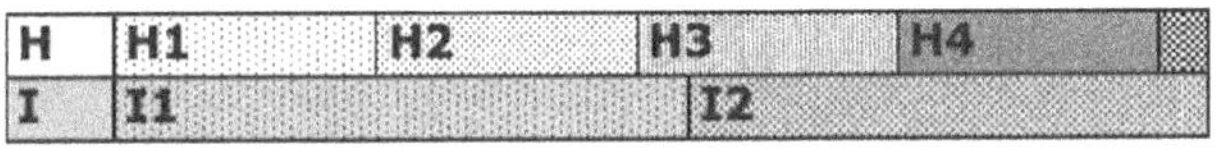

Figure 15.9 Structure of section 1 of *It's Like This Y'All*

pairs of turntables. H1 breaks down into two smaller two-bar phrases, the vocal samples 'It's like this y'all' and 'It's like that y'all' are juggled to create a quaver motif – the first sample used in the first two bars of the phrase and the second in the latter two bars. This pattern is mirrored in H2 (bars 67–70), where two different vocal samples are used – the first sample used in the first two bars of the phrase and the second in the latter two bars. In this development of the phrase, however, the straight quaver rhythm is replaced with a dotted rhythm. H3 (bars 71–4) uses the same samples as H1, and again beatjuggles with the samples, but performs a slower syncopated rhythm, compared to the straight quaver rhythm of H1. H4 breaks down into two smaller phrases – the first two bars utilising the samples from H2, and the final two bars utilising the samples from H1. This phrase is punctuated with snippets of the sample used in the transition from the previous section, 'The game is not over', and by returning first to the sample used in H1 and then to the sample used in the transition creates a sense of balance to the section. Bar 79 gives a sense of pause/anticipation, with a held melodic sample before the section moves to Part I.

Part I

Part I samples 'Intergalactic' and lasts for eight bars, breaking down into two smaller four-bar phrases. In the first four bars, records are beatjuggled across both pairs of turntables to create a syncopated rhythmic pattern with the vocal track. In the final four bars, a longer part of the sample is used – the record on turntable 3 is left to spin for two bars, repeated, whilst on turntables 1 and 2 a rhythm double the time of those created previously in the section is created through beatjuggling. Bars 88 and 89 are a two-bar transition to the next section, at its slower tempo, ending with the sample 'Come in Mr DJ' in the second half of bar 89.

Performative aspects

This section is the most performative in terms of showmanship, possibly in response to the inclusion of DJ performance in the judging criteria. As well as the usual physical gestures, body tricks are integrated into the performance including the performers playing with their hands behind their back, hands under their legs and turning around whilst juggling. In the final part of Part H, where beatjuggling is used to manipulate the sample, the performers beatjuggle and move in unison, which creates a unison rhythmic pattern across the turntables.

Section 4: *Spin for Japan*

Sound sources, sound synthesis, sound quality

In this section, as well as the usual drum, bass and vocal samples, sound sources from traditional Japanese instruments are used. This provides a balanced structure to the piece, bringing back the focus on Japan that was evident in the opening section. Where these traditional sounds are incorporated, the sound sample is played in full prior to being manipulated by scratching. Where this is the case, it is much easier for the listener to hear the change in the sample, in terms of both sound quality and rhythm, and to appreciate the manipulation techniques involved. This different instrumentation offers a contrast to the other sections, starting with simple light texture, before becoming thicker with the inclusion of bass and drum samples.

Order and organisation

This is the final section of the routine and the longest, lasting for approximately 2 minutes and 5 seconds. This is the only section with a different tempo, beginning at 69 bpm and increasing in tempo during the section to 73 bpm. It breaks down into two smaller parts: J and K (Figure 15.10).

Part J

Part J lasts for 13 bars and is structured J1, J2, J3. J1 and J2 are both four-bar phrases, consisting of a steady crotchet-based rhythmic motif created by beatjuggling between turntables 2 and 3. Both performers manipulate the records, changing places and turntables whilst juggling. Both these phrases are also characterised by the use of a spoken sample in the second half of the final bar – 'break down' in bar 93, and 'keep rocking' in bar 97. However, whereas J1 only comprises a drum pattern, in J2 a staccato melodic line is added, mirroring the rhythm of the drum part. In J3, which lasts for four bars (98–101), the drum part is omitted and a new melodic sample featuring a female vocal is included. This plays over the four bars, the performer speeding up the sample over the final two bars of Part J from 69 to 73 bpm (resulting in a pitch increase) to reach the desired tempo for

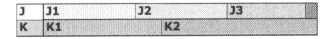

Figure 15.10 Structure of section 1 of *Spin for Japan*

Part K. In the final bar of Part J (102), the vocal sample is left to overhang, before the vocal sample 'Spin for Japan' sounds as an upbeat to Part K.

Part K

Part K lasts for 20 bars (bars 103–22) and consists of drums, bass, vocal melody and other miscellaneous sounds performed across the four turntables. It is structured into K1 and K2 plus a four-bar ending. Part K is characterised by the use of a prominent melodic vocal sample, which is used throughout. This is the same vocal sample as is used in Part J, providing consistency throughout the section. In K1, which lasts for eight bars from bars 103 to 110, the vocal sample played from turntable 1 forms two similar four-bar phrases and is manipulated through scratching across the eight bars. This vocal line is supported by a drum pattern, as well as a bass pattern performed on turntables 3 and 4 through manipulating the faders as well as tapping the record. In K2 a similar pattern is followed, with variation. A different texture is created here, by alternating samples and manipulation techniques between the bars. In bars 111, 113, 115 and 117 the vocal sample is left to play without any scratched manipulation and the drum and bass parts remain silent. In the alternate bars, however, bars 112, 114, 116 and 118, the vocal sample is scratched and the drum and bass parts sound. This builds tension, working towards the climax of the piece. The final four bars of the routine see the vocal, drum and bass parts silenced in bar 119, replaced with a bar-long extended spoken vocal sample that begins on the upbeat to bar 120, 'hope that everyone can live freely, harmoniously and joyfully', followed by the routine culminating in the sound of a record slowing to a halt in bars 121 and 122.

Performative aspects

Again, the performers engage with the audience through physical gestures, including hands in the air, arm gestures and pointing at the crowd. In this final section, as they did in the opening one, the team again point to the slogan on their T-shirts, drawing attention to the Spin for Japan organisation.

SOME CONCLUSIONS

The routine was carefully and thoughtfully structured and divides into clear sections, with parts and subsections linked by transition phrases (Figure 15.11). On a micro level, the routine is given a sense of unity both within and across the larger sections through the use of repeated phrases that are developed on each

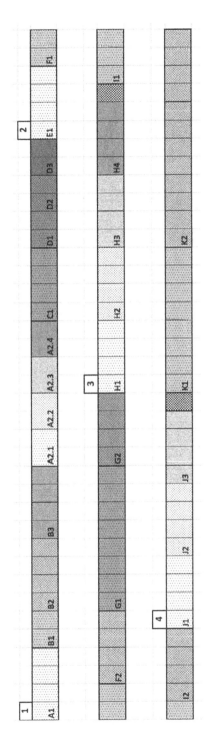

Figure 15.11 The structure and flow of the routine

repetition. However, when we look at the overall structure of the routine, it is possible to see how unity is also provided on a macro level, through the structuring of sections and their individual parts. The length of the transitions, for example, are symmetrical – four bars in length for first and last, two bars in length for the middle sections. The final two sections also include short one-bar internal transitions between their two parts, which punctuate through a pause, providing anticipation. The first and last sections are the longest in duration, but the sections get structurally simpler throughout the routine: section 1 has five parts, section 2 has three parts and sections 3 and 4 both have two parts. In the first two sections the first parts are the longest, establishing sonic motifs, but in the last two sections the longest parts are at the end of the sections, drawing the routine to a close. Through the careful selection of specific sound samples and their live manipulation using a variety of turntable techniques, Kireek have created a performance that is both sonically interesting and emotionally engaging. As I set out in the introduction, this short analysis is not intended as definitive but I hope that by offering some insights covering sound sources, sound synthesis, sound quality, order and organisation and performative aspects, it has offered a starting point for a deeper awareness and understanding of the complexity of turntable team routines and their construction.

References

Broughton, F. and Brewster, B. (2006) *How to DJ (Properly): The Art and Science of Playing Records*. London: Bantam Press.

Carluccio, J., Imboden, E. and Pirtle, R. (2000) 'Turntable Transcription Methodology' Available from http://www.studioscratches.com/wp-content/uploads/2011/01/TTMv1_Eng.pdf (accessed October 26 2015).

DMC (2011) DVD *World Team + Battle For Supremacy 2011*.

Gaskin, S. (2011) Kireek – Reigning world team champ DJs perform at the DMC after party. *Time Out Shanghai*. www.timeoutshanghai.com/features/Bars__Clubs-Event_spotlight/3660/Kireek.html (accessed 9 November 2012).

Gragg, R. (1999) Turntablists are the true visionaries. *ncra.ca*. www.ncra.ca/business/turntablism/ttarticles.html (accessed 20 June 2005).

Kireek (2012) Kireek Myspace page. www.myspace.com/kireekjp (accessed 9 November 2012).

Lambert, E. (2006) Kireek: Up to scratch. *Kansai Scene*. http://archives.kansaiscene.com/2006_10/html/club.shtml (accessed 9 November 2012).

Smith, S. (2000) Compositional strategies of the hip-hop turntablist. *Organised Sound*, 5(2), 75–9.

    (2013) *Hip-Hop Turntablism, Creativity and Collaboration*. Aldershot: Ashgate.

Webber, S. (2003) *Turntable Technique – The Art Of The DJ* (DVD). Quantum Leap.

16 | The analysis of live and interactive electroacoustic music: Hans Tutschku – *Zellen-Linien* (2007)

SIMON EMMERSON

GENRE AND CATEGORY

This is a live electronic and interactive work of concert art music (notated and determinate).[1] Here we confront our first major caveat. I shall approach this piece first and foremost from the point of view of the listener. While few composers really want their audience to 'follow a score', analyses of works such as this have traditionally been anchored on the score as representation of 'the music'. But many more people will have heard the work than have seen the score, so we should begin with the listener and work back to those aspects of the score which illuminate this experience. Of course an interested listener may want to become more informed about the work. Even before a concert performance they may have seen the programme note, read something by the composer on his website, seen a YouTube clip and so on. Or maybe the listener is listening at home to the work from recordings – an audio and a video recording are available.[2] They may have read that it is 'live and interactive'. In giving the music such a description, we make assumptions. Will the listener 'decode' the interactivity? What is 'live' about the relationship? What does that add to the experience of the music?

So, first – what do we hear?[3] What follows does presume access to the materials on the composer's website and is the product of multiple listenings to obtain the detail – a live performance experience cannot ever exactly be reproduced. The problem with thinking we can describe objectively what is heard is that a lot of descriptions cannot avoid the

---

[1] That is, there are no 'free' or improvisatory elements, although standard expressive interpretation is certainly encouraged. We may not know this at first listening – but this is part of the discussion that follows.

[2] These and all score and electroacoustic materials (which will be examined below) are available at www.tutschku.com/content/works-Zellen-Linien.en.php.

[3] Although I shall introduce the score relatively late in this discussion, all music references from the start will be in the form [minutes.seconds range – score page/bar number range] with reference to the available recording and score.

writer's own experience of playing the piano, working with piano sounds in the studio, and listening to many other works using similar materials. Listeners will have their own description but I hope to offer some signposts.

MATERIALS: HEARING, LEARNING AND EXPERIENCE

The work combines live piano and electroacoustic sound. What is immediately apparent is that it is not a trivial listening skill to untangle the live from the electronically produced sound. This is once again a skill based on experience of the instrument and its sound, on the one hand, and electroacoustic sound manipulation, on the other. The soundworld is remarkably integrated – and my intention here is to disentangle the two in order to show how this integration comes about.

The live piano part

There are three basic types of materials in the live piano writing:

1. Chords allowed to 'sound out' (thus usually isolated): these cover the whole range of the instrument from bass (examples at the opening) to treble.[4] First occurrence: Example 1[5] [0.00–0.26 – p.1/bb.1–3] on Figure 16.1.
2. Repetition of single pitches, accelerando–ritardando, or with nervous variation of rhythm, usually continuous but occasionally isolated and separated. First occurrence: Example 2 [0.24–0.36 – p.1/b.4] on Figure 16.1.
3. Clearly shaped rhythmic gestures – these are essentially complex energetic 'outbursts', sometimes formed of a sequence of single pitches or a mix of chords of varying density. The chords are never perceived as polyphonic but more as single sonorities. First occurrence: Example 3 [1.50–1.53 – p.1/b.13] on Figure 16.2.

We hear all three within the first two minutes but these dominate the entire 18 minutes of the work. All three of these sound types articulate a

---

[4] Though little exclusively in the high treble – presumably due to low resonance.

[5] Sound examples, movies and colour images may be found on the website accompanying this book. All examples in this chapter and on the website are used with permission (Hans Tutschku and Xenia Pestova).

Ex.1 [0.00-0.26 – p.1/bb.1-3] Ex.2 [0.24-0.36 – p.1/b.4]

Ex.6 [0.59-1.42 – p.1/bb.8-10]

[material 1]

[material 2]

[visual confirmation of play-trigger relationship needed]

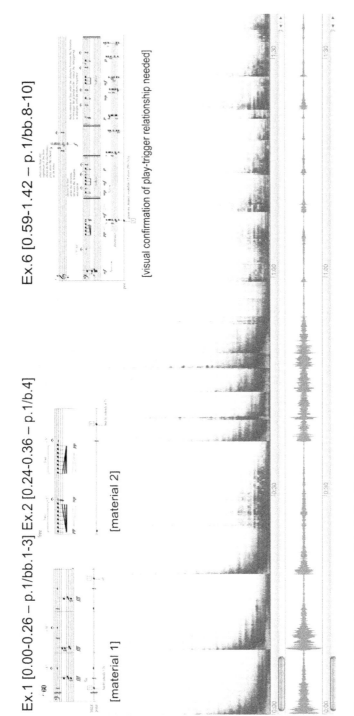

Figure 16.1 *Zellen-Linien* (excerpt) including Examples 1, 2, 6

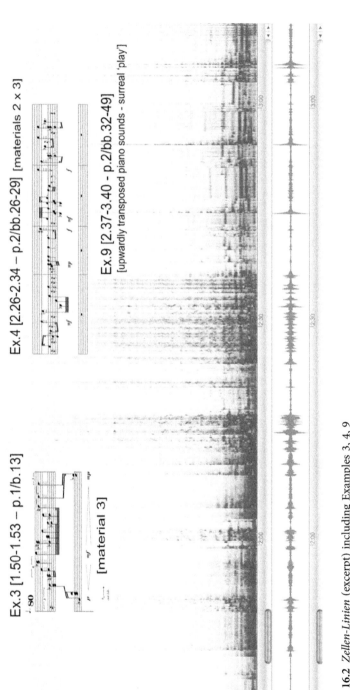

Figure 16.2 *Zellen-Linien* (excerpt) including Examples 3, 4, 9

percussive approach to the piano – and we sense immediately, too, that the dominance of the attack of the note relates to its function as trigger of electroacoustic sounds and processes. There are brief moments where these materials seem to interact and hybridise. At 2.26 (Example 4 [2.26–2.34 – p.2/bb.26–9] on Figure 16.2) a strung out gesture appears to absorb repeated note material (and there are other instances), while at 7.26 (Example 5 [7.26–7.47 – p.5/bb.118–20 and on] on Figure 16.3) cluster chords are articulated in a sudden gestural burst. But in general the three types of material retain their separate identities.

The electroacoustic soundworld

The listener might know the sound of a transposed piano note from experience – even though strictly it sounds more like a xylophone in some registers. We might suppose that the composer has here used piano sounds (pre-recorded or transformed 'live') but there is clearly a continuum from 'obvious' to 'unlikely' recognition of the sound as derived from the piano.[6] That said – there is a strong perceptual gravitational pull towards the instrument in every way. It is anchored centre stage and in every permissible spatial format for performance acts as an apparent source from which the sound flows – there is a natural perceptual pull of the less recognisable sounds towards the instrument, reinforced through this chain of recognisability.

Piano untransformed and 'easily recognisable' transformations

If we hear piano sounds from the loudspeakers, these might have been the result of live performance followed by a delay or might be the result of a pre-recorded soundfile trigger. The former we shall discuss further below (interactivity and causality); the second option is more complex – and may only be apparent with a visual cue. For example the set of eight clearly recognisable piano chords 0.59–1.42 in the recording are an ambiguous case (Example 6 [0.59–1.42 – p.1/bb.8–10] on Figure 16.1). I know from the video that they are pre-recorded and triggered (the performer is clearly playing single notes in the mid-low register – and the chords themselves

---

[6] I emphasise that at this stage I wish to avoid reference to the score – we are listening first and foremost.

Ex.5 [7.26-7.47 – p.5/bb.118-120 and on] [materials 1 x 3]

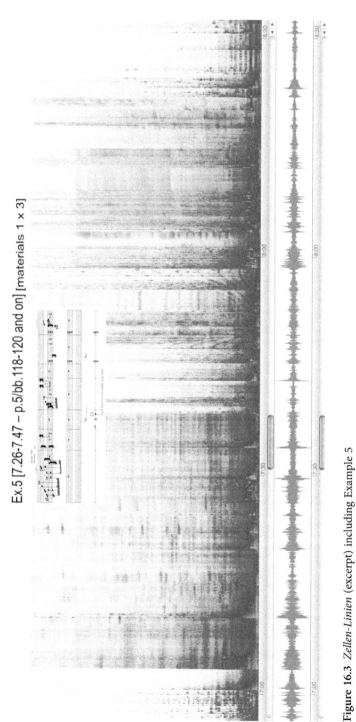

Figure 16.3 *Zellen-Linien* (excerpt) including Example 5

have not been heard before) but would not know from the audio only on first listen.[7]

Easily recognisable transformations include reverse sounds and transposed sounds (usually transposed up comes across more clearly). From 3.40 (and especially 4.00–4.30) obvious piano sounds are heard at a great distance from the piano itself, but clearly related to the live material. These are mixed with their immediate reversed forms in a continuously woven set of 'forward-reverse mirrors'. Sometimes I think the sounds are live and delayed – but they might also be pre-recorded and triggered (Example 7 [3.40–4.34 – p.3/bb.50–69] on Figure 16.4).

Reverse piano sounds are heard relatively low in the mix throughout the opening section's elaboration (0.54 and onwards to 1.01 acting here as a distant echo). But they are also the foreground feature from 4.34 to 5.18 when the piano duets with its mirror – apparently immediate reversal of the performed sounds (Example 8 [4.34–5.18 – pp.3–4/bb.70–80] on Figure 16.4).

With added flanging and phasing (spatial): a play of 'strange spaces'

The use of subtle flange and phase transformations is sparing in this piece and focused in specific sections to create a dreamlike and 'strange' quality to the sound. There is a unique section at 2.37–3.40 (Example 9 [2.37–3.40 – p.2/bb.32–49] on Figure 16.2) which uses upwardly transposed piano sounds in a surreal atmosphere of 'play'. There is a bizarre short section where it is almost as if there has been a mistake in the soundfile and its unsteady pitch shifts lurch to and fro in uncharacteristic rise and fall glissandi.[8]

There are two approaches to the transformation and timbral enrichment of the piano sound – vertical and horizontal – though of course the two may be found together.

Timbral enrichment (vertical)

We often hear the vertical layering of sounds – live and electroacoustic – to produce a wide variety of more or less spectrally denser 'spaces'. The

---

[7] Except that the experienced listener can hear that the *recorded space* is different – the live piano sounds close miked while the chords sound like a classic recording 'in a room'. But this may change in different recordings and performances.

[8] This has a strangely performative feel – a 'sampler keyboard gesture' somehow escaped. Tutschku does indeed play synthesiser and live electronics in his Ensemble für Intuitive Musik Weimar.

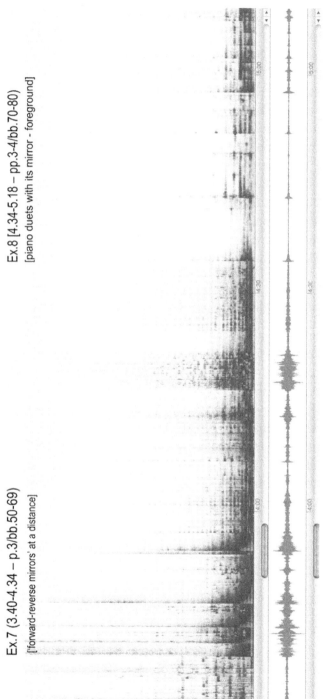

Ex.7 (3.40-4.34 – p.3/bb.50-69)

[forward-reverse mirrors' at a distance]

Ex.8 [4.34-5.18 – pp.3-4/bb.70-80)

[piano duets with its mirror - foreground]

Figure 16.4 *Zellen-Linien* (excerpt) including Examples 7, 8

soundworld retains a piano-like quality even at its most dense. This is probably due to the 'attack-decay' morphology of the piano's sound with longer decay towards the bass. The live piano sound also assists this anchoring process – a lot of the time this layering is triggered simultaneously with the live sound attacks which we can clearly hear (and see). All the material 1 working has this characteristic but it is easiest to perceive in the final section where we hear a variety of sonorities and timbres rooted in, but not variations of, the piano sound (Example 10 [16.49–18.45 – p.12/bb.296–325]).

One of the richest aspects of this work is that there is none of what we might at first hear as 'harmonisation', that is, chords generated electronically from single pitches – or pre-recorded and triggered to sound in this way. In fact the added layers do not resemble the piano itself spectrally in such a simple way – the timbres are more complex, often with a grainy noisier component. Indeed pitch sense (and hence any idea of 'chord') is strongly reduced with this timbral thickening and our perception shifts much further towards the colouristic.

Timbral extension (horizontal)

There are also horizontal extensions and near sustains, prolonging and changing the live piano sound. The ear is drawn to conclude that the piano has somehow been 'frozen' – any such sustain system has inevitably this 'slo-mo' feel to it as if time has slowed down or even been suspended (Example 11 [8.52–9.58 – p.7/bb.148–63]).

Then there is a related family of transformations based on fast repetition – a kind of grainy echo – higher pitched short piano attacks proliferate and are repeated at high repetition speed moving into the ambiguous area between rhythm proper and grainy texture. We hear this clearly at 2.41 onwards where such repetition rates – subtly varied and spatialised so as not to provoke a perception of pitch – approach 30Hz (= ca. 0.033s delay). Perhaps the best example is at 9.58–11.09, a long section of isolated damped attacks (material 2) which trigger the grain trains. Such a repetition transformation would not work with the longer decays of lower pitches and the additional high proportion of transient noise in the attack adds a white noise 'sheen' across the resulting texture. We hear from the loudspeakers an insect (cicada-like) buzzing articulated into gesture shapes and thrown around in space – that briefly crosses its apparent genre boundary into a strange kind of almost natural soundscape (Example 12 [9.58–11.09 – p.7/bb.164–84]).

SPACES: FIELDS OF ACTIVITY, DYNAMIC FRAMES

The available recordings will do little justice to the surround sound of a live performance. I shall return to how we might 'hear out' this space in a later section as it might involve knowledge from the score and programme notes which I wish to approach with caution at first discussion. That said, the stereo audio-only recording does capture a lot of spatial differentiation and movement. I have suggested the two terms 'local' and 'field', further subdivided into event, stage (local) and arena, landscape (field)[9] to help delineate functions in live electronics. I suggested local functions tend to remain rooted in the instrument on stage, probably projected on loudspeakers close to it, while field functions break free from the immediate rooted causality of the instrument and create an arena (quite close to the audience) even a landscape (further away) in which the local sits.

While I hear the two functions very clearly articulated, what is remarkable about this piece is the way there is a continuous exchange between the two. There is no simple boundary; there is a continuum in what I hear. Local seamlessly becomes field – indeed, to a very great extent the local controls the field, but not vice versa. While in general an event in an electroacoustic part could at times appear to *cause* a live event, this is a musical (not a literal) cause.[10] In *Zellen-Linien*, however, this is rarely the case; the sonic flow is predominantly out from the instrument, into the arena and landscape around it. It is a profoundly expansive piece, centred on the performer. Some materials may appear to break free, to become independent of source in the greater distances created by the electronics, but the interactivity remains 'close' to the instrumental gesture.[11]

Space frames: examples

In pure acousmatic and soundscape compositions there is no limit to the spaces that may be represented or implied. Even seated in a small hall we may be led into a world where the boundaries fall and the horizon is as large as our perception may take it. This is the power of loudspeakers to transform perceived space. But if we add a piano, fixed somewhere in the

---

[9] Elaborated in Emmerson (1998b).

[10] I give examples of this in an analysis of Denis Smalley's *Clarinet Threads* (Emmerson 1998a).

[11] I have described two paradigms for human–machine relationship in Emmerson (2009) – the machine as extending the scope and range of the performer (as here), and as creating surrogate other performers (truly interactive).

arena (usually on a stage), it influences our expectations in two ways. There is a performance horizon – the boundary of an acoustic area within which detail sufficient to an appreciation of the performance may be heard. Then there is social space in which the music of this instrument has normally been heard – which may or may not have walls and ceilings – from open spaces and amphitheatres, through village squares, piazzas and courtyards to enclosed spaces. The two interact and have fundamentally influenced the application of mechanical and electronic technologies to music.[12] And as pianos are rarely found in outdoor performance traditions, we start with expectations as to directions and boundaries – both of which our loud-speaker array can challenge.

There are many examples of the small event located clearly in the piano on stage and not really venturing much outside its physical location. Much of material 2 – repetition of pitches – remains static in the piano, although amplification alone tends to enlarge the space to fit the wider stage. Example 12 showed this at work and in addition this is clearly so in the tightly triggered section 13.26–14.14 (Example 13 [13.26–14.14 – p.9/bb.228–45]).

Of course these sometimes trigger much larger events and transform-ations that fill the field spaces. Slightly further out in the space frame array is the arena – but this can still be felt as close. This is best exemplified by the opening chord amplification and transformation – immersing the listener. Note that these are largely based on spectrum enrichment (described above as 'vertical') transformations. Denis Smalley describes spaces which include the more metaphorical spectral space (Smalley 2007). Here these spectral spaces are used to articulate a real space, still anchored to the instrument, but which seems to enlarge its presence to immerse the listener such that we hear inside the sound to a much greater extent.[13]

The field space frames – arena and landscape – have a simple continuous relationship in this work. They cannot clearly be distinguished – there is no obvious boundary. We hear changing distance, but otherwise there is no qualitative distinction. As we have just described, sometimes we are immersed in a relatively close surround sound where clearly the proscen-ium and forward direction is undermined and the listener becomes the focal point in an arena. But these give way to moments where the soundworld seems to expand outwards through invisible walls to way beyond the traditional boundaries of a performance space. There is a dynamic

---

[12] For example, the increasing loudness of the Western orchestra ca. 1750–1930, the replacement of wood with steel for the frame of the pianoforte (ca. 1820s–1840s).

[13] And in a surround sound recording this would be even more pronounced.

relationship of spaces. This is striking in the long section from 14.14 to 16.49 – all four frames are dynamically in operation: windows in the nearer spaces open to the very distant; each space has solo and interactive elements (Example 14 [14.14–16.49 – p.9–12/bb.246–95] – see overview Figure 16.5).

FORM AND FORMING

Discussions on musical form often seem to be conducted as if discussing a finished structure, something that appears to have extension 'outside time' – an architectural view of form. In fact for the listener we are watching (listening to) the *building process* – the forming of the work in time. The composer may work in building blocks and structures, but the listener can only create such things (if at all) in memory after the event. It is difficult for the analyst to think back to such a state – possibly a first listening – and hear how the piece builds up to its totality. For someone who knows a piece well, memory creates much firmer anticipation of the future event and its relation to the past. Furthermore representation on screen enables us literally to see what we are about to hear, and surprises can be anticipated.

Even from early listenings I noted that the forming of the piece emerges from a sequence of characteristic sections each built from a variant of one of the three material types I outlined above and also differentiated clearly by electroacoustic treatment – triggering soundfiles, processing and transformation and very clear differences in spatialisation and spatial 'feel'. The exact number of these refines on repeated listenings but seems to settle on about eight.[14]

(1) 0.00–4.34: an opening section itself differentiated into much smaller parts but retaining a sense of overall introduction to all the material.
(2) 4.34–7.03: a whimsical introspective section, dreamlike and distant (mostly piano solo with apparently minimal electronics).
(3) 7.03–8.25: a much noisier section, becoming increasingly anarchic – the electroacoustic and piano sounds are constantly trying to overcome each other.
(4) 8.25–9.58: moving into sustained piano hits creating another beautifully sustained surreal atmosphere (in the middle to far distance).
(5) 9.58–12.33: quiet and sparse – inside piano plucks and damped hits, insect-like textures come and go and bass resonances re-emerge.

[14] Repeated listenings tend (in this work) to differentiate boundaries and thus subdivide rather than clump together the section memories as they accumulate.

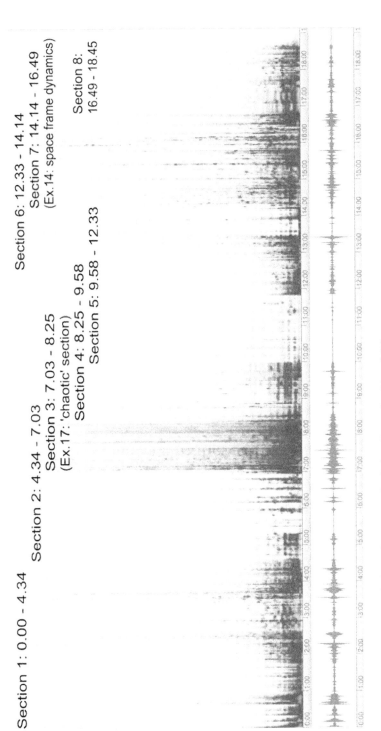

Section 1: 0.00 - 4.34

Section 2: 4.34 - 7.03

Section 3: 7.03 - 8.25
(Ex.17: 'chaotic' section)

Section 4: 8.25 - 9.58

Section 5: 9.58 - 12.33

Section 6: 12.33 - 14.14

Section 7: 14.14 - 16.49
(Ex.14: space frame dynamics)

Section 8:
16.49 - 18.45

Figure 16.5 *Zellen-Linien* whole work overview (including Examples 14 and 17)

(6) 12.33–14.14: piano attacks trigger clear samples, isolated rhetorical gestures re-emerge.

(7) 14.14–16.49: another strange and surreal space is created in the middle to far distance.

(8) 16.49–18.45: an extended sustained chordal section that has a sense of closure and return to the opening material of the work – but breathes much more freely and is for the most part gentler and lighter in touch.

See Figure 16.5 – whole work overview (includes Examples 14 and 17).

Of course, repeated listening also allows a more nuanced interpretation of each section. A look at the score then explodes forever a sound-only memory and overlays this with the performance schema as given by the composer. Our perceived sections do indeed correspond to 'hits' on the advance pedal but there turn out to be many others within these sections. There are 32 patches in all – most of which are clearly distinguishable although not all as pronounced as those we delineated above – I hesitate to call them all scenes even if the composer does.

'POIETIC LEAKAGE' INFLUENCES THE LISTENING PROCESS

There is no such thing as a completely naïve listener – no *tabula rasa*. Expectation plays a key role in how we make sense of music, especially in live performance – expectation stretches all the way from the venue and social circumstance, and what we see around us in preparation (here a piano and an array of technology) to what we may know of other such music. The composer's website gives the listener an opportunity to get to know some of his intentions through notes to, and a score of, the work (in addition to audio and video recordings). We shall treat these as potential new resources for the listener, but with the caution that they need a degree of expertise to read. What do they add to our listening experience? Do we hear what the composer describes?

Programme note (available on the website)

For *Zellen-Linien*:

I wanted to create an 'electronically prepared' piano. [...] Since 1999 I experimented with the real-time analysis of the instrumental gesture of the pianist and with possibilities to control the live-electronics through the gesture of the player.

The composer adds that this work relates to an earlier one, *Das Bleierne Klavier* (*The leaden piano*):[15]

During his playing the musical gestures are traced and interpreted by the computer program to determine a big ensemble of parameters for the generation and playback of the electroacoustic part. This allows for the player a very direct 'action – reaction' between the piano part and the electroacoustic sounds. They become a sort of prolongation of these instrumental gestures. [...] and what is controlling equally the sound spatialization around the public.

The composer does not use the term 'interactive' in the title – this term implies the mutual influence of two agents. In this work the piano clearly directs the electronic part. While the performer may respond expressively to the electroacoustic result, there are no primary 'either/or' decisions to be made. The reciprocal influence is quite low. However, the tyranny of the 'mixed music' (instrument plus 'tape'[16]) stopwatch time line is broken and expressive gestural performance practice is restored to the live performer.

   The question 'Do we perceive the action – reaction?' causality the composer refers to is perhaps the wrong one. It is better to ask how the instrument/electroacoustic relationship enhances our experience music-ally. I have argued elsewhere that we do not hear causes, we hear effects (Emmerson 2011 – discussed further below).[17] But furthermore it is a sequence of such effects that matters – from these we put together rela-tionships. I would argue that the effectiveness of these cause-effect links adds considerably to the *performer's* control and hence freedom and expressivity. The *control intimacy* long discussed[18] in the live and inter-active literature is that between performer and instrument, extended to include the electronics. If this enhances the 'quality of life' of the per-former, then this has a chance of being conveyed to the listener. The listener need not decode each individual cause-effect link, but ideally perceives an immanent quality of control intimacy in the overall result. A sense of enhanced relationship emerges.

   Let us take as an example the model that Tutschku cites, the prepared piano. We need not know what Cage's preparations are – although if we are inquisitive we may ask and get to know from the composer's score

[15] The two works share much material. *Zellen-Linien* is effectively an extended and rewritten version of the earlier work.

[16] Electroacoustic material fixed in time.

[17] I am referring to musical listening. In the primeval forest a twig snap might mean a predator is about to attack – in this listening mode you move rapidly from effect to possible cause.

[18] See F. Richard Moore's (1988) article from the MIDI era – the principles still stand.

notes and maybe visual inspection at a concert. In the listening experience it is the beautiful sequence of sounds which entrances us, not a sequence of 'pictures' of nuts, bolts and rubber strips. So in the present work the composer is free to tell us how the electroacoustic extension of the piano sounds was indeed caused but that need not be a primary aspect of the listening experience. We need not have a sequence of such explanations running through our minds in parallel to the music as experienced.[19]

Gesture and event

In the article 'What is an event?', Gary Kendall (2008) describes his idea of the 'EVENT schema'. This is 'a generic model that captures the essential temporal structure by which auditory experiences may be *understood* as "events"' (Kendall 2008: 2–3) (Figure 16.6). His article applies this idea to several examples of electroacoustic music to show how the many types of event may be 'made sense of'.[20]

Here we encounter an interesting dilemma. Kendall developed and applied this idea to acousmatic electroacoustic music where we cannot see any material cause of the sound beyond the loudspeaker, yet we surmise the gist in relation to the event schemas of the real world. But in a live electronic work we might have sight of the pianist's relationship to the instrument whether in performance or video recording (which we have from the composer here; Figure 16.7). This is then linked to an electroacoustic soundworld to form a three-way relationship – performer, instrument, loudspeaker.

Here we have visual evidence of the preparing and stopping components of the schema which we would otherwise try to 'think in' from experience of the sound alone. In live performance there is at any instant evidence for what is about to happen – anticipation is encouraged and reinforced by the visual. One event's schema may be linked directly to the next – the 'done' state for the first may be the 'enabled' state for the subsequent event. Kendall also suggests that there are event hierarchies, thus at faster micro-levels we may not distinguish individual schemas but these may be grouped in various ways and be perceived as singular events at what he terms the *focal layer*. In *Zellen-Linien* the piano part contrasts static repetition (chords or repeated pitches – material types 1 and 2)

---

[19] I say 'need not' but some kinds of professional listening do indeed encourage this.

[20] He calls the overall sense of a fast-moving set of events its 'gist'.

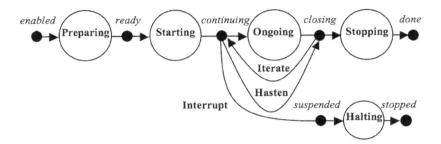

Figure 16.6 Kendall event schema (2008)

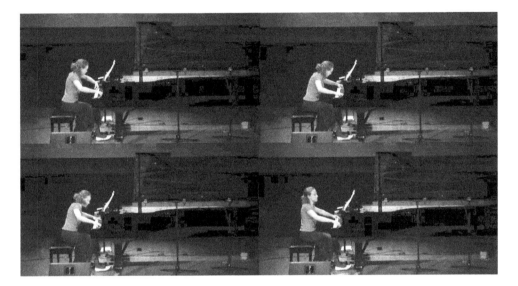

Figure 16.7 'Preparing – starting – ongoing – stopping' (Xenia Pestova – used with permission)

which are singular events with 'outbursts' of clearly shaped lines – the string of short events tends to group together and my focal layer here conceives of these as 'gestures' of varying lengths – material 3.

Towards the score

Our journey may now arrive at the score which is freely available from the composer's website. Scores from the Western tradition need, of course, an expertise in reading their codes. Furthermore these may have been modified and extended with a wide variety of new practices from the second half of the twentieth century. The score is barred and time signatures based on a rational Crotchet appear throughout, though with various tempo indications. Pitches are traditionally notated[21] – with brief exceptions of clusters and inside-piano damped, plucked and glissando sounds. The extension to tradition also lies with the electronics – a simplified instruction line with indications for MIDI pedal hits to advance the (Max) patch 'scene' for electronic processing. These scene numbers each have a characteristic 'mix' of processes – described only very briefly in words in the score, and usually in terms only understandable with the Max patch details to hand.

Max patch

Finally the public availability of the Max patch[22] itself allows the expert listener to discover the electronic side of how the piece sounds as it does. As it is stored in 'standalone' form, it is available to anyone to play with its functions and understand its 'scene changes'. The nearer one goes to the composer's real piano set-up, the more it will resemble the performed and recorded result. But even using your own voice as test sound input reveals an enormous amount about the triggering, information extraction and consequent processing that the patch allows. Similarly for spatialisation, if eight- or four-channel systems are not available, a stereo mix can still reveal much about the spatial positioning and movement trajectories which are generated. And, of course, the sequence of scenes tells us something about the overall dramaturgy and formal evolution of the work.

Unpacking the Max patch opens a Pandora's box for the listener. Some things we heard before are confirmed, some explained. But many new ones now emerge and some old ones replaced; we hear non-piano sounds clearly for the first time,[23] realise which pre-recorded elements return perhaps treated differently, and no doubt express surprise at some of these. Whether we hear more will depend on the individual but we certainly listen differently now we have some detailed knowledge about how this is done.

---

[21] The addition of super treble and low bass staves at two-octave transpositions is a helpful logical extension allowing exceptionally clear cross-stave chord writing.
[22] In several incarnations as the Max program itself has evolved.
[23] The new knowledge that there are 'Chinese percussion' samples does not change the earlier observation about how rooted the electroacoustic sound is in the sound of the live piano.

INTERPRETATION AND MEANING

As noted above, this work comes largely from the percussive tradition of pianism, extended through the 'sound projection' of both the French and the German traditions of mixed electroacoustic music.[24] The technology throws the instrumental sound around us in an intensely immersive experience, clearly an expression of the amniotic drive of a lot of art and media experience in the late twentieth century. The sound surrounds us and we are inside it – to the extent of feeling inside the instrument itself, even inside its spectrum.[25] That said, the work does have a forward direction due to the presence of the live instrument and more importantly the performer's physical presence and embodied gestures – we do tend to focus on the source from which the sound emerges, or which appears to conjure the sound up. The sound flows towards and swirls around us.

Reading the score with respect to the gestures illuminates one aspect of my listening immediately. Many gestures are based on a fixed pitch field which possesses a clear sonority – the gesture morphology 'unpacks' and articulates the sonorities generated by the field, yet the ear is drawn back to its totality which seems to be 'assembled' through memory and repetition. This unifies in principle two of the material types we outlined at the beginning. The gestures are 'unpacked chords', the chord materials 'stacked up gestures', both based on singular sonorities. In fact both the opening chords and the first three gestures emphasise the sonorities drawn from a near complete octotonic pitch set.[26] These are very clear in the gestures which emphasise a high group (Example 16 [p.1/bb.20–1] also Figure 16.8), repeating and permuting its members.[27]

Octave transpositions and doublings are not avoided, and within many of the pitch fields there is an inherently consonant feel disturbed by carefully placed chromatic tension. I cannot help but be reminded of the pitch fields of Stockhausen's *Momente* and Berio's *Sinfonia* which are built and sound similarly. But this is also a sonorous characteristic of octotonic practice – as in the Russian tradition from Mussorgsky to Stravinsky. The opening has the same kind of sonority and gesture as the opening of the coronation scene of *Boris Godunov*.

---

[24] Originally the French focus was on the creative projection of timbral detail while the German focus was on geometric spatial projection – this distinction can no longer be made so clearly.

[25] Barry Truax (1994) has written about this sense of 'getting inside' a sound with respect to granular synthesis – and in this work, too, granulation is a key technique.

[26] G, B♭, B, D♭, D, E, F – only A♭ is omitted (in this section).

[27] These are exactly repeated in the final section (p.12).

grain-rec, hinher,
buf01 (chords 1-16 transposed very high)

Figure 16.8 *Zellen-Linien* octotonic pitch field gestures (staves: treble plus two octaves, treble, bass)

The piano, especially when played percussively, naturally draws us to the inharmonic soundworld as its partial tones are consistently detuned from harmonic series values. Henry Cowell, who formalised the cluster, as well as playing and adding objects inside the instrument, and John Cage, whom he taught and who is generally credited with the invention of the prepared piano, emphasise increasingly the world of inharmonic sonority. Bolts, screws and rubber preparations disturb the standard divisions and tensions of the strings. It is not surprising that many have perceived Indonesian gamelan qualities in the result; the prepared piano becomes a metallophone orchestra.[28] In *Zellen-Linien* similarly, the piano aspires to the condition of a vast metallophone – made most explicit and tam-tam-like at the opening and then deconstructed and reconstructed as the work progresses. Interestingly, different metallophone models emerge throughout the work. This is articulated through the addition of *noise* – very often 'sizzle' and denser grainy noise within the metallic sonority. In Japanese aesthetics, instrumental sound production does not aspire to the totally clean sound (as in the Western classical tradition) but considers breath noise in wind instrument performance and *sawari* – additional distortions and noisy components – in plucked strings essential ingredients of a 'beautiful sound'. Example 17 'chaotic section' [7.03–8.25 – pp.5–6/bb.110–39] – see overview (Figure 16.5).

---

[28] At least in the metal prepared strings – rubber tends to produce damped drum-like sonorities.

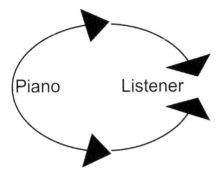

Figure 16.9 Musical and technical space

CONCLUSION

Listening to this piece we can hear how technology has allowed the composer to create an *expanded* or *extended* soundworld.[29] The sounds have a gravitational pull back to the piano in terms of both sound quality and embodied performance. Individual sounds never really attain an 'escape velocity' and an independence from this anchoring. And there is another focus around which the sound travels – the listener. So what emerges as a musical model for this work reflects the ideal distribution of the loudspeakers – the two are in a strongly reinforcing relationship. What we have both musically and technically is an *ellipse* with the piano and listener each at a focal point around which the work flies (Figure 16.9).

References

Emmerson, Simon (1998a) Acoustic/Electroacoustic: The relationship with instruments. *Journal of New Music Research*, 27(1–2), 146–64.

   (1998b) Aural landscape: Musical space. *Organised Sound*, 3(2), 135–40.

   (2009) Combining the acoustic and the digital: Music for instruments and computers or pre-recorded sound. In Roger Dean (ed.), *The Oxford Handbook of Computer Music*. Oxford University Press, 167–88.

   (2011) Music Imagination Technology. *Proceedings of the International Computer Music Conference, Huddersfield, 2011*. San Francisco: ICMA, 365–71.

---

[29] But as noted above, not as radically separated as the sounds of the mechanically prepared piano.

Kendall, Gary (2008) What is an event? The EVENT schema, circumstances, metaphor and gist. *Proceedings of the International Computer Music Conference, Belfast, 2008*. San Francisco: ICMA (unpaginated).

Moore, F. Richard (1988) The dysfunctions of MIDI. *Computer Music Journal*, 12(1), 19–28.

Smalley, Denis (2007) Space-form and the acousmatic image. *Organised Sound* 2(2): 107–26.

Truax, Barry (1994) Discovering inner complexity: Time-shifting and transposition with a real-time granulation technique. *Computer Music Journal* 18(2), 38–48.

17 | Audio-only computer games: *Papa Sangre*

ANDREW HUGILL AND PANOS AMELIDES

Introduction

This chapter addresses the important question of the role of the audience in electroacoustic music by considering a genre in which user agency is paramount: audio-only games. While the primary intention of audio-only games is not necessarily musical, an understanding of the active role of the gamer in relation to the audible environment offers many valuable insights to aid analysis of the burgeoning field of interactive electroacoustic music. Indeed, the distinction between what is intentionally 'musical' and what is not becomes blurred when users take time during gameplay actively to enjoy the sonic experience, and even to become creative within that virtual world. This is a recurring phenomenon in all forms of gaming, but audio-only games offer a distinctively acousmatic experience that equates to an act of composition. Central to this is the construction of narrative using a set of sonic materials that may be interactively mixed and remixed, usually within a spatial field. This is typically common both to gaming and to interactive electroacoustic music, but is also an important aspect of much fixed media electroacoustic music in which narrative is increasingly being rehabilitated as a primary driver of experience. Electroacoustic music therefore has much to learn from an analytical understanding of how gaming goes about enabling the user to construct a narrative path. This is sometimes, even if tacitly, acknowledged by electroacoustic musicians and it may well be the case that recent developments in interactive music have been conditioned by the gaming experience that forms a key part of digital culture.

We therefore analyse the audio-only game *Papa Sangre*, with the intention of informing both games researchers and electroacoustic musicians about some of the key aspects of its interactive composition. Identifying an appropriate analytical method for such an endeavour is in itself challenging, and we consider several approaches within the chapter before proposing a hybrid that reflects the 3D sound perception of location for the gamer, and the flow of affects and effects, triggers and instructions, and all the other events that make up the experience. We use both film and game sound analysis and electroacoustic music analytical techniques to arrive at

355

this hybrid. We place *Papa Sangre* within a historical context of the evolution of audio-only games. We also deploy Pierre Couprie's EAnalysis software tool to show how the various sonic layers interrelate during the game. We conclude by making some observations about how audio-only gaming may inform electroacoustic music making and vice versa.

Background

A preliminary study for this chapter was first published by Andrew Hugill (2012) on the OREMA (Online Repository for Electroacoustic Music Analysis) website on 30 January 2012, under the title 'Towards an analysis of *Papa Sangre,* an audio-only game for the iPhone/iPad'. The article was written in response to discussions that took place during the first symposium of the AHRC-funded project *New Multimedia Tools for Electroacoustic Music Analysis*. One of the project leaders, Leigh Landy, expressed the view that the playing of computer games could produce an algorithmic electroacoustic musical composition, regardless of the intentions of the player. Hugill suggested that the genre of audio-only gaming (which was unknown to all present) offers peculiar opportunities in this respect.

Interactive work presents a particular challenge for analysis. The experiences of the user, who acts as both 'composer/musician' and 'audience' in interactive music, are central in a way that is substantially different to the relatively passive listener at, for example, an acousmatic concert. Hugill consequently adopted an 'aestheticist' approach to the early study, using the 'pleasure framework' first identified by Brigid Costello (Costello 2007: 370–1). *Papa Sangre* was selected because it offered the clearest examples of electroacoustic sound design and processing as part of the gaming experience.

The preliminary study considered only the first three levels of gameplay. To prepare the present chapter, more substantial research into the entire game was conducted. Student subjects were invited to play the game and record their experiences. Accounts of the gameplay given in various gaming forums and a detailed description given on the Enongo blog (Enongo 2012) were added to the documentation. Finally, Panos Amelides joined the analytical team and combined his gameplay experiences with Hugill's own.

Audio games

Audio-only games, or audio games, have a rich history that may be traced back to the Atari game *Touch Me* (1974), a memory test which combined visual and audible signals, but could be played using the sounds alone. A more popular version of the same idea was the Milton Bradley Company's *Simon* (1978), which used a handheld mobile device comprising four coloured buttons that had to be pressed in sequence to match an audio cue. This game became very popular, spawning many imitations, and to some extent defined the generation gap at the time (Edwards 2006).

Text-to-speech (TTS) applications such as MacInTalk, which was installed on Apple computers from 1984, opened up the possibility of audio versions of text-based adventure games. These acquired a wide following, particularly amongst visually impaired gamers, who subsequently represented the primary constituency for audio games. As the video capabilities of computers developed, however, games creators increasingly moved away from text-based games, leaving an ever-dwindling group of audio gamers apparently lagging behind developments. This led to a culture of amateur enthusiasts and very small companies, who either adapted video games for visually impaired users or, increasingly, created audio-only games. This culture is still very much in evidence, particularly on dedicated sites such as audiogames.net. Two typical examples of such games are *Terraformer*, in which the gamer has to fight robots in order to gather terraforming tools, a process which is made possible by 3D sonar navigation, and *Seuss Crane: Detective for Hire*, which is effectively a drama in which the gamer plays the detective.

Meanwhile, console games makers began to show an interest in audio games. Probably the most important early example was Kenji Eno's *Real Sound: Kaze No Regret* (1999), which was made available on the Sega Saturn and Dreamcast platforms. In this game, a narrative builds around themes of fear and love, governed by critical decisions made during the game. Nintendo entered the market subsequently, producing a series from 2006 onwards called *Soundvoyager* in which users navigate using only sound clues. The advent of smartphones has opened up this market still further with many popular new titles coming out in 2012/13, such as *Ear Monsters* (shooting audible monsters), *Freeq* (futuristic audio adventure), *Audio Archery* (archery shooting) and *Zombies, Run* (running game).

Games such as *Papa Sangre* may be said to be a synthesis of all these historical developments, representing a conscious effort to address the visually impaired market while also opening up the experimental potential of audio-only gaming to a wider audience. This is reflected in market share which, while it remains a tiny fraction of the games market as a whole, has nevertheless seen a significant expansion. Interviewed by the BBC in 2005, the co-author of audiogames.net, Richard van Tol, said 'my guess is that about 3,000 audio or blind-accessible games are sold a year' (Adams-Spinks 2005). However, by 2012 the director of the *Papa Sangre* project announced, at a BAFTA 'What's App' event in London, that this game alone had sold 'about 70,000 copies' on iOS (Bennun 2012). It seems most likely that this market has gone well beyond visually impaired users, an impression which is confirmed by the various YouTube reviews and discussions in gaming forums. At the time of writing, Somethin' Else are about to launch a new version of *Papa Sangre* and another audio game, *The Nightjar,* so clearly the market offers significant opportunities.

Mobile phone games are, as Karen Collins points out, 'distinguished from handheld gaming in that games are not the primary intended use of the machines' (Collins 2008: 77). Nevertheless, the capabilities of smart-phones are such that they can now deliver high-quality and, most import-antly, binaural sound through headphones. Their portability and mobility make them ideal devices for visually impaired gamers. The pervasive nature of these media also allow audio games to be presented as a fascin-ating experimental corner of the video games market, something which is apparent in all the marketing for *Papa Sangre*. It is now possible to imagine an audio game achieving the same iconic status within mobile phone gaming as *Simon* did in the pop culture of the 1970s.

Papa Sangre

Papa Sangre is an app for the iPhone and iPad that was developed by a team at Somethin' Else, a London-based content design company, includ-ing Paul Bennun, Ben Cave, Adam Hoyle of Do Tank, Peter Law, Margaret Robertson, Nick Ryan and Tassos Stevens of Coney, with support from 4iP. The game was launched in 2010, and rapidly attracted attention, both for the novelty of the approach and for the quality of the sound design and gameplay. The game was developed in software (including the Verb Session reverberation tool and the HEar binaural encoding tools from IRCAM), but also through playing a theatre game called 'Sangre Y Patatas', a kind of Blind Man's Bluff using nachos on the floor and other sound cues to simulate the gaming interaction (Papa Sangre Blog 2010).

Papa Sangre is a 'first-person' game in which the gamer navigates through a virtual world using only aural cues. Movement is enabled by left–right–left–right touching of the lower half of the screen, corresponding to footsteps which move you forward in time and space. Orientation is adjusted by scrolling the upper half of the screen. There are graphics (feet and a dial) that correspond to these regions, but there is no need to be able to see them.

All the audio in the game is binaural and is designed to be experienced wearing headphones. Some was pre-recorded using a dummy head wearing a pair of microphones positioned inside the pinnae (or outer ears). The resulting Head Related Transfer Function (HRTF) compared the arrival times and intensity differences of the binaural cues received at the different ears in order to simulate a '3D' effect that effectively mimics the way humans actually hear. The same effect may also be applied to synthesised sounds, which was done in *Papa Sangre* by using the Create Signal Library (CSL, pronounced 'sizzle') (Fastlab 2009). This is a C++ library for digital signal processing which offers the scalability, complexity, flexibility and portability that is essential for a game that changes as rapidly as *Papa Sangre*.

Figure 17.1 shows how the reverberant characteristics of the gamer's 'footsteps' are combined with the virtual space or 'room', and any other sounds that are present, to create an overall mix at any given moment. This mix provides the locative precision that enables navigation during the game. In addition to the CSL processes, the pre-recorded 'dummy head' binaural sounds are also fed directly to the gOutMix Mixer to be combined with the synthesised material when triggered by the gameplay. The result is an 'immersive' environment which has the capacity to deliver both general atmosphere and precise location detail.

Papa Sangre is an example of 'survival horror', a genre that is typified by a 'total atmosphere [that] is densely creepy' (Whalen 2004) in which the gamer is powerless, with survival dependent upon successful completion of puzzles and avoiding dangerous enemies. The narrative of *Papa Sangre* plunges the gamer into the land of the dead, a dark and frightening place whose blackness parallels the situation of the unsighted gamer him/herself. The whole story has a Cinco de Mayo, voodoo quality that owes a lot to the tradition of B-movie horror.

The gameplay involves puzzle solving which is constantly hampered by hostile creatures that block your path. These hostile creatures come from voodoo nightmares, such as: flesh-eating snuffle hogs (the main enemy from the start); a slasher bird that tries to 'peck your skull clean' (first introduced at Level 8); the grim reaper, complete with scythe, who multiplies and giggles from Level 9 onwards. Your mission is to 'save a soul in peril', a goal which is announced during Level 1 (Into the Dark):

The sound of a telephone ringing in my left ear (left channel) and I hear a child singing 'twinkle, twinkle little star' in my right ear (right channel). The telephone

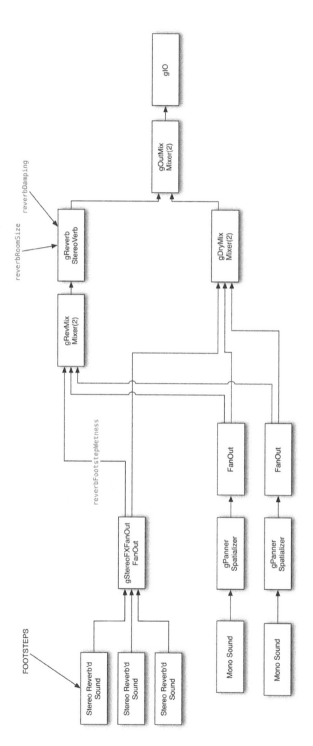

Figure 17.1 *Papa Sangre*: CSL Graph (Bennun 2012)

continues ringing and I hear distant cars and it feels like being in the sidewalk of a big avenue in London(?) as the phone ringing continues. Then, a door closing sound and a click as the player (me?) apparently picks up the ringing phone. At the other end of the line a person with a funny Spanish accent is greeting me in my right ear: *'Buenos dios compañeros. The soul of someone dear to you is in grave danger. To save him you must leave this world and follow me into the kingdom of Papa Sangre. No time to lose!'* (Panos Amelides, gameplay notes)

To achieve this goal, you are aided by a disembodied female voice that has a distinctly 'correct' English accent (Enongo likens her to Catherine Zeta Jones). She provides training and advice, but her role becomes increasingly ambiguous as the game progresses, sometimes disappearing for long periods and at other times appearing to be rather treacherous. In Level 17, for example, she teases the gamer by repeatedly changing location while calling to you to follow her. As Amelides remarks:

Her voice continues to be audible and I have the feeling of being Ulysses and she is one of the Sirens. Is it possible that now she will prove to be untrustworthy, against me and trap me?

She defines herself from the start as the Fluttery Watery Thing (FWT) and has a metaphysical presence that is part narrator, part guide, part trainer and part mischievous fairy.

Red herrings are also often thrown across the gamer's path, especially in the form of morally challenging decisions relating to the central rescue mission. In Level 12 (The River), for example, you are given guidance by the FWT that saving the old man who pleads for help will be 'more trouble than it's worth'. But by Level 18 (Little Girl) you are left to choose whether to rescue the little girl. If you try to do so, her loud voice acts as a further barrier to completing the level. Papa Sangre himself comments: 'You're learning that charity may get in the way.' Such 'lessons' set up the ambiguous ending (Level 25, Elysium), which offers a choice of two possible outcomes to the entire game.

Papa Sangre, whose name immediately conjures up voodoo (the voodoo priests are called 'Papa') and blood ('sangre'), is a grotesque vocal presence who appears only infrequently, at the start (through a telephone) and in the later levels. He is clearly positioned as the 'boss' (Collins 2008: 91) towards whose palace you travel, in the manner of a platform game. His menace is sonified as a cackling laugh, and as sound effects during instructions: 'They [bells] bring Papa to your side and he'll tape you [sound of tape being stretched] and nail you [sound of hammering] and burn you to hell' (Level 24, The Fate Bell). The FWT occasionally fulfils the 'miniboss' role ('Of course you can trust me, I only speak what Papa Sangre says', Level 17).

These strong narrative elements provide the framework for the aural navigations which are the core mechanics of the game. They rely on detailed and accurate listening in three dimensions. The key items on each level are musical notes, which must be gathered before the level may be completed (by finding the exit). So, for example, in Level 12, The River: 'as the slasher bird makes its way back from my right ear to the left ear, crowing the entire time, the music note beeps ahead of me, alternating back and forth between a low and a high, string sound' (Enongo 2012). The player must navigate through many different terrains, avoiding obstacles and enemies, and at varying speeds (walking or running) appropriate to the situation, while constantly adjusting orientation. Failure to do so adequately may lead to 'death' at the hands of an enemy, following which the player is reincarnated (your soul enters a new body) to restart the level. Such operations provide much of the sense of timing, with its attendant tension and release, in the game.

All players commented on how the game developed their listening skills as they learned to 'see with [their] ears' (Level 1, In the Dark). The skills change with the different demands of the various levels, increasing from simple orientation while standing still, to sophisticated skills such as listening while you run, discriminating between sound types, listening past masking sounds, and using aural memory to recall the locations of various sonic objects. These skills require a high level of hand–ear coordination through making manual responses to particular audio stimuli.

Given the filmic qualities of the narrative, it is interesting to compare the function of sound and music within *Papa Sangre* with its traditional role in film and indeed within video games. Michel Chion's *synchresis*, which refers to 'the spontaneous and irresistible weld produced between a particular auditory phenomenon and visual phenomenon when they occur at the same time' (Chion 1994: 63) is clearly incapable of unifying the functional interaction of image and sound in an audio-only environment. Instead, we have to rely on *imagination* to supply the visual component, allowing for some amusing creative possibilities within the game, such as the sound of squeaky toys that are heard when you step on 'bones' that might alert the snuffle hog. The gamer's footsteps themselves, which are the most constant sounds in the game, are examples of this kind of imaginative anomaly, since they have the audible appearance of Cuban heels regardless of location.

This is emphasised still further when considering the role of *music* in the game. As Zach Whalen observes:

In general survival horror games rely on conventions of horror film sound to effectively create the mood of horror required for the game (echoing effects, screeching violins, dissonant bursts of symphonic noise at 'startle' moments, etc.) (Whalen 2004)

In *Papa Sangre*, this role is only partially fulfilled. The primary musical elements are the 'notes' that must be collected. Music that resembles orchestral movie accompaniments only begins to appear at Level 13, Pathway to Pain, which is accompanied by 'a simple, sombre and yet theatrical song, with a longing violin, and deep horns in the background alternating between 3 chords' (Enongo 2012). But even such conventional elements fulfil an ambiguous role, being gradually subsumed into the soundscape of Papa Sangre's kingdom. Thus the ritual drum beating and chanting of Level 15, or the Xylophone Road of Level 16 (in which brass instruments and cymbal clashes denote the right and wrong steps), move from 'music' to 'sound', simultaneously enriching the sonic environment and musicalising the gameplay.

Such subtle and clever orchestration represents an important aspect of the *emotion map* of the game (Collins 2008: 91) which corresponds to the scripted events. In *Papa Sangre* the audio emotions are not simply evoked by the soundtrack, but also *embedded within it*. Collins cites two composers discussing the role of emotion within game sound:

As composer Charles Deenan has described, there are six basic audio emotions: happiness, sadness, surprise, disgust, anger, and fear, and each of these can be mapped to major scripted events. Composer Scott B. Morton (2005) writes: 'The musical arc is often more important than the literal events themselves because it can infer deep meanings ... Is the final boss battle more important than the miniboss battle? Show it in the music. A player should be able to subconsciously interpret the importance level of events based on the music that accompanies them.' (Collins 2008: 92)

Here the 'major scripted events' are themselves sonic events. Thus, the finding of a musical note is accompanied by a 'joyful bell-like sound' (Student B) and the level exit is signalled by a 'sparkling' sound towards which one must navigate, and which, once passed through, provides the release of tension through the sound of a closing door. Searching for these key items provides much of the tension that is enhanced by the various environmental sounds and effects. Screeching ghouls whistle past, buzzing flies (perhaps around corpses) obscure the navigation sounds, crowing birds threaten. Successful navigation often depends on speed as well as direction: sometimes one must move slowly, other times one must run or stand still. The echoing footsteps which are your presence in the world are therefore also significant builders of tension.

This elision of the underscoring of the action, traditionally provided by video-game music and soundtracks into its direct manifestation in the fabric of the game itself, has a direct effect of heightening the emotion. In *Papa Sangre*, the primary emotion is fear, and all the gamers commented on how powerful this is:

- The voice of Papa Sangre interrupts everything and I am suddenly filled with fear and anxiety (Enongo).
- Specifically, emotions are closely related to fear of the unknown, anxiety, nervousness, fear of threat (Amelides).
- The sense of danger is surprisingly realistic, especially given the compromises in verisimilitude that are of necessity made by the game's design. This sense lasts beyond the game, at least for the present author, who experienced a rather unpleasant nightmare that was clearly derived from the gameplay (Hugill).

Such strong emotions are often accompanied by physical symptoms. Gamers make references to exhaustion and 'adrenaline all over my body'. The immersive experience seems to be heightened by its audio-only nature. The gamer *becomes* the medium for the game through which the game-space is projected. All the gamers reported feeling themselves to be *inside* the game, a participant rather than just a 'user'.

Analysis

Traditional game sound analysis (and film sound analysis, for that matter) makes a distinction between diegetic and non-diegetic sounds. Diegetic sounds are those where the source is visible on the screen or is implied to be present by the action of the game, whereas non-diegetic sounds are not. This distinction is not as straightforward as might at first appear, especially when music is added into the game. As Whalen points out:

The music/sound problem is further complicated by a distinction between diegetic and non-diegetic music in that the diegetic music functions similarly to the incidental diegetic sounds that populate an environment. (Whalen 2004)

In a game that consists *only* of sound, the diegetic/non-diegetic distinction may at first appear to be redundant in any case, since there are no visual representations from which the sound may appear to emanate. Yet *Papa Sangre* nevertheless makes use of quasi-diegetic video-game sounds, whose source is implied to be present by the action of the game. In fact the vast majority of its sounds fall into this category, because the gamer's navigations rely upon the locations of the *imagined* objects from which they emanate. Thus the grunting of the snuffle hogs or the giggling of the reapers or the echoes from the walls or the click-clack of your footsteps provides the very location cues on which your survival depends. Even the music, which is deliberately held back until the later levels (perhaps to avoid confusion), is absorbed into this signifying soundscape, as we have seen.

Papa Sangre's world, then, is an acousmatic environment in which the emphasis is thrown very much upon heightened *causal* listening, or 'listening for the purpose of gaining information about the sound's source' (Chion 1994: 25). *Semantic* listening (listening for the purpose of gaining information about what is communicated in sound) is also present, most notably in the spoken instructions of the FWT and Papa Sangre. The extent to which Pierre Schaeffer's *reduced* listening ('listening to the sound for its own sake, as a sound object by removing its real or supposed source and the meaning it may convey') may be present is a matter of gamer's choice. There is relatively little in the game that functions as incidental sound which is barely noticed (*ouïr*), although many levels do feature an 'ambient' sonic environment. The level of understanding (*comprendre*) is deliberately simplified to facilitate gameplay. Since most sounds are in some way a clue, discrimination between sounds (*entendre*) is encouraged (Chion 2009: 11).

Listener choices that are made within the game are generally borne out of necessity, rather than any specifically musical intention. Nevertheless, several of the gamers reported moments at which they enjoyed playing the soundscape of the game for its aesthetic properties as much as for its gaming aspects. This became more frequent as their listening skills developed. As Nicolas Bourriaud remarked, in a very different context:

The artist works in the real field of the production of goods and services, and aims to set up a certain ambiguity, within the space of his activity, between the utilitarian function of the objects he is presenting, and their aesthetic function. (Bourriaud 2002: 35)

An artist playing *Papa Sangre* may well be able to appreciate this ambiguity in the interactions with the game. There remains a further possibility that gamers themselves may also enjoy the same ambiguity and relish the soundscape for the aesthetic pleasures it affords as well as its functional aspects. Leigh Landy, referencing Christopher Small's concept of 'musicking', suggests that this is often the case, whether or not the players themselves realise the fact:

[Small] includes not only composing and performance but also listening and dancing as pertaining to the music experience. Yet, is it not true that the installation and the computer game also form new ways of musicking? (Landy 2007: 8)

Environmental factors beyond the virtual world of the game itself are important. Amongst the players, the very mobility of the iPhone/iPad platform was seen to offer possibilities for enhancing the gaming experience. Student A commented, while playing in a bright, daylit room, that the gaming would be enhanced by playing in a dark room at night. However, the game also proved sensitive to external location in ways which could sometimes be disruptive. Enongo experimented by playing in a pizza parlour:

I realized that I have begun to think of the game as a part of my body, operating within the same framework of rules that applies to sound in the 'real world.' When the voices in the pizza shop became too loud, I started leaning closer to the screen as if that would increase the volume, until I remembered that I could only make the volume of the in-game sounds louder by moving closer to certain objects within the virtual space.

Panos Amelides similarly observed:

I played *Papa Sangre* in the privacy of my room, during the night and with reduced lighting, in order to enhance experience. But, when I tried to play it during the day, in my living room, various sounds coming from outside the house would 'mask' the sound design of the game.

Complete immersion in the virtual environment was therefore seen as a priority for the best (i.e. most frightening) experience.

In their study of the acoustic ecology of first-person shooter games, Grimshaw and Schott introduce a concept of *navigational* listening, in which localisation is designed into the resonating space of the game (Grimshaw and Schott 2007: 476). Building on R. Murray Schafer's soundscape theories, they identify the spatial and temporal elements of a virtual acoustic environment, with 'keynote sounds' (ubiquitous and pervasive background) and *aural figures* or 'signal sounds' (which the player will attend to and interpret). Their category of *causal auditory icons*, which '[have] either a one-to-one mapping or at least display some aspect of caricature in which salient features of the object or action being represented are emphasised at the expense of others' (Grimshaw and Schott 2007: 476) comes closest to describing the function of the vast majority of the sounds in *Papa Sangre*. This framework goes a considerable way towards providing a perceptual and phenomenological approach to analysing audio-only games, but the diegetic/non-diegetic relationships are made redundant by the absence of video.

Other typologies proposed by game audio theory, which are similarly focused upon the relationship between visible objects and sounds, tend to have the same problem. Thus, for example, the IEZA (Interface, Effect, Zone, Affect) framework created by Sander Huiberts and Richard van Tol develops Stockburger's technically derived categorisation of 'sound objects' into *score, effect, interface, zone* and *speech* (Stockburger 2003). They place sounds within a diegetic/non-diegetic field centred on the player, in which *Interface* expresses activity in the non-diegetic part of the game environment, *Effect* expresses activity in the diegetic part of the game, *Zone* expresses the setting or environment (e.g. geographical, topological) within which the diegetic part of the game takes place, and *Affect* the non-diegetic equivalent (e.g. emotional, social and/or cultural) (van Tol and Huiberts 2008). Likewise, Ingre Ekman's division of sounds into diegetic and non-diegetic signals and referents relies upon a perception of the relationship between the video image and the sounds that are heard by the gamer (Ekman 2005).

Most commentators criticise the limitations of the approach adopted by Friberg and Gärdenfors, whose system is based on the implementation, rather than the affect, of the audio. Their typology comprises: *avatar sounds, object sounds, (non-player) character sounds, ornamental sounds* and *instructions*. Van Tol and Huiberts comment:

Besides the considerable overlap between the categories of this categorization (for instance, the distinction between object sounds and non-player character sounds can be rather ambiguous), this approach is very specific to only specific game designs. It says very little about the structure of sound in games. (van Tol and Huiberts 2008)

Despite these reservations, Friberg and Gärdenfors's typology is the only one conceived for audio-only games. They analyse *TiM's Journey,* a game in which 'the avatar is moved around a three-dimensional soundscape to unravel a hidden mystery' (Friberg and Gärdenfors 2004: 150). One stated objective of the game design is 'to maintain an ambiguity between what are object sounds and what are ornamental sounds' (Friberg and Gärdenfors 2004: 151), which is similar in both concept and realisation to the design of *Papa Sangre*.

In audio-only gaming, *every* sound has a function within the game and we may only really speak of quasi-diegetic and quasi-non-diegetic sounds.

The only truly non-diegetic sounds are those created by the physical environment within which the player is seated and which may intrude upon gameplay as already discussed. The diegetic and non-diegetic functions of sounds such as avatar footsteps and music, for example, are only *relative* within an audio-only game. *Papa Sangre* actively plays with this conundrum.

A framework for analysing *Papa Sangre*, therefore, needs to be, to some extent, a hybrid of all the above approaches. It needs to reflect the 3D sound perception of location for the gamer, and the flow of affects and effects, triggers and instructions, and all the other events that make up the dramaturgy of the game. If we consider the sounds of *Papa Sangre*, we may place them within the various theoretical frameworks summarised above as shown in Table 17.1.

Here the *footsteps* represent the presence of the gamer in the game, governing timing and causing triggers to be activated. Scrolling the wheel

Table 17.1 Proposed classification of sounds in *Papa Sangre*

	Ekman	Grimshaw and Schott	IEZA (Huiberts and van Tol)	Gärdenfors and Friberg
Footsteps	Diegetic	Aural figures/causal auditory icons	Effect	Avatar sounds
Instructions	Symbolic/ non-diegetic	Aural figures/causal auditory icons	Effect	Instructions
Character speech	Diegetic	Aural figures/causal auditory icons	Effect	Character sounds
Triggers		Aural figures/causal auditory icons	Effect	Object sounds
Enemies	Diegetic	Aural figures/causal auditory icons	Effect	Object sounds
Masking	Diegetic	Aural figures/causal auditory icons	Effect	Object sounds
Obstacles	Diegetic	Aural figures/causal auditory icons	Effect	Object sounds
Orientation	Diegetic	Aural figures/causal auditory icons	Effect	Object sounds
Soundscape	Diegetic	Keynote sounds/choraplast	Zone	Object sounds
Music	Symbolic/ diegetic	n/a	Affect	Object sounds/ ornamental sounds
Gaming situation	Non-diegetic	Synchretically combined with resonating space	n/a	n/a

in conjunction with the footsteps provides the sole navigational tool. *Instructions* are mainly delivered by the FWT, and occasionally by Papa Sangre. *Character speech*, such as the 'rescued' man or the little girl, frequently includes masking sounds that become obstacles to navigation since they obscure the cues.

The most important sounds in the game, after the footsteps, are the *trigger* sounds and the *orientation* sounds. Examples of trigger sounds include:

- a joyful bell when one collects a musical note;
- the exit sound – a sparkly 'composite sound-object including bell-like, musical notes and whistling sounds' towards which one navigates to end a level;
- entry to level sounds (e.g. low violins, Level 3);
- 'dying' sounds (e.g. snuffle hog attacks);
- danger sounds, such as the 'finger bones'/squeaky toys (Level 3), the wooden and metal strips on the floor at Level 13, the chessboard squares (alternating silent and noisy) in Level 14, or the xylophone road (Level 16).

Orientation sounds include ticking clocks, snoring hogs, iterative bells, dripping water and a host of other locative clues. Above all, one tries to navigate towards the musical notes: in *Papa Sangre,* the gamer is constantly heading towards the abstraction of music, accompanied by the metaphysical FWT and drawn by the spectral Papa Sangre. The narrative journey, paradoxically, is away from the diegetic towards the non-diegetic.

Enemies are characterised by the sounds they make, which are occasionally extended to include technology (such as the reaper's scythe in Level 9), and *obstacles* similarly have a direct sonic effect that is quasi-diegetic (such as the 'squishy guts' of Level 7). A more ambiguous role is played by the various distracting or masking sounds, such as: swarming bees or bugs (Level 2), splashing water (Level 8), screaming bird (Level 8), chickens (Level 19), and the fake bells of Level 24 from amongst which one must distinguish the Fate Bell. These become both obstacles and part of the soundscape, and their purpose is simultaneously navigational and incidental to the general gameplay.

Music, as we have seen, operates in a similarly ambiguous way, being quasi-non-diegetic at first but shifting into a more diegetic soundscape function. Two other aspects of the game that are not covered by the critical literature are *haptic* clues (in the case of *Papa Sangre* a phone 'rumble' when one hits a wall), which form part of the navigational game, and the curious invitations to *synaesthesia* offered during the game narrative, such as the FWT's comment: 'That piercing feeling is fangs. That smell is the rotten breath of a hungry hog.' The synaesthetic invitations remind one that *Papa Sangre* has as much in common with radio drama as with film.

The game subsumes both text-based adventure games and console games within its essentially radiophonic soundworld.

A hybrid, gamer-centred typology may therefore be a more appropriate framework for analysis. Sounds may be categorised as: spatio-temporal (locative, transient, stationary); by agency (gamer, game character, game); ecological (keynote, aural figures, causal auditory icons); and by affect (emotion, sociocultural, haptic, synaesthetic). To test this typology, we will examine the beginning of a level of captured gameplay, using the toolset created by Pierre Couprie in his EAnalysis software (Couprie 2013). The level in question is Level 3, The Kennel. The gaming experience may be summarised verbally as follows:

Low violins comprise the entering soundscape of Level 3. The voice of the TWF begins: 'You are at the entrance to the palace of bones. It is guarded by a hog (hog's snoring). The hog is asleep in the kennel next to a musical note. The hog will eat you if it catches you. If you trip and fall, the hog will wake and chase you (animal growling and running away?).'

Fear is pre-eminent by the appearance of the hog (= danger), which is depicted through two distinctive sounds escorting the narration: the sound of hog's snoring and the sound of hog's attacking. That makes me more alert in order to avoid a 'fatal' mistake.

At this stage I am aware that if I walk towards the wrong place, my 'death' will surely come, so I listen carefully. To locate the position of the animal growling in the distance is not an easy task. Now, I hear the first note I need to collect, blinking in the distance on the right. I turn the wheel to the right and walk towards the note; I hear the snuffle hog growling in the distance. I turn until I hear the musical note placed at the centre. I still do not know if the growling is in close distance to me. As I walk towards the note, the growling snuffle hog's sound gets louder and suddenly I am listening (terrified) as the snuffle hog eats 'me' (I now know it is a male character) while I scream desperately. The whole situation is annoying as I hear the sounds of the snuffle hog eating me. But, the TWF says:

'Careful near a snuffle hog. If it catches you, it eats you. But your soul remains to try again in a new body' (metallic sound follows that statement and a sound of a falling body).

Figure 17.2[1] shows the start of the level, indicating the layering of sounds that enable clear identification of each element. The low 'rumble' at the

---

[1] A colour version of this figure is available on the website accompanying this book.

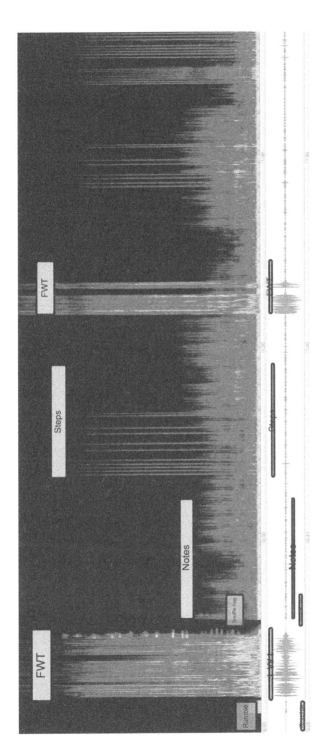

Figure 17.2 Level 3, start

start continues throughout the level, creating a sustained menacing atmosphere that is typical of survival horror. However, the level is low in both pitch and amplitude, giving it immediately a quasi-non-diegetic environmental status. Under our typology this is a stationary game sound that serves as a keynote and has an emotional affect of general menace. At this stage in the game, such 'atmospheric' sounds do not interfere with the gameplay.

The next layer is the snuffle hog, whose amplitude varies according to proximity but whose frequency band remains low. These are transient sounds that are causal auditory icons which have no locative value, produced by a game character. Once again the emotional affect is fear.

The FWT's instructions are voiced by a female game character, giving the high pitch, but are also very prominent, overriding all other signals. Her presence is stationary, because she is always heard in the same proximity regardless of the location. The ecological function is of an aural figure, and the affect is reassuring, guiding, encouraging, at least during this level.

The musical note is pitched at C5 on this occasion. The musical notes vary in pitch and instrumentation throughout the game, creating the semblance of a melody, although this is never heard in its entirety. As may be seen from the sonogram, the note is periodic and repetitive, but with a sharp attack and only slight decay. This shape makes it quite distinctive even at the low levels that occur when the player loses 'sight' of it or some other sound intrudes upon it. The notes are locative and stationary, produced by the game, and attractive in affect.

The pace of the loud footsteps is controlled by the gamer, so their peaks are high but their spacing is irregular. These are always heard at the same level of amplitude, since they represent the presence of the gamer. In this example the gamer comes to an uncertain standstill at 0' 51". Realising this after a short time, the FWT reappears with further encouragement and instructions. The footsteps appear to be transient, since they are always on the move, or locative, since the orientation changes, but in fact are stationary, because they always sound the same. The orientation is only achieved by hearing changes to the world around the gamer, not by any audible change in the footsteps themselves. The only exception to this is when one hits a wall, which triggers a haptic clue and a 'coming to attention' sound of the footsteps.

Notice how there are four elements present during any period of time. This is a pattern that is maintained throughout the game and is presumably derived from the well-documented psychoacoustic phenomenon that four layers of sound are in general the maximum that may be perceived separately by the average listener (Landy 2012: 108). In practice, the perceptual aspects for the gamer are limited to the orientation and trigger sounds only, since environmental and footstep sounds give little new information. Consequently, as the game increases in difficulty, the number and complexity of orientation and trigger sounds increases as the game evolves.

Conclusion

In her study of 'play along' games, Kiri Miller remarks how virtual performance games such as *Guitar Hero* and *Rock Band* 'foster a creative, imaginative listening orientation in which the players feel responsible for producing the music through moment-to-moment embodied engagement with the "inner time" of the song' (Miller 2012: 111). There is a parallel here with the heightened listening and pleasurable manipulations described by the players of *Papa Sangre*.

Most studies of audio-only gaming (e.g. Friberg and Gärdenfors 2004; Röber and Masuch 2005; Roden *et al.* 2007; Papworth 2010) have concentrated upon design and technical issues, with minimal discussion of aesthetic content. Music analysis has almost completely avoided the genre. But, at its best, the playing of *Papa Sangre* can become an act of performance, or even composition, as one orients oneself within the sonified world. Players repeatedly referred to improving their 'performance' with reference to sound manipulation and especially to the importance of sonic or musical memory.

The experience of playing *Papa Sangre* created vigilance in regards to memory, where one should always remember the instructions/clues given only through sound. For example, a direction one needs to take towards a particular path in a video game is clear due to the sense of vision; you see the path and you go. In Papa Sangre, the path is related to a sound(s) and the player uses his sonic-memory in order to complete his goal. In another context (such as improvisation), this would pass perfectly well for a description of music-making.

The contribution an understanding of such active on-the-fly creativity can make to electroacoustic music is to improve our understanding of the construction of narrative. Radiophonic studies have already contributed a great deal in this respect, but the major difference here is the active agency of gamer-cum-composer-cum-performer. Nor is this necessarily a solitary experience: social gaming enables the possibility of ensemble.

Electroacoustic music that is narrative-driven tends to provide very clear aural signposts to help the listener decode the composer's intentions. In an era of active audio-only gameplay, this may be capable of further sophistication. While the aural signposts of audio-only games are, as we see in the case of *Papa Sangre*, also very clear, their manipulation by the user can lead to quite complex results that go beyond the simple requirements of gameplay. Thanks to such developments, today's audience may be trusted more readily to construct their own experience from the material provided. In other words, gaming is paving the way to active listening in all contexts.

Acknowledgements

We would like to thank the following for their help: Paul Bennun (Somethin' Else), Michael Gatt (OREMA), Adam Hoyle (Do Tank Studios) and Tassos Stevens (Coney).

References

Adams-Spinks, Geoff. 2005. Blind gamers get their own titles. *BBC News*. http://news.bbc.co.uk/1/hi/technology/4112725.stm (accessed 17 July 2013).

Bennun, Paul. 2012. Papa Sangre: CSL graph. Private email.

Bourriaud, Nicolas. 2002. *Relational Aesthetics*, trans. Simon Pleasance and Fronza Woods. Paris: Les presses du réel.

Chion, Michel. 1994. *Audio-Vision*. New York: Columbia University Press.
 2009. *Guide to Sound Objects: Pierre Schaeffer and Music Research*, trans. John Dack and Christine North. www.ears.dmu.ac.uk (accessed 20 July 2013).

Collins, Karen. 2008. *Game Sound: An Introduction to the History, Theory, and Practice of Video Game Music and Sound Design*. Cambridge, MA: MIT Press.

Costello, Brigid. 2007. A pleasure framework. *Leonardo Journal* 40(4), 370–1.

Couprie, Pierre. 2013. *EAnalysis*. www.pierrecouprie.fr/?p=468.

Edwards, Owen. 2006. Simonized: In 1978 a new electronic toy ushered in the era of computer games. *Smithsonian Magazine*, 1 September. www.smithsonianmagazine.com/issues/2006/september/object.php; http://web.archive.org/web/20061111115352/www.smithsonianmagazine.com/issues/2006/september/object.php (accessed 16 July 2013).

Ekman, Inger. 2005. Meaningful noise: Understanding sound effects in computer games. *Proceedings of the Digital Arts and Cultures Conference*, København, Denmark.

Enongo. 2012. Musicology in the flesh: Papa Sangre explorations. http://enongo.wordpress.com (accessed 16 July 2013).

Fastlab. 2009. The CREATE Signal Library (CSL) project. http://fastlabinc.com/
     CSL/ (accessed 17 July 2013).
Gärdenfors, Johnny and Friberg, Dan. 2004. Audio games: New perspectives on
     game audio. *Proceedings of the ACM SIGCHI International Conference on
     Advances in Computer Entertainment Technology.*
Grimshaw, Mark and Schott, Gareth. 2007. Situating gaming as a sonic experience:
     The acoustic ecology of first-person shooters. *Proceedings of the DiGRA 2007
     Conference, September 24–28, University of Tokyo, Tokyo, Japan,* 474–81.
Hugill, Andrew. 2012. Towards an analysis of *Papa Sangre,* an audio-only game for
     the iPad/iPhone. www.orema.dmu.ac.uk (accessed 20 July 2013).
Huiberts, S. and van Tol, R. 2008. IEZA: A framework for game audio. www
     .gamasutra.com/view/feature/131915/ieza_a_framework_for_game_audio
     .php (accessed 21 July 2013).
Landy, Leigh. 2007. *Understanding the Art of Sound Organization.* Cambridge,
     MA: MIT Press.
     2012. *Making Music with Sounds.* New York: Routledge.
Miller, Kiri. 2012. *Playing Along: Digital Games, YouTube and Virtual
     Performance.* New York: Oxford University Press.
Papa Sangre Blog. 2010. www.papasangre.com/blog/ (accessed 28 January 2012).
Papworth, Nigel. 2010. iSpooks: An audio focused game design. *Proceedings of the
     5th Audio Mostly Conference: A Conference on Interaction with Sound.*
Röber, Niklas and Masuch, Maic. 2005. Playing audio-only games: A compendium
     of interacting with virtual, auditory worlds. *Proceedings of the 2nd DIGRA
     Games Conference, Vancouver, Canada.*
Roden, Timothy, Parberry, Ian and Ducrest, David. 2007. Toward mobile
     entertainment: A paradigm for narrative-based audio only games. *Science of
     Computer Programming* 67(1), 76–90.
Stockburger, A. 2003. The game environment from an auditive perspective. In
     M. Copier and J. Raessens (eds.) *Level Up, Digital Games Research Conference*
     (PDF on CD-ROM). Utrecht: Faculty of Arts, Utrecht University.
Whalen, Zach. 2004. Play along – an approach to videogame music.
     Game Studies: The International Journal of Computer Games Research 4, 1.
     www.gamestudies.org/0401/whalen/ (accessed 18 July 2013).

18 | Some questions around listening: *Vancouver Soundscape Revisited* by Claude Schryer

KATHARINE NORMAN

Introduction

The primary question faced by anyone attempting a musical analysis is ostensibly quite straightforward: 'How does this work?' The motivation for asking the question is (ostensibly) universal, however expressed: a desire to gain greater understanding and knowledge and to apply both to one's musical endeavours, whether listening, composing or performing. Pick up your tools, and off we go.

Ah, but it is never that simple. Even within the bounded, but increasingly difficult to bound, purview of 'electroacoustic music' it is often difficult to know which analytical implements to grab for most effect. Electroacoustic music does not fall into an aesthetic or a school any more than instrumental music and, in addition, making a functional distinction between the electroacoustic and instrumental is sometimes problematic. There are no 'one size fits all' electroacoustic music analysis tools. But at least *musical* analysis is primarily to do with sounds and how they are placed, including a concern with their intrinsic nature, the ways in which they have been constructed and formed, and the manner in which the relationships between sonic components have been prioritised, defined, composed and performed – isn't it? Particular agendas and foci might be essential to a certain work or aesthetic, be they sociological, cultural or performative, but understanding how things were 'put together' as music rests, somewhere fundamental, on tools that deal with sound.

That attitude is of course ridiculously naïve. A great deal of music has little to do with sound in isolation, and often the analyst is left scrabbling around for some relevant device that they were *sure* they owned, and will recognise if they can only just see it for looking. Popping round to borrow useful interdisciplinary tools (or bits of them) from someone else in cultural studies, sociology, ethnography, or some other more applicable field is useful and desirable, and I am going to do it myself. Interdisciplinary borrowings can be extraordinarily fruitful in contributing to and helping to amplify musical analysis and yet, by virtue of their intent, such tools often do not go quite far enough when it comes to thinking about how the music *sounds*, and conjecturing as to why it sounds that way, to understanding more about how it is put together, and gaining greater knowledge or insight in to what it is all 'about' in listening terms.

Analysis of any piece of music requires repeated listening, and electroacoustic music in 'fixed media' especially assists in enabling that. This 'return' listening is undertaken in a more interrogative manner than a first listening to the work and brings an accretion of applied thought, conjecture and, one hopes, discovery and greater understanding. At its best, analysis provides deeper knowledge of the specific work and yet also suggests ways of thinking that can be generalised as applicable to other, broadly similar, compositions. An analysis that aims at this kind of wider relevance must start from listening, but needs to probe further than a first-person, phenomenological response.

The work in question

This chapter considers, as a case study, a work from a broad repertoire that is sometimes called 'soundscape' composition: Claude Schryer's *Vancouver Soundscape Revisited* (Schryer 1996). Using source materials recorded in the city, this composed portrait of Vancouver is, I suspect, also an analytical exploration of listening and re-listening, using composition itself as an analytical tool.

Itself a borrowed portmanteau word, 'soundscape' already lugs behind it a certain amount of baggage relating to landscape studies, ecology and various assumed motivations on the composer's behalf, not to mention certain other assumptions as to what the listener should best attend to. One of the chief assumptions, quite often and perhaps occasionally because it is easiest to talk about, is that all such work is – or should be – 'message driven', addressing either ecological or sociological concerns.

Additionally, there appears (to me, at least) to be a bias towards discussing works where the nature of the sonic landscape recorded is somehow extraordinary to most people's experience, whether through being unusually quiet or 'natural', from a 'threatened' environment or, conversely, presenting loud, 'gargantuan' industrial or noisy environments that most people would not experience in daily life. For such works, a tendency towards exoticism in sound is often difficult to detach from analytical discussion. When work is made from recordings of places and the people in them (or not in them), ecological and anthropological concerns can define the analytical approach and tools. Rather than being intent on musical analysis this becomes another, equally valuable but different, exercise – that of 'doing anthropology in sound' (Feld and Brenneis 2004).

One might argue that musical analysis might, and should, include all these approaches, dependent on circumstances. I would be the first to promote interdisciplinary study that is responsive to the situation, but in this chapter I would like to focus my analytical approach on listening and sound. I would like to branch outwards from that starting point in relation to work in which the original place and provenance of the recorded material remain significant in the finished work. The motivations behind such works may be diverse and similarly interdisciplinary, the treatment of sounds may vary, and many will have extra-musical priorities, but they all at some level, I suggest, address the embodiment of *listening* in a place.

The listening in question

In works such as *Vancouver Soundscape Revisited*, where the sound materials are documentary recordings of a pre-existent sonic environment and are still recognisable as such, the listener is encouraged to employ listening behaviours comparable to those employed in everyday experience; behaviours in which memory, recognition, personal and learned response, and all kinds of other interpretive responses are implicit – quotidian listening, if you will. If the composer (or performer/improviser) has made a point of retaining that connection, and worked to draw attention to this, then the way in which the listener individually experiences the work is evidently important to its meaning.

To complicate matters further, as is so often the case in music made from recorded sounds, the compositional process itself is one centred on a listening analysis of the available materials by a composer who, often, was present at the time of recording – and so initially experienced the sounds in the context of a particular time and place. That temporal disjunction between 'sounds from then' and 'listening now' is, I think, an important and defining aspect of this kind of work. However, the 'embodiment of listening' doesn't require the composer's presence at the time of recording as a necessity, but rather that it is in some manner 'enacted' as part of the composition – something I will go on to discuss in relation to Schryer's work.

The analysis in question

This brings questions about the subject of analysis, in relation to a work in which listening is deemed material. What is being interrogated – the work or the listener's response (and that includes the 'listening composer', as perceived in the work), or the relative success in representing 'listening' to another listener? In what way do these differ, and would gravitating analytically more towards either one or the other influence the kinds of questions asked, and the kinds if understanding gained? It all becomes rather circular.

What tools will work? If each individual's subjective listening to the work is, effectively, part of its performance – or (let's be brave) of its content – by what means can that individual response be analysed usefully, or at all, outside of undertaking some massive interpretive phenomeno-logical analysis study for every listener, for every single work that qualifies? Even if that were possible, what knowledge would result?

An effective musical analysis of such work might entail retaining, *as an analytical tool*, the ways in which we listen in daily life and, more than this, becoming self-consciously aware of how the many facets of 'ordinary' experience contribute to what appears to be wholly aural experience, but rarely is. This is an analytical approach that benefits from incorporating thinking such as Eric Clarke's ecological listening (Clarke 2005) or the many and various writings by composers and theorists on different 'listening stances', including my earlier writing (Norman 1996) that draw attention to associative and referential con-nections to sound.

A conscious attention to the multifarious nature of aural experience in everyday life, via a 'thick description' (to borrow an anthropological term itself borrowed from elsewhere), might facilitate an analysis of 'meaning-making' in work made from documentary sounds. For instance, if both sonic and social meaning are so integrated within an environment that changing or accentuating one might do irrevocable damage to the other, a listener–analyst might concentrate on describing this, identifying to what extent – and how – a composer succeeds in achieving an effective balance between them, or how and why they would choose not to.

If a work's *raison d'être*, or a fundamental part of it, is the relevance of quotidian listening in everyday meaning-making, then the work becomes itself a reflexive form of musical and extra-musical analysis – one that proceeds by means of a creative analytical methodology more commonly known as 'composition'. As I hope I will be able to indicate through describing and investigating Schyrer's work in relation to its compositional context, composing itself might be examined as a form of analysis.

Some questions around listening to *Vancouver Soundscape Revisited*

Why was the work composed?

Context – place, time and provenance – can sometimes be illuminating. For *Vancouver Soundscape Revisited*, knowing more about the context of composition helps to inform part of the analytical journey in that it has a direct bearing on the focus, and probably the compositional approach, of the work.

Schryer was one of four composers commissioned to make a piece during a four-week residency at the Sonic Research Studios, Simon Fraser University (SFU), organised with the assistance of composer and theorist Barry Truax. This formed part of the Soundscape Vancouver '96 project, directed by Hildegard Westerkamp, to whom *Vancouver Soundscape Revisited* is dedicated (Schryer 1996/2007). The composers were invited to use materials from two collections of recordings of Vancouver: those made during the work of the World Soundscape Project (WSP),[1] between September 1972 and August 1973 (recorded by Howard Broomfield, Bruce Davis, Peter Huse and Colin Miles); and a new collection, made between 1991 and 1995 (recorded by Robert MacNevin and Scott Morgan). The completion of recordings for the second collection was the instigation for the project. While none of the composers was from Vancouver (two were Canadian, two German – the project was held in collaboration with the Goethe Institut in Vancouver), all four were already deeply sympathetic to the focus on acoustic ecology initiated at SFU by the WSP. A year later, Schryer went on to become co-founder of the Canadian Association for Sound Ecology.

At the end of the residency the works were presented in concert at SFU, in conjunction with a symposium, held the next day, at the Goethe Institut. Shortly after the project, Truax released a double CD of extracts from both the 1970s and the 1990s recordings alongside documentaries and the four compositions, mixed down from eight-track to stereo format, so extending the life of the project and enabling listeners, worldwide, to encounter these

---

[1] There is insufficient space here to rehearse the history of the WSP's early period of activity, which is well documented elsewhere. The more pervasive 'tradition' the group's work initiated, of considering the natural soundscape through an artistic lens, has continued at Simon Fraser University, in the main part due to composer Barry Truax's presence on the faculty and Westerkamp's proximity, living in Vancouver. The interested reader is directed to http://britishlibrary.typepad.co.uk/sound-and-vision/2013/07/ for an informative summary of the group's original work in context.

responses to the Vancouver soundscape (Cambridge Street Records 1996). This CD set is an important documentation: of the Vancouver city sounds-cape over time and of a project in which artistic response was prioritised as a means of bringing people closer to appreciating the social, ecological and aesthetic relevance of the soundscape and their place within it. With the passing of time, an increasing concern with the audible environment from an interdisciplinary perspective that includes the arts has further heightened the prescience of this work.

What is 'revisited'?

On the face of it, the *Revisited* in the work's title is an uncomplicated wordplay: the earlier sound recordings had been 'revisited' in conjunction with those from the more recent collection as the reason and means of composition; in the work, Vancouver is 'revisited' by the composer and by the listening audience. Also revisited, however, is a variety of asynchronous listening activity.

The sound recordists' listening

The source materials for *Vancouver Soundscape Revisited* are in part a documentation of the sound recordists' listening choices. Microphones in hand, they were the original aural explorers, intent on sound. More questions, now. Were they in search of typical, interesting or unusual sound environ-ments? To what extent were they influenced by their knowledge of the city and of any personal 'favourites' in the soundscape? Did they set out with a script as to place and time to record? Even if so, which were those recordings born of happenstance, from catching an unexpected and glorious sound environment? A sociohistorical study of the WSP's work, including inter-views with the recordists, might well reveal more detail but my point here is simply that listening is already embedded in the materials. As in a first-person narrative, that listening presence becomes a role for reader-listeners to identify with. This tendency is made explicit in the central movement, 'Walk', which is a recording of someone walking in a quiet forest environment. The footsteps cease, but the environment continues while everyone stops to listen.

The composer's listening

Schryer was handed recorded sources that documented places and times about which he could have no personal memory. Perhaps this is a strong position – with only sound to go on, his initial encounters with the recordings would necessarily have had a listening-focused intimacy (although no listening is devoid of imagination). As he selected, trimmed, moved about or abandoned sounds he would no doubt have perceived, created or destroyed apparent connections between the different recordings, each time inscribing a deepening relationship to them as materials with meaning. It is this process of composing that remains vivid in his memory:

... long hours in the SFU studio, editing and trying different mixes in order to create 'music' from the sounds. It was fun.

... I did not have a particular set of events in mind. I listened to the material and composed a 'composition' based on what I liked.

... I don't recall any intention in comparing decades or eras but this might well have been a compositional strategy as I was playing with the perception of place and space through the recordings. (Schryer, personal correspondence, 6 August 2013)

This refreshingly candid description of process is not only honest but very true to listening experience in life, where preferences are often bound up with personal psychology and/or the experiences that an individual has come to associate with particular sounds: one person may like the calming sounds of quiet rain while another prefers the exhilarating roar of the ball game. In choosing materials that he 'liked', Schryer moved towards creating a representation that reflected his worldview: *Vancouver Soundscape Revisited* is, like any expressive portrait, as much an impression of its maker as of its subject.

The listening audience

Waiting expectantly, and possibly quite in the dark, the original audience would have included Vancouver residents interested in the subject of the project – their home city and its sonic identity. The first performance was over an eight-channel diffusion system that 'transformed the traditional concert hall environment into an electroacoustically enhanced place for soundscape listening' (Truax 1996). Multichannel 'immersive' diffusion was not uncommon in the mid-1990s but must have been a more unusual experience for at least some people in the audience, for whom both city and concert hall were thus de-familiarised.

The first audience members would have brought their listening experience of Vancouver with them to the concert hall, almost literally still ringing in their ears. Listening to Vancouver through the work, this audience would have noticed familiar and unfamiliar sounds and would perhaps have been more attuned to the difference between contemporary and archive soundscapes than we are able to appreciate from this distance.

A composer working with soundscape recordings is also working in the knowledge that the work will invite others' thoughts, memories, imaginings and associations. No listener is a *tabula rasa* (not even a newborn child), and listening is never immune to individual bias. For any soundscape work there is inevitably going to be quite a listening party.

How are things put together?

There are nine short movements, each with a title (a seven-movement release exists – 'Noise' and 'Walk' were dropped[2]). The longest movement is just under four minutes in duration and many of the others are considerably shorter:

1. Eagle 1:52
2. Fire 3:50
3. DroneSong 1:27
4. Noise 1:30
5. Walk 0:41
6. Industry 2:11
7. Horn 2:08
8. Beans 2:28
9. Blowin' 1:32

It is worth reflecting further on the choice of a multimovement form because it appears more usual for 'soundscape' compositions to adopt expansive proportions, in which long durations and slow rates of change assist a contemplative listening engagement: examples that come to mind, from works made by the 'WSP composers' at around the same period, include Hildegard Westerkamp's immersive *Talking Rain* (1998) at 17 minutes and Barry Truax's four-movement *Pacific* (1990), 36 minutes in duration.

In terms of relative durations of movements, the original nine-movement version of *Vancouver Soundscape Revisited* seems roughly

[2] The shorter version is on Schryer (1997) solo CD *Autour*, Empreintes DIGITALes – IMED 9736.

mirrored around movement 5, 'Walk'. As already mentioned, this is also the only movement to reference 'a listener', explicitly. This mirroring around 'Walk' is not rigorous in terms of duration but does seem to extend to aspects of the other movements' individual character: 'Eagle' and 'Blowin'' are both relatively slow paced, mostly outdoors, and feature that familiar sound for inhabitants of British Columbia – steady rain; 'Fire' and 'Beans' both place a particular, opening emphasis on Chinese culture and are somewhat similar in the 'density' of activity and number of environments presented; 'DroneSong' and 'Horn' both feature 'song' (a maudlin drunken song and the opening notes of the Canadian national anthem, respectively) and horns; 'Noise' and 'Industry' each build dense layers of mechanical or industrial sound. Whether this arrangement was intuitive or not, the result is a group that is distinctive in its variety of depiction, and from its members being arranged much as one might hang a series of portraits in a gallery space – ready for visitors to appreciate as a whole or individually.

Within each short movement, duration and the rate of events are also compressed. This is not a work that 'speeds up' the world through a helter-skelter time-lapse ride; neither is it the inverse, a series of 'close-ups' that examines small things in microscopic detail. Rather, the proportions of reality are preserved, as in a set of miniatures that each fit a whole view within a tiny frame. Miniature representational forms are seductive because they invite wonder at their achievement (i.e., at both the result and the maker's skill) and also position the viewer (or listener) in a different, externalised relationship to the recognisable things depicted. They demand a temporary re-scaling of one's perception that recasts their dimensions as the normal frame of reference. Through this magic coercion they become a convincing world. We lean forward, peering in amazement. The return to life-size experience resumes our place in another world that had, for a few minutes, paused in consciousness. For time-based miniatures, however, this sorcery is compromised, because time does not pause or 'wait' and there is no direct equivalent to staring, spellbound, at an exquisite portrait, three inches in diameter. One approach for listening might be to miniaturise the perception of time passing: to maintain the proportions, materials and context of time passing in the world (or in a larger work) – a perceptual quality – but to re-scale this perception so that everything happens 'as might be expected', except in a compressed, miniaturised manner. I think that 'Eagle', the first movement of *Vancouver Soundscape Revisited*, achieves exactly that.

'Eagle'

'Eagle in forest, music in Chinese shop, soft rain, train whistle and echoes of the 9 o'clock gun' (Schryer, CD liner notes for 'Eagle').[3]

Figure 18.1 provides a brief descriptive summary of the clearly recognisable material in 'Eagle'. The number of 'environments' or events noted does not necessarily correspond to the number of sound sources used. There is no reliable way of distinguishing aurally between the 1970s and the 1990s sources; the knowledge would be of largely historical rather than analytical interest in any case, since the 'Vancouver' created by Schryer is a portrait that transcends time and place.

'Eagle' commences outside (a relatively quiet outdoors ambience is audibly apparent, and the CD liner notes confirm it is a forest). In the background, an engine hums – perhaps a distant small plane. After a few seconds, an eagle's cry: the single, loud and high-pitched squawk is an unequivocal announcement of presence.

Fast tempo, exuberant Chinese flute music fades in above the quieter, outside world, which rises into the foreground once more before receding. The music, which sounds broadcast rather than live, continues and a Chinese-speaking voice is briefly heard. This new place is an inside environment, as is apparent from the resonance of the voice (the liner notes confirm it is a shop). For a short while, three possible places co-exist: the outdoor ambience, the shop, and the music.

Now, the sound of steady rainfall emerges, rapidly overwhelming the existing sounds to become the spectrum-hogging foreground, and continuing to build in amplitude. This sound dominates for 20–30 seconds, quite a long period by comparison to the preceding shifts. The rain sounds fade, not by the composer's intervening 'fade out' but in the recording itself, as the shower gradually ceases and dissolves into occasional drips and drops. When both the weather and the spectrum clear, small 'peeping' birds start up. After the rain, we are left standing beneath trees in a habitat where birds are unbothered by human presence or any traffic noise.

During the cessation of the rain, another ambience had started to appear, still quietly: an outdoor environment with the very distant sound

---

[3] Audio example 1: 'Eagle' (duration 1:52). All music examples are to be found on the website accompanying this book. All music examples reproduced by kind permission: Eagle, Fire, DroneSong, Blowin' from *Vancouver Soundscape Revisited* (1996) by Claude Schryer (SOCAN, SODRAC)/Ymx média (SOCAN, SODRAC). Previously released in 1997 on the compact disc *Autour*, empreintes DIGITALes (IMED 9736). Colour versions of Figures18.1 and 18.2 are to be found on the website accompanying this book.

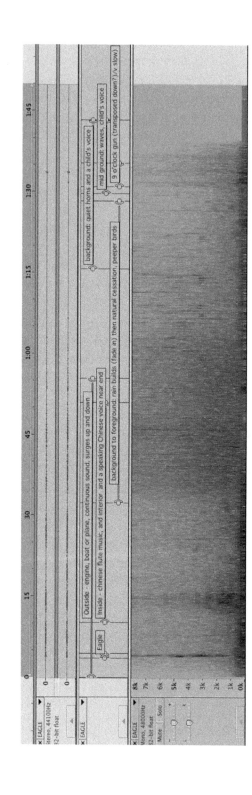

Figure 18.1 'Eagle' events and spectrum

of children's voices, and a breathy train whistle (identified as such in the liner notes). The quality of the voices indicates an expansive, open area, perhaps a beach. This guess seems reinforced by the closer sounds of lapping waves. A few seconds later comes the muffled and 'unusual' sound (in this context) of a reverberating cannon shot – only the echoes, not the shot itself. Schryer's notes describe it as 'echoes of the 9 o'clock gun', an enduring landmark in Vancouver that is fired across the harbour each evening at 9pm.

This is not a cut and paste collage where the listener is relocated abruptly from one place to another. Instead, environments 'fade up' gradually, giving the impression that they have already been going on for some time and are just now coming into aural focus. With the exception of the rain ceasing, which provides a moment of stillness rather than departure, the ambient environments leave by means of a gradual 'fade out', maintaining the aural illusion that they are continuing elsewhere. It is the listener's 'earpoint' that has moved on: as in traversing a real city, one foreground ambience is overtaken by another as the listener – not the environment – travels from place to place. At 1:52 in duration, 'Eagle' may be a short movement, but it is slow listening. One sound environment after another has successively entered, become the focus of listening and then faded out as another enters. This is the kind of leisurely exposition that might ensue in an expansive 'soundscape' work – but here the structural proportions are compressed within a miniature form.

The first movement of any multimovement work, when not simply an introductory flourish, has a dual role to play: as a movement that is self-sufficient in form and content, and as a 'scene-setter' that indicates the scale and aesthetic direction of the work as a whole. 'Eagle' performs both roles so convincingly that the next movement, 'Fire', seems epic at nearly four minutes in duration.

How are things connected musically?

Schryer describes *Vancouver Soundscape Revisited* as an 'impressionistic portrait of the musicality and poetry of the soundscapes of Vancouver' (Schryer, CD liner notes). His choice of the word 'musicality' is a little odd, or seems so initially. It might be better replaced, in the sense I think he means it, with the rather more clumsy 'inherent musical properties', but one has to allow a certain artistic licence. Even so, when composers talk of finding what is 'inherently musical' in a natural soundscape, they are addressing some other complexities around listening that are, I think, hard to pin down.

Taxonomies of sound or listening can be restrictive, possibly best treated as an untrustworthy starting point for any kind of musical study or analysis. All I will offer are a few passing considerations, as a precursor for examining specific aspects of *Vancouver Soundscape Revisited*.

There are sounds in the urban or rural 'natural' soundscape that might be deemed 'musical' by human listeners. These have sonic tendencies in various, overlapping combinations and are likely to appeal to listeners as having form, pattern, or appreciable euphony or timbral fascination. They might include sounds that have been constructed, or are biologically produced, to function as aural communications – birdsong, animal cries, or human speech or clapping, for instance. There are also sounds that imaginative listeners can endow with similar intent because they demonstrate apparent patterning or organisation, while knowing this is not really the case – the rhythmic drumming of rain on a roof, for instance. An implied or quasi-anthropomorphic 'fictionalised intent' can be attributed to everything from machine noise, foghorns, telephones and bells to the waves, the wind in the trees or the breathy sound of a distant train whistle. What is more, all these examples have the potential to be listened to, or re-contextualised, as music because all have contours that are, or seem, organised and so are, or could be with some intervention, 'like music'. Making, perceiving and imagining music from the inherent properties of sounds is, as Schryer himself puts it in relation to making his work, 'fun' – a form of imaginative play.

There are obviously many other sounds that are appealing for sonic or other reasons and which have meaning for many, or for a few, listeners. There are sounds that in their natural context might not be perceived as 'musical' or sonically interesting. They might well either go unnoticed or be regarded as obtrusive noise (a plane passing overhead might be either, depending on the listener and the context) but could become suddenly noticeable by their absence. One might take the view that people have the ability, in the right circumstances, to locate 'musical' or at least interesting properties in all humanly perceivable sounds. Certainly, a great many sounds are considered 'of interest' in *Vancouver Soundscape Revisited*. Footsteps, humming machinery, and even the clamour of the crowd at a raucous ball game – all these appear, re-contextualised as a potentially musical experience. In each case, the natural properties of the sounds are preserved.

On the whole, there is very little *overt* audio processing in this work and audible manipulation of sound is not a foreground concern. *Vancouver Soundscape Revisited* conceals its sonic artifice in the service of different goals that focus on noticing qualities within the natural soundscape, rather than transforming its identity beyond recognition. Nevertheless, there is a great deal going on behind the scenes to create organised, musical connections through careful, understated structural devices that are built through sound and listening. A brief look at the spectrum for 'Eagle', for instance, reveals an acute ear for registral space and the timbral characteristics of sound environments. The spectrum is orchestrated (whether consciously or not) to be roughly symmetrical over the movement's duration, with the central rain section occupying all frequencies and either side reducing the information to lower frequencies. The eagle cry cuts a sharp peak across the higher audible spectrum. Balancing this, at the other end of the piece, the echoing of the 9 o'clock gun causes a brief surge in the lower frequencies.

While it might on first, or even subsequent hearings, appear quite free-composed in its ebbing and flowing of environments and juxtaposition of seemingly diverse sound sources, 'Eagle' is quite rigorously constructed. The Eagle's screech and the 9 o'clock gun's alert, the spectrum's symmetry, and the relative proportions of each episodic shift of ambience: all these are carefully placed to elicit and guide listening through a composed sonic narrative.

'Fire' and 'DroneSong'

'Chinese firecrackers, folkdancing, Krishna musicians, baseball game, tennis, mechanical piano, gulls in the harbour, 9 o'clock gun, electronic telephone. Main Street bus, various natural and processed boat horns and sirens' (Schryer, CD liner notes for 'Fire').[4]

If footsteps or engines can be induced to elicit 'musical' responses, recordings of music in the soundscape can, conversely, acquire weighty extra-musical meaning. In addition to naturally occurring sounds with 'musical' potential – defined pitch, rhythmic pattern or attractive timbre, for example – archive recordings of a vibrant, culturally varied and reasonably cosmopolitan, city included music of various kinds. *Vancouver Soundscape Revisited* makes some inspired, and entertaining, connections between them.

Figure 18.2 provides a descriptive table for 'Fire'. Like 'Eagle', and like other movements, 'Fire' is composed as a series of overlapping layers that fade in and out of aural focus, in what appears to be a stream of consciousness progression in terms of connections between them. However, on

---

[4] Audio example 2: 'Fire' (duration 3:50).

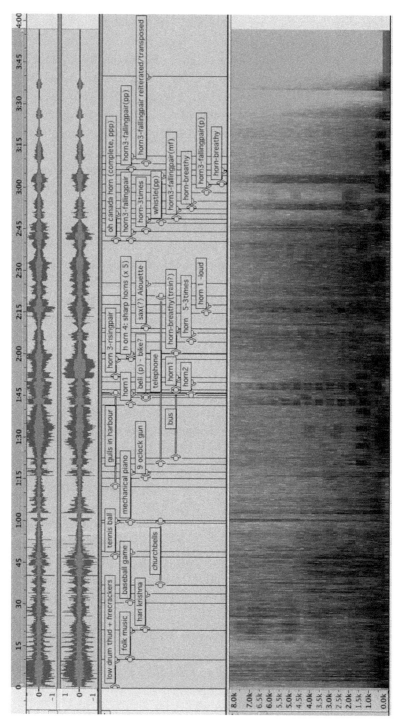

Figure 18.2 'Fire', main events and spectrum

further investigation, the composition is rigorously, and subversively, conventional in its musical construction.

'Fire' opens with a compressed succession of environments in which music, rhythm or ritual form a part: the thud of an iterating drum beat on a low C sharp (approximate pitch). Above this, exuberant Chinese firecrackers percuss the air; jovial folk music takes up the beat with another integral low, heavy pulse; next, Hare Krishna singers pass by to the sounds of cymbals in a slightly faster tempo and as they fade (and in a nice cultural irony) Christian church bells ring a change on the same melodic pitches, although barely audible under a different congregation – a raucous baseball game crowd. In a surreptitious insertion, the rhythmic back and forth of a game of tennis, panned to and fro, provides a new 'beat'. This evolving sequence is summarily dismissed by the foreground sound of a coin in a slot, and a player piano strikes up an exuberant honky-tonk waltz. In the course of a minute the music has moved from fireworks and street music, through dancing and religion, to games and then a 'machine music' impersonation of performance. The ambience has moved too: from outside to inside, from the street to the tennis court and, finally, to the close-up 'non-space' of a recorded player piano – music for hire.

The material may be diverse, and the cultural journey disorienting, but other 'musical' connections are subtly integrated. Figure 18.3 outlines the main shapes for the more discernible pitched material (notation indicates approximate pitch).

Having put the money in the slot, it pays to spend a bit more time with the prominently featured nickelodeon (a player piano that requires a nickel in the slot to play). There was a Player Piano Museum in Vancouver for a relatively short period in the 1970s,[5] so perhaps this was the source. Here, a musical instrument that provided one of the earliest ways of 'recording' performed music became the subject of recording and is revisited in the work for its multilayered meaning as music, recording machine and piece of social history. Like many aspects of *Vancouver Soundscape Revisited*, there are layers and 'punning' meanings for its role in this movement.

The piano, along with a crowd of mewling seagulls, is banished with the firing of the 9 o'clock gun (more later, on its recurring presence). The phone rings, and nobody picks up. As it continues, an orchestrated chorus

---

[5] See www.legacy.com/obituaries/rutlandherald/obituary.aspx?n=doyle-h-lane&pid= 143611083#fbLoggedOut www.mmdigest.com/Archives/Digests/201006/2010.06.21.01.html. An online collection and sound archive of this and other player piano collections can be found at http://avantgardeproject.conus.info/.

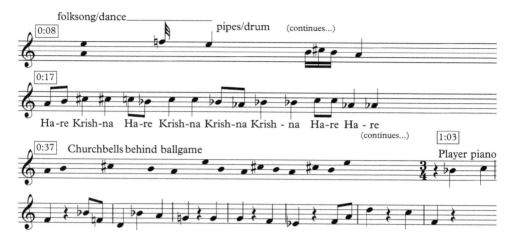

Figure 18.3 Pitch contours for material at beginning of 'Fire'

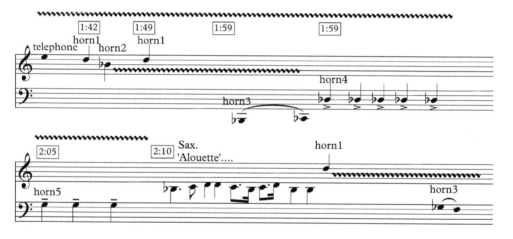

Figure 18.4 Pitch shapes for main events in final part of 'Fire'

of boat and other horns ensues, and then accompanies a few bars of a French-Canadian folksong, 'Alouette', busked on sax (or possibly clarinet; either way, 'horn-like' in timbre). Figure 18.4 indicates the main pitch shapes up to this point.

The snatch of 'Alouette' leads into a more abstract 'horn call chorus' with obviously processed sounds. The train whistles and foghorns are now breathy, extended and otherworldly and the sounds are transposed, time stretched and probably filtered in various ways. The processing has been handled with care to preserve the qualities of the materials and, since they have already appeared previously, their original, normal appearance remains in listening memory. There has been a transition from a conventionally 'musical' orchestration of pitched horn notes, amusing to the knowing ear, to a new dreamscape that draws 'musical' properties' from a functional, 'real-world' sound. Two kinds of 'musicality' converge.

Can you read the signs?

'DroneSong'

Boats drones, a drunk singing in an alley, seagull cries and ship horns. (Schryer, CD liner notes for 'DroneSong')

There is amusement to be had in 'Fire' but in 'DroneSong',[6] the third movement of *Vancouver Soundscape Revisited,* there's a moment of silliness that turns out to be more poignant than it first appears.

An enthusiastic male drunk, with occasional contributions from his more reticent sidekick, meanders aimlessly through a song (unidentifiable to this author). Behind him is a quiet outdoors ambience. The words are so slurred as to be virtually unintelligible but the slow song-form melody is easily followed, as is the general (probable) theme of unrequited or lost love. The song's melody ends with a melodic move from major third to tonic note at the end of the verse. At the end of the final verse, the singer pauses melodramatically on the penultimate note, milking the approaching cadence to the full. The tonic note is inevitable, and predictable. What's less predictable is that a clique of foghorns will leap on stage to snatch the final two notes, in the aural equivalent of a photobomb prank.

The final foghorn to grab the tonic note converts it to the first note of a distinctive falling semitone motif (heard also in 'Fire'). For some of the Vancouver audience that particular sound would have had an extra twist, as a little piece of history. The distinctive mournful call is the recorded sound of the original diaphone foghorn at Point Atkinson lighthouse, at the entrance to Vancouver Harbour. By 1996, this was a sound long gone from the natural soundscape, but it might have been a nostalgic blast from the past for any middle-aged Vancouverites among the audience. In 1976 the foghorn's well-known plaint had been replaced by an electronically operated air-horn (also appearing in *Vancouver Soundscape Revisited* and evocative in its own right) and that year, 1996, the air-horn had been replaced with an automated electronic foghorn 'beep' (all three can be

---

[6] Audio example 3: 'DroneSong' (duration 1:13).

heard in sequence at www.sfu.ca/sonic-studio/handbook/Soundmark.html). The foghorn, of any kind, was finally silenced for good in 1998.

Modernisation and increased technological capabilities bring about incidental changes to the soundscape in ways that might not be anticipated or considered important in the grand scheme of things. Any lighthouse keeper would be glad not to have to hand-crank a steam-powered horn repeatedly during the early hours of a foggy night. Yet, as objects and habitual actions – and their sounds – fall out of use, their demise also silences the human experience that surrounded them. Soundmarks, as Murray Schafer (1994) termed these aural 'natural signs' in the soundscape of a community, are not really about sound at all: they are about people, listening and noticing them, and associating them with personal and collective memory and experience. They are sounds to which we have grown attached. Many sounds preserved in the WSP and subsequent SFU recordings have by now faded from the soundscape or become less important to the majority of listeners. Sounds like the Atkinson foghorn and the player piano were already 'living relics' when recorded. They were disinterred for contemporary, and future, ears in *Vancouver Soundscape Revisited* but what they originally stood for – their social history – was going, or had gone.[7]

Two other distinctive Vancouver 'soundmarks' that are still very much around, at time of writing, are used more than once in the work: the Heritage Horns (known locally as the 'O Canada' horns) and the 9 o'clock gun. The Heritage Horns, ten air-horns on the top of the Pan Pacific hotel at Canada Place (near the waterfront), blast out the first four notes of the Canadian national anthem at 12 noon each day. They were moved from their original location on the top of the BC Hydro building in the downtown area (the electric company funded their construction for the 1967 Expo) but, at 115 decibels, are still audible in much of the city centre and several miles beyond. The Heritage Horns are granted a movement of their own ('Horn') in *Vancouver Soundscape Revisited*, in addition to a couple of guest appearances in other movements. However, it is the 9 o'clock gun that becomes an aural 'leitmotif' in the work, firing in at least five of the nine movements. The gun (actually a cannon) always fires as a single, echoing shot across the aural landscape, its sound disrupting the existing

---

[7] A work of art is not obliged to consider and address such issues, although of course it can. In a documentary comparing the 1973/1996 Vancouver soundscapes, on the CD *The Vancouver Soundscape*, Truax and Westerkamp introduce the listener to an informational survey of the sounds important to Vancouver's soundscape, including the foghorns at Point Atkinson. The documentary was made in 1996. Since 1998 there has been no foghorn at Point Atkinson.

ambience and echoing through what follows – similar to its presence in real life. Schryer's use of the sound is judicious and thoughtful – for *any* listener to *Vancouver Soundscape Revisited*, not just those already 'in the know', this sound's recurring presence creates a soundmark experience. It keeps turning up, recognisable and reliably 'the same'. A real-world sound-mark acts out the role of soundmark within the context of the work.

Vancouver Soundscape Revisited references two other sounds that are important to the local soundscape as signposts to its culture and environment. The bald eagle's brief but piercing cry, which opens the work, is more than a distinctive sound. An eagle sighting in Vancouver city is a fairly unusual occurrence, greeted with admiration or pleasure, but the bird is emblematic of British Columbia. Only a few minutes out of Vancouver the eagles gather in large numbers each winter and, like other indigenous animals, it is central to First Nations culture and stories. The other sound symbol is also a wry reminder of the region: in both the first and the last movements of *Vancouver Soundscape Revisited*, the sound of persistent rain is prominent, its presence serving as a frame.

What really matters?

As a composed work about listening to the sonic and social environment, *Vancouver Soundscape Revisited* is concerned with acoustic, or sound, ecology. This interdisciplinary approach considers the relationship between living beings and the environment, and the sonic impact of human activity.

However, there is no shouting about the 'health' of the soundscape in *Vancouver Soundscape Revisited*. Not even in 'Noise', an energised collage constructed from a fast succession of layered 'man-made', post-industrial sounds – machinery, sirens and alarms. Although this movement draws attention to mechanical sounds that have supplanted quiet in routine aspects of our daily and working lives, it also makes a gentle point about human communication. At the beginning and end of the movement is the same recording of a male voice calling over the hubbub of a human crowd: 'You cannot hear me? ... There's too much noise going on.' He is asking people to stop and direct themselves towards what he has to say. The ambience is in fact not that loud (the bald eagle cry at the beginning of the work, with its natural sudden transient at a high amplitude, would be far more likely to break health and safety rules). His words are a request to listen.

The most deafening moment in the work comes when there is no sound at all. Not even a whisper. The fifth movement, 'Industry' is more obviously 'thematic' in terms of meaning than others, making use of sounds relating to 'work' and human industry. The composer's manipulation of the sounds – his 'work' – is also clearly audible. 'Industry' commences with the sonic arrival of a seaplane that starts as a filtered timbre and gradually comes in to land in 'reality', moving on to a tree being felled, the sounds of the stock exchange, and machine noise. People doing things.

Taking the high moral ground about post-industrial 'noise' would be naïve in a portrait of one of the most liberal, affluent cities in the developed world – a city consistently rated as one of the most desirable locations in which to live. The quiet of non-mechanised subsistence farming is surely a far more disturbing aural picture of incomprehensible levels of rural poverty and social deprivation. Instead, *Vancouver Sounds-cape Revisited* could be interpreted as making a different point. At just over one minute into 'Industry' the sound is 'cut off'. There is a 'dead' silence of six long seconds before humanity returns with what sounds like the opening of metal folding doors and then an electronic till roll, totting up the cash.

That silence might just speak volumes on how industry's cessation would *not* return humans' existence to a tranquil Arcadia. Without industry, without the working and making and building communities of human activity and knowledge, and its products, the city would be diminished, and so would its inhabitants. The diaphone foghorn and its successors, the O Canada horns, the player piano, the 9 o'clock gun? – all absent from the soundscape. The social conscience and resources needed to develop and preserve the parks and forests where people are at liberty to look up at an eagle or paddle in the sea? – unlikely to mature. The time-saving technology that provides opportunities for people to rest for a while? – not available. When 'Industry' stops sounding for those few silent seconds, *Vancouver Soundscape Revisited* does not revisit a pre-industrial utopia to my ears, it warns of loss. Are these few seconds of silence a critique of some of the more idealistic tenets of Schafer's early thoughts on 'acoustic ecology', in which he prioritised a 'lo-fi', pre-industrialised soundscape? Perhaps I am hearing too much. *Vancouver Soundscape Revisited*'s metaphors are in flux and open to wide interpretation – I think that's no bad thing.

There has been an amount of rather prescriptive polemic about how sound environments could, or should, be, and one has to tread this directive path with care and a sense of perspective. It is noticeable that some composers with a strong interest in acoustic ecology and soundscape have stepped back from making protests or admonishments about the soundscape the entire focus of their creative work (Truax, for example). Schryer's sincere concern for environment and acoustic ecology is evident in both his writings and his compositions but he expresses his opinions on acoustic ecology in flexible, accommodating terms:

Acoustic ecology is all about listening and awareness of the acoustic environment and though I agree that one must indeed 'do' something with the acoustic environment, as Schafer and others have done so very well, I think there is more than one way of being 'active', including being actively passive by allowing an environment [to] be musical by itself. (Schryer 1998)

This might appear on first reading an undirected approach to the soundscape, but it is evident from this analysis that *Vancouver Soundscape Revisited* is far from that. Rather, the listener is guided, almost unwittingly, through an indirect tour of the city that mimics – in miniature – the process of 'finding one's way around' a new place: walking from one district to another, noticing one thing or another, and coming to 'know' how things fit together in both social and sensory terms. This journey is encouraged through the careful superimposition of layers of largely unprocessed sound, each source retaining its original sonic identity and its implied (or listener-imagined) time and place. While the relationships between sounds are often carefully composed, it is rare that *overt* connections are made or melded. Instead, the approach to 'meaning' and metaphor is more tangential, and I would venture to suggest more sophisticated than is sometimes the case in electroacoustic music in general. Coming to 'know' something through personal endeavour is different from being told, and the knowledge gained this way is strong and sustainable. Schryer is an excellent teacher.

Blowin'

Windy Forest. 'Blowin' in the wind' buskers, geese, frogs, distant squirrel, quiet rain. (Schryer, CD liner notes for 'Blowin'")[8]

At last, a song in the air. The final movement opens with the wind, rising in the forest with a white noise turbulence that is almost indistinguishable from the sound of rushing water. Next comes another friendly pun: the emergence of buskers singing the refrain from Bob Dylan's 'Blowin' in the wind', the song adopted so widely by the civil rights movement that it became a general anthem for protest, much performed later by middle-class kids with not quite so much to complain about (I count myself among them).

---

[8] Audio example 4: 'Blowin" (duration 1:32).

Finally, the rain descends again and the soundscape gradually subsides to nothing, returning the listener to their present environment, to their own thoughts, and to another time and place. Like all portraits that offer more than superficial appeal, *Vancouver Soundscape Revisited* invites a number of readings, of which this was just one.

In conclusion

It is not my place to tell you how to listen. It is your place, your world and your pair of ears that encounters the work. Nevertheless, in considering effective tools for analysing work such as Schryer's *Vancouver Soundscape Revisited*, in which a recognisable sonic environment from the 'real world' is composed, constructed and considerably changed and manipulated to sonic and extra-musical intent, it is helpful to consider those listening tools we might collectively share, and to build ways of making a useful, communicable critique. I believe we all have those tools already; they inhabit quotidian listening experience.

In a 'soundscape' work, the listener, I suggest, is placed in a world where ordinary listening cohabits with an attention to sonic relationships, gestures, qualities and patterns that is more characteristic of 'listening to music'. The success of the work lies in appreciating and working with how these two differ and how they have been combined.

References

Clarke, E. F. (2005) *Ways of Listening*. Oxford University Press.

Feld, S. and Brenneis, D. (2004) Doing anthropology in sound. *American Ethnologist* 31(4), 461–74. https://quote.ucsd.edu/sed/files/2014/01/Feld_Brenneis-2004.pdf (accessed 29 September 2014).

Norman, K. (1996) Real-world music as composed listening. In K. Norman (ed.), *A Poetry of Reality: Composing with Recorded Sound, Contemporary Music Review*, 15 (1–2). New York: Taylor and Francis.

Schafer, R. M. (1994) *The Soundscape – Our Sonic Environment and the Tuning of the World*. Rochester, VT: Destiny Books.

Schryer, C. (1996/2007) Report: Soundscape Vancouver '96. http://wfae.proscenia.net/library/articles/schryer_vancouver.pdf (accessed 29 August 2013).

(1998) Electroacoustic Soundscape Composition. *e-contact 1.4*. http://cec.sonus.ca/econtact/Ecology/Schryer.html (accessed 1 September 2013).

Truax, B. (1996) The Vancouver soundscape. www.sfu.ca/~truax/vanscape.html (accessed 29 August 2013).

Recordings

Cambridge Street Records. (1996) *The Vancouver Soundscape 1973/Soundscape Vancouver* 1996, Cambridge Street Records CSR2CD 9701.

Schryer, C. (1996) *Vancouver Soundscape Revisited.* On *The Vancouver Soundscape 1973/Soundscape Vancouver 1996*, Cambridge Street Records CSR2CD 9701.

(1997) *Autour.* Empreintes DIGITALes – IMED 9736.

Index

9 781107 544055